D1560250

OXFORD HISTORICAL MONOGRAPHS

Editors

BARBARA HARVEY   A. D. MACINTYRE
R. W. SOUTHERN   A. F. THOMPSON
H. R. TREVOR-ROPER

ENGLISH DIPLOMACY

1422–1461

JOHN FERGUSON

OXFORD
AT THE CLARENDON PRESS
1972

Oxford University Press, Ely House, London W. 1

GLASGOW NEW YORK TORONTO MELBOURNE WELLINGTON
CAPE TOWN IBADAN NAIROBI DAR ES SALAAM LUSAKA ADDIS ABABA
DELHI BOMBAY CALCUTTA MADRAS KARACHI LAHORE DACCA
KUALA LUMPUR SINGAPORE HONG KONG TOKYO

*Printed in Great Britain
at the University Press, Oxford
by Vivian Ridler
Printer to the University*

PREFACE

THE debts I have incurred in writing this book are formidable. First and foremost, I wish to thank my supervisor, Dr. Pierre Chaplais, who permitted me to pillage both his thought and notes for ideas and information. Then I am deeply obligated to my superiors in the Public Record Office, especially Mr. H. C. Johnson, Mr. L. C. Hector, and Mr. R. E. Latham, who not only allowed me to postpone my work for them while I finished this study, but also generously put their own paleographic and linguistic talents at my disposal. In addition I am indebted to my examiners, Mr. G. A. Holmes and Mr. C. A. J. Armstrong; to Professor R. B. Wernham, Professor Elizabeth Brown, and especially to my friend and teacher Professor G. P. Cuttino—all of whom read the typescript. Finally, I should like to thank Professor W. R. Dynes, whose encouragement and linguistic and editorial skills substantially shortened the time necessary to complete this book.

J. F.

CONTENTS

LIST OF ABBREVIATIONS

Note: Documents from the Public Record Office are cited by letters and numbers only for which a key can be found in the bibliography. Chronicles are cited by the author's name.

A.C.A.	Archivo de la Corona de Aragón.
A.G.N.	Archivo General de Navarra.
Beaucourt, *Charles VII*	G. du Fresne de Beaucourt, *Histoire de Charles VII*, 6 vols., Paris, 1881–91.
B.M.	British Museum.
B.N.	Bibliothèque Nationale.
Cal. Close Rolls	*Calendar of the Close Rolls*, London, 1892–1938.
Cal. Pap. Let.	*Calendar of Papal Registers: Letters*, London, 1893–1955.
Cal. Pat. Rolls	*Calendar of the Patent Rolls*, London, 1893–1955.
Chichele	*The Register of Henry Chichele, Archbishop of Canterbury*, ed. E. F. Jacob (Canterbury and York Society, vols. xlii, xlv–xlvii), Oxford, 1938–47.
College of Arms	W. H. Godfrey, *The College of Arms* (Survey of London, vol. xvi), London, 1963.
Correspondence Bekynton	*Memorials of the Reign of King Henry VI. Official Correspondence of Thomas Bekynton, Secretary to Henry VI*, ed. G. Williams (Rolls Series), 2 vols., London, 1872.
Deutsche Reichstagakten	*Deutsche Reichstagakten*, ed. J. Weizsäcker et al., 16 vols., Munich, 1867–1921.
Dickinson, *Arras*	J. G. Dickinson, *The Congress of Arras, 1435*, Oxford, 1955.
D.N.B.	*Dictionary of National Biography*, ed. S. Lee et al., 63 vols., London, 1885–1921.
Hist. MSS. Com.	Historical Manuscripts Commission.
Mansi	*Sacrorum conciliorum nova et amplissima collectio*, ed. J. Mansi, 31 vols., Venice, 1758–98.
Palgrave, *Antient Kalendars*	*Antient Kalendars and Inventories of the Treasury of His Majesty's Exchequer*, ed. F. Palgrave, 3 vols., London, 1836.

Proc. P.C.   *Proceedings and Ordinances of the Privy Council
                             of England*, ed. H. Nicolas, 7 vols., London,
                             1834–7.

Regesta   *Regesta historico-diplomatica ordinis S. Mariae
                             Theutonicorum, 1198–1525*, ed. C. Joachim
                             et al., 2 vols. in 3 pts., Göttingen, 1948–50.

Register of Cambridge   A. B. Emden, *A Biographical Register of the
                             University of Cambridge to 1500*, Cam-
                             bridge, 1963.

Register of Oxford   A. B. Emden, *A Biographical Register of the
                             University of Oxford to A.D. 1500*, 3 vols.,
                             Oxford, 1957–9.

Rot. parl.   *Rotuli parliamentorum, ut et petitiones et placita
                             in parliamento*, 6 vols., London, 1767–77.

Rymer   *Foedera, conventiones, literae et cujuscunque
                             generis acta publica inter reges Angliae et
                             alios quosvis imperatores, reges, pontifices,
                             principes vel communitates*, ed. T. Rymer,
                             20 vols., London, 1704–35.

V.C.H.   *Victoria County History*.

Wedgwood, *History of   J. C. Wedgwood (in coll. with A. D. Holt), *A
  Parliament: Biographies*   History of Parliament*, vol. i: *Biographies of
                             Members of the Commons House, 1439–1509*,
                             London, 1938.

INTRODUCTION

O N 21 May 1420 Henry V of England and the King of France's plenipotentiary, Queen Isabel, stood before the high altar of the Cathedral of Troyes. They had come to hear the recital of the articles comprising a treaty of peace between England and France, a treaty which is of fundamental importance for mid-fifteenth-century diplomacy. When the reading was finished, the parties to the agreement swore the required oaths and affixed their seals.[1] To obtain peace King Charles had, by affiancing his daughter Catherine to Henry V, adopted the English king as his son; this adopted son also became his heir, for the *soi-disant* dauphin was disinherited as a consequence of his participation in Duke John of Burgundy's murder. Moreover, King Henry became Regent of France during the lifetime of his father-in-law, owing to Charles's sickness, and on the French king's death he was to be immediately proclaimed King of France. Elaborate precautions, however, secured France from subjection to England. During Charles VI's lifetime Henry was never to style himself King of France. He was neither to encroach on the rights, lands, or revenues of the crown nor (except in very special circum-stances) to issue in his own name letters of pardon, remission, and the like. Justice to all according to French law, appoint-ment of suitable governmental functionaries, defence of the rights, customs, and privileges of the magnates, towns, and communes of France, and maintenance of the Parlement of Paris's authority—these represent some of the demands made on the English monarch. Although Charles enjoined the new regent to reduce places held by rebels to sub-mission, those landowners, ecclesiastics, and educational institutions who took an oath of obedience were to retain their possessions. While Charles lived, Normandy and the lands conquered by the English retained an independent

---

[1] J. H. Wylie and W. T. Waugh, *The Reign of Henry V*, iii. 202–6; P. Bonen-fant, 'Du meurtre de Montereau au traité de Troyes', *Académie royale de Belgique, Mémoires*, lii (1958), 168–70.

status, but were to be re-joined to the crown on Henry's accession. (For some reason no mention was made of Gascony's fate: claims obfuscated by almost two centuries of wrangling were perhaps best left unstated.) 'Burgundians' whose lands Henry had confiscated in Normandy or elsewhere would have their property restored if it had not already been re-granted; otherwise lands captured from the 'Armagnacs' would serve as compensation—provided such grants did not diminish the rights of the crown.[1]

It is a historical commonplace that a government whose constitution is monarchical both in theory and in fact has its foreign policy made by the king. And as long as the Plantagenets occupied the English throne their desire to make good their claims to continental possessions (whether allodial, feudal, hereditary, or acquired by treaty) overrode any other considerations.[2] Professor Unwin's transfer to Edward III of Bishop Stubb's appraisal of Richard I's attitude towards England regarding his continental ventures finds a further application with reference to the Lancastrian kings; for all these monarchs their island kingdom was primarily a source of supply.[3] Only when the development of the mighty Valois and Habsburg states in the sixteenth century could no longer be ignored did England abandon the dream of a continental empire.[4]

To a lesser extent other general factors were at work moulding the framework of English diplomacy, though the decision-makers may not have been consciously aware of them. The most conspicuous of these, perhaps, is the development of warfare.[5] The continuation of the practice begun at Falkirk (1298)—using the long bow in a defensive position against both mounted and unmounted cavalry—

[1] For a different interpretation of the provisions of this treaty see A. Bossuat, 'Le Parlement de Paris pendant l'occupation anglaise', Revue historique, cxxix (1963), 19–40.
[2] J. le Patourel, 'The Plantagenet Dominions', History, l (1965), 289–308.
[3] G. Unwin, 'The Economic Policy of Edward III', Studies in Economic History: The Collected Papers of George Unwin, ed. R. H. Tawney (London, 1927), p. 130.
[4] R. Wernham, Before the Armada (London, 1966), p. 12.
[5] C. Oman, 'The Art of War in the Fifteenth Century', Cambridge Medieval History, viii, ed. C. W. Previté-Orton and Z. N. Brooke (Cambridge, 1936), 649–59; id., The Art of War in the Middle Ages, A.D. 378–1515, revised and ed. J. H. Beeler (Ithaca, 1953), pp. 116–51.

served the English well at the opening of Henry VI's reign. French knights, who had not grasped the lessons of Crécy, Poitiers, and Agincourt, fell easy victims to the English archers at Cravant (1423), Verneuil (1424), and the Battle of the Herring (1429). If, however, the English forgot themselves or became excited as at Baugé, defeat was the result—here the Duke of Clarence outran his archers and was killed. Moreover, by 1429 La Hire, Xaintrailles, Dunois, and others of Charles's commanders were coming to appreciate the weaknesses as well as the strengths of English tactics: the English archer performed most efficiently from a pre-established defensive position. Thus the English army must be taken by surprise, attacked while on the march, at night, in ambush. Once the French fully understood these facts and were able by clever manœuvres, such as feints, similar to those William is reputed to have used at Hastings, to lure the archer from his established position, it was only a matter of time until by sheer weight of numbers they drove the English from the continent. It is interesting that the use of artillery, even though a customary part of an English army after 1346, apparently played an insignificant role in the French wars. Although the Bureau brothers used cannons to reduce Norman fortresses to submission in a matter of weeks where it had taken Henry V months, the Turks at Constantinople were the first to use artillery to bring down an ancient fortification at great speed (and then it took six weeks to breach the triple walls).[1] Yet the French, at the end of the war (Formigny, 15 April 1450) and at Castillon-la-Bataille, heralded a new era in the history of warfare when they, in the first instance, used cannon fire to harass English archers from their position, and, in the second, where they turned the cannon on the advancing troops.

Geography had not yet assumed the leading place it occupied in later formulations of Britain's 'eternal interests',[2] but it could not be ignored. Although the country normally produced enough corn to feed the population, evidence

[1] See S. Runciman, *The Fall of Constantinople, 1453* (Cambridge, 1965).
[2] R. H. Tawney, *Business and Politics under James I* (Cambridge, 1958), pp. 21–4.

suggests that weather conditions in the late Middle Ages were less favourable for growing corn than in the past. In years of scarcity like the late 1430s corn needed to be imported from the Baltic. By Henry VI's reign England no longer manufactured enough salt for preserving food.[1] Spices like cinnamon and saffron would not grow on the island, nor could the exotic luxury goods in such great demand be obtained at home, but had to be purchased from the Italian merchants. Finally, the manufacture of cloth depended on imports of dyes, alum from Genoa, and a small amount of wool brought from Spain. But the importance of England's geographical situation must not be overstated. The Channel was held to be so insignificant militarily after the ratification of the Treaty of Troyes that the royal navy was disbanded; by 1435 Henry VI's advisers had disposed of all thirty of his father's ships, though they ultimately acquired two new ones.[2] The absorption of Brittany into the kingdom of France and the disintegration of Burgundy at the end of the fifteenth century, Professor Wernham has suggested, stripped away the twin buffers separating England and France. This fact and England's growing dependence on Antwerp as an outlet for her booming cloth trade underlined the significance of the Channel and the need for a navy.[3]

The economic factor is highly important, and at the same time problematic, for generalizations about economic conditions in fifteenth-century Europe are hazardous, even for the specialist.[4] Political fragmentation exacerbated by particularism produced a wide variety of economic policies and a concomitant succession of poverty and wealth in relatively small geographical areas. Sources for the period are not particularly abundant, and where they exist they are often incomplete, inaccurate, or misleading. And in no case were the sources ever intended to provide the information needed for the statistical analysis favoured by modern

[1] A. R. Bridbury, *England and the Salt Trade in the Later Middle Ages* (Oxford, 1955), p. 105.
[2] C. F. Richmond, 'The Keeping of the Seas during the Hundred Years' War: 1422–1440', *History*, xlix (1964), 283–98.   [3] Wernham, *Armada*, pp. 11, 20.
[4] See for example R. Lopez, H. A. Miskimin, C. M. Cipolla, 'Economic Depression of the Renaissance ?', *Economic History Review*, xvi (1963–4), 519–29.

economists. Yet the importance of the economic determinants for foreign policy in wartime is plain, and one has
no other recourse than to rely mainly on the general con-
sensus of opinion of modern authorities.[1]

Europe entered the fifteenth century in the midst of a
period of economic contraction. The population, which
began to decline in the fourteenth century, fell by at least
30 per cent. before 1450. In the hundred years following
1350 the number of inhabitants in Toulouse, for example,
dropped by 22,000 to 8,000.[2] In rural areas the catas-
trophe slightly reduced the area of land under cultivation
and raised the cost of labour. But the plague, which had been
largely responsible for the fall in population, mainly struck
the very old or the very young, so the labour force did not
correspondingly decline. Furthermore, less productive lands
were abandoned for those more fertile. As a result the supply
of corn surpassed the demand and corn prices fell, while the
cost of other commodities stayed the same or continued to
rise. In the cities economic contraction added impetus to an
old policy of protectionism, an effort to secure the most
favourable trading conditions possible for native merchants
at foreigners' expense.

In England the conversion from wool to cloth trade also
characterizes this period. Perhaps no other episode in
English economic history, aside from the industrial revolution in the nineteenth century, has received so much
attention from scholars, though the effect of this change on
diplomacy has not been so widely canvassed. Between 1348

---

[1] What follows is primarily based on J. Heers, *L'Occident aux xive et xve siècles.
Aspects économiques et sociaux* (Nouvelle Clio, 1963), no. 23; L. Génicot, 'Crisis:
From Middle Ages to Modern Times', *The Cambridge Economic History of Europe*,
i, 2nd edn., ed. M. M. Postan (Cambridge, 1966), 660–741; R. de Roover, 'The
Organization of Trade', pp. 70–107, H. van Werveke, C. M. Cipolla, 'The Eco-
nomic Policies of Governments', pp. 281–361, 397–429, E. B. and M. M. Fryde,
'Public Credit with Special Reference to North-Western Europe', pp. 430–533,
ibid, iii, ed. M. Postan, E. Rich, and E. Miller (Cambridge, 1965); E. Carus-
Wilson and O. Coleman, *Englands' Export Trade, 1275–1547* (Oxford, 1963);
E. Power, *The Wool Trade in English Medieval History* (Oxford, 1941); H. A.
Miskimin, 'Monetary Movements and Market Structure—Forces for Contraction
in Fourteenth and Fifteenth Century England', *Journal of Economic History*, xxiv
(1964), 470–90; John H. A. Munro, *Wool, Cloth, and Gold: Bullionism in Anglo-
Burgundian Commercial Relations, 1384–1478* (Ann Arbor, 1965).

[2] Génicot, 'Crisis', p. 664.

and 1399 the export of wool dropped by one-third, and that figure was halved during the following years. One scholar has argued recently that by converting the amount of wool that went into making cloth back into raw wool one finds that the total production of wool declined only slightly, but his calculations have not yet commanded general acceptance.[1] In any event the production of cloth has less economic significance for foreign policy than raw wool, since cloth was never able to bear the high customs duty placed on wool, for English cloth, unlike the fine wool the island produced, had to compete with Flemish and Italian wares. Conversion from wool to cloth export reduced revenue from the customs by 50 per cent. between 1350 and 1430.[2] Since England was a country that relied on direct taxation only in times of emergency, halving one of the principal sources of royal revenue became especially significant in time of war.

In addition to the declining incomes of all landowners, receipts from the crown's estates were further diminished by the king's unbounded munificence. Suffolk's willingness to accept an excessive number of grants from the king was one of the charges against him laid before parliament in 1450. The king was the poorest man in the kingdom, the chroniclers lamented.

A reduced income and increasing expenses, especially after Lancastrian France became unable to pay for the war, made it necessary to borrow. That foreign bankers played a less important role at the end of the Hundred Years' War than they had at the beginning might be explained by their fear that Henry VI like Edward III would repudiate his obligations and ruin them—the Lancastrians had a bad reputation about forgetting their debts. But there is a much more basic explanation: the shift from exporting wool and the protectionist policies of English merchants so reduced the share foreign merchants had in the export trade that the promise of lower tariffs gave them little incentive to back the king. (At least part of the £26,500 they did lend was extracted by force.) As a result the king had to rely on

---

[1] A. R. Bridbury, *Economic Growth* (London, 1962), p. 27.
[2] Fryde, 'Public Credit', p. 464.

native merchants, who obtained a monopoly on the sale of
wool, and the rich men in his kingdom for loans. Cardinal
Beaufort, whose financial dealings Mr. McFarlane studied,
lent the government almost £100,000 in the 1430s, about
half the sum the Lancastrians borrowed from him during
his life.[1] Nor was it unnatural for men who had such a heavy
stake in the government to demand some influence in
determining policy. The cardinal's role in diplomatic
relations with Burgundy and France is only a case in point.
That by the 1450s the economic situation had placed the
crown at the mercy of its creditors, who refused to advance
more funds, goes far to explain why there was no English
army on the continent again until 1475.

Unlike England, royal income in France came chiefly
from direct taxation.[2] Since the country produced no important item of export and was largely self-sufficient, she
played little part in foreign trade. Of the provinces of France,
Normandy was reputed to be among the wealthiest, and the
English saw no reason why she should not contribute pro-
portionately to the cost of the war. Because Henry V had
relied more and more on loans and direct taxation of his
English subjects towards the end of his reign, his son's
councillors decided to let Bedford and his government bear
most of the cost of the war as well as that of administering
the central government. Under optimum conditions and by
following an enlightened economic policy the duke might
have succeeded. But the territories in northern France,
outside Normandy, subject to the Lancastrians had been
repeatedly devastated by war and were never firmly under
English control for a long enough period to provide substantial revenue, and Gascony was never wealthy enough to
contribute to the war in the north. Nevertheless, Bedford
could expect an annual income of about £84,000 in the
early years of his regency.[3]

[1] K. B. McFarlane, 'Loans to the Lancastrian Kings: the Problem of Inducement', *Cambridge Historical Journal*, ix (1947-9), 56.
[2] R. A. Newhall, 'The War Finances of Henry V and the Duke of Bedford',
English Historical Review, xxxvi (1921), 172-97; A. Bossuat, 'Le rétablissement de
la paix sociale sous le règne de Charles VII', *Le Moyen Âge*, lx (1954), 137-62; R.
Doucet, 'Les finances anglaises à la fin de la guerre de cent ans (1431-1433)', ibid.
xxxvi (1926-7), 265-332. [3] Newhall, 'War Finances', p. 197.

Unfortunately, neither the duke nor his brother was an enlightened economist. Henry V's reform of the coinage came to little when the Armagnacs began to circulate counterfeit copies. Failure to clear the north of Armagnac enclaves prevented an attack on internal economic barriers. Moreover, these enemies in the north made it necessary to protect the populace by maintaining garrisons in Normandy which should have been in the field. Though Henry VI was King of France, the English soldier saw the war as a chance for conquest rather than the quelling of a rebellion. What had been taken from the enemy was booty.[1] From this notion a wave of confiscations had followed. At one time Bedford personally held the lands of Alençon, Anjou, Maine, Harcourt, Mortain, Beaumont, and Dreux, while Queen Catherine drew 22,500 *livres* from the Vexin.[2] These expenses, added to the sums spent on the futile sieges of Mont-Saint-Michel and the ruthlessly successful exploitation of Normandy's financial and human resources, slowly bankrupted Lancastrian France, forcing Bedford to pawn some of Charles VI's jewels and to enter into negotiations with the pope for the right to tax the clergy—a liberty he ultimately took without papal permission. Nevertheless, only the military disasters of 1428–9—amounting to the loss of an army put in the field at enormous expense—shattered the finances of Lancastrian France.[3] It was at this moment that Cardinal Beaufort, backed by a paid army, intervened in French affairs.

It must be pointed out that even today no satisfactory account of the role of public opinion in determining foreign policy exists. Mr. H. G. Richardson has argued learnedly and eloquently that the Commons played an insignificant part in medieval politics.[4] When they opposed the king's policy—and this happened seldom—it was to support the principles of the lords who dominated the council. Although

---

[1] Bossuat, 'Rétablissement', p. 139 argues that the English got the idea of confiscation from Armagnac and Burgundian practice in 1413 and 1418.

[2] Doucet, 'Finances anglaises', p. 280.

[3] Normandy alone furnished 71,000 *livres* for the siege of Orléans, (ibid., p. 323).

[4] H. G. Richardson, 'The Commons and Medieval Politics', *Transactions of the Royal Historical Society*, 4th ser. xxviii (1946), 21–45.

the Commons could influence policy by withholding supplies, they never made a practice of using their power in this way; the argument to the contrary reflects a tendency to read history backwards. In matters of foreign policy the Commons' avowal that they were incapable of giving advice on an invasion of Flanders in 1383 serves to corroborate this restrictionist view.

Yet the fact of Henry VI's minority greatly inflated the insignificant role the Commons had played in the past. The constitutional settlement of 1427 (reflecting an earlier decision) provided that during the minority the executive authority of the kingdom would be vested in parliament and the council; therefore, we may expect to find increased parliamentary activity in the sphere of diplomacy. In October 1423 the Commons, in keeping with its enhanced prerogative, 'doe send certain by name to the Duke of Gloucester, for vouchsafing to make them privy to the treaty of the Scotish ambassadour for delivery and marriage of the Scotish king, which they liked wel',[1] and again that year they thanked the lords 'que lour pleust de faire les communes, d'avoir notice et conisance par declaration de monsieur le chaunceller a eux jatarde faite, de la tretee sur les maters touchantz le roi d'Escoce . . .'.[2] In the following years the Commons confirmed the appointment of ambassadors to treat with the Scots at Durham, presented a bill to exhort the council to send ambassadors to prevent a duel between Gloucester and Burgundy, recommended that the council grant the Duchess of Bavaria 5,000 marks because of her great friendship and alliance with England, requested that the king write to the pope on behalf of the Archbishop of Canterbury, and enacted that certain princes of the blood should be sent to negotiate with the dauphin.[3] In the king's ninth year, although the Commons petitioned for the repeal of the statute forbidding English merchants entry to the King of Denmark's dominions, the only answer they received was that the king expected to hear from his

[1] R. Cotton, *An Exact Abridgement of the Records in the Tower of London*, ed. W. Prynne (London, 1657), p. 568.
[2] *Rot. parl.* iv. 199.
[3] Cotton, pp. 569, 588, 699; *Rot. parl.* iv. 277; C 49/16/3.

ambassadors shortly and would then take the matter into consideration;[1] but they met with more success in urging him to send envoys to the pope, to Spain, and to Scotland concerning a peace with Charles VII. During the parliament that met in 1432 'Iames the kyng of Scottes, sent ambassadors, to conclude a peace, with the duke of Gloucester, which, (because the kyng was absente) referred the matter to the iii estates, [and] after long consultacion, (not without greate arguementes) a peace was graunted and concluded ...'.[2] In 1435 certain English merchants had the audacity to complain of the ineffectual and costly embassy lately sent to Flanders.[3] Thus in the early years of the reign parliament played an appreciable role, serving in an advisory capacity, in the conduct of diplomacy; however, this activity should not be overemphasized. The matters that concerned parliament were those which directly affected its members: trouble on the Scottish border caused immediate misery and suffering at home, unsuccessful diplomatic relations with Denmark and Flanders endangered the profits of English mercantile interests, the problem of the French war assumed importance only when it pressed the pockets of the gentry too severely.

When Henry came of age in November 1437 the main reason for parliamentary diplomatic activity disappeared and thereafter its interest in foreign policy, except in matters that touched its purse or grave instances of treason, declined. In 1444 parliament, limiting the scope of its activity further, agreed that the provisions in the Treaty of Troyes forbidding the conclusion of a treaty with the dauphin 'be voyd, irryt, cassed, adnulled, and of non forse ne effect...',[4] and Anglo–French relations received no other notice from them until 1447 when the chancellor announced to the parliament meeting at Bury St. Edmunds that English ambassadors had completed the preliminaries for a treaty with France.[5] In 1450 parliament undertook to impeach the Duke of Suffolk because he 'hath deceyvably and traiterously, by his letters

---

[1] *Rot. parl.* iv. 378.
[2] E. Hall, *Chronicle of Lancaster and York (1399–1547)*, ed. H. Ellis (London, 1809), p. 166.
[3] *Rot. parl.* iv. 371.   [4] Ibid. v. 102–3.   [5] Ibid. 128.

and messages, discovered and opened to your seid grete ennemye Charles, callyng hymself kyng of Fraunce, all instructions and informations geven to your seid ambassiatours, afore their commyng into Fraunce . . .',[1] but it was more treason than foreign policy which concerned this parliament. And Mr. Richardson admitted that Suffolk might have been saved in 1450 if Henry VI could have raised some support in the lower house of parliament. Perhaps the times had changed, for the refusal to lend more money for the war certainly helped to put a quick end to what had become an unpopular policy.

The sources do not suggest to what extent decision-makers in fifteenth-century England manipulated or were manipulated by factors such as these in formulating specific foreign policies. That they did not align these factors into matrices and base decisions on the application of a theory of games, however primitive, to these matrices in order to determine 'the strategy which maximises the minimum pay-off'[2] is patently clear from the history of the period. It seems unlikely, for example, that England had an economic policy designed to further her foreign policy. That is not to say that economic considerations did not influence the course of the war. The protectionist policies of England's merchants created conflicts with foreign governments. Abandoning the wool trade cost England some of the coercive power she had wielded in the Low Countries a century earlier, while the loss of foreign creditors put her at the mercy of natives with less easily controlled ambitions. The growth of the cloth trade led to an effort to expand markets, especially in the Baltic, where Hanseatic merchants were faced with a similarly contracting economy.

Although they may have failed to understand the general determinants of a foreign policy, in practice English kings during the later Middle Ages relied on the ancient formula of encircling the enemy with a series of offensive alliances. Edward I's and Edward III's pursuit of this ancient policy has often been described. Henry V adopted a similar plan.

[1] Ibid., 178.
[2] S. Beer, 'An Operational Research Approach to the Nature of Conflict', *Political Studies*, xiv (1966), 124.

However, without a forceful and determined ruler a monarchical government is not likely to follow a consistent
programme in its relations with other princes. The reign of
Henry VI in England provided a clear-cut demonstration of
this hypothesis. Whatever propaganda the English spread to
increase the acceptance of the double monarchy, the fact
remained that there were two kingdoms and they were to
remain separate, albeit under the same sovereign. And
France, like Ireland a century later, did not always seem to
have the same interests as England. In England itself
Gloucester's failure to make himself the undisputed regent
produced a struggle for power[1] that militated against the
pursuit of a consistent policy abroad, with one exception.
Even King Henry roused himself to write numerous,
undoubtedly sincere letters, seeking the best way to obtain
peace in the Church universal.

If this analysis of the factors influencing foreign policy
and the account of those who made it reflect the Anglo–
French conflict at the beginning of Henry VI's reign with
reasonable accuracy, they may clarify some of the difficulties
in the text that follows. Generalizations and theories of
history—why things happen—are always more stimulating
than a recitation of the facts—what happened. But generalizations on inadequate evidence, as everyone knows, produce
faulty theories that tend to pass into circulation as fact. Thus
a large part of this essay is devoted to determining what
happened in England's negotiations with foreign powers
during Henry VI's reign. England's relations with the
empire and with the Spanish kingdoms in the mid fifteenth
century are virtually unknown. Other parts of the picture—
negotiations with France and Rome, for example—have
been painted innumerable times in tedious detail. In other
words, this study is not an exhaustive recital of English
diplomatic relations in the mid fifteenth century, for as
Basin said, 'De quibus per singula referre nec opus est et
fastidiosam nimis sua prolixitate hystoriam legentibus
redderet.'[2] Where the narrative is well known it has been

---

[1] See for example the letters to the Count Palatine sent in the name of 'Henrici,
eadem gracia, regis Anglie et Francie et domini Hibernie consiliarii' (E 28/41/109).
[2] Basin, i. 90.

summarized to make room for items of particular interest; elsewhere the repeated going and coming of envoys about whose missions very little (or nothing) is known is recounted in an attempt to establish the facts. In any event a list of all known English agents who went abroad or who negotiated with representatives of foreign powers in England, as well as a list of those foreigners who came to England on diplomatic business is provided in an appendix. Moreover, the intrusion of letters concerning merchants and their affairs often impedes the progress of the narrative. But not until one sees the frequency and persistence with which such letters appear does the importance of the economic factor and of public opinion (or at least one segment of it) become evident.

The possible sources for a study such as this, which potentially comprises all European diplomacy for half a century, are embarrassingly plentiful. I do not pretend to have seen all, or even most of them; to do so would take a lifetime. Yet I do not think future discoveries will alter the outline presented here, only the details. In England the most important manuscript collections have been searched with reasonable diligence. A limited amount of time on the Continent necessitated selecting a few libraries; inevitably some choices were less fortunate than others that might have been made. The transcriptions of the second appendix comprise a small selection culled from the documents, offered in support of statements in the text.

Finally, the structure of this book calls for a word of explanation. It comprises a series of chapters on English diplomatic activity in the individual states of fifteenth-century Europe. Only in the introduction and the conclusion is an attempt made to delineate the constants of English foreign policy during this period; that is, there is no effort to present an integrated chronological account of English diplomacy during Henry VI's reign. The reasons are two. One main purpose of this study is to set out the facts, to find out what actually happened. The result of marshalling the available information has tended at times to obscure the wood for the trees; however, until the trees are studied the forest cannot be accurately mapped. Setting out the details of English foreign policy from 1422 to 1461 raised a weightier reason for adopting the old-fashioned approach of treating each state separately: if this book shows anything, it demonstrates that, with one exception, the English did not think about foreign policy in the long term. Rarely did the king's council formulate any logical and consistent ground rules for making effective decisions. The silent acquiescence of the English council to Gloucester's invasion of the Low Countries provides sufficient evidence on this point. Mid-fifteenth-century English foreign policy was more often a matter of the passions than of reason.

As far as Henry VI's advisers focused their thoughts on England's relations with the Continent, the problem was France (thus the first chapter of this book), and those who faced the problem could only propose the ancient device of encirclement—a policy which in Anglo-French relations dates from Edward I's reign, if not earlier. Consequently, bankruptcy in the realm of innovation appears at every crisis. This rigid conservatism, together with the power struggle in the royal council, reduced the likelihood of diplomatic triumphs to complement the early military victories of the reign, and in fact served to diminish the advantages to be won from them.

The chapters that follow the Anglo-French story immediately point up these tendencies and clearly demonstrate the shortcomings of the English government. The prospects of a fruitful alliance with Aragon and Navarre, for example, were sacrificed to the unrealistic pursuit of renewing an ancient connection with Castile. Money fiefs, like those Edward III designed, were resurrected and they served Henry VI even less than they had his ancestor. Thus the question of the money fiefs conceded to the Count Palatine and to the Archbishop of Cologne and his cronies in the Rhineland precedes an effort at assessing the importance of England's disjointed communications with the secular powers of Italy and the clashes with the Baltic states. The chapter on England and the Empire introduces a different strand of international politics—the problem of the church councils. Here one might suggest that meagre were the fruits of supporting the pope against the councils,

while antipathy and at times genuine distaste for the conciliarists accompanied by childish, sterile bickering over
precedence obscured the role the council might have played
as an international forum for the settlement of the differences between England and France.

The following chapter on England and the papacy moves
on two levels: the international duel between papal absolu-
tism and conciliarism, and the more parochial struggle
over provisions. Slavishly content to back the pope on the
international level, Henry's ministers staunchly defied him
in domestic matters. And in this they achieved their one
resounding diplomatic victory.

The final chapter constitutes an excursion into admini-
strative and legal history, aiming to examine Roman law
as the framework for settling differences between princes.

These then are the strands—the military, the economic,
the religious, the determination to resist foreign appro-
priation of political patronage—from which the cloth of
English foreign policy was woven. But the woven cloth of
history did not resemble the fine woollen fabric for which
the English weavers were deservedly famous. Instead,
because the loom was often simultaneously operated by men
working at cross purposes, because some threads were
broken and others missing completely, the fabric of English
diplomacy disintegrated in times of stress.

I

ENGLAND AND FRANCE

ALTHOUGH chroniclers differ in recording the details of
the provisions Henry V made, as he lay dying at
Vincennes, for the governance of his kingdoms,
there is little doubt that the arrangements represent a
clarification and expansion of the plan embodied in the
Treaty of Troyes: a viceroy to control the government of
France while the incapacitated Charles VI lived, a Normandy independent of the French crown, and a separate
government for England.[1] By the terms of Henry's political
testament, the regency of France was to fall to Philip of
Burgundy, preparations for the defence of an independent
Normandy to John of Bedford, the regency of England to
Humphrey of Gloucester. The dying king could not know
that Charles VI would follow him to the grave in less than
two months and thereby render Bedford's function an
anachronism, for Normandy was to be reintegrated into the
kingdom of France. Nor could he know that the royal
council in London would refuse to accept a viceroy. Furthermore Henry had drastically underestimated the ambition of
both his brothers. From the beginning Bedford seems to
have been discontented with his brother's dispositions.
Although in governmental orders dated at Rouen on 15
October, he styled himself *Jean duc de Bedeford gouvernour
de Normandie*, five days earlier he had made an indenture
with the Earl of Suffolk for garrisoning Coutances and

---

[1] Monstrelet, iv. 109–12 gives Henry's death-bed speech in full, allotting the regency of France to Burgundy or Bedford, the government of England to Exeter;
he is followed in this by Waurin, ii. 422 and le Fèvre, p. 62. P. Cochon's *Chronique
normande* states simply, 'Et, après sa mort, fu mons^r de Bethfors eslu regent le
royaume' (p. 290). Juvenal des Ursins, who thought Bedford accompanied Henry's
body to England, wrote in a similar vein, while Guillaume Gruel's *Chronique
d'Arthur de Richemont* ignores the subject and Morosini, ii. 222–6, heard that
Henry V died at Paris from leprosy and that the king's death was followed by that
of his son, a brother, and about forty barons. See also T. Livius, p. 95; Elmham,
p. 333; and Chastellain, i. 328–32.

Saint-Lo in which he called himself regent of France.[1] Less than a month later, he introduced the phrase *fils du roy* into his style, signifying his right to govern France on the grounds of consanguinity.[2] And as he returned from King Charles's entombment at Saint-Denis, the duke had the king's sword borne before him; thus he advertised his intention of becoming France's regent.[3] King Charles was buried on 18 November and within a week the Duke of Bedford had adopted the style he was to use until his death, with the exception of the time Henry VI was actually in France, *Jehan regent le royaume de France duc de Bedford.*[4] Whether Duke Philip had already seen the advantages of forgoing this honour it is not possible to tell; in any case there is no evidence that he openly opposed the self-made regent.[5]

Bedford took his title of regent (or *prorex* as he called himself)[6] literally; he conceived his duty as that of governing a France quite unfettered by the control of the English council. Although he had a council in Paris and another in

---

[1] B.M., Add. Charter 11484; *Chronique du Mont-Saint-Michel*, ed. S. Luce (Société des anciens textes français, 1879–83), vol. i, *pièces diverses*, no. xv.

[2] *Jehan filz du roy Dengleterre duc de Bedford et gouverneur de Normandie* is the style he adopted in a letter to Richard Woodville, treasurer general of the duchy, on 8 Nov. 1422 (B.M., Add. Charter 87). Slightly earlier, on 26 Oct., he laid claims to the regency in England on similar grounds (*Calendar of Letter-Books Preserved among the Archives of the Corporation of the City of London. Letter-Book K.*, ed. R. Sharpe (London, 1911), p. 4). Grants, such as the gift of the hôtel de Préaux to Woodville (A. Longnon, *Paris pendant la domination anglaise (1420–1436)* (Paris, 1878), n. liv), were, however, made in the name of the young king, as were remissions of punishment for crimes (P. le Cacheux, *Actes de la chancellerie d'Henri VI concernant la Normandie sous la domination anglaise (1422–1435)* (Rouen and Paris, 1907–8), vol. i, nos. x, xi, *et passim*).

[3] 'Item, le duc de Bedfort, au revenir, fist porter l'espée du roy de France davant luy, comme regent, dont le peuple murmuroit fort, mais souffrir à celle foys le convint' (*Journal d'un bourgeois de Paris, 1405–1449*, ed. A. Tuetey (Paris, 1881), p. 180).

[4] The next day, in fact, the Parlement de Paris was officially informed that Henry VI was now King of France (*Chartularium universitatis Parisiensis*, ed. H. Denifle (Paris, 1897; Brussels, 1964), iv. 410). The letter containing Bedford's 'royal style' is dated at Paris, 24 Nov. 1422 (B.M., Add. Charter 11486).

[5] The argument developed here and much of what follows is based on the important article by C. A. J. Armstrong, 'La double monarchie France–Angleterre et la maison de Bourgogne (1420–35)', *Annales de Bourgogne*, xxxvii (1965), 81–112.

[6] The inscription of Bedford's tomb at Rouen reads: JOHANNES DUX BETFORDI NORMANNIAE PROREX (A. Deville, *Tombeaux de la cathédrale de Rouen* (Rouen, 1833), p. 167).

Rouen to advise him, the duke had the last word on any important *ordonnance*. He personally approved appointments and gifts, and he was commander-in-chief of the army as well as the formulator of foreign policy.[1] To strengthen his personal position the duke agreed to marry Burgundy's sister Anne, which cost Philip 50,000 *écus*.[2] Moreover, at Amiens in April 1423 Bedford entered into a mutual alliance with the Duke of Brittany and another with the same duke and Philip of Burgundy.[3] The form of the alliances markedly resembles the treaty of brotherhood in arms concluded between the Dukes of Clarence and Orléans in 1412.[4] Each of the three contracting parties promised (because of their friendship, nearness of kin and—in the second treaty—marriage ties) to be 'en bonne et vraie amour, fraternite et union' as long as they lived, to assist either of the others with a modest contingent of troops, and to use all his power to better the conditions of the poor in France. Having sworn to abide by the provisions of the treaty, the principals affixed their seals and signed their own names to the treaty, while to the second agreement the three ducal secretaries added their signatures as witnesses.[5]

---

[1] B. J. H. Rowe,' The *Grand Conseil* under the Duke of Bedford', *Oxford Essays in Medieval History Presented to Herbert Edward Salter* (Oxford, 1934), pp. 207–34. There were some Englishmen on the *conseil* but they were in a minority. Contact between the governments of England and France was maintained by messengers and occasionally by more important deputations. The Bishop of Beauvais, the Abbot of Fécamp, and the Abbot of Mont-Saint-Michel, for example, headed an embassy to the English council, which remained in London from 21 Jan. to 9 Mar. 1423 (E 101/322/7; E 28/43/8; *Proc. P.C.* iii. 123). And on 15 May 1423 the English council drafted letters of credence for the Bishop of London who was going to the Duke of Bedford (E 28/41/66).

[2] Armstrong, 'La double monarchie', p. 84. P.R.O. 31/8/143 contains a list of jewels and precious vessels the Duke of Burgundy gave to Bedford in 1423.

[3] P. H. Morice de Beaubois, *Mémoires pour servir de preuves à l'histoire ecclésiastique et civile de Bretagne* (Paris, 1742–6), vol. ii. coll. 1135–6; Rymer, x. 280–1; 1136–8; *Inventaire sommaire des archives départementales du Nord, Série B*, ed. A. le Glay *et al.* (Lille, 1862–1906), B. 297.

[4] L. Douët d'Arcq, *Choix de pièces inédites relatives au règne de Charles VI* (Mémoires pour servir à l'histoire de France, 1863), p. 359, cited in M. Keen, 'Brotherhood in Arms', *History*, xlvii (1962), 1–17.

[5] Miss E. Carleton Williams has written that the Duke of Bedford required Duke John of Brittany to read aloud every clause of their agreement to make certain that the duke had no doubts about his commitments (E. Carleton Williams, *My Lord of Bedford, 1389–1435* (London, 1963), p. 100). I have been unable, however, to find any corroboration of this statement.

At approximately the same time similar treaties seem to
have been drawn up between Bedford and Gloucester
and between Bedford, Gloucester, and Queen Catherine.[1]
Although the agreement between the two brothers is more
formal and written in Latin, its purpose remained the same
—to strengthen the regent's hold on France. After a proem
which averred that civil contracts between princes strengthen
their friendship, the treaty provided that, saving the infant
King Henry, the two dukes would serve and aid one another
above all others, neither believing false accusations against
one another nor supporting each other's enemies. Nor would
they make any alliances without the other's consent. Having
sworn on the Gospels to uphold this agreement, John and
Humphrey in the presence of three witnesses were to append
their seals and sign manuals. Once he had consented to such
a treaty Gloucester, despite his ambition, would not be likely
to violate it by attempting to supplant Bedford in France.
Since the only surviving evidence of this alliance is an undated copy, its implementation remains in doubt. The
content seems to rule out a date before Henry V's death,
while the form seems to presuppose the physical presence of
the contracting parties. But Bedford left England in May
1422 and appears not to have seen his brother again before
1426, when such an alliance was unlikely. Whether the two
last-named alliances were concluded or not they provide
striking testimony of the Duke of Bedford's efforts to
construct a system of personal alliances which would secure
him against attack as Regent of France.[2]

As part of this enterprise, Bedford began picking up the
threads of Henry V's web of alliances. The twenty-sixth
clause of the Treaty of Troyes set forth the procedure for
including the French and English kings' allies;[3] after
notification that the treaty had been concluded, the princes
had eight months' grace to signify their willingness to be
incorporated in it. Letters had been sent but the response
was slow. The Prince of Orange refused outright;[4] the
Count of Foix—like the Duke of Brittany—temporized;
while the King of Navarre demanded Champagne and Brie

---

[1] *Correspondence Bekynton*, i. 138–45.   [2] Ibid. 145 n. 1.
[3] Rymer, x. 902–3.   [4] Juvenal des Ursins, p. 352.

as the price of his adhesion. Castile and Aragon did not answer and Pope Martin refused his sanction. Only Sigismund, the Count Palatine, and Amédée of Savoy, all of whose friendship had been secured in advance, signified their desire to be included before Henry died.[1] Thus the regent found himself burdened with the ungrateful task of coaxing oaths of allegiance from greedy friends and recalcitrant vassals. In the past Henry had conducted negotiations from a position of strength guaranteed by his military successes; Bedford, though hardly less skilled as a general, had yet to win the respect of France's neighbours. Henry V's death had roused the dauphin's supporters to new military efforts; recruits were sought in Lombardy and Castile, Lower Normandy was attacked, and Meulan taken by surprise.[2] The tedious, unfruitful *pourparlers* with the Spanish kingdoms are to be described and the Count of Foix's indecision only produced exasperation.

The count had ardently upheld the dauphin until March 1420, when he abruptly changed sides. No doubt the count was angered when he learned that the dauphin's party at Montereau had slain his brother Archambaud, and the highly coloured account he received from the Burgundian agent, Gui de Brosse, who had brought Charles VI's promise of revenge, must have enraged him still further. Equally persuasive was Henry V's offer of either the constable's sword or the government of Languedoc, not to speak of the threat a developing *entente* between Armagnac and Navarre presented.[3] Although Jean's actions soon gave tangible proof that he had changed sides, he delayed offering the documents formalizing the agreement in hope of extorting either more substantial emoluments from Henry or some promise from the dauphin, if once again he switched sides. After the Treaty of Troyes came into effect the English king, warned that the Castilians were contemplating an

[1] Beaucourt, *Charles VII*, i. 325–6.
[2] R. A. Newhall, *The English Conquest of Normandy, 1416–1424* (Yale Historical Publications, vol. xix, 1924), pp. 290, 294, 296.
[3] L. Flourac, *Jean Ier comte de Foix, vicomte souverain de Béarn* (Paris, 1884), pp. 81–2; P. Tucoo-Chala, *La Vicomté de Béarn et le problème de sa souveraineté* (Bordeaux, 1961), p. 95; C. Samaran, *La Maison d'Armagnac au xve siècle et les dernières luttes de la féodalité dans le midi de la France* (Paris, 1907), pp. 48–9.

invasion of Gascony, decided to add greater inducements to secure Foix's promised aid in the south. Count Jean graciously accepted the *vicomté* of Lautrec and the lieutenancy of Languedoc, but demanded the county of Bigorre and other lands as well as 400 francs per month for his personal expenses as Lieutenant of Languedoc and for the wages of his officials. Envoys from Foix with these new demands arrived in northern France late in 1421; by the following March Henry capitulated on condition that the count put an army of 1,000 men-at-arms and 1,000 archers in the field by 1 June. In return, on 3 March the envoys promised their count's adherence to the Treaty of Troyes.[1] The summons to arms came too late to raise an army by June and before anything else was done both Henry V and Charles VI were dead.[2]

Jean of Foix regretted his promise to assist the English almost as soon as he had made it. Even in the early months of 1422 his envoys were trying to discover what the terms of his reconciliation with the dauphin would be.[3] With envoys from the Lancastrian French the count simply adopted delaying tactics. The ambassadors sent to receive his letters ratifying the promises he made to Henry V were side-tracked. A new embassy followed, but Foix was in Toulouse; when still another group of agents caught up with him in Béarn the count presented them with a schedule modifying his previous agreement.[4] Then Pierre Guiraud appeared in Bayonne about 3 July 1423 with letters from Henry VI, but the count politely refused him a safe conduct on the perfectly legitimate grounds that the count could not assure the safety of Henry's messenger because his route would pass through territory held by England's enemies.[5] Letters from the royal council at Bordeaux Foix would not answer since the letters did not contain the sender's name: he did not know who had sent them, or so he claimed.[6] Finally, the Captal de Buch, Sir John Radcliffe, and four assistants, armed with specific instructions to see that 'sur

[1] E 30/412. [2] Flourac, *Jean Ier*, pp. 84–6.
[3] Ibid., p. 87. [4] Rymer, x. 273.
[5] Jean was not disposed to remove the obstacle by coming to Guiraud. Flourac, *Jean Ier, p.j.* no. xxv, pp. 261–2.
[6] Flourac, *Jean Ier, p.j.* no. xxvi, pp. 263–5.

ce [the formal adherence to the Treaty of Troyes] il leur face response certaine et clere' or return the 12,600 *écus* given him to raise an army in Languedoc,[1] sought out Jean, but they had no more success than those agents who had gone before. And in fact the council at Bordeaux remained ignorant of the count's reconciliation with the dauphin for eight months after its conclusion.[2]

The regent was not, however, deterred by these set-backs. Duke John of Brittany, pressed by Henry V (who must have recognized that the Duchess of Brittany, his wife's elder sister, had as strong a claim to the French throne as Queen Catherine) and encouraged by his brother Richemont (who wanted his freedom and Henry's good offices in his marriage venture) finally sent envoys to the English king with power to swear his adherence to the treaty.[3] Henry died before the Breton envoys reached Vincennes; however, in return for a bribe of lands worth 15,000 *livres tournois* and his promise not to make a treaty with the dauphin without including the Duke of Brittany, Duke John's ambassadors swore to the treaty before Charles VI on 8 October 1422.[4]

While Bedford was consolidating his power and un-knotting the diplomatic tangles which surrounded him, the pope mounted another peace offensive. Both the regent and the dauphin had informed Martin of the deaths of Henry and Charles. Although he was inclined to give neither much support,[5] Martin wrote to Bedford as well as to the English council announcing the mission of Bishop Albergati of Bologna for bringing about the end of hostilities. Also on 25 November 1422 he commissioned the Cardinal of Porto (Louis, Duke of Bar) for the same purpose. Finally, he wrote

[1] Appendix II, no. 7.　　　　　　　　[2] Flourac, *Jean Ier*, p. 87.
[3] E. Cosneau, *Le Connétable de Richemont* (Paris, 1886), p. 55.
[4] Ibid., p. 68; Beaucourt, *Charles VII*, ii. 333 n. 5. Apparently there is no evidence for Dr. Knowlson's assertion that Duke John and the Breton estates were insulted by Philip of Burgundy's promise to secure Brittany's adherence to the Treaty of Troyes (G. Knowlson, *Jean V, duc de Bretagne, et l'Angleterre* (Rennes, 1964), p. 118). On the contrary, the estates expressed their approval of the friendship between Brittany and Burgundy (Plancher, *Histoire de Bourgogne*, *preuves*, vol. iii, p. cccxix), an unlikely act if the estates had found Duke Philip's behaviour insulting.
[5] For England and the papacy see below, pp. 120–45. The dauphin and Martin V were at odds because Charles had sworn to uphold the *Ordonnances* of 1418, which the pope wanted repealed (Beaucourt, *Charles VII*, ii. 313–14).

to Amédée of Savoy (who, although he had married John the Fearless's sister, maintained his former connections with the French crown) to suggest that he renew his peace initiative, since the accession of two new monarchs seemed auspicious. Amédée proposed a meeting between the Burgundians and the French under his supervision at Bourg-en-Bresse; Charles sent a large embassy, but Philip's envoys treated the conversations with reserve. They arrived, five weeks late, to confront the Savoyard duke with copies of all Burgundy's treaties and alliances with the English. In the light of all these, they asked him what he advised. But Amédée did not flinch. 'I know', he said, 'that no agreement can be reached at the moment, but I have at least broached the question in order to know the dispositions of both Burgundy and Charles so that at the right time and place the matter can be settled.'[1] Even though—still mindful of the snub he had received from Henry V—he refused to send an embassy to Bedford, proposing that the three parties concerned in the war meet for a general peace conference under his mediation, the Burgundian envoys did secure his promise to write.[2] But both Bedford and Philip were lukewarm towards this scheme. Instead of setting out for Chalon-sur-Saône as Amédée planned, Philip had gone to Amiens to secure his friendship with Brittany and Bedford.

Meanwhile in England the Duke of Gloucester's pretentions to govern the country as regent had met with a sharp rebuff. Thanks to Bishop Beaufort's supporters in the council, Duke Humphrey's office was restricted to 'Protector and Defensor' and its prerogatives curbed by elaborate hedges.[3] Furthermore, he had to yield the position to Bedford when the latter was in England. Nevertheless, like Bedford he began to dabble in diplomacy. Shortly after Henry V's death Humphrey married Jacqueline, Countess of Hainault and Countess of Holland.

So few clues remain of Henry V's policy in the Low Countries that it is difficult to form a clear picture of his

---

1 Beaucourt, *Charles VII*, ii. 323.

2 Plancher, *Histoire de Bourgogne*, iv. 65–6; Beaucourt, *Charles VII*, ii. 321–3.

3 This title had been settled by 5 Dec. 1422 (Vickers, *Humphrey, Duke of Gloucester*, p. 114). See also B. Wilkinson, *Constitutional History of England in the Fifteenth Century (1399–1485)* (London, 1964), pp. 10–14, 225–31.

intentions. That he willingly permitted, if he did not encourage, Jacqueline of Hainault's flight from her husband
is not open to reasonable doubt.[1] In England conspicuous
honours were heaped on this lady: she received a monthly
stipend[2] and held the infant Henry VI at the baptismal font.[3]
To bind her more firmly to the English cause she was
apparently admitted to the Order of the Garter,[4] which
entailed a promise on the countess's part never to fight with
a fellow member. Such an ally obviously provided England
with a valuable hostage for the Duke of Burgundy's faithful
support. But is this all the English had in mind? Though
it is not possible to invest Henry with foreknowledge of the
coming of Arras, he had clearly considered the disastrous
consequences that would ensue from some such eventuality.
Is it not likely that he was making some plans to meet this
contingency? As early as 1418 he had tried to affiance
Bedford to Jacqueline, in whose name the lands of Holland,
Limbourg, Hainault, Zeeland, and Friesland were governed.
In 1421 he had concluded an alliance with the Doge of
Genoa, which specifically named Jacqueline as an English
ally.[5] Furthermore, if the story that Benedict XIII annulled
Jacqueline's marriage to Jean of Brabant is true and if the
countess and Gloucester were married shortly after Henry's
death, then either the king knew of, and consented to, these
arrangements or his reputation as a diplomat needs drastic
reinterpretation. By marrying Gloucester to Jacqueline,
England had a permanent surety for Burgundian support.
If this did not hold the Burgundians, then Gloucester could
be set up in the Low Countries in opposition, and the
Italian merchants, who were already deserting Bruges, could
be enticed to Holland.[6] It is not inconceivable that Henry
also knew the dauphin was trying to open negotiations with

[1] Wylie and Waugh, *Henry V*, iii. 290–2.
[2] The Duchess of Holland's stipend was confirmed three days after Henry VI's accession. On 15 Oct. 1422 she received £50 and a further £200 in Nov. and Dec. (E 404/39/5; E 403/658/mm. 1, 3, 6).
[3] *Chronicles of London*, ed. C. L. Kingsford (Oxford, 1905), p. 74.
[4] G. Beltz, *Memorials of the Order of the Garter* (London, 1841), pp. lxi, lxii.
[5] Rymer, x. 117.
[6] J. van Houtte, 'La genèse du grand marché international d'Anvers à la fin du moyen âge', *Revue belge de philologie et d'histoire*, xix (1940), 107–12.

the council of Flanders.¹ What Henry could not anticipate was that his early death followed by Gloucester's unsuccessful attempt to rule England as regent would loose him on Burgundy at the wrong time. The narrative of Gloucester's continental venture can be briefly summarized, as it has been recounted in detail on several occasions.² Late in 1423 both Duke Humphrey and the Duke of Brabant agreed to submit their differences to the arbitration of Bedford and Philip of Burgundy, assisted by a large body of councillors at Paris; but the arbiters were not able to reach a satisfactory verdict, and shifted the burden to the pope's shoulders. But Pope Martin, always looking for ways to turn a situation to the advantage of the Holy See, was in no hurry to give a decision; as a result Gloucester invaded the Low Countries, established himself and Jacqueline at Mons, and senselessly allowed his troops to pillage his wife's lands, but failed to take decisive military action against his opponents.³ When his brother cut off reinforcements he beat a hasty retreat to London, ostensibly to prepare for a duel with Philip, whom Gloucester had called a liar.⁴ From London he periodically dispatched aid to his stranded consort.

What is interesting about this episode is the Regent of France's reactions. Gloucester initiated the invasion of the Low Countries without so much as a word of opposition from the English council. But almost immediately the Duke of Bedford set the machinery for arbitration in motion.⁵

¹ In Oct. 1421 Hannequin Poallet from Tournai was arrested in Ghent, the letters he was carrying from the dauphin to the Flemings impounded and sent to Duke Philip (Brussels, Archives Générales du Royaume, Conseil de Flandres, 21799, f. 11ʳ).

² F. von Löher, *Jakobäa von Bayern und ihre Zeit* (Nördlingen, 1862–9); E. le Blant, *Les Quatre Mariages de Jacqueline, duchesse en Bavière* (Paris, 1904); Vickers, *Humphrey, Duke of Gloucester*, pp. 125–61; Plancher, *Histoire de Bourgogne*, iv. 71–2, 90, 95–6, 98–9.

³ *Chronique des Pays-Bas*, ed. J.-J. de Smet (Corpus chronicorum Flandriae, 1856), iii. 387–9.

⁴ E. de Dynter, *Chronique des ducs de Brabant* 57, ed. P. de Ram (Brussels, 1857), iii. 865–6.

⁵ Gloucester was besieged by messengers from Bedford almost as soon as he landed at Calais. The accounts of the receiver general for 1424–5 contain numerous payments to these messengers (B.N., MS. français 4491, ff. 17ʳ⁻ᵛ, 31ʳ; MS. français 4485, pp. 365–6, 376; B.M., Add. Charters 3579, 3580).

When this broke down he wrote to Martin V begging for a quick decision, and since the pope gave no sign of compliance another council was summoned to Paris to adjudicate the case. As a warning the regent had the county of Ponthieu, which had been settled on Jacqueline by her first husband, the Dauphin Jean, re-united to the French crown on 15 July 1424.[1] By this time Duke Humphrey with almost 6,000 men had established himself in Jacqueline's counties and refused to abide by the arbiter's verdict. With no apparent compunction Bedford cut off his brother's reinforcements. The Protector of England, however, had not ended his continental venture, for late in 1425 he began raising troops for another invasion.[2] This was the last straw; Bedford decided to put an end to his brother's adventuring.[3] On 25 December he notified Duke Philip of the impending invasion; consequently, the English troops that disembarked near Zierikzee in Zeeland early in 1426 were quickly massacred.[4] Although he put a stop to Gloucester's active intervention on the Continent, the regent could not stop the English council's response to the Duchess of Gloucester's pleas for assistance in the following year:[5] 'considering the great troubles, dangers and distresses' of the duchess the council ordered 9,000 marks to be assigned to her.[6] And they went a step further, composing a letter to the

---

[1] Archives Nationales, J. 520, no. 34. There is also a transcript of this document in the Public Record Office (P.R.O. 31/8/136).

[2] Vickers, *Humphrey, Duke of Gloucester*, pp. 169–70.

[3] On 29 Dec. 1425 the Council of Flanders sent a messenger, Guerardin du Bois, to the ducal chancellor with letters containing a message from Guillebert de Lannoy 'escriptes a Eclo ce meisme jour' saying 'que le duc de Clocest' avoit miz sus certaine quantite de gens darmes et d[e] trait pour venir en Hollande ou en Zeelande comme mons' le regent le royaulme lui estant nagair' a Calais avoit mande a mon dit s' de Bourgogne affin que hastivement il pleusist a mon dit s' le chanceller traire pardevers le dit mess' Guillebert en la ville de Brug' pour oir sa credence et charge quil avoit de mon dit s' le duc touchans la dite matiere' (Brussels, Archives Générales du Royaume, Conseil de Flandres, 21801, f. 16ᵛ).

[4] On 14 Jan. 1426 the Council of Flanders wrote to the bailiffs of Sluis because they had heard that 'mon dit s' avoit desconfiz les diz Engloiz et leurs alliez mais ancoir' ilz nen avoient eu aucunes seures nouvelles' (ibid. f. 17ʳ).

[5] On 26 May 1427 the English council ordered the exchequer to pay 100 marks to Louis de Montfort and Arnaud de Gent, knights, who had come to the king from the Duchess of Holland (E 404/43/337).

[6] E 404/43/350. I can find no evidence, however, that this sum was actually paid.

regent recommending Jacqueline's cause. Since these moves had stirred up rumours of another English invasion, the exasperated regent averred that although he had great personal regard for both his brother and his sister-in-law their policy did nothing but stir up dissension in the two kingdoms.[1] Mr. C. A. J. Armstrong has pointed out that contrary to general belief, the invasion of Hainault actually served to shore up the bond between the regent and Burgundy.[2] Forced to relax his insistence that the crown lands of France were inalienable, Bedford at last granted Philip some of the spoils he had anticipated when he became a party to the Treaty of Troyes.[3] As a whole the regent's gifts to the Duke of Burgundy were niggardly. Rather than allow Philip to establish himself at Orléans (spring 1429) Bedford preferred to bring the siege to an unsuccessful conclusion.[4]

The regent's decision to continue the siege of Orléans almost terminated the double monarchy. Philip left Paris in a rage and ordered the withdrawal of his troops before the besieged city; a crippling blow which eventually cost Bedford the victory.[5] By the end of the summer Burgundy had resumed negotiations with the French at Arras. This setback followed by the defeats at Jargeau, Meung, Beaugency, and Patay, and revolt in Normandy virtually wiped out the Lancastrian-French army. That the regent's government survived can no doubt be explained in large part by the exertions of his wife as mediator. Just as important, however, was Cardinal Beaufort. When the English council learned of Talbot's rout at Patay, Beaufort was in England

---

[1] Archives du Nord, B. 1189. He also wrote a similar letter to Gloucester. And the Parlement of Paris wrote in Aug. to exhort peace between Burgundy and Gloucester (Clément de Fauquembergue, ii. 242).

[2] Armstrong, 'La Double Monarchie', p. 101.

[3] Professor Bonenfant suggested that Philip had negotiated the Treaty of Amiens with Bedford hoping to acquire some of the territorial concessions Henry V had promised but never granted (P. Bonenfant, *Philippe le Bon* (Brussels, 1955), p. 39).

[4] Armstrong, 'La Double Monarchie', p. 90. When Bedford refused to make a truce on the terms stipulated Philip sent a herald to inform the Orléanists that he was withdrawing his army, thereby giving them the encouragement they needed to hold out until reinforcements arrived (G. Cousinot, *Chronique de la Pucelle*, ed. M. Vallet de Viriville (Paris, 1892), p. 270).

[5] Beaucourt, *Charles VII*, ii. 407.

raising an army to renew the Hussite crusade. With little apparent hesitation the cardinal turned his army aside from the Holy War and led them to France. His gift was not, however, without a price: he demanded a voice in the French government. Thus in October he joined Hugues de Lannoy, Jean de Luxembourg, and the Abbot of Mont-Saint-Michel in their talks with Charles VII's agents and arranged for a peace conference at Auxerre the following year. The same day that the cardinal was admitted to the French council Philip was made Lieutenant General of France, having already relieved the regent of Paris's government.[1] These concessions evidently satisfied the duke, for in February 1430 he began making plans to renew the war with 1,500 men-at-arms and 1,500 archers in return for an additional concession—the county of Champagne as an apanage.[2] But Burgundy's military ventures brought no success and by November the duke was complaining that he received no support from his allies. (Bedford had gone to Rouen, where apart from retaking Château-Gaillard and a few minor victories nothing was accomplished.)[3]

Failure—whether through inability or indifference—to come to Philip's aid embittered relations further. Heralding his growing estrangement from the double monarchy, Philip established the Order of the Golden Fleece as a rival to the regent's own knightly order,[4] he absented himself from Henry VI's coronation at Paris, and took a wife whose links with England were mostly historical. Bedford's response to these pricks suggests that the actions of both dukes obeyed a kind of *lex talionis* in which reprisal and counter-reprisal succeeded one another. Anne of Burgundy represented her husband at Philip's wedding;[5] when she died in 1432 the regent chose his second wife from among Philip's rivals, and finally when both dukes found

---

[1] Beaucourt, *Charles VII*, ii. 413. Henry VI granted the government of Paris, Chartres, Melun, Sens, Troyes, Chaumont-en-Bassigny, Amiens, the Tournésis, Saint-Amand, and Ponthieu to Philip on 13 Oct. 1429 (Archives du Nord, B. 302).
[2] Ibid., B. 302.   [3] Beaucourt, *Charles VII*, ii. 39.
[4] It seems that Bedford used his knightly order to attach nobles on the border between Burgundy and France to his cause (A. Bossuat, 'Les prisonniers de guerre au xve siècle, la rançon de Guillaume, seigneur de Châteauvillain', *Annales de Bourgogne*, xxiii (1951), 7–35).
[5] Cardinal Beaufort, however, attended personally (*Brut*, pt. 2, pp. 437–8).

themselves at Saint-Omer they departed without meeting, neither wishing to demean himself by calling on the other.

At the curia the Duke of Bedford adopted a more direct strategy, while the English proceeded with their evasive negotiations. In March 1424 an Anglo-French embassy arrived at the Roman court in hopes of reaping reward for English connivance in breaking up the council of Siena. Among the envoys was Jean de la Rochetaillée, Bedford's agent at the council. He requested *inter alia* that the pope create some cardinals of Anglotropic disposition, that the pope in his letters address Henry VI as King of France and England, that he abandon the case concerning the Duke of Gloucester's marriage since Bedford and Burgundy had been accepted as mediators, and he assured the pontiff that in future he must resign himself to a mere one-third of the common services and one-half of the annates, so that the French clergy would not be pauperized. Further, Rochetaillée asked that the pope henceforth provide benefices only to one of the three upright and deserving persons secretly named beforehand and that some French churchman be accorded knowledge of the cases pending before the curia.[1] It seems that some rather lively and heated discussion followed the delivery of this credence at the Holy See.

By early in 1425 the pope had trained his sights on Bedford, for in October 1424 the latter had presumed to call an assembly of French prelates and others from the three estates to discuss the disposition of benefices. Here it was announced that 'l'intencion et volenté dudit (duc) de Bedford estoit de maintenir et faire maintenir l'eglise de France et les personnes ecclesiastiques de ce royaume en leur libertés et franchises anciennes . . .'.[2] To Bedford Martin wrote on 2 February taking as his theme the often quoted commonplace 'quod super omnes reges regnant et domini dominantur'.[3] From this it followed, the pope argued, that

---

[1] '. . . de persona notabili et benemerita tali provisione digna unus ex tribus per eum ad hoc serenitati vestre secrete nominandis . . . potestatem facultatem et licenciam cognoscendi de quibuscumque causis de quibus recursus habendus esset ad sedem apostolicam sive per simplicem querelam aut appellacionem vel alias quovis modo . . .' (P.R.O. 31/8/136).

[2] Clément de Fauquembergue, ii. 144.

[3] An echo of Proverbs 8: 15. Raynaldus, *sub anno* 1425, no. vii.

the duke should endeavour to preserve the liberties of the church and to beware 'scandalosis hominibus' who seek to disturb the peace of the church.

At this time Bedford did not know that his chances of extorting concessions from the pope had been considerably reduced. Charles VII had written to the pope (10 February) to effect a reconciliation with the Holy See and had dispatched envoys to formalize this accord.[1] But the news travelled rapidly and by 1 May Bedford had decided on a course of action.[2] Dr. John Gentill, a Gascon in the English diplomatic service, was] dispatched with a response to an earlier letter from the pope's inveterate enemy Alfonso V of Aragon. What the English wanted was to support Alfonso's professed desire for a reduction of the time until the next general council.[3] (Now, however, the Aragonese monarch was on the point of invading Castile and was unable to make use of English support.)[4] Without waiting for a reply,[5] Bedford continued his efforts to embarrass this pope who found the very idea of a council so abhorrent. A further letter to Bedford written towards the end of May must have considerably exacerbated the regent's hostility. In this letter the pope asserted that a peace

---

[1] The chroniclers Waurin, Le Fèvre, and Monstrelet (under the wrong date) mention the French embassy to Rome that made the formal reconciliation with the pope. Waurin, ii. 178–9; Le Fèvre, ii. 114; Monstrelet, iv. 231.

[2] Giuliano Cesarini appears to be the bearer of this news. On his way to England he stopped in Paris and on 3 Apr. he 'apporta ceans lettres closes du Pape, contenans creance, exposée par ledit docteur . . . afin que la court voulsisit toujours perseverer et entendre à la tuition et defence des drois, auctorité, privileges et preeminences du siege du Romme et de l'eglise universal' (Clément de Fauquembergue, ii. 169).

[3] '. . . pro requirendo abbreviacionis termino proximi generalis consilii celebrandi' (B.M., Cotton MS. Cleopatra C. IV, f. 177ᵛ; (N. Valois, Le Pape et le Concile (Paris, 1906), i. 84–5, no. 4).

[4] 'Primo exponantur . . . domini regis occupacio in factis arduissimis Castelle ad presens inevitabilibus talibus quod circa alia non posset commode intendere de presenti' (A.C.A., Registro 2680, ff. 8ᵛ–9ʳ; K. A. Fink, 'Martin V und Aragon', Historische Studien, Heft 340 (1938), p. 187 n. 9).

[5] Alfonso informed Sigismund on 25 Feb. that he had not encouraged the English and the Castilian kings 'pro expetenda scilicet instantissime tam in capite quam in membris reformacione sancte matris ecclesie . . .' (A.C.A., Registro 2678, f. 141ᵛ; Fink, 'Martin V und Aragon', p. 125 n. 21). The preceding autumn Sigismund had written to Henry VI certifying his willingness to send a messenger to the pope on the subject of a general council (Regesta Imperii, XI, Die Urkunden Kaiser Sigmunds (1410–1437), ed. W. Altmann (Innsbruck, 1896–1900), no. 5992).

settlement must be reached and that an effort to bring this about could not be repudiated without grave offence to God.[1] Before the middle of the next month it had been determined to send William, Abbot of Beaulieu, and Walter de la Pole, knight, to Rome with the demand for a council,[2] and a letter to the keepers of the port of Dover dated 11 July contained an order to provide sufficient shipping for this embassy.[3] The abbot actually left London on 20 July with twenty-four mounted men in his retinue.[4] This embassy may have been accompanied by Pierre de Rouville, whom Bedford empowered to explain to the pope on 7 August 'aucunes matieres touchant l'onneur de mondit seigneur et le bien universel de sancte eglise'.[5] But this embassy, like so many Anglo-papal conversations, achieved nothing, even though it had threatened the pope with the possibility of using secular authority to obtain ecclesiastical reform.[6] The pope simply delayed responding to the thrust, for he believed that his aim of reducing the English to obedience was in sight. Valois France had submitted to him and the Iberian political situation prevented Aragon from supporting the Lancastrians. This delay turned to his advantage, for by the end of the year Gloucester had come so near causing a rupture in the Anglo-Burgundian alliance that Bedford was compelled to come to an agreement with the pope in the hope of securing his support in settling the case.

If this accommodation with Martin V solved one of Bedford's problems, it created another. During the early years of the fifteenth century the French clergy had slowly

---

[1] Raynaldus, *sub anno* 1325, no. vi.

[2] 'En ce temps furent envoyés devers le saint père à Romme, notables ambassadeurs de France et d'Angleterre pour luy sommer de convoequier concille de Constance' (le Fèvre, ii. 116). See the warrants for issue dated 9 June and 4 July (E 404/41/331, 332, 346). The tellers rolls record that the abbot received £121. 6s. 8d. and de la Pole £40 advance on their wages (E 405/2/38/mm. 1rb, 4rb). The exchequer paid the abbot's advance on 13 and 19 June; on the latter day de la Pole, who contrary to the statement on the tellers rolls received an additional £50, took his advance (E 403/671/mm. 8, 13; 673/m. 10).

[3] *Cal. Close Rolls, 1422–4*, pp. 172–3. This letter was delivered by the king's messenger John Davenport, who received 3s. 4d. for his services (E 405/2/38/ m. 4rb).

[4] E 101/322/11. He returned to London the following Feb.

[5] B.N., MS. français 26048, no. 447; Valois, *Le Pape et le Concile*, i. 85 n. 1.

[6] Mansi, vol. xxix, coll. 464–5.

secured freedom from papal impositions such as provisions, reservations, and annates that Bedford's act had restored. By this accommodation with the pope the regent alienated all the greater ecclesiastics in his dominion with the possible exception of Pierre Cauchon and the University of Paris, whose clerks generally received more lucrative provisions when they were papally provided than when distribution was locally controlled. As the war progressed and the French treasury became emptier Bedford was forced to turn to these ecclesiastics for financial support. Having sounded the pope on a scheme to collect a double tenth (nominally for the Hussite crusade, but in fact for the war in France) and a special subsidy, the regent approached the French clergy at the Synod of Sens 19 January–10 May 1429. Although each of the bishops present owed his position to the English or the Burgundians, they flatly refused to contribute anything to the government's war chest.[1]

In retrospect, it seems surprising that Arras did not come some years before 1435. Credit for its postponement seems equally divided between events at Charles VII's court (the disfavour into which the constable Richemont fell and Charles's *rapprochement* with Burgundy's enemies Sigismund and the Duke of Austria) and the efforts of Cardinal Beaufort.[2] As we have seen the reversal of Bedford's fortune in war had given the cardinal an opportunity to act. In return for his army, the cardinal assumed a place in the French council, and when Henry VI landed in France for his coronation the regent was forced to relinquish his absolute control of the government, though it was returned when the king departed. Having secured a place in the government and reduced the regent's authority, Beaufort turned his attention to pacifying Duke Philip. Beaufort had early given evidence of his desire to consolidate the Anglo-Burgundian alliance. Returning from Germany in 1428 he had passed through Cologne where he tried his hand at mediating between Burgundy's vassal the Duke of Cleves, his brother and Archbishop Dietrich.[3] The following year his arbitration of the differences between Duke Philip and the

---

[1] S. Luce, *Jeanne d'Arc à Domrémy* (Paris, 1886), pp. ccxvi–ccxxvi.
[2] Armstrong, 'La double Monarchie', pp. 109–10. [3] See below, p. 113.

Hollanders resulted in the more successful Treaty of Delft.
Next, Beaufort secured both the government of Paris and
the office of lieutenant general for the Burgundian duke. If
(as the negotiations of 1429 suggest) he had come to France
to make peace, the plan was abandoned, for Philip, having
received the rewards he expected in 1420, was ready to
renew the war. But lack of success turned Philip against the
war: he renewed his negotiations with Charles VII, and in
December 1431 he informed Henry VI of an agreement he
had made with Charles that was designed to lead to peace.[1]
'La guerre pour laquelle supporter ne m'avez aidié ne
secouru comme besoin estoit . . .', he writes, was too costly
to be pursued.[2] The cardinal quickly and correctly assessed
Philip's changed attitude; he visited the Duke of Bedford
at Corbeil and tried to reconcile the two dukes at Saint-
Omer. When this failed he approached Charles VII directly
and persuaded the reluctant French to offer a four months'
truce at the conference to be held at Corbeil in July. The
English delegates were accordingly furnished with the
protocol Beaufort extorted from the French monarch, but
the regent's chancellor, the Bishop of Thérouanne refused
to ratify it. Defeated, the cardinal withdrew. The Burgundians at Basel received orders that same month to separate
themselves from the English delegation. As long as the
regent and his council could act independently of the
English government, adopting contrary foreign policies,
there was no chance to save the Anglo-Burgundian alliance.
At Arras the English made an attempt to avoid the problem
of contrary aims by sending an embassy representing both
governments, an experiment they had tried at Basel, but
neither side really wanted peace.[3] The French hoped to
compel Burgundy to a separate peace—that way the English
could be bought off for less—while the English only came
to the conference to negotiate a truce, secured by Henry VI's
marriage to one of Charles's daughters, realizing that peace
would involve abandoning claims to land and renouncing

[1] Beaucourt, *Charles VII*, ii. 443.
[2] Plancher, *Histoire de Bourgogne, preuves,* iv, p. cix.
[3] Dickinson, *Arras, passim*. The chronicler Basin thought, however, that the
French proposals were eminently reasonable (Basin, i. 189).

the title King of France.[1] Thus it was a foregone conclusion
that the Anglo-French negotiations would come to naught;
for the English refused to abandon Henry's rights to the
French crown and the French refused to negotiate unless he
did. On 6 September 1435 the English delegation departed,
leaving the French and Burgundians to conclude a separate
agreement.

While the alliance between Burgundy and the double
monarchy slowly dissolved, the regent had other pressing
diplomatic problems to solve. The wax seal impressions on
the Treaty of Amiens were hardly set before the mercurial
Duke of Brittany began scheming to escape from the
entanglement of the French war. Thus he took advantage
of Philip the Good's discomfiture by the Duke of Gloucester
to conclude an agreement whereby the Breton-Burgundian
alliance remained intact if either party became reconciled to
the dauphin, and as a *pro forma* concession to Philip, his
reconciliation with the la Marche pretenders to Breton rule
was not to invalidate the treaty. Seeing his role as that of a
grand mediator, the Breton duke succumbed to the entreaties of the dauphin's mother-in-law and consented to an
arrangement made at Nantes (May 1424), which provided
for an Armagnac-Burgundian *rapprochement* and peace with
England.[2] Within the next month the Constable Richemont,
John V's brother, had quarrelled with Bedford, who would
not release him from his nominal status as a prisoner,[3] and
fled to Brittany where he cast off his English allegiance; in
return the dauphin presented him with the constable's
sword in March 1425.[4] Over-confident because of the ease
of changing alliances, at Saumur on 7 October 1425 the

[1] On 6 Sept. the ambassadors for Eugenius and from Basel declared that Henry
was not King of France and that 'il soit content de ses lepards' (*Chronique des Pays-
Bas*, iii. 422).

[2] Knowlson, *Jean V*, p. 128; Cosneau, *Richemont*, p. 77.

[3] Henry V evidently intended to use his prisoner Richemont in the same way
that he planned for Jacqueline of Bavaria and for the Duke of Orléans—as a
security for his allies' good behaviour. John V would be neutral, if not friendly, as
long as his brother was in English hands. However, in Feb. 1420 John V was
captured by rival claimants to the ducal throne and imprisoned. King Henry,
yielding to the pleas of John V's wife, Queen Catherine's sister, paroled Richemont
so that he could help secure his brother's release (ibid., p. 56).

[4] Ibid., p. 56.

duke made one with the dauphin's cause and later betrothed
his eldest daughter to one of the dauphin's supporters.[1]
Then he audaciously accused Bedford of breaking the
Treaty of Amiens by treating with John's rivals, the la
Marche and their mother. Such rash behaviour makes it
difficult to agree with Dr. Knowlson's description of John V
as a Machiavelli *avant la lettre*; perhaps a more conservative
estimate, say a second-rate Louis XI, comes nearer the
truth. In any case his folly was soon manifest. On 15 January
1426 Bedford declared war on the duke for breaking the
Amiens treaty. It did not take John V long to realize that
he had underestimated the Regent of France; opinion in
England might be divided between factions in the council,
but on the Continent Bedford had the last word always—and
he was not a man to abide treachery. Having quickly
arranged a short truce, the Bretons were favoured by chance:
although warfare began again during September, the regent
was compelled to break it off in October, when he returned
to England to settle the quarrel between Gloucester and the
cardinal. In the interval no effort was spared to persuade
Burgundy and the dauphin to compose their differences and
come to Brittany's aid. But the Duke of Burgundy was
impressed neither by the clumsy revelation of a supposed
English plot to assassinate him nor by the Breton ambassadors' assertion that their duke had refused to make peace
without Philip's consent, and the dauphin continued in-
active.[2] The regent returned to France in the early summer
of 1427 and reopened the war. It took only three months
to reduce John to obedience; on 7 September he ratified his
peace with Bedford and swore once again to uphold the
settlement of 1420.[3] From this treaty until late in the war
Brittany's diplomatic importance was eclipsed by larger
problems. Brittany's defeat coupled with Richemont's fall
from favour the next year must have played a decisive role
in postponing the failure of the regent's alliance system
until 1435.

[1] Knowlson, *Jean V*, p. 132.
[2] A. Desplanque, *Projet d'assassinat de Philippe le Bon par les Anglais (1424–
1426)* (Mémoires de l'Académie Royale de Belgique. Savants étrangers, 1867),
vol. xxxiii.
[3] Knowlson, *Jean V*, p. 137; Cosneau, *Richemont*, pp. 147–8.

London greeted the news of Burgundy's treachery at Arras with a fury reserved especially for foreigners. Bruges merchants returning from Portugal were captured and their goods confiscated.[1] The heralds Toison d'Or and Franche-Comté, who came as ambassadors from Philip bearing the duke's entreaty that England accept the French proposals for peace and assurance that he did not interpret his treaty with Charles VII as an offensive alliance against the English crown, were arrested—narrowly escaping with their lives—and their letters impounded.[2] On 10 October the chancellor, Bishop Stafford, gave parliament the news officially and invited it to make generous provision for an army to punish Burgundian perfidy.[3] Futhermore, the changed political situation called for a reappraisal and a readjustment in foreign policy. Bedford had died before learning the outcome of Arras and the *grand conseil* in France had been merged with the councillors sitting at Rouen for more than a year. It seems unlikely that the English government seriously considered reconstituting the double monarchy, rather they assumed full control of foreign-policy making. The most pressing task was to re-establish, following the pattern of Edward III's German policy, close connections with the princes of the Empire and with Sigismund, whose hostility towards Philip was well known. Cities of the Low Countries, such as Dordrecht, Amsterdam, Rotterdam, Leiden, Delft, and Middelburg, having been reminded of their economic link with England, were encouraged to revolt.[4] And Charles of Orléans, who had been captured at Agincourt, was offered his freedom if he would make war against Philip.[5] Henry even offered to make peace with Charles VII if he would invade Burgundy.

The Burgundian army's cowardly performance before Calais and the rapine of the English soldiers were followed

---

[1] On 17 Mar. 1436 Henry wrote to Duke Philip denying that he had any part in the seizure of these merchants (Archives du Nord, B. 571).

[2] Monstrelet, vi. 190–1.

[3] *Rot. parl.*, iv. 481. Philip's old enemy Humphrey of Gloucester was appointed lietenant of Calais on 1 Nov. 1435 (Rymer, x. 641).

[4] J. Stevenson, ed., *Letters and Papers Illustrative of the Wars of the English in France during the Reign of Henry VI* (London, 1861), i, p. x; E. Scott and L. Gillodts van Severen, *Le Cotton MS. Galba B. I* (Académie Royale de Belgique, 1896), pp. 428–34.   [5] Beaucourt, *Charles VII*, iii. 87–8.

by a revolt in Flanders. Charles VII, having concluded the
Treaty of Arras, proved indifferent about fulfilling it. And
the emperor, having openly defied Burgundy, began to
incite the citizens of Liège to revolt. The pro-English
faction among Philip's advisers argued that peace between
England and France was the only way to end his difficulties; but if by adroit manœuvres he could secure the
Duke of Orléans's release to reconcile Henry and Charles,
then not only would the war cease but the son of his father's
assassin would be in the duke's debt. Furthermore, Philip
must have been aware of the Bastard of Orléans's plans to
free his brother: if Amédée of Savoy, who was also a friend
of both the Count of Armagnac and the Duke of Brittany,
could be won over, the English government could be
approached through him. The success of this plan, the
Burgundian councillors warned, might confront Philip with
a coalition of French nobles dedicated to reducing his
power.[1] Moreover, a longing for peace was spreading over
all western Europe. The Duke of Brittany's ambiguous
position was exploited to approach the English. The Council
of Basel and the pope exhorted the English to make peace.
At Eugenius's request, the King of Portugal offered himself
as a mediator.[2] The war was going badly for the English:
though they saved Calais in 1436, they lost Paris; the next
year Nemours and Montereau fell. That same year the
harvest failed, famine was widespread in France, and
attempts to buy grain from the Teutonic Knights met with
little success.[3] Consequently, the Duchess of Burgundy's call
for negotiations in 1438 did not fall on deaf ears in the
English council now that the peace party was slowly gaining
the upper hand. Envoys were sent to the duchess late that
year, though they were not to negotiate with her traitorous
husband.[4] In turn the duchess won over the French king and
plans were laid for a conference at Gravelines.

---

[1] Beaucourt, *Charles VII*, iii. 80–3.

[2] Ibid. 89, 91. On 10 May 1438 the pope wrote to the King of England marvelling
that the plan to send the Duke of Orléans to treat for peace between France and
England had not matured (P.R.O. 31/8/40/f. 152).

[3] See below, p. 96.

[4] In May the council discussed sending the Bishop of Norwich, the Earl of
Stafford, Lord Beaumont, the Deans of York, Salisbury (or of Exeter or Lincoln),

But the Burgundians had no more success at ending Anglo-French hostility at Gravelines than they had at Arras.[1] The chief members of the English embassy headed by Cardinal Beaufort arrived in Calais on 26 June; the French appeared a few days later. By 6 July all the preparations had been made for the conference and after a preliminary skirmish over the wording of the letters of proxy, the envoys got down to work. Proceeding in the usual manner—by alternate proposals—the envoys soon collided against the solid refusal of the English to abandon claim to the crown of France. At this point the English instructions are of interest, for the king had written that if this was the only point standing between the two parties he had instructed the cardinal personally on the matter. What concession Henry had been prepared to make is unknown. Beaufort made no reference to his secret and sent agents back to England for new instructions so that the conference could proceed to the question of a truce, seeing that peace was unobtainable. Perhaps a healthy respect for his opponents at home counselled prudence, for the new instructions, which he received in September, suggest a more intractable attitude; with Beaufort out of the kingdom the advocates of continuing the war found their cause easier to pursue. There was no question of abandoning Henry's claim or his style, though the territorial demands were further reduced and Orléans would be temporarily freed to work for peace. Nothing further could be done beyond concluding a mercantile agreement that patched up Anglo-Flemish differences brought about by the attack on Burgundy in 1436.

Because Cardinal Beaufort's henchman, the Archbishop of York, returned to England insistent on pursuing the way of peace (which entailed setting the Duke of Orléans free) he provoked the last great duel between Gloucester and the cardinal (now represented by the peace party), and the duke's defeat signalled the end of the independent and conflicting

---

or Richard Caudray (*Proc. P.C.* v. 95). On 23 Nov. 1438 the envoys appointed were Sir Thomas Rempston, John Rinwell, merchant, Dr. William Sprever, Robert Whittingham, and Dr. Stephen Wilton (Rymer, x. 713, 714).

[1] Dr. Thomas Beckington's account of this embassy is printed in *Proc. P.C.* x. 334–407.

diplomacy conducted by the king's uncles which had wrecked England's alliance system and played a large part in causing her to lose the war. Hereafter—that is until the Duke of York opened negotiations with the French and the pope's legate—English policy was uniform, if it was not successful.

The logic and careful reasoning of Gloucester's argument shows an acute, well-trained mind, but a mind which years of defeat and frustration had blinded to subtlety.[1] The duke chose the method of direct attack and clothed his argument in a vicious personal diatribe against the cardinal. The Cardinal of England was disobedient, dishonest, and a purveyor of bad advice; therefore his plan to release Orléans was no more likely to benefit England than Beaufort's adventures at Arras and Gravelines. Indeed both he and the Archbishop of York should be removed from the council. There were excellent reasons for holding on to Duke Charles, and Gloucester gave them: releasing Orléans would complete his reconciliation (which Beaufort had begun at Calais) with Philip of Burgundy, who would have otherwise remained his mortal enemy. Henry V had warned of the dangers implicit in Charles's release before France was conquered. It was evidently known that Charles VII was unable to govern personally and that the nobles of France would be likely to take advantage of the duke's 'subtilite and cauteleux disposition' by making him Regent of France. Any promise Orléans made to the English he would later renounce, claiming it had been made under duress. (He was in fact a prisoner.) Gascony, particularly vulnerable at this time, would be in even greater danger owing to alliances between Orléans, Armagnac, and Foix. Further, Orléans, who acknowledged Charles VII's sovereignty, would be unlikely to undertake any business for the English that would subject his lands to confiscation by the French king. And finally, the king's reply intimates that Gloucester suggested Orléans had picked up valuable information for France while he was in England.

---

[1] One part of Duke Humphrey's argument is printed in Stevenson, *Wars*, ii. 440–51; another copy of this document survives in B.M., Add. MS. 38690, ff. 4^r–5^v. A second part of the duke's argument is in the Bodleian Library in Oxford (Ashmole MS. 758, ff. 705^r–713^r).

However cogent, Gloucester's argument presented in this fashion was certain to be vetoed. The reasons that moved the king to reject Gloucester's argument were couched in more general terms.[1] Apart from secret things that could not be revealed to the public, the overriding reason was peace. Basel and the pope could not be pacified until all Christian princes united their efforts to achieve it. The king had discovered (like Edward III) that the possibility of conquering all the vast area of France was unlikely. Since it was not dishonourable to sue for peace—his father had done so—and since it was time to end the suffering of his people, Henry had approached King Charles, but Charles was unwilling to negotiate until Orléans was free. In addition to paying an attractive ransom, the duke would reduce the influence of Charles's advisers who were hostile to England, and he had promised both orally and in writing to work actively for peace. Furthermore, the law of arms forbade keeping a man in prison who was willing to ransom himself. As for the information he could give the French government, it was much less than other prisoners, who unlike Charles had been free to wander about the country, could give. Thus on 2 July 1440 Charles and the English agreed to the terms of his liberation.[2] He was in Calais on 5 November and six days later, when there was no question of duress, he swore once again to uphold his engagement. If the councillors who authorized this plan expected immediate results, they were doomed to disappointment. The French king was displeased by the excessive friendliness Orléans showed Burgundy as well as by the magnificence of Charles's retinue and refused to receive him. Rebuffed, the duke left Paris and actively entered into preparations for a league of princes against the king.[3] The exact purpose of this league is unknown, but it certainly included a plan to draw England into the design. In 1441 the Duke of Alençon, who had allied himself to Armagnac and Brittany as early as 1438, befriended the English by warning them that Argentan was about to be delivered to the French through

---

[1] Stevenson, *Wars*, ii. 451–60; there is another copy in B.M., Add. MS. 38690, ff. 6ʳ–8ʳ.   [2] P. Champion, *Vie de Charles d'Orléans* (Paris, 1911), pp. 308–15.
[3] Beaucourt, *Charles VII*, iii. 194.

treachery.[1] The capture of Pontoise by Charles VII's army and the conference at Nevers gave the members of this league pause to think, but in the early spring the Duchess of Burgundy sent messengers to Cardinal Beaufort and Suffolk and in two months' time renewed her conversations with the Duke of York.[2] Surely it is no coincidence that the Count of Armagnac's envoy appeared in England at exactly this time proposing a marriage alliance between Henry and one of the count's daughters.[3] Before the end of the summer the Duke of Burgundy was at Dijon laying plans for the marriage of Margaret of Anjou to the Count of Nevers. By October 1442 the Duchess of Burgundy and York had reached agreement on a truce between England and Burgundy, which she ratified the following April.[4] Moreover, the Duke of Brittany renewed his final peace with England at the end of the year.[5] Although no positive proof survives, the indirect evidence points suspiciously towards a league with the English against the French king. Nor do we know what rewards were offered the English, but they must have been sufficiently attractive to arouse Gloucester, the leader of the war party in England, to urge English acceptance. Fortune, however, favoured the advocates of peace. Charles VII descended upon the Count of Armagnac with his army, putting an end to the prospects of that marriage alliance.[6] But the Duchess of Burgundy and York resumed their lively flow of correspondence so that when Suffolk came to France in 1444 he felt constrained to secure an offer of one of King Charles's daughters for York's eldest son.[7]

[1] Beaucourt, *Charles VII*, iii. 202–3.

[2] Beaucourt, *Charles VII*, iii. 259.

[3] Jean Batute arrived in England on 24 Apr. 1442 and remained until 21 July, when he sailed from Plymouth (E 404/59/281, 282).   [4] *Proc. P.C.* vi. 12.

[5] Archives du Nord, B. 306; Beaucourt, *Charles VII*, iii. 262. Cardinal Beaufort wrote to the Duchess of Burgundy on 16 June 1443 promising to see that the truce York had concluded was executed. However, he warned, Burgundians fighting for Charles VII would be attacked when they crossed into territory not covered by the truce (Archives du Nord, B. 306).

[6] It seems to have been common gossip in England that Suffolk put an end to the idea of an Armagnac marriage in England. 'In this same yere wer diverse embassatoures sent in to Guyan for a mariage for the King for therles doughter of Arminak which was concluded; but be the mean of therle of Suthfolk, it was lett and put aparte' (*Brut*, pt. 2, p. 510).

[7] Basin says that Charles refused to give one of his own daughters to the English

Having bought off the Duke of York and seen Armagnac subdued, Suffolk thought to conclude peace with France. The duke with his associates Moleyns, Roos, Hoo, the secretary Richard Andrew, and Wenlock presented themselves to Charles on 17 April 1444. As in so many negotiations in the past the question of sovereignty stood in the way of peace; however, Charles privately proposed to Suffolk that he would give the English Normandy, Gascony, and all the lands the English held before raising the question of the crown in return for Henry's renunciation of his rights. Since the duke had no power to make such an arrangement, he agreed to make a truce during which time French ambassadors would come to England to conclude the peace.[1] And he settled the arrangements for the marriage of Henry VI with Margaret of Anjou. For both sides the truce was advantageous: the English, though their aspirations had been blasted, would hold outright an economically valuable part of France, and Charles for a concession would check Burgundy's expansion in Lorraine as well as seal off his *rapprochement* with England. But subsequent events were to show that the French king was even cleverer; he had outwitted the English embassy.

Suffolk returned with his party to England in late July amid wild rejoicing, and received public thanks in parliament for what he had accomplished.[2] Though almost a year passed before Charles commissioned his envoys to Henry's court, they formed part of a grand embassy headed by the Archbishop of Reims and including ambassadors from the King of Castile, King René, the Duke of Brittany, and the

king because of the unhappy marriages between Frenchwomen and English kings in the past (Basin, i. 290, 292). On Queen Margaret and her marriage see A. Joubert, 'Le Mariage de Henri VI et de Marguerite d'Anjou', *Revue historique et archéologique du Maine*, xiii (1883), 313–32 and for King René, R. Allain, 'La politique domaniale du roi René en Provence (1431–1480)', *Positions des thèses* (École des Chartes, 1947), pp. 9–16.

[1] Henry VI confirmed the truce that was made on 28 May to last until 1 Apr. 1446 on 27 June (Rymer, xi. 59).

[2] In fact the truce seems to have been generally welcomed. Basin says that France was exhausted (Basin, i. 290), and both Jean de Stavelot and Adrien de But mention it favourably (Jean de Stavelot, p. 536; Adrien de But, i. 275). On the treaty's reception in Normandy see C. de Beaurepaire, *Les États de Normandie sous la domination anglaise* (Évreux, 1859), p. 68.

Duke of Alençon.[1] (Burgundy claimed that his agents had
not received safe conducts.) The envoys were received by
the king himself, who accorded them a warm greeting, but
when the time came to get down to business Suffolk learned
to his dismay that Charles had withdrawn his offer of Normandy and reduced his definition of Gascony. Having
consulted their instructions the French envoys proposed a
slightly more generous definition of Gascony, but pointedly
added (when Suffolk reproached them about Normandy)
that England had no claim to Normandy before the question
of the crown was raised—indeed Charles VII had a better
claim to the crown of England than the Lancastrians.[2] To
prevent an immediate rupture of the truce Charles's ambassadors suggested that Henry and Charles could best settle
the differences between them at a personal interview and that
they had powers to extend the truce until 1 November 1446
so that Henry could come to France in safety. Suffolk had no
room for manœuvre; rather than face the storm his failure
would raise in the council, he took himself to Windsor and
persuaded Henry to agree to the personal interview.[3] On
15 August 1445 the English truce with France was prorogued until All Saints' Day the next year.[4] The French
embassy departed taking Moleyns with them to obtain a
further extension of the truce.

Charles must have been overjoyed at the ease of his
success. He raised difficulties about extending the truce and
sent Moleyns home, though two of the French king's agents
were soon hastening after him. The ostensible purpose of
Cousinot and Harvart's expedition was to prorogue the
truce, but they also had letters from King René saying that
restoring his county of Maine would speed up peace

[1] A contemporary journal of this mission is printed in Stevenson, *Wars*, i. 87–
182. To prepare for negotiations the king ordered the treasury 'an in alle othir
places that ye have any of oure evidence' for the agreements made between Henry V
and Charles VI to be searched and the documents brought to the council to be
deliberated upon (E 404/61/278). And parliament voided the clause of the Treaty of
Troyes which prohibited negotiations with the 'dauphin' without the consent of the
three estates of both realms (*Rot. parl.* v. 102–3).

[2] On the use of this theme as propaganda see P. S. Lewis, 'War Propaganda and
Historiography in Fifteenth-Century France and England', *Transactions of the
Royal Historical Society*, 5th ser. xv (1965), 1–22.

[3] Beaucourt, *Charles VII*, iv. 162.   [4] Rymer, xi. 97.

negotiations. In return for handing over Maine René offered a twenty years' truce.[1] On 19 December the Treaty of Tours was prorogued until 1 April 1447 and three days later Henry wrote to his father-in-law stipulating the terms of surrender.[2] Who was responsible for persuading Henry to yield to this proposal? Henry was not mad in 1445, but he was easily led.[3] Perhaps he made the grant to please his young wife, who had promised King Charles to work towards this end.[4] It is even more likely that she was seconded by Suffolk,[5] for the peace plan which was the main prop of his influence in the government was in danger of collapsing. Acceding to René's request was the one frail straw which he had to seize.

Failure to find satisfactory terms on which to form a peace settlement once again revealed the schizophrenic quality of English diplomacy. While Henry and the English council assured Charles of their fervent desire for peace, the Lieutenant of Normandy and his advisers assumed a more bellicose attitude.[6] The submission of Maine to the French quickly revealed the differences between the English parties. Although representatives of the French and the English government had met at Évreux (in April), Louviers (in May), and Mantes (in December) to regulate differences arising from the truce, they accomplished little. Nevertheless, Adam Moleyns and Lord Dudley had met Charles in July to assure him of Henry's ardent desire for peace; Charles thanked them for their sentiments but expressed

[1] Beaucourt, *Charles VII*, iv. 163–4.
[2] Rymer, xi. 113 is the confirmation of this agreement dated 3 Jan. 1446.
[3] For the most recent investigation of Henry VI's character and periods of insanity see R. L. Storey, *The End of the House of Lancaster* (London, 1966), pp. 29–42, and J. R. Lander, 'Henry VI and the Duke of York's Second Protectorate, 1455 to 1456', *Bulletin of the John Rylands Library*, xliii (1960–1), 49–69, who argues that Henry may have been ill in 1455, but he was not insane.
[4] As early as 17 Dec. Margaret and Charles had corresponded about the delivery of the county to King René (Stevenson, *Wars*, i. 164). The embassy, comprised of Moleyns and Lord Dudley, which Henry VI sent to France in 1446, also carried letters of credence from the queen to Charles VII (B.N., MS. français 4054, f. 79).
[5] For a not wholly satisfactory exoneration of the Earl of Suffolk see C. L. Kingsford, *Prejudice and Promise in Fifteenth-Century England* (Oxford, 1925), pp. 146–76. Professor Jacob (*The Fifteenth Century*, *1399–1485* (Oxford, 1961), pp. 473–5) and Dr. Storey (*House of Lancaster*, pp. 43–60) have redressed the balance.
[6] Beaucourt, *Charles VII*, iv. 285–7.

his surprise that no progress was made towards turning
Maine over to King René. In September he sent a stronger
message on this subject, hinting that the personal interview
had better be postponed until Henry's officials in Normandy
complied with his orders; however, rather than face a
renewed outbreak of war Charles allowed (22 February
1447) the truce to be prorogued until 1 January 1448.[1]
Later that year it was extended, first until 1 May and then
to 1 January 1449, in return for more specific orders about
delivering the French county, and in October a convention
opened in Maine to arrange the English evacuation.[2] In
spite of Henry's protests the envoys seized every excuse for
delaying proceedings, and not until the spring of 1448 was
the county evacuated.[3] Charles's victory was a Pyrrhic one,
for the Englishmen who left moved to Mortain and Saint-
James-de-Beuvron, previously evacuated because their nearness to Brittany made them excellent sites from which to
lead raids in the Breton marches.

If the replacement of York by Somerset was calculated
to ensure a closer co-operation between the governments
at Westminster and Rouen, it was a failure. Somerset
allowed, if he did not actively encourage, violations of
the truce with France.[4] When Charles sent envoys to
complain about these infractions Somerset first threatened
to arrest the French agents and then sent them back
with a haughty letter to the king, which lacked any
of the usual signs of courtesy. Charles was not slow
to complain to the English that York had never written
such insulting letters and that something had to be
done about the English on the Breton marches.[5] The
answer he received through his envoys in Normandy was
that these towns were in the Breton march and not on the
frontier of France; since the Duke of Brittany was an
English ally, the occupied places were none of Charles's

[1] Rymer, xi. 151.
[2] Beaucourt, *Charles VII*, iv. 296.   [3] Ibid. 311.
[4] Ibid. 310.
[5] '. . . les quellez [lettres] ilz [Gaucourt et Cousinot] ne voulurent recevoir ne
prendre charge dicelles porter, pour ce que par le duc Dyork et autres seigneurs du
sang du dit prince nepveu navoit este acoutume estre fait le temps passe' (Stevenson,
Wars, i. 209–20).

business.[1] The French riposted that Brittany was not an English ally, and Duke Francis's agent agreed. With the convention thus deadlocked, Somerset wrote for more specific instructions but received a vague answer telling him to do what he thought best, though he might try to adjourn the meeting and treat with Brittany alone. Somerset adopted this programme and the envoys undertook further useless discussions in November 1448 and January 1449. In response to numerous complaints from the French king, Henry promised to send envoys in May, but before they set out an English mercenary took the Breton town of Fougères (24 March 1449) by surprise.[2] When the English made only feeble efforts to restore the town, Charles concluded an alliance with the Duke of Brittany to help him reduce it to obedience.[3]

The evidence that Fourgères had been taken with the knowledge of the English government is clear. François de Surienne, a knight of the Garter and a member of the king's council, had received money from Suffolk and had gone to England in 1448 to see him. On the other hand a Tudor propagandist writing for Henry VII claimed that Surienne had acted without the knowledge of either Henry VI or Somerset. Since 'the said sir Frauncis de Surienne the Aragonys which was fellow and brother in armes to the said sir Giles de Bretaine', Duke Francis's brother, had been unable to obtain Gilles's release from prison and since King Charles had subsequently murdered Gilles, the Aragonese knight had no alternative except to attack Brittany. In any case Charles had broken the truce first by allowing Duke Francis, an English ally, to do homage.[4] It is difficult to imagine what persuaded the king's councillors, who had adopted a totally different policy up to this point, to reverse themselves. The estates of Normandy had declared to Somerset their unreadiness for war and the poverty of the country. But whatever prompted this foolhardy policy it succeeded admirably for the French. During the years

[1] Beaucourt, *Charles VII*, iv. 315.
[2] A. Bossuat, *Perrinet Gressart et François de Surienne, agents de l'Angleterre* (Paris, 1936), pp. 301–52.
[3] Beaucourt, *Charles VII*, iv. 315.
[4] B.M., Add. MS. 48005, ff. 92ᵛ–96ʳ.

following the 1444 truce Charles had successfully reorganized his army, while the English government did nothing about its forces in France, preferring to concentrate on the disgrace of the Duke of Gloucester. Less than eight months after Surienne surprised Fougères Charles entered Rouen. By the summer of 1451 he had occupied the whole duchy and had turned his attention to Gascony, where Dunois, Armagnac, Albret, and Foix moved to encircle Bordeaux on the landward side. When no relief came from England the city capitulated (24 June 1451).

Only Calais, which was reinforced with about 500 men in August, remained in English hands and Charles laid plans for taking it, but the Duke of Burgundy, fearing that Charles would be too powerful if he held the port, put a new peace plea in motion.[1] Despite Henry VI's personal dislike, the English and Burgundians had renewed the truce of 1443 in 1446 and the next year extended it for four years.[2] Philip followed this beginning by exhorting Henry to send an army against the Turks; of course he would have to make peace with France first. He wrote in the same vein to the King of France and sent an embassy to Nicholas V which was instructed to persuade the pope to send legates to France and England. Nicholas complied and designated Cardinal d'Estouteville (to Charles) and Nicholas of Cusa (to Henry).[3] Charles, resenting Burgundian intervention, suggested without success that the cardinal delay his visit. Apparently Nicholas of Cusa never came to England, nor is there any official record of a visit by the Cardinal of Ravenna. In any case peace was unlikely. The English, smarting under the blow of their sudden defeat, replied to Philip that a truce or peace now would be dishonourable;

[1] Symptomatic of the worsening relations between France and Burgundy is the curt answer Charles's envoys received when they requested Philip to attack Calais (B.M., Add. MS. 48031, f. 28ᵛ).
[2] Rymer, xi. 161, 171.
[3] The cardinals were empowered to negotiate peace on 13 Aug. 1451. The true purpose of d'Estouteville's mission was to secure the abrogation of the pragmatic sanction. To remove the stigma of working for the pope against the interests of France, the cardinal opened an inquest at Rouen in May 1452 to rehabilitate Joan of Arc (P. Doncœur and Y. Lanhers, *La Réhabilitation de Jeanne la Pucelle, l'enquête du cardinal d'Estouteville en 1452* (Documents et recherches relatifs à Jeanne la Pucelle, 1958), vol. iv.

when Charles had been driven from France there would be
time to talk of a Turkish Crusade.[1] Charles on the other
hand was unwilling to make peace for less than the submission of Calais, a price the English would never willingly
pay. Although the French conquered Gascony in 1453, the
assault on Calais (and on the Channel Islands) failed; it
would be more than a hundred years before it succeeded.

In England the loss of Normandy precipitated the fall of
the Lancastrian government.[2] The main advocates of peace,
who had lately fostered a disastrous war, Aiscough, Moleyns,
and Suffolk, were murdered. In Kent the populace rose
under Jack Cade and marched on London. The king, who
until this time had shown little capacity for overcoming his
ingrained aversion to holding the reins of government,
went mad, and the struggle for control of affairs became a
contest between the queen[3] and the Duke of York. English
diplomacy had turned full circle. The epilogue to Henry
VI's reign is nothing more than a struggle between factions
in England for the friendship of France or Burgundy. At
first Charles and Philip declined to offer aid to either side,
preferring to see what course England's domestic troubles
took. Thus Charles congratulated James II of Scotland on
his raids against northern England, but he remained silent
when a herald from James proposed a co-ordinated attack on
Calais and Berwick, and pretended to be unable to supply
military aid.[4] The invitation to join the Scots, who were
about to reverse their alliance, and exterminate the Lancastrians was not accepted. James, whom Margaret may have
contacted during York's power, changed his mind again;
he sent Henry VI a letter of defiance (10 May 1456) but
broke off the attack when Margaret regained control of the

[1] B.M., Add. MS. 48031, ff. 29ʳ–30ʳ.
[2] The most intelligible studies of the Wars of the Roses are K. B. McFarlane,
'The Wars of the Roses', *Proceedings of the British Academy*, l (1965), 87–119, and
Storey, *House of Lancaster*.
[3] C. L. Kingsford's estimate of Queen Margaret (*Prejudice and Promise*, pp.
154–79) has recently been corrected by A. L. Myres, 'The Household of Queen
Margaret of Anjou, 1452–53', *Bulletin of the John Rylands Library*, xl (1957–8),
pp. 79–113, 391–431. 'A study of Margaret's revenues', Professor Myres has written, 'confirms the impression of her as a woman eager for power and ever watchful
to gain and keep all the income she could' (p. 68).
[4] Beaucourt, *Charles VII*, vi. 132–4, 138–9.

government in October.[1] At the same time as she entered into conversations with the Scots, the queen contacted Charles's government. Her overtures received little encouragement. Perhaps the queen was predestined to failure; as a French-woman negotiations with the government at home and with its traditional ally Scotland were normal, as Queen of England such negotiations took on the odour of treason. Although York, on the other hand, negotiated with both the French and the Burgundians, he was not slow to renew the friendship he had established with the Burgundians more than fifteen years earlier.[2] His embassy to Charles in May 1458 was paralleled by conversations between Warwick and Burgundian agents at Calais the next month, followed by renewed talks in England and at Bruges in August. In October the English agents proposed a marriage alliance between the sons of Henry VI, Somerset, and York, and the daughters of Philip's heir, the Duke of Bourbon, and the Duke of Guelders. Charles VII must have learned about this series of negotiations, for when the envoys broached an even more preposterous matrimonial alliance—Prince Edward, and the sons of York and Somerset to daughters of Charles, Orléans, and Maine—the French king promised to consider it and declared himself ready to make peace. News of this meeting was followed by an increased Burgundian interest in the Yorkist cause. The struggle between Burgundy-supported Yorkists and French-backed Lancastrians was on, and the Yorkist victory led logically to the Anglo-Burgundian alliance of 1467.

---

[1] *Correspondence Bekynton*, ii. 139-41.
[2] Beaucourt, *Charles VII*, vi. 260–3.

II

ENGLAND AND THE SPANISH
KINGDOMS

O N 29 May 1418 the Burgundians, having gained
entrance to the city by treachery, overran Paris. The
dauphin abandoned his Armagnac allies to their fate
and fled to the south where he set himself up as regent for
his father, despite the fact that Charles VI, though insane,
was still alive and claimed to be ruling for himself. Princes
concerned with French diplomacy were thus confronted
with the alternative of treating either with the Burgundian
puppet, Charles VI, or with the *soi-disant* regent. Neither
French regime underestimated the importance of foreign
recognition and support. Of the European states, France's
'chief and principal' ally Castile as well as the other kingdoms of the peninsula furnished prime targets for both the
puppet master John the Fearless and the dauphin. The race
to Spain was soon on.

Since the mid fourteenth century Castile had consistently
sided with the French against the English.[1] When Edward
III's daughter, who was betrothed to Alfonso XI's only son,
died of plague at Bordeaux in 1348, the probability of an
enduring Anglo-Castilian alliance evaporated. In the following years France backed the Trastámara family's attempt to
rule Castile and Leon and while that family ruled, the English—especially since John of Gaunt had wed the daughter
of the rival claimant to the Castilian throne and from time
to time asserted her right to it—were unable to entertain
any serious hope of *rapprochement*. Furthermore, the realities of their economies militated against lasting friendship.

---

[1] G. Daumet, *Étude sur l'alliance de la France et de la Castille au xive et au xv^e
siècles* (Bibliothèque de l'École des hautes études, 1898), fasc. 118; P. E. Russell,
*The English Intervention in Spain and Portugal in the Time of Edward III and
Richard II* (Oxford, 1955); L. Suárez Fernández, 'Política internacional de Enrique
II', *Hispania*, xvi (1956), 16–129.

Castile, like England, consumed vast quantities of luxury goods for which she paid chiefly by exporting wool, which was sold in competition with the English to the Low Countries. In the years following the Black Death the Castilians relied more and more on this source of income, for economic contraction resulting from the plague ruined her industry. Castile also operated a considerable merchant marine which was increasingly menaced by the growth of English shipping and English piracy.[1] For these reasons France had a sure ally once the basic treaty with the Trastá-maras received ratification (1368). Thereafter renewals of the treaty at the accession of a new monarch—Enrique III (1391), Juan II (1408)—marked the only significant negotiations between these countries.

In 1418, however, Juan II was only thirteen years old and his mother Queen Catherine, Henry IV of England's sister, was regent. Catherine had laboured unstintingly for an Anglo-Castilian alliance, but the most she had obtained was a truce in 1414 between Henry V and her son.[2] Early in 1417 Henry charged the Mayor of Bordeaux to head an embassy to Castile where the king hoped to resuscitate the 1414 truce, or (if that failed) to have himself included as an ally in the treaty of 1411 between Castile and Portugal. In addition the English envoys had instructions to persuade Juan to break his alliance with England's enemies in France.[3] But the situation at the Castilian court was not propitious: Charles VI had already secured France's inclusion in the 1411 treaty,[4] the queen's passion for wine had recently proved fatal and her muddle-headed son had proclaimed the end of the regency and the beginning of his personal rule. In these circumstances it is hardly surprising that the Anglo-Castilian treaty was not renewed. However, neither the Armagnac nor the Burgundian agents fared much better

[1] J. Vicens Vives, *Aproximación a la historia de España*, 2nd edn. (Barcelona, 1960), pp. 123–9; id. *Manual de historia económica de España*, 3rd edn. (Barcelona, 1964), pp. 193, 244.

[2] Beaucourt, *Charles VII*, i. 302–3; Wylie, *Henry V*, i. 91–3.

[3] Rymer, ix. 419; *Proc. P.C.* ii. 205; H. Ellis, *Original Letters*, 3rd ser. (London, 1846), i. 63.

[4] On 15 Aug. 1411 (L. Suárez Fernández, *Relaciones entre Portugal y Castilla en la época del infante Don Enrique, 1393–1460* (Escuela de estudios medievales, vol. xxxiv, 1960), pp. 177–8.)

initially, for the Castilians preferred to temporize;[1] both French governments had asked for ships to transport Scottish soldiers to France.[2] When the Dauphin Charles sent another embassy in April 1419, news that Rouen had fallen buttressed his cry for help; and the Castilian monarch, now sufficiently alarmed, hastily concluded that the dauphin best represented Castile's interests in France and agreed to lend him forty ships for three months, provided, of course, that Charles bear the expense.[3] Early in the next year these ships commanded by Bracquemont defeated the English off La Rochelle, but further aid was denied by the outbreak of war between King Juan's brothers-in-law, the *infantes* of Aragon and the royal favourite Don Alvaro de Luna, who were all vying for control of the supine king.[4]

Aragon's primary concern in the early fifteenth century centred upon finding a successor to Martin the Humane. Having done so she found herself—after a brief interlude when the new Aragonese monarch, Ferran d'Antequera, busied himself in Castile rather than at home[5]—with Alfonso V, a king hankering for a Mediterranean empire and thereafter anxious to dissociate himself as much as possible from the wars between England and France. Consequently in 1415 when Henry V had proposed marriage to Ferran's eldest daughter Maria, who was later to marry

---

[1] See the remark in Plancher, *Histoire de Bourgogne*, iv. 65: 'L'Espagne, le Portugal et l'Allemagne regardoient nos divisions comme un accès de vertige, qu'il estoit dangereux de contracter . . .'.

[2] Beaucourt, *Charles VII*, i. 309; B.-A. Pocquet du Haut-Jussé, *La France gouvernée par Jean sans Peur* (Paris, 1959), nos. 195, 225, 332. The Castilians also sent ambassadors to the Franco-Burgundian government (ibid., no. 20).

[3] Beaucourt, *Charles VII*, i. 311–12. On 22 July the city of Bayonne wrote to Henry V that the King of Castile was proposing to ally with the dauphin, to besiege Bayonne, and to send his fleet to Scotland for reinforcements for the dauphin's army (Rymer, ix. 783). Another appeal for help followed on 5 Sept., but by this time Henry had already ordered the sheriffs of Devon and Cornwall to be ready to intercept the Castilian fleet (Rymer, ix. 794–5; *Cal. Pat. Rolls, 1416–22*, p. 268). See also E. W. M. Balfour-Melville, *James I, King of Scots* (London, 1936), p. 78.

[4] B. Fazio, *De rebus gestis ab Alfonso primo Neapolitanorum rege commentariorum libri decem* (Lyon, 1560), p. 22; J. Calmette, *Histoire de l'Espagne* (Paris, 1947), pp. 140–1.

[5] For a brief contemporary biography of Ferran see F. Pérez de Guzmán, *Generaciones, e obras semblanzas* (Madrid, 1775), pp. 210–17. I have been unable to locate a copy of the new edition of this text by R. B. Tate (1966).

Juan II of Castile, the Aragonese king turned aside the English advance, though he offered to substitute his second daughter for Maria.[1] Furthermore, the Duke of Clarence's scheme to replace Ferran as king with the Count of Urgell, wrangling at the Council of Constance about precedence, and English overtures to Queen Joanna of Naples, which aimed at having either Gloucester or Bedford adopted as her heir, did nothing to encourage a spirit of amity between the two countries—especially since Ferran had raised his second son Joan to the vice-regency of Sicily, Sardinia, and Majorca, hoping thereby to make him an attractive husband for Queen Joanna.[2] Finally, though economic factors furnished no motive for outright hostility (Catalonia manufactured cloth from the little wool she produced), the trade in spices and citrus fruits for wool and tin was never valuable enough to make common policy worth considering.[3] Yet in 1417 Alfonso[4] accorded a three-year safe-conduct for English merchants trading in his country. Less than three months later (4 October), however, he agreed to a vague covenant with the dauphin and Louis of Sicily,[5] having apparently ignored Charles VI's request for a fleet.[6] As a result Aragon

---

[1] Wylie, *Henry V*, i. 96–7. Apparently Ferran's sole interest in this alliance was the support Henry V would be obliged to give Aragon's efforts at Constance to have Benedict XIII recognized as the legitimate pope (I. Macdonald, *Don Fernando de Antequera* (Oxford, 1948), p. 231).

[2] L. Loomis, 'Nationality at the Council of Constance', *American Historical Review*, xliv (1939), 517–20; A. J. Ryder, 'The Evolution of Imperial Government in Naples under Alfonso V of Aragon', *Europe in the Late Middle Ages*, ed. J. R. Hale, J. R. L. Highfield, B. Smalley (London, 1965), p. 333.

[3] Vicens Vives, *Manual*, pp. 194–5; *Historia social y económica de España y América*, ed. Vicens Vives, ii (Barcelona, 1957), 334–5, 338. For English imports from Catalonia carried in Florentine galleys see W. B. Watson, 'The Structure of the Florentine Galley Trade with Flanders and England in the Fifteenth Century', *Revue belge de philologie et d'histoire*, xxxix (1961), 1073–91; xl (1962), 317–47.

[4] 'Senyoreja lo dit realme pacificament molt anys; fou Rey molt virtuos magnanim, piados e molt saui . . .' (P. Tomic Caualler, *Historias e conquestas dels excellentissims e catholics reys de Aragó e de lurs antecessors los comtes de Barcelona* (Barcelona, 1886), p. 282). But Vespasiano, though extolling Alfonso's piety, generosity, and honesty, notes his secretiveness and tendency to play vicious practical jokes on envoys from states he disliked (V. de Bisticci, *Renaissance Princes, Popes and Prelates*, ed. M. Gilmore, trans. W. George and E. Waters (New York, 1963), pp. 59–83).

[5] Beaucourt, *Charles VII*, i. 304.

[6] J. Vielliard and R. Avezou, 'Lettres originales de Charles VI conservées aux archives de la couronne d'Aragon', *Bibliothèque de l'École des chartes* (1936), vol. xcvii, no. xxi; B.M., Cotton MS. Vespasian C. XII, f. 164.

stood in an indifferent position with respect to England's war with France, until Henry V rashly concluded an agreement with Alfonso's inveterate enemy, Genoa, in 1421.[1]

Portugal, aside from chronic border disputes and occasional outbreaks of armed hostility with Castile, increasingly disengaged from her earlier European involvement to devote her efforts to the exploration of the African coast and to the search for new trade routes to the East. Richard II had established Anglo-Portuguese friendship as a part of his diplomatic policy focused upon creating between the 'kings now reigning, their heirs and successors, and between the subjects of both kingdoms an inviolable, eternal, solid, perpetual and true league of friendship'.[2] Thus in May 1386, having previously lent some English archers to help the Portuguese win their independence from Castile, Richard ratified the true and perpetual friendship between the two countries. John of Gaunt (1387) strengthened the ties of friendship by marrying his daughter Philippa to João I (1385–1433). But when Henry V sent the learned Dr. Lyndwood to ask for fighting men, the Portuguese government temporized.[3] Although they responded with an embassy the next year and a fresh mission set sail for Portugal in turn, the Plantagenet cause seems to have received no material assistance.[4]

The kingdom of Navarre was surrounded on three sides by states either overtly hostile or at least indifferent to the English interest: Castile to the south, Aragon to the east, and Foix to the north. In this situation the Navarrese could not take a strong pro-English position, though their friendly relations with the English based in Gascony were mutually desirable in terms of a balance of power.

The Treaty of Troyes caused considerable embarrassment in the Spanish kingdoms. In the interval between its conclusion and King Henry's death, negotiations were put in hand to secure the adhesion of the Spanish monarchs. The King of Navarre's almoner, Master Pierre de Fontenay,

---

[1] See below, p. 77.

[2] H. Livermore, *A New History of Portugal* (Cambridge, 1966), pp. 102–4.

[3] Wylie, *Henry IV*, ii. 330. Lyndwood's proxy is dated 14 Jan. (Rymer, x. 167; E 101/322/1).

[4] E 403/658/m. 14; Rymer, x. 270; E 403/666/m. 14.

who was also a French royal councillor, and Master Pierre
de Venisse were picked as representatives of Charles VI and
Henry V to solicit Don Carlos of Navarre's adhesion.[1]
Their instructions intimated that Carlos, being informed of
the final concord between England and France, ought to
offer his adherence to the treaty and to call together the
three estates of his kingdom so that they might understand
the turn of events. The envoys were also to ask Carlos for
a small army—about 200 men under his son's command—
to fight the dauphin; the expenses of these forces would be
borne by the French and English. In addition to promoting
the Castilian court's adhesion to the treaty, as well as the
Count of Foix's, the King of Navarre was asked to form an
alliance with Henry V. Don Carlos astutely responded that
it would delight him to fulfil these requests (and he would
signify as much to Henry and the Chancellor of France in
writing), if the counties of Champagne and Brie, which
belonged to him by right of his Évreux ancestors, were
returned.

Incompetent to deal with such a demand, the envoys
apparently pressed on to Castile, where similar entreaties
fell on deaf ears. Passing through Navarre on the return
journey, Fontenay and Venisse picked up guides who
conducted them to San Sebastián and thence to Bayonne.[2]
From Bayonne the envoys called on the Count of Foix before
continuing northwards.

Henry had embarked for England shortly after these
agents set out; he returned to France in June 1421 and
proceeded to the siege of Meaux; Fontenay and Venisse
found him at Rutel in December and made their report.[3]
When Henry heard Navarre's outrageous demand, he icily
replied that his duty as Regent of France was 'to protect
and increase—not to diminish—the rights of the French

---

[1] They seem to have departed after 15 July 1420 (Pocquet du Haut-Jussé, *La France*, no. 950). Appendix II, no. 5 contains a 'Memoire pour le Roy de Navarre duc de Nemox'.

[2] The envoys seem to have remained around Navarre throughout the spring and summer of 1421. The Navarrese messenger Miguel Dalmassu obtained safe conducts for them to go to the King of Castile and other messengers conducted them first to San Sebastián and then to Bayonne (A.G.N., Cajón 119, no. 27; Compto del tesorero, t. 365, ff. 61ʳ, 65ᵛ; Cajón 107, nos. 3 (xxviii, xxx), 4 (iii), 5 (cxiv), 6 (iv, viii, xvii, xxx), 14 (xxiv)).   [3] Appendix II, no. 5.

crown, of which the counties of Champagne and Brie are but a part'. Don Carlos would be well advised, Henry continued, to content himself with the 16,000–20,000 *livres* of land he held as Duke of Nemours. The matter was dropped for the time; however, before Meaux capitulated in May, the French regent summoned Fontenay to his camp at Saint-Faron. Assuring Fontenay of England's and France's regard for Navarre, Henry encouraged him to estimate the price at which Carlos would sell his support. The price Fontenay hazarded was high: 25,000 *livres* of land near the Duchy of Nemours. Justification for this figure lay in claims the Navarrese monarch had on the French government—122,500 *livres tournois* for rent that was in arrears. In no hurry for decision since Meaux was to capitulate the next day, Henry departed for Senlis, instructing Fontenay to rejoin him in the Forest of Vincennes. Before Master Pierre had reached the forest, however, Henry had died.

Shortly after Bedford assumed control of the French government and French diplomacy he appointed the Archdeacon of Sens, the Dean of Reims, and the Lord of Montferrat to inform the King of Navarre that both Henry V and Charles VI were dead and to explain how matters stood with the new government in France.[1] They were particularly to emphasize that the part of France loyal to Henry V and Charles VI obeyed Henry VI and his uncle the Duke of Bedford, who because of the nearness of kin was regent. Moreover, if Navarre harboured any doubts concerning the new regent's ability, let them be swept away by the telling of the great victories Bedford had obtained over the rebellious parts of the kingdom, especially Champagne, Picardy, and Brie. Since the duke's regency had been so successful, Bedford confidently renewed Henry V's attempt to incorporate Navarre into the Treaty of Troyes and once again asked Don Carlos to write to the Kings of Aragon and Castile to discourage their giving the dauphin aid, and to the Count of Foix that he fulfil the promises he had already made. Rather than dismissing the Navarrese claims out of hand, Bedford and his advisers scrutinized each item minutely. It was quite true that the King of Navarre descended

[1] Appendix II, no. 6.

from St. Louis and that he had been a faithful vassal, but he ought to recall that Nemours had been raised to the status of a duchy in 1404 by adding to its lands the *châtellenies* of Château-Landon, Grez-sur-Loing, Lorrez-le-Bocage, Chéroy, and Pont-sur-Yonne which the king's family had exchanged for its rights to Champagne and Brie.[1] Therefore, it was manifest that the French government did not rightly owe the King of Navarre any of the sums claimed. And if the three estates of Navarre proved unwilling to swear to uphold the Treaty of Troyes, they ought to be content if the king acted alone. Although Bedford willingly conceded that an open declaration by Carlos in favour of Henry VI's government might be followed by invasion from Castile, Don Carlos's statement that rents from the counties of Champagne and Brie would be adequate compensation for such a risk was injudicious, since he left himself open for the reminder that by failure to declare himself he stood the chance of having Nemours confiscated. (Bedford also promised to bring an army to Navarre's aid if she were attacked.) The reply to this embassy has not survived.

In January 1420 the dauphin had deputed a large number of ambassadors to wait on the Kings of Castile and Aragon to renew their respective alliances, but the embassy's head, the Archbishop of Tours, died, and by the time the party finally reached Barcelona via Castile, Alfonso had sailed to Sardinia,[2] the first leg of his journey to Naples. So although the dauphin's agents secured a promise—one that was never honoured—of twenty armed galleys and forty smaller boats from Castile, they accomplished nothing in Aragon. An even grander embassy in 1426 yielded only a few knights sent to respond to the dauphin.[3] Because of slow communications, the English fared only a little better. In June 1421 Henry V had bravely warned Alfonso that assisting the dauphin could cost the Aragonese England's good regards; however, Henry apologized for the infrequent exchange of

---

[1] *Dictionnaire topographique du département de Seine-et-Marne*, ed. H. Stein and J. Hubert (Paris, 1954), p. xvi n. 1.

[2] From Sardinia he went to Corsica and nine months later to Naples only returning to Aragon in Nov. 1423 (F. Soldevila, *Història de Catalunya* (Barcelona, 1935), p. 51).

[3] Ibid. 490.

messages and indicated that Alfonso's agents would be welcomed at the English court.[1] By this time the Aragonese monarch had reached Naples and became embroiled in Italian politics, yet he found time to entrust Lluís de Falcs, the knight whom Henry V had sent to Italy, with a favourable reply.[2] Lluís went to Henry and returned with a message that the English king was sending plenipotentiaries to Rome to treat with Alfonso's agents, but no Englishmen ever appeared,[3] and Alfonso returned to Aragon.

Bedford's first message as regent had no more original purpose than to inform Alfonso of English success in France, to repeat the late king's warning about helping the enemy, and to ask for an alliance.[4] He was ignored. Yet this unimaginative policy did not quickly find a replacement. Falcs was back in England by March 1425 with a message that Alfonso would send other envoys to Rome.[5] (The solemn embassy appointed in March 1424[6] to treat with the Aragonese monarch left Rome before the Aragonese arrived.) It is not possible to gauge how far these early meetings succeeded in breaking down the mutual apathy existing between the two states. Alfonso refused to back the English desire for a new ecumenical council, but the chaos at the Castilian court, which was to bring Alfonso to the brink of war in Spain, and the dauphin's ill-concealed ambitions to expand towards the south provided compelling reasons for an alliance designed as a counterweight to the Franco-Castilian league. A reasonably well-governed Castile might think twice before attacking Aragon, if the attack would bring an English invasion through Gascony. With Castile checked, Alfonso's imperial design might advance unhindered.[7] The advantages for the English do not appear so compelling; it is true that Alfonso might induce his brother, the King of Navarre, to join a league with England—a nice riposte to the turncoat Foix as well as to

---

[1] *Proc. P.C.* ii. 285–6.   [2] E 404/39/167; *Proc. P.C.* iii. 54.
[3] A.C.A., Registro 2692, f. 43.
[4] Appendix II, no. 1. It is interesting to note that Alfonso did not mention this embassy in his recital of Anglo-Aragonese relations in 1431.
[5] E 403/655/m. 4.   [6] Rymer, x. 319.
[7] On Alfonso's general diplomatic policy see J. Vicens Vives, *Juan II de Aragón, 1398–1479: monarquía y revolución en la España del siglo XV* (Barcelona, 1953), p. 187.

the threats of invasion by Castile—and that Aragon would conceivably furnish a recruiting ground for soldiers, but no informed observer would have been sanguine enough to think that Alfonso would allow any treaty with England to deflect his attention from the conquest of Naples more than momentarily.

In Castile the ferocious quarrel that had broken out between Enric, Pere, and Joan, Alfonso's brothers, and Alvaro de Luna continued unabated. Enric had captured the king at Tordesillas in July 1420, but he and Alvaro escaped to Montalban, and subsequently Enric was himself arrested. To secure his brother's release and put an end to this civil war which resulted in attacks on the Aragonese frontier, Alfonso returned to Aragon in November 1423. By then the situation proved to be out of control and in 1425 he was preparing to invade Castile,[1] when the Castilians released Enric. The Castilian imbroglio may well explain why the dauphin's embassy to Juan II in 1422 apparently never arrived. In fact it seems that except for the renewal of articles concerning trade relations in 1424 the dauphin abandoned Castile to her folly until 1426.[2] When at the Count of Foix's insistence Charles picked up the threads of his old alliance, he had good news to tell: Burgundy and Gloucester were in open conflict. The time was opportune for renewing their alliance and Castile, if she would contribute 2,000 men-at-arms and five or six hundred archers, could share the honour of driving the English from the Continent. To this dubious invitation the King of Castile replied that discord in his own country made it impossible for him to think of sparing so many men.[3] Undaunted, Charles dispatched still more envoys in 1428 to secure a renewal of the Franco-Castilian alliance and to obtain a fleet to punish the Duke of Brittany, who had recently been compelled to support the English once more. That the French had lost their copy of the treaty[4] and had to ask the Castilians for another did not enhance their prospects for success, and indeed they

[1] A. Beccadelli, *De dictis et factis Alfonsi regis Aragonum libri iv* (Basel, 1538), f. 4.
[2] Beaucourt, *Charles VII*, ii. 312.   [3] Ibid. iii. 391–3.
[4] Charles left the royal archives behind when he fled from Paris in 1418 (Daumet, *France et Castille, p. j.* no. 59, p. 231).

evidently received no encouragement. Nevertheless another ambassador set out for the south in 1429, but he died before completing his mission.[1]

At first the English had no success in Castile. Apparently, Don Juan did not bother to answer Bedford's embassy, which sought Castile's adherence to the Treaty of Troyes. The regent had instructed his ambassador to remind Don Juan of the embassy Henry V and Charles VI had sent to inform the Castilians of the dauphin's complicity in the Duke of Burgundy's murder, and of the peace made between England and France which Castile was invited to join. Also the duke's agents had to explain the current situation in France—how Bedford had become regent and how many adversaries he had subdued. Then they were to press for an alliance including a provision of military aid for Bedford's army and the refusal of such aid to the dauphin. In case the King of Castile did not want to enter such negotiations, he ought to be urged to send his envoys to Henry VI and to Bedford. Meanwhile, he ought to recall any aid he had lent the dauphin.[2] These requests and admonitions, needless to say, went unheeded. Nor did the Gascon, Dr. John Gentill, who sailed from Plymouth to Lisbon in the summer of 1424, have better luck, though his way had been paved in advance by the Duke of Bedford, who granted safe conduct to Spanish and Portuguese merchants trading at Harfleur.[3] The French regent's notable lack of success in Spanish diplomacy evidently gave the English government an opportunity to reassert their control in the matter. The turn of events in Castile reduced the chance of failure. By 1428 the Castilians again found themselves at the brink of war with Aragon and Navarre[4] and became more deferential to the English. They sent an impressive embassy composed of a bishop, a doctor of laws, and one of the king's secretaries to London early in 1429 accompanied by Sancho Esquerra, who had negotiated the commercial relations with the dauphin in 1424.[5] The instructions of this embassy presumably

[1] Beaucourt, *Charles VII*, iii. 395.   [2] Appendix II, no. 8.
[3] E 101/322/8; *Ordonnances*, xiii. 58.   [4] Beccadelli, f. 9.
[5] Rymer, x. 411. The embassy is misdated by a year in *The Brut, or the Chronicles of England*, ed. F. W. D. Brie (Early English Text Society, 1906), orig. ser. no. 131, pt. 2, p. 443.

entailed holding preliminary discussions leading to some
sort of truce between the two countries. How well they
succeeded is not known. In any event early in the next year
two more ambassadors from Castile requested safe conducts
from Henry VI[1] and in turn were followed during the
summer by Sancho de Roxas, Bishop of Astorga, with his
retinue. On 6 November the lords of the council ordered the
chancellor to draw up letters of proxy that gave the Bishop
of Norwich, Lord Cromwell, and Dr. Lyndwood full powers
to treat for a truce on land and sea with the King of Castile's
agents.[2] The clauses of the truce must already have been
agreed upon for the negotiations were completed two days
later,[3] despite a brawl at the Crown Tavern in Fenchurch
Street in which the publican 'debadet with ambassitours of
Spayne and rede blode of oon of them, a gentleman flowed'.[4]
The English king ratified the truce on 20 November. One
of the clauses of this truce specified delivery of the English
ratification between Christmas and 1 March following at
Bayonne,[5] but that ratification, sealed with the great seal in
white wax and attested by the Duke of Gloucester as *custos
Anglie*, is still in the Public Record Office;[6] this might
indicate that the truce was never put into effect, but the
Commons, meeting at Westminster on 12 January 1431 (to
revise the Treaty of Troyes so that Cardinal Beaufort and
the Dukes of Bedford and Gloucester could negotiate with
Charles VII), seem to have thought that the Castilian
truce was operative.[7]

Don Carlos of Navarre died in 1425 and his daughter,
Blanca, the wife of Alfonso V's brother Joan, inherited the
title to the throne, though her husband ruled. This marriage
alliance, obviously, resulted in a closer connection between

---

[1] The safe conducts were granted on 8 Mar. 1430 (Rymer, x. 452).

[2] *Proc. P.C.* iv. 69-70.

[3] The English had been considering the treaty for some time. On 9 Oct. the
treasury had relinquished an alliance with Castile sealed with a gold seal so that it
could be transcribed (Palgrave, *Antient Kalendars*, ii. 93-4).

[4] *Brut*, pt. 2, p. 456.   [5] Rymer, x. 476.

[6] E 30/439.

[7] *Rot. parl.* iv. 371: '. . . and also ye Kyng of Spayn, send hider but late agoo his
Ambassadeurs, which entred tretee of Pees, ye which tretee is yit hangyng bytwyx
the Kyng our soverain Lord and him, for yeim, yeire Reumes, lordshippes and
Subgitz.'

Aragonese and Navarrese foreign policy,[1] which the unsatis-
factory relations with Castile made desirable. But progress
towards an agreement with the English was slow. The
standard-bearer of Navarre sent messengers with letters for
Henry in July 1427[2] and in the autumn Henry granted
Aragonese merchants the same rights of safe conduct as
Alfonso had conceded to the English in 1417.[3] The next
year a chain of dynastic matrimonial ties, even though they
were not exactly what the English had in mind, linked
Aragon more closely to England: Alfonso's sister Leonora
married the heir to the Portuguese throne, Duarte, in hope
of alliance against Castile, and Philip the Good made plans
to wed the Portuguese princess Isabel.[4] Furthermore, on 16
September 1428 Navarrese envoys did homage to Henry VI
for the Duchy of Nemours.[5] Then on 13 July 1428 the
council selected Sir John Lescrope, Master Peter Partridge,
and Master John Stokes to treat with Alfonso's ambassadors
in Rome; what this accomplished is not known.[6] But a year
passed before another meeting important enough to occasion
letters of proxy was planned. Meanwhile a French embassy
had appeared in Barcelona requesting armed assistance.
Alfonso cunningly proposed to furnish lavish support—for
a price: the lands of Carcassonne, Beaucaire, Montpellier
with all their castles, cities, towns, and vassals.[7]

In June 1429 the Aragonese monarch, abandoning hope
of a peaceful settlement, invaded Castile.[8] Learning of the
preliminary negotiations for an Anglo-Castilian truce and

---

[1] *Les Vies et quelques gestes des roys de Navarre* (Paris, 1595), p. 20ʳ⁻ᵛ.

[2] E 403/680/m. 10.   [3] B.M., Cotton MS. Vespasian C. XII, f. 35ʳ.

[4] Le Fèvre, ii. 155; G. Zurita, *Anales de la corona de Aragon* (Zaragoza, 1610),
f. 181ʳ⁻ᵛ describes Leonora's wedding feast: 'Et quant au regard des metz et entre-
metz pavons et aultres oyseaulx revesters et armoyes, entre lesquels y eult v banières
de ceneq royaulmes premiers d'Angleterre, de Castille, [de Portingale] et de Navarre
et d'Arragon.'

[5] Archives Nationales, JJ 619, nos. 25, 26; A.G.N., Cajón 125, no. 9.

[6] Rymer, x. 405, 407–8. Sir John's request for letters of protection survives among
the Privy Seal and Council files (E 28/50/5). Since this embassy was also charged
to visit the emperor and the Roman court they may have expected to find Alfonso
in Italy, when in fact he was in Aragon (*Proc. P.C.* iii. 301).

[7] Zurita, *Anales*, f. 184ᵛ.

[8] B.N., MS. lat. 5956a, f. 190; Daumet, *France et Castille*, p. 82; F. Pérez de
Guzman, *Crónica del Rey Don Juan II* (Biblioteca de autores españoles, vol. lxviii,
1877), p. 482.

that the Castilians had exhorted the French to make war on Aragon and Navarre, Alfonso intensified his diplomatic conversations with England.[1] Jaume Pellegrini, the Aragonese vice-chancellor, Lluís de Falcs, and Mateu Pujades departed the following April for Navarre to explain their instructions to Queen Blanca.[2] From Navarre Pellegrini, Falcs,[3] and Charles de Beaumont, the Queen's standard-bearer, made their way to England.[4] The three envoys landed early in the summer, but the parley soon reached an impasse. The king was in Paris for his coronation, neither side had sufficient authority to make a binding agreement, and the English made it plain that the king would not accept any alliance that did not include his kingdom of France. Yet the royal council, even though they had instructed an embassy the previous 16 July to treat with Alfonso's envoys in Rome,[5] signified its willingness to send ambassadors with full powers to conclude a treaty at Bayonne.[6] Apparently the solemn embassy from Castile, which arrived in England to conclude a truce as the envoys from Aragon and Navarre were ending their discussions,[7] prompted the latter to make their offers even more attractive, since they were unable to prevent the Anglo-Castilian truce, for Falcs proposed that Henry VI marry one of Queen Blanca's two daughters.[8] The English councillors replied that they dare not discuss this matter without the

---

[1] Thomas Spofford, Bishop of Hereford, Andrew Holes, Robert Fitzhugh, and Henry Herburg were appointed to treat with the Aragonese for amnesty in July 1429, but what they accomplished towards this end remains unknown (C 81/691/ 2110; Rymer, x. 433; *Proc. P.C.* iii. 348). These ambassadors may also have thought Alfonso was still in Italy, for the Bishop of Hereford was on a pilgrimage to Rome (*Cal. Pat. Rolls, 1422–9*, p. 541). Fitzhugh's protection also stated that he was going to Rome (C 76/111/m. 4).

[2] Zurita, *Anales*, ff. 197ᵛ–8ʳ; Appendix II, no. 11.

[3] Falcs had previously been awarded land in Gascony for his service to the English crown (*Archives historiques de la Gironde*, xvi. 226, 227; C 61/121/m. 1).

[4] A.C.A., Registro 2692, f. 131ᵛ, mentions Falcs and Pellegrini, but not Pujades. A.G.N., Compto del tesorero, t. 398, f. 123ᵛ, is a payment to Beaumont.

[5] *Proc. P.C.* iii. 348.

[6] Ibid. iv. 56–9.

[7] The Aragonese ambassadors remained in England until Oct. E 404/47/118, 127 are warrants authorizing payments to the Aragonese and Navarrese agents.

[8] Blanca, who was to marry the King of Castile, and Leonora, later betrothed to Gaston IV of Foix (*Les Vies et quelques gestes des roys de Navarre*, f. 20ʳ–ᵛ). Tomic Caualler, *Historia*, pp. 282–3 mentions only one son.

presence of the king's uncles, but they would write to the king to discover his wishes in the matter.

Since Aragonese envoys were still in England in October, it is hard to see how any successful negotiations could have been carried out at Bayonne the next month. Yet on 7 November the council ordered the exchequer to advance Dr. John Gentill a part of his wages for going to Bayonne for the discussion of certain things concerning the king's welfare;[1] in Gascony the Mayor of Bayonne, Thomas Burton, and the Bishop of Bayonne, Guillaume Arnaud de la Borde, who had served as the King of Navarre's ambassador to Constance,[2] were to join Gentill to give the embassy greater prestige.[3] Eight days later at Lérida, Alfonso, who had evidently been informed by letter, issued full powers for Pellegrini and one of his Aragonese councillors, Mateu Pujades, to make a perpetual league with 'Henry, by the grace of God, King of England and France', which the Aragonese would swear to uphold on the cross and the Four Gospels.[4]

The instructions for these envoys contained no definite proposal apart from a project for some sort of treaty linking England, Aragon, and Navarre in a general alliance against Castile. A tedious rehearsal of the misdeeds of Juan II's advisers and their attempts to deprive the *infantes* of Aragon of the property that they had inherited from their father in Castile was to serve as a partial explanation of why Alfonso and his brother wanted a league against that country. The reason the alliance had not been made sooner was to be explained by the failure of the English envoys to appear when they were expected. Nevertheless Alfonso—because of the kinship and the high regard he had for the Duke of Burgundy and the King of Portugal—had sent his envoys to Bayonne with full and sufficient powers to conclude a league.[5]

The Aragonese arrived on schedule and waited for Gentill's appearance throughout November and December.[6]

---

[1] *Proc. P.C.* iv. 70. Rymer calls him Philip rather than John (Rymer, x. 473; E 404/47/141). He received an advance of £66. 13s. 4d. (E 403/696/m. 4).

[2] *Gallia Christiana*, i, coll. 1318–19; von der Hardt, iv, nos. 1029, 1031, 1036, *et passim*.   [3] C 81/692/2292; Rymer, x. 477.

[4] Appendix II, no. 9.   [5] A.C.A., Registro 2692, ff. 41ʳ–43ᵛ.

[6] I can find no evidence for Balasque's statement that negotiations lasted from

When he did not come in January, the envoys wrote to Alfonso for further instructions.[1] Alfonso advised them to withdraw, after arranging with the mayor of Bayonne to be informed if the English came. The English envoys finally assembled in April and notified the Navarrese court, which sent Pamplona Herald to inform Alfonso.[2] Pujades, Pellegrini, and Falcs duly reappeared—after a stop in Navarre to inform the queen of their instructions[3]—and the negotiations got under way.[4] But almost immediately the Aragonese, who may have been recalling the practice of their *Cortes*, suddenly became exercised by a question of law; did a minor have the right to appoint a proctor? In the *Cortes* the usual practice was for the minor's tutor or guardian to serve as his representative.[5] Unable to resolve this difficulty they solicited Alfonso's advice;[6] it was the opinion of his advisers, the king replied, that the English king was not able to appoint proctors to deal with such serious matters as this proposed alliance contained, but they should let this letter of proxy form no impediment to the progress of negotiations, though they should try to get another signed by either six or twelve men elected by the three estates of England.

The treaty the Aragonese and Navarrese had come to make was one of mutual assistance;[7] the friends and enemies of Alfonso and his brother were to be the friends and enemies of King Henry, except that the pope and the emperor were to be excluded. Within four months of a request for aid Alfonso would supply 1,000 horsemen or 1,500 cross-bowmen at his own expense for a period of six months. If they served after this time it would cost the King of England each month fifteen florins for every horseman or ten florins per cross-bowman. In return the English were to supply within four months of the request 1,500

---

7 to 16 Nov. Alfonso's letter seems to rule out this possibility (J. Balasque, *Études historiques sur la ville de Bayonne* (Bayonne, 1862), iii. 473).

1 A.C.A., Registro 2687, f. 36ʳ.

2 Pamplona Herald was sent to notify Alfonso when the English ambassadors arrived at Bayonne (A.G.N., Compto del tesorero, t. 402, f. 111ʳ; t. 403, f. 75ʳ).

3 Appendix II, no. 10.   4 Appendix II, no. 11.

5 G. Martel, *Forma de celebrar cortes en Aragón* (Zaragoza, 1641), p. 18.

6 Appendix II, no. 3.   7 A.C.A., Registro 2692, ff. 131ᵛ–132ᵛ.

archers for six months; after that, Alfonso would pay ten florins per month per archer. At this point the Aragonese introduced a saving clause into the instructions: Aragon and Navarre would not be obliged to furnish aid to England before the English had sent their archers southwards. Further, if Gentill, the Bishop of Bayonne, and Thomas Burton insisted that Alfonso's brothers confirm the agreement, then the Aragonese envoys were to insist on confirmation by both Bedford and Gloucester. Finally, Pujades and his associates were to convey Alfonso's consent to a marriage alliance between England and Navarre.

The English, on the other hand, hoped to conclude an alliance which did not contain a clause of mutual assistance.[1] If such a clause was insisted upon, the ambassadors were to say that they had no power to conclude such an agreement. The matter of mutual assistance was so important—*materia satis ponderosa*—that it would have to be discussed by the lords and magnates of the kingdom in the coming parliament. Meanwhile it would be possible to discuss the nature and amount of aid to be included in the treaty. On this point Alfonso had had second thoughts, for he wrote to his envoys on 10 May instructing them to raise the number of archers required from the English to 2,000 on the principle that one horseman was worth two archers. In return he would supply 2,000 cross-bowmen. If it were impossible to obtain agreement on these new figures, they could revert to the old ones.[2] Once again Alfonso made it clear that the English would have to furnish aid to him before he sent any soldiers to France. In the same letter Alfonso sent supplementary instructions about the proposed marriage alliance. The envoys were to press the younger daughter of Joan and Blanca on the English king; the English envoys reported that the matter had been discussed with the Duke of Gloucester and the council and that after much thought the council concluded that they were not able to assume such a grave responsibility as selecting a wife for the young king.

When the Aragonese reported that it was against the customs of the kingdom for the king to restrain knights who wished to go abroad to fight, in answer to the English demand that the Aragonese cease supporting the dauphin, negotiations broke off. But an agreement was reached to hold a further conversation in Bayonne the next year when the English had sufficient power to discuss mutual aid.

The following February (1432) the English council once again sent an embassy to Bayonne.[1] The Bishop of Dax, Thomas Burton, Bayonne's mayor, and the Dean of Saint-Seurin,[2] the English ambassadors, this time held out little hope for an agreement satisfactory to both sides. Their instructions flatly rejected the idea of mutual assistance; the English were so occupied with their own wars that they were unwilling to take on the burden of fighting in the Spanish peninsula, and in any event it had proved impossible to reach agreement about the wages of the troops.[3] Yet the English king was prepared to forbid any of his subjects to furnish aid to Aragonese enemies and to allow unhindered mercantile intercourse between the countries, in return for similar concessions.

Precisely what went wrong with this proposed alliance is problematical. Both countries wanted something for nothing. Alfonso had contrived a five-year truce with Castile shortly after he initiated conversations with the English;[4] consequently he was unlikely to be in a mood for substantial concessions. All he wanted was an ally against Castile, and a pacified Castile (even with an unratified English truce) did not present so formidable a threat to his imperial schemes as in the past. On the other hand, an unrestricted promise of mutual assistance would quickly draw him into an unprofitable war with Charles VII. Although trade between the two

---

[1] C 81/694/2461.

[2] On Bernard de la Planche, Bishop of Dax, see *Gallia Christiana*, i. 1055; he was also one of the judges in the court of sovereignty in Gascony (E 101/191/1/38). As a reward for his services the bishop was made a member of the king's council at Bordeaux (C 81/696/2671; C 61/125/m. 16). For Burton see Balasque, *Bayonne*, iii. 472–3. Pierre Arnaud 'deu Vescomtau' was the Dean of Saint-Seurin from 16 Oct. 1430 to 2 Oct. 1444 (J. A. Brutails, *Cartulaire de l'église collégiale Saint-Seurin de Bordeaux* (Bordeaux, 1897), p. xxvii). He was also one of the judges in the court of sovereignty (E 364/70, 75, 84, 91).

[3] B.M., Cotton MS. Vespasian C. XII, f. 170ʳ; Appendix II, no. 4.

[4] J. Yanguas y Miranda, *Diccionario de antigüedades del reino de Navarra* (Pamplona, 1840), p. 161.

countries was approaching its most profitable period, the amount of money involved was negligible. In March 1443, for example, Catalan merchants were to send £582. 17s. 4d. worth of spices, commercial and industrial goods to England in Florentine galleys and to buy cloths valued at £16. 6s. 8d.; the value of imports from Alfonso's kingdom reached £405. 6s. 8d. the next winter, but the Florentine cargo alone in the same fleet was worth three times as much.[1] And the English government's inability to control piracy was rapidly smothering the small trade carried on directly between Southampton and Barcelona.[2] Furthermore, Alfonso had obtained from Henry VI's envoys just the friendly sentiment he wished to hear. Their military reverses about this time must have given the English pause to wonder whether the option of a dynastic alliance ought to be squandered on one of the King of Navarre's daughters. There was no question of extra soldiers to send to Spain if Aragon and Navarre made war on Castile again.

If English diplomatic ventures had ground to a halt by 1433 in Castile, Aragon, and Navarre, the alliance with Portugal, Professor Russell has shown, 'lived on as a reminder of a commercial relationship important to both parties, but as an instrument of political or military power it had already served its time out'.[3] It is true that the Duke of Coimbra received the livery of the Garter from Gloucester Herald in 1427,[4] and that the crown prince attended Henry VI's coronation at Westminster,[5] but the other correspondence remaining from Henry VI's reign is, with one exception, of little significance. Sometime before the summer of 1444, perhaps in the summer of 1442 or the autumn of 1443,[6]

[1] Watson, 'Florentine Galley Trade', pp. 342–3, 338–9.
[2] There are numerous documents in the city archives at Barcelona to illustrate the most notorious case of English piracy on Catalan ships, the plunder of goods belonging to En Joan Lull in June 1436. In 1442 he was still trying to recover his goods. The case is briefly mentioned in N. Coll Juliá, 'Aspectos del corso catalán y del comercio internacional en el siglo xv', Estudios de historia moderna, iii (1953), 167. (Archivo Histórico de la Ciudad de Barcelona, Lletres Closes, 1442–4, f.43ʳ.)
[3] Russell, English Intervention in Spain and Portugal, p. 548.
[4] Devon, Issues of the Exchequer, p. 400; E 403/666/m. 14; Rymer, x. 405; E. H. Fellowes, The Knights of the Garter, 1348–1939 (London, 1939), p. 66. In 1428 the crown prince was installed in the order also (E 404/46/157).
[5] Brut, pt. 2, pp. 436–7.
[6] Rolando d'Almada and a pursuivant were in England during July and

a suggestion was put forward that Henry VI marry Afonso V's sister or his widowed mother, the King of Aragon's sister.[1] Perhaps the Portuguese regent, Dom Pedro, hoped this alliance would strengthen his resistance against the *infantes* of Aragon, who, having reasserted their dominance in Castilian politics, were trying to oust him from the regency.[2] We do not know how seriously the English considered this proposition; in any case they soon decided a French marriage was more advantageous. And Portuguese interest must have declined after the defeat of the *infantes* at Olmedo (May 1444) and the death of the queen mother.

Otherwise, for the rest of Henry VI's reign announcements of election to the Order of the Garter, renewal of Richard II's treaty, and claims made by merchants for goods taken without just compensation comprise the chief reasons for the passage of diplomats between the two countries. On 25 November 1435 King Duarte promised to observe his father's alliance with England, and the next year Henry VI ratified his confirmation and ordered the livery of the Garter to be sent to the king.[3] The accession of Afonso V in 1438 signalled a re-confirmation of the treaty (1439–40), though Afonso did not become a member of the Order of the Garter until 1447.[4] The bestowal on the Portuguese knight Rolando Alvaro Vasquez d'Almada on 11 July 1445 of the Order of the Garter[5] furnished the occasion of copying out the *Liber regie capelle* by Dean William Say for the young

---

Aug. 1442(*Proc. P.C.* v. 208; E 403/745/mm. 2, 13). The pursuivant returned the next year (E 404/60/64).

[1] A.C.A., Registro 2939, ff. 79ᵛ–81ʳ.   [2] Livermore, pp. 113–16.

[3] In 1436 the garter was delivered to the Portuguese king (Rymer, x. 639, 641). In 1443 the livery of the garter was sent to the Duke of Viseu (E 404/60/64; E 403/751/m. 1). King Afonso V was elected in 1447 and Garter King of Arms took another livery to Portugal in 1455 (Fellowes, pp. 33, 77; E 403/811/m. 7). On 25 Nov. 1435 the King of Portugal promised to observe his father's alliance with England; the next year Henry VI re-confirmed the alliance. In 1439–40 and in 1472 the alliance was again confirmed (Rymer, x. 625, 631, 735, 752; C 81/772/505a).

[4] The letter dated 13 Sept. 1439 in which Henry asks for the restitution of goods taken from an English merchant and another dated 13 June 1454 in which a Portuguese knight complains that his ship was seized by English pirates near Southampton provide fair examples of the level of Anglo-Portuguese diplomacy during the last years of Henry VI's reign (E 28/63/51, 84/45). There are two more similar letters in B.M., Cotton MS. Nero B. I, ff. 49ʳ–ᵛ, 52ʳ.

[5] Fellowes, p. 67.

Afonso V.[1] Although Afonso may never have seen this richly illuminated work, it does provide evidence for the impressive appearance of the English court on the eve of civil war.

Despite English efforts to reform their alliance system after 1435, they made little headway in the Spanish kingdoms. An English embassy went to Barcelona and Pamplona in 1436, and at the end of the year ambassadors from Barcelona and Pamplona came to England.[2] If the purpose of these meetings was to continue discussions of an alliance, they got nowhere. After this a flurry of messages passed between England and Navarre, but their content is unknown.[3] Moreover, although the King of Navarre had made a great show of trying to persuade the Count of Foix to raise the siege of Mauléon in 1449, when he refused the Navarrese monarch departed.[4] And in 1452, at Castilian insistence Charles VII declared war on Navarre.[5] Yet England was so little regarded that Aragon and Navarre made no attempt to forge a stronger friendship based on their common enmity towards France.

Alfonso V of Aragon sailed for Italy in May 1432 to bring his long war with the Angevins to a successful conclusion.[6] His attitude, at first hostile to the papacy, then ambivalent while he negotiated, first with Felix V and the council at Basel and then with Eugenius, to see who would recognize his Italian claims, was likely to meet with little sympathy in

---

[1] *Liber regie capelle*, ed. W. Ullmann (Henry Bradshaw Society, vol. xcii., 1961), 10 *et passim*.

[2] A.G.N., Cajón 139 no. 29; E 403/727/m. 12.

[3] A.G.N., Cajón 139, nos. 29, 30; 140, no. 21; Compto del tesorero, t. 427, ff. 78ʳ, 101ʳ; E 404/53/337. Queen Blanca died in 1442 and soon after the conflict between her son and her husband over the right to govern the country began (*Les Vies et quelques gestes des roys de Navarre*, ff. 20ʳ⁻ᵛ). See also J. Calmette, *Louis XI, Jean II et la révolution catalane, 1461–73* (Toulouse, 1903).

[4] *Recueil des chroniques de Flandre* (Corpus chronicorum Flandriae), ed. J. J. de Smet (Brussels, 1837–65), iii. 434–5.

[5] For more than ten years Navarre and France had been discussing the question of the Duchy of Nemours (Yanguas y Miranda, *Diccionario*, p. 164).

[6] See the letter from the Genoese to Henry VI telling him about their naval victory in which they captured both Alfonso and Joan II of Navarre (E. Martène and U. Durand, *Veterum scriptorum et monumentorum historicorum, dogmaticorum, moralium amplissima collectio* (Paris, 1724), i, coll. 1584–6; Yanguas y Miranda, *Diccionario*, p. 163). Despite this temporary setback Alfonso entered Naples in 1442 and concluded the Treaty of Terracina with the pope in June 1443 (Raynaldus, *Annales ecclesiastici, sub anno* 1443, no. 1).

England.[1] In June 1444 Alfonso sent his knight Felip Boyl
to the emperor, the Dukes of Burgundy and Orléans, and
the King of England to solicit their backing for a crusade to
wrest the Church of the Holy Sepulchre (*la sancta casa de
Hirlm*) from the Muslims.[2] There is no doubt that Alfonso's
desire to lead a crusade was sincere. There is equally little
doubt that he expected no support from England. Once
Boyl got to England, he was to keep open the negotiations
for a treaty, which had presumably been resumed when civil
war in Castile erupted again in 1439. But the King of
England should know that Alfonso was against the proposal that Henry marry either the sister of the King of
Portugal or the queen mother. If the English insisted on the
alliance, Boyl was to say he had insufficient power to discuss
it and that Henry would have to send an embassy to Alfonso.
Such elaborate precautions, however, were unnecessary.
Boyl apparently did not reach England until the end of
1445;[3] by that time the marriage with Margaret of Anjou
had been arranged. A further instance of the lack of information about England available in Naples was Alfonso's
message to the semi-retired Gloucester: Alfonso was displeased that nothing had been done about the losses of his
merchants En Francesc Pujades and En Joan Lull, and he
intended to look into the matter further.

An England mistress of half of France and capable of
intervening decisively in the great councils of the church
was a power to be reckoned with. But an England on the
verge of expulsion from France, struck down by civil war,
and saddled with an incompetent king was a different
matter. Alfonso accepted his election to the Order of the
Garter and kept communications between the two countries
open,[4] but his Neapolitan scribes did not even know the name
of England's king;[5] this represents a surprising indifference

---

[1] See below, p. 140.   [2] A.C.A., Registro 2939, 79ᵛ–81ʳ.   [3] E 404/62/46.
[4] Fellowes, p. 60; E 28/78/3; E 404/65/125, 195. In the early 1450s he dispatched
a number of letters to England in order to obtain safe conducts for his merchants
(J. M. Madurell Marimón, *Mensageros barceloneses en la corte de Nápoles de Alfonso
V de Aragón, 1435–1458* (Barcelona, 1958), nos. 193, 194).
[5] There is a copy of a letter in Barcelona dated 2 Nov. 1450 addressed 'serenissimo et illustrissimo principi Ludovico regi Anglie' and another dated 14 Jan. 1452
headed 'serenissimo rey [*sic*] et illustrissimo principi L. regi Anglie etc' (A.C.A.,
Registro 2655, f. 97ᵛ; 2658, f. 81ʳ).

to English assistance in view of the growing hostility between Charles VII and Aragon over Marie d'Anjou's claims
to property in Spain and Alfonso's bid for Cerdagne and
Roussillon.[1] Nor was Alfonso's successor more interested.
In case there was any startling development Alfonso
and Joan after him could be warned by the Valencian diplomat Vicent Clement.[2] Henry VI's court pleaded with
Joan for an alliance in June 1459, but the Aragonese
monarch sent the English agent back with an ambiguous
reply because he was negotiating with Charles VII.[3] Not
only was the English government's stability risky, but trade
between the two countries had come to a standstill: as
early as 1448 the Florentine galleys brought spices from
Barcelona worth only £9. 3s. 4d.[4]

Franco-Castilian diplomatic relations may have broken
off about 1428 for fourteen years as Beaucourt thought,[5]
but it brought little profit to England. Ambassadors of the
two countries quarrelled violently at Basel over precedence.[6]
The Castilian fleet, which had been borrowed to escort
Margaret of Scotland to France,[7] assisted the Duke of
Burgundy's siege of Calais in 1436, according to the
Brut.[8] And in 1442 the Castilians suggested concerting an
attack on Bayonne and Bordeaux with a French assault on
Calais, though nothing came of the proposal.[9] The King of
Castile sent a herald bearing letters and an ambassador to
Henry in 1445, but there is no evidence that a full-scale
embassy (as Adrien de But's chronicle suggests) came to

[1] Calmette, *Histoire d'Espagne*, p. 151.
[2] Appendix II, no. 13. Although the Aragonese monarch encouraged Clement
to write news letters and to support his causes at the English court, he was hardly a
resident ambassador. Most of his diplomatic career was spent on missions for the
English to the Continent. *Contra* A. Fernández Torregrosa and R. B. Tate, 'Vicent
Clement un valenciano en Inglaterra', *Estudios de historia moderna*, vi (1956–9),
133–9.
[3] A. Fernández Torregrosa, 'Aspectos de la política exterior de Juan II de
Aragón', ibid., ii (1952), 111–12.
[4] Watson, 'Florentine Galley Trade', p. 344.
[5] Beaucourt, *Charles VII*, iii. 250.
[6] L. Suárez Fernández, *Castilla, el cisma y la crisis conciliar (1378–1440)* (Escuela
de estudios medievales, vol. xxxiii, 1960), pp. 348–54; V. Beltrán de Heredia, 'La
Embajada de Castilla en el concilio de Basilea y su discusión con los ingleses acerca
de la precedencia', *Hispania Sacra*, x (1957), 5–31.
[7] Balfour-Melville, *James I*, p. 219.
[8] *Brut*, pt. 2, p. 469.   [9] Beaucourt, *Charles VII*, iii. 250.

assure the English of Charles VII's good intentions about making peace.[1] Castile had been nevertheless included in the Anglo-French truce of 1444.[2] Two years later John Lord Dudley, and Thomas Kent travelled to Aquitaine and to the Castilian court, but all they secured was an eight months' truce that was never extended. Likewise the strained relations between the courts of Castile and France in the last decade of Henry VI's reign were not turned to England's advantage.[3] In 1454 Juan II had sent the famous Rodrigo de Arévalo to Charles with a protest about French liberality in granting safe conducts to English merchants. The English, the Castilian ambassador claimed, used safe conducts as a guise for spying and piracy.[4] Issuing safe conducts or making truces with common enemies without Castile's consent was a violation of the treaty between the two countries; if this practice did not stop, the Castilians would begin to issue their own safe conducts. Yet less than three years later the Castilian envoys at Lyons agreed to supply the French with six galleys and ten smaller ships for their war effort.[5]

In fact Anglo-Castilian relations were not patched up until Edward IV's reign, when Louis XI's policy in Aragon forced Enrique IV to initiate conversations with England. The English ratification of a perpetual alliance with Castile is dated 10 September 1467;[6] however, the Spider King once again escaped being trapped in his own web and accommodated French policy to the Castilians. Not until the union of Castile and Aragon, the Treaty of Medina del Campo, and the marriage alliance of Henry VII's reign did the two countries finally reconcile their differences.

[1] E 404/62/82; A. de But, *Chronique d'Adrien de But*, ed. K. de Lettenhove (Chroniques relatives à l'histoire de la Belgique sous la domination des ducs de Bourgogne . . ., 1870), i. 281.

[2] B.M., Add. Charter 3996 is an order to publish in the *vicomté* of Auge Henry VI's letters patent declaring that the King of Castile had been included in the truce dated 28 May 1444.

[3] Rymer, xi. 187; C 61/135/m. 4; E 101/324/14. Such incidents as John Arundel's refusal to release a Castilian ship taken in time of truce showed the Castilians that little could be gained by treaty with the King of England (C 49/50/8).

[4] R. H. Trame, *Rodrigo Sánchez de Arévalo, 1404-1470* (Catholic University of America, Studies in Medieval History, 1958), pp. 78-9.

[5] C. de la Roncière, *Histoire de la Marine française* (Paris, 1900), ii. 290.

[6] E/30/528.

III

ENGLAND AND THE GERMAN PRINCES

WHATEVER the instructions Henry V imparted to his heir's councillors as the king lay dying at Vincennes, it is fairly certain that they must have included the advice to maintain the *status quo* as far as England's system of alliances was concerned. As regards the Empire this meant renewing the Treaty of Canterbury with Sigismund and strengthening this alliance by agreements with the lesser princes clustering about France's eastern border. Of these German princes the most powerful, apart from the Count Palatine, was the prince-archbishop Dietrich von Mörs of Cologne. The Archbishops of Cologne, unlike most of the other German princes, had been English allies since the days of Richard II, when Frederick of Saarwerden had done homage to the king for an annual payment of £1,000.[1] Henry IV had apparently felt no need of this alliance, or if he did no record of payment of the archbishop's annuity has survived in England. Henry's son, however, renewed the alliance in 1416, and the archbishop's envoys did homage to the king while he was at Canterbury with Sigismund. Negotiating from a position of strength, Henry reduced the size of this money-fief to 500 nobles. By 1419 the king, as part of his plan to surround the French with enemies, had extended arrangements of this type to the Archbishops of Mainz and Trier, and during the winter of 1421–2 the king tried to extract the armed support provided by these agreements to bolster his soldiers in France.[2] The Count Palatine, as we shall see, heeded the royal request, but for a reason as yet unknown the Archbishop of Cologne

[1] Wylie and Waugh, *Henry V*, iii. 32, n. 3. In fact friendly relations between England and the Archbishopric of Cologne can be traced back to the closing years of the thirteenth century (F. Trautz, *Die Könige von England und das Reich, 1212–1377* (Heidelberg, 1961), p. 113).

[2] Wylie and Waugh, *Henry V*, iii. 174–5.

did not.[1] Thus it is not surprising to find that although they may have made some attempt to have the treaty renewed, Henry VI's advisers turned a deaf ear to Archbishop Dietrich's entreaties and he received no more of his accustomed stipend for the time being.

By 1435, however, the English had lost their initiative in the war and Burgundy's growing coolness must have given them as much cause for alarm as his expansionist policies gave the Archbishop of Cologne, his brother the Bishop of Münster, and his protégé the Count of Mark.[2] Consequently, once the English had grasped the realities of the Congress of Arras they immediately began to put their house in order. On 15 December the council decided to send Master Stephen Wilton and Sir Robert Clifton to the Archbishop of Cologne, the Bishop of Liège, the Duke of Guelders, the Count of Mörs, and the emperor.[3] Wilton and Clifton remained abroad for three months. Although the actual purpose of the mission is unknown, it seems fairly clear that the duties of these ambassadors involved patching up Henry V's alliances with the imperial princes, for at Arras Cardinal Beaufort and the Earl of Suffolk had approached the Duke of Guelders with this end in mind. The Duke, apparently before Wilton and Clifton reached him, took occasion to write to Henry reminding him of the conversations at Arras. To this letter the king answered that he was about to send envoys to Basel who would confer with the duke on their way to the council.[4] In July the king dispatched another letter to Guelders assuring the duke that he had not heard (and if he had he would not have believed) that Guelders rendered assistance to Burgundy in the siege of Calais; furthermore, the king assured the duke of England's friendship.[5]

---

[1] Nevertheless on 5 May 1422 the archbishop ordered a quittance to be drawn up for 1,000 gold nobles that he had received from Henry V (E 30/428).

[2] For Dietrich von Mörs's territorial policies see G. Droege, *Verfassung und Wirtschaft in Kurköln unter Dietrich von Moers (1414–1463)* (*Rheinisches Archiv*, i, 1957).

[3] *Proc. P.C.* iv. 308. The draft of the instruction and the order to the chancellor to draw it up survive in the chancery warrants, C 81/701/3147, 3148. The letter of proxy is printed in Rymer, x. 621. On 16 Dec. Clifton and Wilton received £66. 13s. 4d. (E 403/721/m. 11). The particulars of Wilton's account also survive in a badly damaged form: (E 101/323/3).   [4] *Correspondence Bekynton*, i. 104.

[5] Ibid. 125. This letter is surely misdated 1435 for 1436.

At about the same time the Count of Mark and the Bishop of Münster empowered agents to treat with Henry's council for alliances. Although no contemporary record survives, it is obvious from what follows that one indenture was drawn up by Johannes Upingrave, Arnold de Brempt, and Johannes de Coelfelda on behalf of the bishop and another in which they acted for Mark with the English ambassadors. Then the German envoys returned home to secure ratification of their agreements. When the ratifications were finally delivered more than a year later, the English declared that they could not accept them because the agreement had been contracted by agents with insufficient powers. Since neither the English nor the German powers have survived, it is impossible to determine the justice of this claim. It seems likely that the English, realizing that these alliances were more advantageous to the princes with their fear of Burgundy, decided to negotiate for better terms. And in any case the king wanted a satisfactory explanation of why the Burgomaster of Danzig, who had been in England and whom the king had commissioned to take messages back to the Hanseatics, had been arrested by the Bishop of Münster.[1]

Just after the dispatch of the letter demanding an explanation for the arrest, the king rewarded Johannes Upingrave, Arnold de Brempt, and Johannes de Coelfelda who had returned to England as ambassadors of the Archbishop of Cologne with £45. 4s. 9d. for their expenses and three gilded cups worth £25. 3s. 4d.[2] The response to the initiative of the archbishop's agents was entrusted to Dauker Petersson, one of the archbishop's messengers, the following September. On the return journey this messenger was pursued by pirates, so he threw the letters with which he had been entrusted overboard just before his ship was overtaken. Captured, he was imprisoned at Mont-Saint-Michel. In January 1438 Henry wrote to Archbishop Dietrich lamenting the arrest of the messenger,[3] but the next month he was able to report that the pirates had released Petersson, who had returned to England and reported the failure of his

[1] Ibid. 215. [2] E 404/53/171; E 403/735/m. 11.
[3] Proc. P.C. v. 86.

mission to the chancellor. In the same letter Henry added his assurances that this delay was no sign of unwillingness to renew his alliance with the archbishop, who may have heard of the failure of his brother's attempts by this time.[1]

In the midst of these efforts to establish a belt of hostile neighbours on Burgundy's eastern flank, the English learned from some merchants that the Emperor Sigismund had died and that it would be necessary to renew the Treaty of Canterbury with his successor as soon as he was chosen. To facilitate the ratification the king wrote to Archbishop Dietrich asking him to use his influence to this end.[2] And later in March a German knight in English employ at Cologne, Sigismund, was advanced £20. 13s. 4d. through a Florentine merchant for his good offices.[3] In May the archbishop sent a messenger to England presumably to inform the king of Albrecht of Austria's election as King of the Romans on 18 March.[4] Thanking the archbishop, Henry urged him to labour unceasingly to heal the schism between the pope and the Council of Basel and promised that he would shortly send ambassadors to the German electors to see what could be done in this matter.[5] On 19 April Dietrich had written to the King of England to inform him of the efforts extended on behalf of the English with regard to their alliance with the emperor, and the next day he followed this letter with another on the same subject. Henry finally answered both of these letters with two of his own written on 15 and 17 July.[6] In these letters the king expressed his gratitude to the archbishop for his efforts, and instead of reverting to the agreement made between him and Henry V, the young king promised to add 2,000 nobles to the archbishop's money fief.

Almost a year passed, however, before the English thought again of renewing their alliance with Cologne. In February 1439 the Bishop of St. David's, Sir John Lescrope, and Sir

---

[1] *Correspondence Bekynton*, i. 220; E 403/279/m. 12.
[2] i. 246.   [3] E 403/729/m. 15.
[4] E 404/54/299; E 405/2/39/2rb; E 403/731/m. 3.
[5] *Correspondence Bekynton*, i. 94.
[6] Ibid. 131; Staatsarchiv Düsseldorf, Urkunde Kurköln no. 1928; T. J. Lacomblet, ed., *Urkundenbuch für die Geschichte des Niederrheins* (Düsseldorf, 1858), iv, no. 229.

John Tiptoft received commissions to treat with the archbishop.[1] If they ever departed, they accomplished nothing tangible. In May Archbishop Dietrich once again dispatched Arnold de Brempt with letters to England, and the instructions he received in turn from the English, which he was to expound to the archbishop, show that no advance in the negotiations had occurred since the previous spring. Arnold was to offer the king's thanks once more for the good offices of the archbishop regarding the Anglo-imperial alliance and to say that the king would remain content about further progress of the business. Further, the king was prepared to raise the archbishop's stipend from 500 to 600 marks, to agree that the 1,200 marks which the archbishop had told Arnold to collect would be paid off by raising the annual stipend to 800 marks temporarily, and to have the question of homage and the services owed to the king worked out by ambassadors of the two parties.[2] Brempt returned to Cologne, but was back in England the following November to discuss some secret matter with the royal council, who replied that since the business concerned the king so deeply they would soon send fully instructed envoys.[3] In spite of this flurry of excitement the treaty with Cologne came no closer to completion. Another archiepiscopal agent, who had arrived about the same time as Brempt, was sent home because the Englishmen appointed to treat with him found his powers insufficient.[4]

In the meantime King Henry wrote to the Count of Mark to explain why the negotiations concluded in 1436 had come to nothing; in the same letter he empowered William Lyndwood and Sir John Lescrope to treat with the count's envoys for an alliance comprising mutual aid and homage.[5] Two months later a similar letter was sent to the Bishop of Münster. Within ten days of the date of the latter commission identical treaties with Mark and Münster had been

---

[1] Rymer, x. 716.

[2] Staatsarchiv Düsseldorf, Urkunde Kurköln no. 1944. There is a faulty transcription of this document in Lacomblet, iv, no. 231.

[3] *Correspondence Bekynton*, i. 73.

[4] Ibid. 75; E 404/56/137.

[5] C 76/119/m. 29; the original survives in the Staatsarchiv Düsseldorf, Urkunde Kleve-Mark no. 1581.

concluded.[1] In return for an annual pension of 400 nobles both promised to render homage to the king and to serve him at English expense with 100 men as long as the contracting parties should live. For each *dux* the royal vassals supplied the English promised to pay two nobles per day and from there the scale diminished until the wages for valets, archers, and cross-bowmen were computed at 6*s.* per day. On 22 December Isbrand de Merwyck did homage to the king for both the count and bishop in the presence of the Earl of Suffolk, Thomas Beckington, and other lords. A week later the king informed the Bishop of Münster that the treaty had been concluded,[2] and before the end of the next month Archbishop Dietrich had likewise been informed. Moreover, Merwyck accepted a commission to call on the archbishop to inquire about his health and to inform him that the English envoys would be sent to Cologne as soon as the present session of parliament was over.[3]

True to his word the English monarch sent a letter to Cologne saying that he was about to send his envoys with full powers to conclude the treaty, and five days later Hertonk van Klux (who had received a letter of credence on 13 May) and William Swan were appointed.[4] However, the alliance was destined to be postponed again. Something, as yet unexplained, went wrong during the course of the negotiations; Swan was sent back to England, though Hertonk remained in Germany.[5] On 4 July Dietrich commissioned ambassadors to try once more to conclude the treaty. By the end of July they were in England. John Lord Tiptoft, Adam Moleyns, John Stopingdon, the master of the rolls, and William Swan were instructed to examine carefully the powers of Gumbrecht de Nurnai, Lord of Alpen, and Master Theolman of Lins'; if sufficient, they were to be incorporated in any agreement the ambassadors made.

[1] Rymer, x. 141–5, 745–50; Dumont, vol. iii, pt. i, p. 543; Lünig, *Das Teutsche Reichs-Archiv, Spec. Cont. I, Fortz. iii,* p. 207 prints the treaty under the date on which homage was performed. The part of the indenture delivered to the Count of Mark survives in the Staatsarchiv Düsseldorf, Urkunde Kleve-Mark no. 1603. The English counterparts of both indentures also survive (E 30/1337, 451).

[2] *Correspondence Bekynton,* i. 214.

[3] Ibid. 98, 77.

[4] Ibid. 94, 85; Rymer, x. 770.

[5] *Correspondence Bekynton,* i. 166.

Further, they were to demand homage from the archbishop and the service of 300 soldiers in time of war. In other matters the English ambassadors had the same instructions that had been embodied in Arnold de Brempt's credence to the archbishop.[1] The treaty must have been substantially complete by 22 July, for that day the English ambassadors withdrew £533. 6s. 6d. from the exchequer to be handed over to the archbishop by two Italian merchants, and the two ambassadors received £266. 13s. 4d., while £13. 6s. 8d. in addition was allotted to their servants.[2] However, the indentures were drawn up only a month later.[3] The archbishop promised to be the king's *fidelis* for as long as he and Henry lived; he would protect and defend English subjects and vassals going through his realm whether on business or trading; and he would furnish the king with 300 fighting men. Gumbrecht and Theolman would do homage to the king before the Bishop of Bath and Wells. In return, Henry vowed to pay Dietrich a yearly pension of 600 marks in semi-annual instalments plus a bonus next Michaelmas of 200 marks and on succeeding Michaelmas days for the five years following. After this only 600 marks would be paid to the archbishop, his envoy having sufficient power to make a quittance. Moreover, the king promised to be a good lord and to protect Cologne merchants in England. At the end of the month the king wrote to thank the archbishop for the co-operation of his envoys,[4] and two days later sent a longer note under the signet and signed by the secretary Thomas Beckington, containing the responses Gumbrecht and Theolman were to relay to Cologne.[5] In this document the king affirmed his desire to further the pacification of the church and to find a means of accommodation with France.

After the conclusion of the treaty the frequency with

---

[1] *Proc. P.C.* v. 126–30; the original is also preserved. C 47/30/9 (19).

[2] E 403/739/mm. 16, 17; E 404/56/306, 307, 308. Garter King of Arms, who 'ad estee continuellement en nostre service sur les ambaxiatours de lercevesque de Coleyn par lespace de dys semaignes', received £6 for his services (E 404/57/45; E 403/740/m. 2).

[3] Rymer, x. 839.

[4] *Correspondence Bekynton*, ii. 59.

[5] Staatsarchiv Düsseldorf, Urkunde Kurköln no. 1947; Lacomblet, iv, no. 241.

which messages were exchanged between England and
Cologne declined appreciably. In October 1440 Henry
wrote twice to Archbishop Dietrich: once to secure a safe
conduct for Richard Chester, who was on his way to Rome,
and later to recommend Pietro del Monte, who intended
to pass through Cologne on his way back to Rome.[1] On
22 December the English confirmation of the treaty with the
archbishop was drawn up,[2] and the following day a letter
inquiring about the archbishop's health and stating that the
king was quite well was drafted.[3] For the next five years the
situation remained the same. In 1441 Johannes de Frowenbergh, a servant of the archbishop, was in England twice—
in February and again in November—while the king sent
Vicent Clement, who had been in Rome, to the archbishop
with secret instructions in August.[4] Occasional messengers
passed between the two courts during the next four years and
a group of miners were imported from Cologne to work
mines in Cornwall (during the autumn of 1447).[5] No doubt
the war that broke out in June 1444 between the archbishop,
his town of Soest and the Duke of Cleves, his deposition by
Eugenius IV in 1446, and the renewal of the war in 1448
fully occupied the archbishop. In any case it was not until
the end of 1448 that Dietrich and the King of England
resumed regular and frequent correspondence.

On the first of October that year the archbishop reopened
his complaint to the king about the payment of his pension:
it was long in arrears. Since no answer came from England,

---

[1] *Correspondence Bekynton*, ii. 136; i. 36.

[2] Ten days earlier two letters, of which one had been drafted as early as 27 Aug.,
were drawn up specifying that the alliance between Henry VI and Archbishop
Dietrich did not oblige the latter to an offensive league against the Dukes of Guelders, Cleves, or Burgundy (Staatsarchiv Düsseldorf, Urkunde Kurköln no. 1979).
The draft of the letter excluding Cleves and Guelders from this alliance can be
found in E 28/63/80; it also contains a note that a similar letter is to be drawn up
'ut non vocetur prescriptus archiepiscopus contra eum qui se nominat ducem
Burgundie'. The Guelders–Cleves letter is printed in Lacomblet, iv, no. 242.

[3] *Correspondence Bekynton*, i. 209.

[4] *Proc. P.C.* v. 176, 181; E 404/58/91; E 403/743/m. 3; *Correspondence Bekynton*,
i. 131.

[5] In Feb. 1443 the council decided to grant Johannes Rosencrans 250 marks for
journeys he made to Cologne on the king's behalf; later in the month the council
discussed sending a merchant and a clerk to Cologne to demand restoration of
English goods seized there (Rymer, xi. 19; *Proc. P.C.* v. 228; C 76/130/m. 15).

Master Johannes de Dubio and Johannes Roulandzwerde were commissioned to remind the king of his obligation.[1] They arrived in England early in the new year (by 20 February), but not until the end of March did they succeed in eliciting an answer about the payment of the pension. The answer they received was not the one they had hoped for; the king simply replied that the grievous wrongs England had suffered at the hands of the French made him unable to honour his debt at the present time.[2] Despite this unfavourable reply, Henry saw no reason why he should not ask for Dietrich's good offices three months later when envoys from Cologne informed him that the Duke of Bavaria's son (the future Philip the Upright) was about to be married to one of the king's enemies.[3] Whether the archbishop responded favourably to this entreaty we do not know; in any case it was not until many years later that Philip, having himself foiled the matrimonial plans laid by his uncle, finally married.[4] This correspondence was, however, only a side issue. When he learned of the failure of his request for payment the archbishop became incensed and once again dispatched letters to the English court stating in no uncertain terms what he proposed to do if payment was not immediately forthcoming. John Ardenbury, the archbishop's pursuivant, was in England before Christmas;[5] in February Gerard Byllestrayne set out for England with letters stating that if the archbishop had not received some payment by June he would be forced to seize the goods and persons of all English merchants in Cologne in order to compensate his church for the money owed it. Delaying as long as he dared, Henry waited until April to answer; the wars in France, he averred, had so exhausted England that there would be great difficulty in paying straight away. However, if the archbishop would show a little patience, the king would shortly send envoys to him to discuss the matter

---

[1] E 28/78/2; E 403/773/m. 14; E 404/65/124.

[2] Staatsarchiv Düsseldorf, Urkunde Kurköln no. 2209.

[3] Ibid., no. 2216; E 403/775/m. 2.

[4] H. J. Cohn, *The Government of the Rhine Palatinate in the Fifteenth Century* (Oxford, 1965), p. 12.

[5] E 28/79/59; E 404/66/91; E 403/778/m. 7. The king rewarded him with £5 for his journey.

and see what could be done about it.¹ Evidently the English
realized that the archbishop did not threaten idly, for on
9 May Thomas Kent and a pursuivant received a warrant
allowing them to draw advances on the exchequer because
they were about to set out on a mission to the Duchess of
Burgundy and to the Archbishop of Cologne.² Two days
later the king wrote to Archbishop Dietrich asking for a
safe conduct for Kent, and on 14 May he was commissioned
to pay the archbishop's annuity.³ But once again the English
—this time by a fortunate accident—escaped paying. The
ship carrying Kent and the pursuivant was captured by
pirates off Skagen and the English agents thrown in prison.

The last episode in England's relations with the Archbishop of Cologne during Henry VI's reign proved what the
English had already guessed: Dietrich von Mörs's threats
were not to be lightly taken. In 1451 he had sent Isbrand de
Merwyck, an envoy by now well acquainted with the
delaying tactics of the royal council, to the king. Nevertheless,
his experience had not enabled him to secure a favourable
hearing of his instructions in October when Henry finally
apologized for keeping Isbrand in England for so many
months; other occupations had prevented royal attention to
this envoy.⁴ In February 1454 Isbrand was back in Eng-
land.⁵ In June the Archbishop of Cologne finally erupted.
Henry VI now owed him 40,000 florins; in addition to the
embassy mentioned above the archbishop had sent two
English merchants, John Aleyn and Rutger Tong, with
letters to the chancellor and to the Earl of Somerset, whom
they described as regent, to beg for the money and to warn
the English what would happen if the archbishop was not
paid. The archbishop had even provided these merchants
with copies of the king's original letters of obligation. To
these entreaties the English council had responded that they
wished to pay the debt, but that the money was not available.

---

¹ Staatsarchiv Düsseldorf, Urkunde Kurköln no. 2243; E 28/80/30 and E 404/
666/137 concern warrants for the herald's reward of £10.
² *Proc. P.C.* vi. 92; E 404/66/164; E 403/779/m. 3.
³ Staatsarchiv Düsseldorf, Urkunde Kurköln no. 2247; Rymer, xi. 269.
⁴ E 404/68/61; E 404/64/72; Staatsarchiv Düsseldorf, Urkunde Kurköln no.
2302.   ⁵ E 403/795/m. 13.

Consequently Dietrich began seizing the merchants in his territories together with their property. To obviate the dangers such action entailed for the English merchants in Cologne, these merchants undertook to pay the royal debt. That June, Aleyn and Tong promised to pay 2,000 florins of the amount owed to the archbishop with the understanding that under no condition could they ever institute a suit to recover the sums; however, they were free to try to collect the money from the English exchequer.[1] And in December two other merchants undertook for all the English merchants in Cologne to attempt to collect the debt from the English exchequer.[2]

What this suggests about England's link with Dietrich von Mörs is that Henry VI's advisers wanted to recreate Henry V's system of alliances—but with a difference in purpose. Henry V had established an aggressive alliance against France and hoped to use it to obtain troops for his army. By the end of the fourth decade of the fifteenth century, when the English were actively rebuilding this system, an alliance for such an end was no longer feasible. What the English needed was a defensive alliance. If they could secure the support of the Rhenish princes, at least Burgundy might think twice before embarking on a long and expensive struggle with England. Furthermore, if the English were far-sighted enough to grasp Burgundy's ultimate aim—the reconstruction of the ancient kingdom of Lotharingia—this defensive alliance would have been doubly satisfying, for it served to bolster the lesser princes on the duke's borders and thus check his ambition. And the attraction of the alliances for the German princes must be seen primarily in this light. Except for Cologne, which had lucrative economic connections with England, these princes had little to gain by an alliance with England other than securing a strong ally in the form of a feudal lord who would deter the Duke of Burgundy's ambition insofar as it might threaten absorption of these regions into his realm. Further evidence that this interpretation must be correct stems from two facts: (1) England paid only a small fraction

---

[1] Staatsarchiv Düsseldorf, Urkunde Kurköln no. 2348.
[2] Ibid., no. 2364.

of the sums she owed to the Archbishop of Cologne, who in turn demanded a letter from Henry VI explicitly stating that his alliance was not to be interpreted as including an aggressive pact against the Duke of Burgundy; and (2) the Bishop of Münster and the Count of Mark received no financial benefit from their treaties. For their part the English seem never to have demanded soldiers from these vassals.

Certainly the most expensive alliance England established with the German princes was her connection with Lewis, Count Palatine of the Rhine. As a result of conversations in London early in 1401 between envoys of the Emperor Rupert, Lewis's father, and Henry IV, the king's daughter Blanche was betrothed to the count and it was agreed that he would receive a dowry of 40,000 nobles, of which 16,000 were to be paid at the time of the wedding and the remainder in instalments during the next two years. Henry IV, who found the first payment almost impossible to collect from his subjects, seems to have been able to raise only a further 1,000 marks during his entire reign.[1] No doubt Blanche's death in 1406, while not discharging the English of their obligation to pay, at least relieved them of any sense of urgency.

Count Lewis, however, was not one to forget such a debt. During the summer of 1415, as Henry V was preparing to depart for his campaign in France, two of the count's envoys arrived in England to press for payment of the sums owing their master. Henry, who was having difficulty enough in raising the funds necessary to conduct his war in France, responded courteously to the envoys, recognizing his obligation but stating that owing to the present financial stringency he was able to spare nothing.[2] Lewis continued to press for payment, and once Henry decided to buttress his alliance with the Emperor Sigismund by forming

---

[1] Wylie, *Henry IV*, i. 166–7, 256. *Correspondence Bekynton*, vol. i, pp. cxii–cxv has an incomplete and somewhat inaccurate account of this alliance. W. Holtzmann, 'Die englische Heirat Pfalzgraf Ludwigs III.', *Zeitschrift für die Geschichte des Oberrheins*, new ser. xlii (1929), 1–38. In view of the large sums paid into the Palatine treasury it is disappointing that H. Cohn (*The Government of the Rhine Palatinate in the Fifteenth Century* (Oxford, 1965)) found no information regarding this alliance.

[2] Wylie, *Henry V*, i. 467.

subsidiary alliances with the lesser princes of the Empire, he revised his obligation to the Count Palatine by turning it into an annuity (apparently worth 1,000 marks a year). Since no copy of this agreement seems to have survived, it is impossible to tell exactly when it went into effect or what its provisions were—whether it was primarily the simplest and most convenient way to satisfy a debt of honour, or whether it provided more substantial backing for the English cause, in view of the fact that Lewis served in the English army with 700 men during the summer campaigns of 1420.[1] While the first recorded payment of this annuity is dated the next year,[2] it seems unlikely that Henry established some sort of agreement similar to the contemporary alliance binding him to the Archbishop of Cologne. Furthermore, it is rather unlikely that Henry VI's councillors would have paid out almost £10,000 between 1423 and 1445 merely to fulfil the promised dowry of a princess who had been dead for seventeen years.

Despite the fact that King Henry had been dead for five months, Johannes Labanum, Canon of Worms, the count's attorney appeared in London in January 1423 to collect his master's pension, and the council, which had debated the matter the previous month,[3] ordered the exchequer to deliver the customary 1,000 marks.[4] Finding it so easy to extract money from the king's councillors, Lewis issued a further commission on 11 April 1423 for the collection of that year's annuity.[5] Again the council, which discussed the matter on 8 and 9 May,[6] decided to allow the payment and authorized the treasurer to pay the pension as it came due without resort to the council. On 17 May, in accordance with this decision the exchequer handed over £666. 13s. 4d. to Bernard Cresz and Otto de Lapide for the count's 'good service',[7] and these envoys in turn gave the exchequer a

---

[1] Wylie and Waugh, *Henry V*, iii. 211–12. As early as Aug. 1419 King Henry had been urging the count to join him in Paris with men ready for fighting.

[2] E 30/1414. The receipt annexed to this letter of proxy bears the date 13 June 1421.

[3] *Proc. P.C.* iii. 12.   [4] E 403/658/m. 7.   [5] E 30/428 A.

[6] *Proc. P.C.* iii. 76.

[7] E 403/660/m. 5. The quittance for this sum was also dated 17 May 1423 (E 30/428 A).

receipt for this sum. Three days later the council drafted a letter to Lewis, probably to be delivered by his returning envoys, stating that they were sending ambassadors in order that the league formed between the late king and count might be renewed just as they hoped to renew Henry's agreement with the Archbishop of Cologne.[1] No evidence seems to have survived indicating that the English ever sent this promised embassy nor does a copy of any agreement survive, but the fact that the annuity was regularly paid until 1429 points to a satisfactory understanding between the two parties.[2]

By 1429 English finances had deteriorated appreciably,[3] and the pressures of the renewed struggle in France meant that commitments not vital to the prosecution of the war were likely to fall into abeyance. Whether the Count Palatine complained about this state of affairs we do not know. In fact it is not until 1434, apparently, that the count's envoys turned up in London again to discuss the non-payment of the annuity.[4] The following September Lewis, seemingly having received a favourable reply to his messages, empowered Otto de Lapide and Frederick de Mitra to collect the customary 1,000 marks.[5] This time they did not receive the sum immediately. In February Henry deputed Master John Stokes, Master Stephen Wilton, and Richard Selling, who were about to undertake negotiations with the Grand Master of the Teutonic Order and the Hanseatic League, to negotiate with Lewis about the

---

[1] E 28/41/109.

[2] On 18 Oct. Count Lewis commissioned Johannes Potte, Johannes Dans, and Ertiner Swert, citizens of Cologne, to receive his annuity for 1423; before 13 Nov. 1424, when it was finally paid, Johannes Rynk and Tydemann Spegyn had been substituted for the above envoys (E 30/1584; E 403/669/m. 4). The king defaulted in 1424 and 1425, but the count's agents (appointed 14 Jan. 1426) received the following 20 June 1,000 marks and seem to have been satisfied about the other 1,000 marks within five days (*Proc. P.C.* iii. 178; E 30/1246 (2); E 403/675/m. 4; E 30/1246 (1)). In 1426 Henry once again failed to provide the count with his wages, so when the payment for 1427 fell due, envoys were duly commissioned to receive these sums. Lord Hungerford paid them from the exchequer before 25 Nov. (Rymer, x. 379, 383). Again in Oct. 1428 the agents were empowered to collect the annuity and in time (28 Feb.) they received the demanded sums (E 30/1372, 1411).

[3] A. Steel, *Receipt of the Exchequer, 1377–1485* (Cambridge, 1954), p. 176.

[4] The agent was awarded £40 for his troubles (E 403/715/m. 12).

[5] E 30/1427.

money that was owed him.[1] The initial conversations with
the German ambassadors seem to have proceeded smoothly
to a speedy conclusion, for within a week of the dating of the
English commission Lapide and Mitra had received a
year's annuity for the duke, in addition to two silver-gilt
cups worth £19.[2] The same day Stokes and Wilton accepted
advances on their wages so that they could undertake the
second part of the mission,[3] discussion with the Hanseatic
League at Calais and Bruges.

In August Henry ordered another commission for Stokes
to treat with the Count Palatine about the payment and
manner of payment of the money owed to him by the king.[4]
Stokes's efforts evidently met with some success, for on
1 March Henry wrote to Lewis thanking him for
granting him temporary respite for paying his annuity and
certifying that he had sent new letters of obligation to him
by Johannes van Wypenord alias Rosencrans of Cologne.[5]

These new agreements, in spite of the king's good
intentions, did not result in prompt satisfaction of the debt.
The first instalment, after the respite granted by the count
had passed, was paid to agents of certain merchants from
Cologne named in the count's letter of proxy.[6] But during
the next four years Henry paid not one penny of the amount
owed, although Lewis IV sent an envoy to remind Henry of
his obligation (even though the old count had died). The
king's reply was that he was sorry about the delay, but there
was nothing he could do about it since his revenue from
customs duties had been less than anticipated and the cost
of the war in France more.[7] The young count Lewis was not
to be put off indefinitely by these excuses; he waited almost
a year before he wrote to the King of England. This time he
affirmed that his patience had run out; his annuity had not
been paid for four years; consequently, he was sending his
ambassadors to demand payment of the arrears.[8] Now the
council decided it would be wise to pay off this annoying
obligation. The king wrote to the count thanking him once

---

[1] Rymer, x. 604, 605.   [2] E 403/717/m. 4.   [3] E 403/717/m. 3.
[4] Rymer, x. 622.   [5] Ibid. 633.
[6] Ibid. 659; E 30/445.   [7] *Correspondence Bekynton*, i. 183.
[8] Ibid. 180.

again for his patience, saying that he hoped he was now fully content,[1] but it was not until the next February (1441) that the exchequer finally disgorged the required £3,200.[2] After such a staggering payment, it is not surprising that, except for two small sums (one of 100 marks and another of £16. 13s. 4d.),[3] the exchequer defaulted in 1441, 1442, and 1443. In March 1444 the Count Palatine commissioned envoys to receive these funds.[4] Then the note on the issue rolls dated 9 April 1445,[5] which recorded the payment of £2,200 to Master Nicholas de Wachenheim, the count's proctor, brings to a close this phase in the history of Anglo-German relations.

From these two episodes of English diplomacy in the mid fifteenth century it is obvious that as far as Henry VI's advisers focused their thoughts on the Continent the problem was France, and those who faced the problem could only propose the ancient device of encirclement—a policy which in Anglo-French relations dated from Edward I's reign, if not earlier. To lay too much blame at the feet of the English government would be a mistake—similar manœuvres had been more or less successful in the past and might be again. Nevertheless, for a country fighting a defensive war, such conservatism, such bankruptcy in the realm of innovation that appeared can only be called lamentable.

---

[1] *Correspondence Bekynton*, i. 182.   [2] E 403/740/m. 41.

[3] The latter payment seems to be a reward to the count's agents rather than an instalment of the annuity (E 403/747/mm. 4, 1).

[4] E 30/482.

[5] They had received 100 marks in July 1444 and the same month the council issued the order for the final payment, although it was another nine months before the money was actually delivered (E 403/753/m. 9; E 28/73/74). Nothing seems to have come of the scheme to pay these envoys in a joint undertaking by the treasurer and the keeper of the wardrobe in the summer of 1444 since all three parts of the indenture setting out this plan survive in the Public Record Office (E 30/479, 483, 1657).

IV

ENGLAND AND THE ITALIAN
CITY-STATES

MODERN scholars tend to assess the cultural and political history of fifteenth-century Italy largely in forward-looking terms. Paralleling the growth of Renaissance art and humanistic scholarship in Italy and their export to the rest of Europe at the end of the century, the development of the concert of Italian states as concretized in the Most Holy League of 1455 and the regular diplomatic relations established in consequence have been regarded by some scholars as the prefiguration of the sixteenth-century European state system.[1] Other historians have stressed the rise of Italian national consciousness in the fourteenth century, leading to a sense of exclusiveness from 'barbarian' Europe.[2] This view is also teleological, for it looks forward to the political unification of the Italian peninsula that was only achieved in 1870.

Common to most modern treatments of pre-Risorgimento Italy, then, is a sense of substantial unity underlying local differences. But from London in the mid fifteenth century things must have looked very different. For one thing the map of Italy was quite variously illuminated: some states of special concern such as Genoa and Florence were never forgotten, while other large areas were scarcely visible at all. Venice, in particular, had not yet attained the status of cynosure that it was to enjoy in the Tudor age. Moreover, in several territories foreign links were perhaps rightly seen as dominant. Sicily had been ruled by the Aragonese ever since the Vespers of 1282 and in our period, in 1442, Alfonso the Magnanimous definitely absorbed Naples into his sea-borne dominions. Thus southern Italy was more

[1] G. Mattingly, *Renaissance Diplomacy* (London, 1962), pp. 60 ff.
[2] D. Hay, 'Italy and Barbarian Europe', *Italian Renaissance Studies: A Tribute to the Late Cecilia M. Ady*, ed. E. F. Jacob (London, 1960), pp. 28–68.

appropriately treated as part of an east–west axis extending across the Mediterranean than as an integral part of the peninsular complex.[1] During the Avignonese captivity the central belt formed by the States of the Church had been insignificant in every way. With the return of the curia to a much dilapidated Rome the territory became a kind of rat-hole down which money disappeared in the form of papal taxes, with no appreciable compensating benefits, as far as the English could see. Only secondarily did the Eternal City figure as a goal of pilgrimage, though this function received a fillip in the successful Jubilee of 1450. For the English, however, the really important parts of Italy were the commercial and banking states of Tuscany and the seafaring Republic of Genoa. Since the papacy is treated elsewhere, our attention in this chapter will be focused almost exclusively on this 'chest area' of the peninsula. It is true that Lombardy was also traditionally associated with trans-Alpine banking, but by our period the term Lombard was applied indiscriminately to any Italian money-lender. Milan the English tended to view largely in terms of the Alpine complex and the Empire, while Savoy, under its ambitious Duke Amadeus VIII, could be treated as one of the peripheral duchies of France.

Despite these considerable differences of emphasis, historians of the fifteenth and twentieth centuries would probably find a considerable area of agreement in regarding the emergence of Florence as a major power in the peninsula as the most significant fact in the political history of Italy in the early fifteenth century. Heretofore numerous small states dominated the scene; from these four prominent territories had emerged by the late fourteenth century: Milan and Venice in the north, Naples and the States of the Church in the south. With the defeat of the democratic government and the final assertion of oligarchic principles in 1382, the city of Florence, situated on the banks of the Arno, assumed her place in the struggle for land that is so characteristic of the other chief Italian cities of this period. Under the direction of the Albizzi–Capponi–Uzzano

[1] E. Dupré Theseider, *La politica italiana di Alfonso d'Aragona* (Bologna, 1956), pp. 59 ff.

triumvirate Florence fought doggedly (1390–1402) to halt Gian Galeazzo Visconti's successful expansion from Milan through Perugia, Siena, Pisa, and Bologna to the gates of Florence.[1] Only Gian Galeazzo's sudden death in 1402 saved Florence from becoming a tributary of the Milanese state. The collapse of Milan following the duke's death gave Florence the opportunity to gobble up the port city of Pisa before she faced a more serious menace—King Ladislas of Naples had moved northwards and occupied Rome by 1408. Attempts to form a league based on support of Ladislas's Angevin rival to the Neapolitan throne came to nothing and Florence escaped conquest only by that king's unexpected death in the summer of 1414. The following eight years of peace witnessed the reconstruction of the Duchy of Milan by the French-allied Filippo Maria,[2] whose success almost immediately nullified the effect of Henry V's peace with Milan's vassal Genoa.[3] By 1421 Filippo Maria's depredations in the Romagna reached such a pitch that Florence found herself once again at war. With the aid of Venice this war was concluded in 1428. However, the next year the Florentines, having tried to absorb Lucca into their territory, were at war with Milan. This war dragged on until 1433; its notable lack of success brought down the oligarchy and set Cosimo de' Medici over Florentine affairs.

With foreign policy so complicated by the local situation and Italian wars so frequent and costly, the Florentines apparently saw little advantage to be gained by throwing their weight on either the English or the French side. Yet the English did provide much of the wool essential for the Florentine textile industry (in addition to tin and hides) and in return took quantities of luxury goods. Because of this trade the two governments remained friendly, if distant. The collapse of the Bardi and the Peruzzi in the 1340s as a result of Edward III's refusal to honour his debts was followed by a revival which lasted until about 1375 (when

---

[1] F. Schevill, *Medieval and Renaissance Florence* (New York, 1963), ii. 336–53.
[2] Beaucourt, *Charles VII*, i. 338, 341.
[3] Dumont, *Corps diplomatique*, ii, pt. 2, 155–7; Wylie and Waugh, *Henry V*, iii. 358–9.

these bankers finally withdrew from England).[1] But a new era of successful commercial relations began in the 1390s. This period lasted until the Medici came to power and still depended primarily on the wool trade, though by the end of the period cloth was becoming as important. Florence's acquisition of Leghorn in 1421 signalled a further expansion of Anglo-Florentine trade, for like Venice she began manning a fleet to sail regularly from central Italy—with the exception of the years 1449–55, when Florence was at war with Naples—bearing such goods as spices, the famous cloth woven from silver and gold threads, fruit, and wine.[2] (After 1421, Genoa's trade, on the other hand, consisted mainly of alum from her mines in the Near East and blue dye in return for wool and cloth.)[3]

In the middle 1430s the difficulties at home of the Alberti family, who dominated Anglo-Florentine trade in this period, are well known.[4] Excluded from public office from 1393 to 1435, the Alberti were subjected to crippling taxation and refused diplomatic help abroad. Demands for payment for wool bought in England by the royal council were answered with pleas for respite from Florence.[5] To these pleas the English king responded that wool bought three years earlier had not been paid for and that the seller called for letters of marque and reprisal, as was his right.[6] When the payment did not arrive, Henry authorized the issuance of letters of marque against the Alberti.[7] Ten years later the Medici, inconvenienced by these letters against their predecessors, arranged to pay the debt.

Medicean foreign policy did not differ significantly from its predecessors';[8] the two goals—safety and territorial expansion—remained constant. But the threat to Florence's

---

[1] G. A. Holmes, 'Florentine Merchants in England, 1350–1450', *Economic History Review*, 2nd ser. xiii (1960), 193–208.

[2] M. E. Mallett, 'Anglo-Florentine Commercial Relations, 1465–91', ibid., xv (1962), 251; id., *The Florentine Galleys in the Fifteenth Century* (Oxford, 1967).

[3] J. Heers, *Gênes au xve siècle* (École pratique des hautes études–vi° section: Centre de recherches historiques, 1961), pp. 406–10.

[4] L. Passerini, *Gli Alberti di Firenze*, 2 vols. (Florence, 1869–70).

[5] Holmes, 'Florentine Merchants', pp. 197–8.

[6] *Correspondence Bekynton*, i. 250–4.

[7] *Cal. Pat. Rolls, 1436–41*, p. 389.

[8] Schevill, *Florence*, pp. 358–62.

territorial integrity was greater. Initially there was little to fear from the south: Naples, following the death of Queen Joanna in 1435, witnessed a long and confusing struggle between Alfonso and the Angevins, while the States of the Church were at the mercy of Milan's condottiere Sforza. In the north, however, Cosimo renewed the alliance with Venice as protection against the rapacity of Filippo Maria. The Milanese were defeated at Anghiari in 1440, but the intrigue resulting in Sforza's succession as Duke—despite French attempts to have Charles of Orléans chosen—cost Florence Venice's friendship. A new war broke out with Venice and her ally Alfonso opposed to Florence and Milan; this war dragged on until 1454, when it was settled by the Peace of Lodi. And Genoa, which had shaken off the Milanese yoke in 1435, was forced by Alfonso's implacable hatred to accept the suzerainty of René of Anjou's son, thus placing the city firmly within the French sphere of allies.[1]

Notwithstanding the difficulties occasioned by the withdrawal of the Alberti, trade between England and Florence continued at such a prosperous level that a branch of the Medici bank, which included agents in London, opened in June 1439 at Bruges,[2] though the Milanese bank owned by the Borromei met with such reversals that it closed the same year.[3] Furthermore, the English king felt no compunction about having his secretary, Thomas Beckington, write a letter to Cosimo de' Medici on behalf of Tito Livio Frulovisi, the author of the *Vita Henrici Quinti*.[4] Anglo-Florentine trade proved even more successful than the Medici bankers

---

[1] V. Vitale, *Breviario della storia di Genova* (Genoa, 1955), i. 153–65.

[2] R. de Roover, *The Rise and Decline of the Medici Bank, 1347–1494* (New York, 1966), p. 320.

[3] G. Biscaro, 'Il Banco Filippo Borromei e Compagni di Londra (1436–39)', *Archivio Storico Lombardo*, 4th ser. xix (1913), 37–126, 283–386.

[4] Archivio di Stato di Firenze, Mediceo avanti il Principato, filza xi, carta 202. This original signet letter bearing Beckington's autograph initial *B* is dated 26 Aug. 1440. On Livio's itinerary after leaving England see T. Livio, *Vita Henrici Quinti regis Anglie (1413–22)*, ed. T. Hearne (Oxford, 1716); J. Wylie, 'Decembri's Version of the Vita Henrici Quinti by Tito Livio', *English Historical Review*, xxiv (1909), 84–9; C. L. Kingsford, *The First English Life of King Henry the Fifth* (Oxford, 1911); and C. W. Previté-Orton, 'The Early Career of Titus Livius de Frulovisiis', *English Historical Review*, xxx (1915), 74–8. See also R. Weiss, 'Humphrey, Duke of Gloucester, and Tito Livio Frulovisi', *Fritz Saxl, 1890–1948: A Volume of Memorial Essays from His Friends in England* (London, 1957), pp. 218–27.

had anticipated; consequently the London agents under Gerozzo de' Pigli were detached from the Bruges bank to form an independent branch.[1] Probably acting on Pigli's advice the Florentine government decided to settle the Alberti debt because of the difficulties the Florentine merchants had met in England and especially because their general safe conduct had expired.[2] (The merchants thought —no doubt rightly—that the safe conduct would not be renewed until they had made some provision for paying off the debt.) Thus in return for an agreement to remove the debt in sums of 580 ducats per year for eight years, the king was asked to grant the Florentines a general safe conduct for the following ten years and the right to the same tax advantages as native English merchants enjoyed.[3] Further, Vicent Clement, a sometime royal envoy passing through Florence on his way to Lyons, was fêted and asked to write to London on Florence's behalf.[4]

In spite of Florentine efforts to buy favour they met with little success. Part of the English merchants' objection to the Italians was that they purchased most of their wool under the king's licence and shipped it from Southampton and Sandwich rather than buying it from the Staple at Calais.[5] Moreover, in the past foreigners bore the brunt of the wool taxes and hence the cost of the war, as Mr. McFarlane argued,[6] but by the mid fifteenth century English merchants handled 88 per cent of the declining wool trade and 55 per cent of the cloth trade.[7] Consequently, Englishmen were

---

[1] Roover, *Medici Bank*, p. 321.

[2] A. del Vecchio and E. Casanova, *Le rappresaglie nei comuni medievali e special-mente a Firenze* (Bologna, 1894), pp. 88 ff.; L. Einstein, *The Italian Renaissance in England* (New York, 1902), pp. 250–1; A. Grunzweig, *Correspondance de la filiale de Bruges des Medici* (Commission royale d'histoire de Belgique, 1931), pp. 7–10.

[3] Grunzweig, 'Les fonds du consulat de la mer aux archives de l'État de Florence', *Bulletin de l'Institut historique belge de Rome*, x (1930). 25–8.

[4] Grunzweig, *Correspondance Medici*, p. 10.

[5] R. Flenley, 'London and Foreign Merchants in the Reign of Henry VI', *English Historical Review*, xxv (1910), 647–8; A. A. Ruddock, *Italian Merchants and Shipping in Southampton, 1200–1600* (Southampton, 1951), pp. 162–86; Roover, *Medici Bank*, p. 326.

[6] K. B. McFarlane, 'England and the Hundred Years War', *Past and Present*, xxii (July 1962), 3–13.

[7] E. Lipson, *The Economic History of England* (London, 1937), i. 564; A. R. Bridbury, *Economic Growth*, (London, 1962), p. 36.

shouldering more of the cost of the French wars than they ever had before. A greater responsibility for the cost of war naturally stimulated a demand for larger profits and goes a long way towards explaining the jealousy of special favours granted to foreign merchants and the search for new and more profitable markets.

The search for new markets, especially urgent following the sharp decline of Gascon trade after 1453, led English merchants to challenge the primacy of the Italians in the Mediterranean. Not unnaturally wishing to protect this trade the Genoese Giuliano Gattilusio lay in wait for Robert Sturmy's ships which set out from Bristol in 1457 and sank them.[1] When the English learned of Gattilusio's attack, Genoese merchants in England were arrested and their goods confiscated. The Genoese commune's effort to show that Gattilusio was a Greek pirate acting on instructions from Charles VII was disregarded, for the English were hardly likely to collect damages from the French king. In the end extrication from the web of reprisals cost the Genoese government £10,970.

Success against the Genoese was not the end of anti-alien feeling in England. The climax came in the form of riots in London during early May 1456 and in July of the next year. The Italians—that is, Venetians, Genoese, Florentines, and Luccans—then signed a mutual agreement to withdraw to Winchester for three years with the penalty for returning to the City set at £200.[2] But they may have lingered in London anyway, because trade was so profitable. In 1458, for example, the Genoese possessed goods worth £16,300 in England.[3] The Venetian galleys were making regular trips by 1460 and in the same year Henry VI and the Genoese concluded a truce for four years on the condition that the

[1] E. M. Carus Wilson, 'The Overseas Trade of Bristol', *Studies in English Trade in the Fifteenth Century*, ed. E. Power and M. Postan (London, 1933), pp. 224–30; J. Heers, 'Les Génois en Angleterre: la crise de 1458–66', *Studi in onore di Armando Sapori* (Milan, 1957), ii. 809–32.

[2] Flenley, 'London and Foreign Merchants', p. 654. There was similar unrest in Southampton, whose prosperity declined despite the activities of the Italian merchants (O. Coleman, 'Trade and Prosperity in the Fifteenth Century: Some Aspects of the Trade of Southampton', *Economic History Review*, xvi (1963–4), 9–22).

[3] J. Heers, 'Les Génois en Angleterre', p. 824.

Genoese accord no aid to the *soi-disant* King of France, the Castilians, or the Scots, and that the English give no assistance to Joan of Aragon.[1]

Although the return of Venice's galleys and the Genoese truce may be thought to herald better times for the Italian merchants, Edward IV's reign did not immediately usher in a period of prosperity. The Medici bank may have operated a profitable business in England until 1455, but from that time bad management coupled with Edward IV's voracious demands for loans—by 1468 he owed the company £10,500 —temporarily closed the London branch in 1473.[2] The crippling reverses caused by the Sturmy affair and the exhaustion of the stockpile of alum in Chios following their loss of the Near Eastern mines in 1455[3] did not end Genoese activity in England; ruin came after Edward IV's accession when these merchants suffered from a lack of credit.[4]

All told, the activity of the Italian city states played a minor role in the diplomatic manœuvering occasioned by the last years of the Hundred Years' War. They contributed no considerable support to the English navy nor did the bankers finance—at least during Henry VI's reign—the war to the extent they had a century earlier. On the whole it seems that the trade was more essential for the Italians than for the English, for twice the Italians consented to pay considerable sums in return for a continuation of their privileges to trade. If these merchants had once borne a considerable portion of the financial burden of the war in its earlier phases, neither they nor the English were particularly mindful of this. On the other hand, it is only just to point out that it was not the lack of government which followed Henry VI's lapse into insanity in the middle of the century which ruined the Italian merchants in England; rather it was the financial policy of the first of the 'new monarchs'.

---

[1] Rymer, xi. 441–3. [2] Roover, *Medici Bank*, pp. 328–34.
[3] M.-L. Heers, 'Les Génois et les commerces de l'alun à la fin du Moyen Âge', *Revue d'histoire économique et sociale*, xxxii (1954), 39.
[4] J. Heers, 'Les Génois en Angleterre', p. 824.

V

ENGLAND AND THE BALTIC

THE origin of Anglo-Hanseatic relations dates from the mid twelfth century when merchants from Cologne began to establish themselves in London.[1] It was only a matter of time before these merchants and others, who came chiefly from towns lying on the southern and eastern coasts of the Baltic Sea, recognized the advantage of collective bargaining and joined together to form a corporation. The headquarters of this organization, the Steelyard, became fixed on the north bank of the Thames slightly west of London Bridge. With the appearance of factories resembling the London Steelyard in Novgorod (the Peterhof) and in Bruges (the *Kontor*), these north German merchants also began to meet at home to discuss common economic problems and to co-ordinate their activities abroad. Not until the second half of the fourteenth century, however, was a stimulus provided—in the shape of troubles with Flanders and the unification of the Scandinavian countries—to weld the Hanseatic cities into a formal union.[2]

Unlike fifteenth-century Englishmen, modern scholars have noted that the unified front presented by the Steelyard masked widely divergent interests within the confederation. By the beginning of the fifteenth century Lübeck, which was the most important of the Wendish group of cities, had emerged as the leader of the Hanseatic League. Both geographically and historically she was well placed for this role. Situated on the Baltic at the base of the Jutland

---

[1] K. Kunz, 'Das erste Jahrhundert der deutschen Hanse in England', *Hansische Geschichtsblätter*, vi (1891), 129–52.

[2] D. Bjork, 'The Peace of Stralsund, 1370', *Speculum*, vii (1932), 447–76. The best of the recent general studies of the Hanseatic League are those by A. von Brandt, 'Recent Trends in Research on Hanseatic History', *History*, xli (1956), 25–37; K. Pagel, *Die Hanse* (Brunswick, 1963); and P. Dollinger, *La Hanse (xiie– xviie siècles)* (Paris, 1964). W. Stein, *Beiträge zur Geschichte der deutschen Hanse bis um die Mitte des fünfzehnten Jahrhunderts* (Giessen, 1900) is too superficial to be of use.

Peninsula, Lübeck controlled trade that came from the south by sea as far as the Elbe, where it was unloaded and carried across the peninsula. Lübeck then transported the goods by sea to towns further east, many of which she had established as colonies. As early as the end of the fourteenth century, however, the eastern colonial towns were rapidly loosening their ties with the mother city. Corn and timber comprised their chief exports and these towns were finding it more profitable to carry goods directly by sea rather than pay Lübeck's tolls for the overland haul, since these commodities were relatively inexpensive in relation to their weight. The historical process may be aptly likened to the vicissitudes of the ancient Greek leagues, which were organized partly on a territorial and partly on a colonial basis. Their history exhibits a continual tension between hegemony, in which one state dominated the others, and autonomy, in which each state managed its own affairs.[1] The working of similar centripetal and centrifugal tendencies is clearly evident in the Hanseatic League.

The presence of the Teutonic Knights in this region accounted for a further development of centrifugal tendencies. Although they exercised authority over the Hanseatic towns of Prussia and Livonia, the Knights traded independently—indeed in competition with the towns. Yet the Grand Master was the protector of the Hanseatic League and provided these cities with a nominal sovereign prince through whom diplomatic relations could be conducted. Since the end of the fourteenth century the Order had been embroiled with both Denmark and the League in a struggle for supremacy in the Baltic. The differences between the Knights and Denmark were longstanding and particularly thorny.[2] The imposition of tolls on ships going through the Sound gave the Danish king a means to restrict Prussian trade with the Atlantic seaboard, and in 1419 Poland joined an alliance with Denmark against the Order. Nor were Prussia's relations with the Wendish cities much more

---

[1] A. J. Graham, *Colony and Mother City in Ancient Greece* (Manchester, 1964); T. T. B. Ryder, *Koine Eirene; General Peace and Local Independence in Ancient Greece* (Oxford, 1965).

[2] L. Koczy, *The Baltic Policy of the Teutonic Order* (Toruń, 1936), pp. 83–6, 94.

cordial. In 1422, for example, the Grand Master refused to intervene on behalf of these cities with Holland, because the Order had just secured its own trading privileges there. In turn the Hanseatic cities began secret negotiations with the King of Denmark, and Rostock forestalled the Grand Master's attempt to recruit archers from that city for his war with Poland. It was, in fact, only when the Order was faced with the Prussian cities' refusal to assist in the war with Poland that the Grand Master came to terms with the League and supported the cities in their confrontation with Denmark.

In the east the efforts of the Order to connect its possessions in Prussia and Livonia by permanently annexing the intervening Lithuanian province of Samogitia brought them into conflict with Poland and Lithuania. Outbreaks of hostility disrupted the flow of raw materials to the west such as timber, copper, amber, and furs from Cracow and Lemberg through the Prussian port of Danzig (Gdańsk) as well as shipments of cloth (from England and Flanders), dried fish, and salt to eastern markets. In addition to the disasters of war, which caused the Knights' lands to be ravaged in 1410, 1414, 1422, and 1431–3, the Order had to face the problem of crop failure in 1412, 1415–16, and 1437–9. All this, combined with a decline in the number of labourers available and devaluation, meant that Prussia had less corn to sell.[1] Consequently, these disruptions contributed in time to the contraction of trade in north-eastern Europe and a concomitant effort on the part of ports like Danzig, which handled 70 per cent of the Prussian trade by the early fifteenth century,[2] to protect their monopoly from dilution by foreign merchants.

In considering English relations with the Baltic the importance of another power must be taken into account. The kingdom of Denmark stood astride the gateway to the Baltic; consequently, the English viewed the consolidation of the Scandinavian countries in the late fourteenth century with mingled apprehension and interest.[3] As early as 1380

---

[1] F. L. Carsten, *The Origins of Prussia* (Oxford, 1954), pp. 102–4, 112.
[2] Ibid., pp. 126–7.
[3] I. Andersson, *A History of Sweden* (London, 1956), pp. 71–81; K. Gjerset, *History of the Norwegian People* (New York, 1932), p. 37.

Queen Margaret of Denmark secured a personal union of her kingdom with Norway by having her son Olaf proclaimed king, but the Danish sovereign was barred from gaining a firm hold on the country until the Union of Kalmar came into effect in 1397. In the meantime the queen defeated Albert of Mecklenburg, the German interloper in Sweden, and brought that country under Danish control. According to the provisions of the Union of Kalmar, these three Scandinavian countries were to make common cause in matters of foreign policy; ultimate decisions rested, of course, with the Danish monarch, though he was expected to ask the council of the country in which he was residing for advice. Henry IV of England seems to have recognized the multiple advantages of an alliance with this new power in the north: the strength it would add to his none too sure claim to the English throne, unobstructed passage through the Sound into the Baltic, a counter to play against the Hanseatic League. Thus he entered into negotiations with Queen Margaret for the marriage of his daughter Philippa to the queen's heir Eric of Pomerania (Olaf had died prematurely) in 1401.[1] Although he waited for five years as he watched Denmark's varying fortunes, noted the security of his own title, and at the same time measured the deterioration of his own relations with the League, Henry dispatched Philippa to Denmark in 1406 for the solemnization of her marriage. Thanks to this close alliance Anglo-Danish friendship flourished with little incident until the late 1420s when English merchants insisted in trading directly with Iceland in defiance of the injunction that they must first pass through the Hanse-controlled staple at Bergen. Only the far more pressing problem of Danish conflict with the Hanseatic League about Denmark's attempt to reassert control over Schleswig prevented this issue from precipitating a real crisis in the alliance.

In England the shift in the export trade from raw wool to manufactured cloth that took place in the second half of the fourteenth century meant that English merchants who

---

[1] Wylie, *Henry IV*, ii. 134–54; L. Daae, 'Erik af Pommerns, Danmarks, Sveriges og Norges konges giftermaal med Philippa, Prindsesse af England', *Historiske Tidsskrift*, ii (1880), 322–74.

previously had only to go as far as Calais or Bruges to dispose of their goods were now forced to seek out new markets at a greater distance from home.[1] It is in this light that the struggles of the English with the north of Europe during the fifteenth century must be seen. The search for wider markets led English merchants to demand from the Hanseatic cities the same privileges their merchants enjoyed in England, especially exemption from certain customs charges and the right to establish factories on German soil. Contraction of trade in the Baltic stiffened the reluctance of the German cities to grant such rights. Nevertheless, the English merchants pressed their demands successfully during most of Henry VI's reign. Not until the instability of the government revealed itself in the middle of the century in its failure to keep the seas reasonably free of pirates was the Hanseatic League able to unite with some effectiveness against England. And in fact it took almost a quarter of a century and a piece of luck for them to turn the tables completely—in return for ships to carry him back to England in 1471, Edward IV confirmed the Hanseatic League's privileges in England, making no mention of reciprocal rights.

But we must retrace our steps. Relations between England and the Hanseatic towns had been troubled since 1398 when the Grand Master of the Teutonic Order withdrew the privileges granted to English merchants in the treaty of 1388.[2] After desultory skirmishing on both sides, an

---

[1] M. Postan, 'The Trade of Medieval Europe: the North', *The Cambridge Economic History of Europe*, ii, ed. M. Postan and E. Rich (Cambridge, 1952), 227–30, 244–5. The fourteenth century is summed up in F. Keutgen, *Die Beziehungen der Hanse zu England im letzten Drittel des vierzehnten Jahrhunderts* (Giessen, 1890).

[2] There are four important monographs relating to Anglo-Hanseatic diplomacy during the fifteenth century: F. Schulz, 'Die Hanse und England: von Eduards III. bis auf Heinrichs VIII. Zeit', *Abhandlungen zur Verkehrs- und Seegeschichte im Auftrag des hansischen Geschichtsvereins*, ed. D. Schäfer (Berlin, 1911), vol. v; K. Engel, *Die Organisation der deutsch-hansischen Kaufleute in England im 14. und 15. Jahrhundert bis zum Utrechter Frieden (1474)* (Göttingen, 1914); W. Stein, 'Die Hanse und England beim Ausgang des Hundertjährigen Krieges', *Hansische Geschichtsblätter*, xxvi (1920–1), 27–127; M. Postan, 'The Economic and Political Relations of England and the Hanse from 1400 to 1475', *Studies in English Trade in the Fifteenth Century*, ed. E. Power and M. Postan (London, 1933), pp. 91–153. None of these studies contains an entirely satisfactory account of the diplomatic relations between England and the Hanseatic League during Henry VI's reign;

agreement was reached (during December 1409)[1] by which damages of more than £10,000 were awarded to the Grand Master and privileges equivalent to those the Hanseatics enjoyed in England were restored to the English merchants in Prussia.[2] Inasmuch as piracy in the North Sea and the Channel continued unabated and the £10,000 was only partly paid,[3] direct confrontation seemed inevitable. But the political situation in the rest of Europe brought more important problems to the fore. Vitold, the Grand Duke of Lithuania, had stirred up a revolt in Prussian-held Samogitia.[4] In their attempt to crush it the Knights met a resounding defeat at Tannenberg, where the Grand Master Ulrich von Jungingen was killed. The Order had to pay reparations, and Samogitia was returned to Lithuania for Vitold's lifetime.

At the same time a constitutional crisis in Lübeck fully occupied the minds of the west Germans, while Henry V's renewal of the Anglo-French wars made strong policy against the German merchants unlikely in England. The League did approach Sigismund to secure his intervention with the English; at his invitation Hanseatic and English representatives met at Constance in the summer of 1417, but the negotiations were unsuccessful.[5] Not long after, Sigismund abandoned the Hanseatic cities to their own devices. Finally in 1420, frustrated by this notable lack of success, the Grand Master once again forbad the establishment of English factories in Prussia. Before the English had

Engel, Postan, and Schulz especially are surveys of a much broader period and are concerned more with economics than with foreign policy. Although Stein treats a few years around the middle of the century rather exhaustively, his account, based almost entirely upon printed Hanseatic documents, is vitiated by a strong bias in favour of Lübeck. The following sentence is only one sample: 'Zudem hatte es [Lübeck] ohne Zweifel das Recht und die Einsicht in das wahre Gesamtinteresse der Hanse an seiner Seite' (p. 91).

[1] There seems to be an error in dating this treaty 1408 in Postan, 'England and the Hanse', p. 111.

[2] For a concise summary of the events leading up to the treaty concluded on 4 Dec. 1409 see J. L. Kirby, 'Sir William Sturmy's Embassy to Germany in 1405–6', *History Today* (Jan. 1965), 39–47. Mr. Kirby apparently overlooked the 380-page dossier prepared for this embassy (B.M., Add. MS. 48009, pp. 25–405).

[3] Schulz, p. 66.

[4] E. Lönnroth, 'The Baltic Countries', *The Cambridge Economic History of Europe*, iii, ed. M. Postan, E. Rich, and E. Miller (Cambridge, 1963), iii. 359–60.

[5] Schulz, p. 70.

agreed what action to take, Henry V died and the final
decision was left for his son's council.

Pressed by merchants demanding restoration of rights in
Prussia corresponding to those that Prussian merchants
received in England and in need of money to prosecute the
war, the royal council (acting upon a ruling by the king's
judges) decided on 23 October 1423 that the merchants of
the Steelyard were to contribute to a subsidy of 3d. in the
cask and 12d. in the pound for tonnage and poundage.[1]
The Hanseatic merchants refused to pay this tax, claiming
that their charter (which now needed confirmation) granted
them exemption; the council threatened to revoke all the
Hanseatic privileges. On the other side the possibility of
arresting the goods and persons of all Englishmen in their
cities was placed under consideration at a diet meeting in
Lübeck, and the Grand Master appointed envoys to go to
England for money owing to him from damages.[2] But they
were unable to reach agreement. In lieu of concord on the
state level the German merchants and the officials of the city
of London reached a working agreement on 20 February
1427. In return for a promise to pay a customs duty of
3d. on each pack of wool exported, 40s. annually to the
sheriffs and four barrels of herrings (worth 13s. 4d. each),
two of sturgeon (worth 80s.), and two of wax from Poland
(also worth 80s.), the city promised to drop its claims against
the Hanseatic merchants and to recognize their privileges.[3]

The English council sent Dr. John Norton to attend the
coronation of King Jagello's fourth wife.[4] Norton's instructions have not survived, but there is little reason to doubt
that he attended the congress of sovereigns where Eric of
Denmark, Jagello of Poland, and the King of the Romans
met to thresh out their difficulties.[5] Perhaps Norton hoped

---

[1] *Proc. P.C.* iii. 117. On 3 July the justices of the King's Bench and of Common
Pleas declared the Hanseatic merchants in England liable to pay tonnage and
poundage (*Select Cases in the Exchequer Chamber before all the Justices of England,
1377–1461*, ed. M. Hemmant (Selden Society, li, 1933), p. 27).

[2] Postan, 'England and the Hanse', p. 114; C. P. Cooper, *Appendix A to the
Report on the Foedera* (London, 1869), p. 130.

[3] *Urkundliche Geschichte des Hansischen Stahlhofes zu London*, ed. J. M. Lappenberg (Hamburg, 1851), no. lxxii.

[4] E 101/322/9, 620/23; E 364/59.

[5] O. Halecki, 'Problems of the New Monarchy: Jagello and Vitold, 1400–34',

to profit by the conflict between the Poles and the Teutonic Knights, whose cause Sigismund had espoused, in order to forge some sort of alliance against the Wendish cities, but it is more likely that the embassy's aim was to assist Sigismund's mediation between the Knights and the Poles.[1] In any case by the time Norton returned to England (February 1425) conditions in the north pointed to the inevitability of a clash between Denmark and the Count of Holstein—a conflict that would ultimately involve both the north German cities and the Knights.

In the last quarter of the fourteenth century Queen Margaret had defined the primary goal of Danish foreign policy: the expansion of Denmark to the south at the expense of the Germans. King Eric pursued this same course with so much vigour that he got into a war when he tried to force the Count of Holstein to give back the Duchy of Schleswig, which Queen Margaret had granted as a hereditary fief in 1386. When Eric decided to impose a tax on all ships passing through the strait between Scania and Seeland in order to raise money for the war, building castles at Malmö and Landskrona (and probably at Hälsingborg and Elsinore as well) to ensure its collection,[2] the League joined the conflict by imposing an economic blockade on Denmark and refusing to carry iron and copper from the Berslagen mines in Sweden. Although the Danish king finally made peace with the League in 1436, the economic blockade had bitten so deeply in Sweden that a revolt broke out two years later which led directly to Eric's deposition. The significance of this conflict for England lies chiefly in the fact that the closing of the Baltic trade route seriously hurt English merchants; to compensate for this loss Eric encouraged the English merchants who were beginning to revive trade with

The Cambridge History of Poland (to 1696), ed. W. Reddaway, J. H. Penson et al. (Cambridge, 1950), p. 223. See also M. Biskup, Zjednoczenie Pomorza Wschodniego z Polską w połowie XV w. (Warsaw, 1959); the author has provided a partial summary of his work in M. Biskup, 'Die Polnisch-preussischen Handelsbeziehungen in der ersten Hälfte des 15. Jahrhunderts', Hansische Studien: Heinrich Sproemberg zum 70. Geburtstag (Berlin, 1961), pp. 1–6.

[1] Again in 1429 an Englishman attended the congress at Tuck where problems concerning the empire, Poland, and Lithuania were discussed, but there seems to be no mention of this envoy in English sources (Halecki, p. 226).

[2] L. Palle, A History of the Kingdom of Denmark (Copenhagen, 1960), pp. 110–11.

Iceland,[1] though he did not hesitate to complain that merchants from Hull were sailing to Iceland without his licence, that Englishmen had killed some of his subjects, captured others, spoiled their goods, and burned down many churches.[2] Eric's hope must have been that the English would both weaken the Hanseatic control of the Bergen staple and furnish him increased revenue. Thus it is not surprising that the council decided to permit some of the king's subjects to fight for Denmark.[3]

With regard to the Hanseatic League, the English ignored Sigismund's intervention on their behalf to obtain compensation for an attack in 1402, at the same time conspicuously honouring a Polish knight in England with a collar and twenty marks.[4] Moreover, Henry VI confirmed his grandfather's charter that authorized English merchants in Prussia and other countries to unite in a corporate body and choose a governor.[5] And at last the king answered the Grand Master's claim for money owed to him since Henry IV's reign. It did not appear to the king or to the parliament (which had been consulted in this matter) that he was responsible for his grandfather's debt; nevertheless, if the Grand Master would send envoys to discuss paying off the sum in annual instalments, the king would see what could be done.[6] The final measures against the League were taken in March 1431 when parliament raised the subsidy of tonnage and poundage from 6d. to 3s. and later instituted a new way of reckoning this fee.[7] These last drastic measures persuaded the Steelyard merchants that war was imminent and they prepared to flee to Bruges.[8] The Prussians and the cities of the eastern Baltic did not immediately grasp the seriousness of the situation, for the Grand Master and representatives of the cities of Riga, Dorpat, and Danzig were

[1] *Diplomatarium Norvegicum*, ed. C. A. Lange and C. R. Unger (Christiania, 1849–1919), vol. v, no. 580.

[2] *Proc. P.C.* iii. 207.

[3] *Diplomatarium Islandicum* (Copenhagen, 1857–1922), iv. 324–32.

[4] *Regesta Imperii* XI: *die Urkunden Kaiser Sigmunds (1410–1437)*, ed. W. Altmann (Innsbruck, 1896–1900), no. 6760; Rymer, x. 386; *Proc. P.C.* iii. 282.

[5] Rymer, x. 400. A copy of this *inspeximus* also survives in the corporation books of King's Lynn (*Hist. MSS. Com. 11th Report* (London, 1887), app., pt. iii, p. 203).

[6] *Proc. P.C.* iv. 45–6.   [7] Schulz, p. 81.

[8] Dollinger, p. 373.

busy negotiating an agreement regarding the amount of money the King of England owed them.[1] Moreover, the Grand Master apparently gave little thought to Henry's letter concerning the seizure of the *Anna of Bristol* in Danzig.[2] In fact not until the summer of 1434 was a decision taken to send envoys to England; the envoys arrived in October and immediately raised the question of damages. The vociferous complaints raised by English merchants prevented the taking of any important decision. Consequently, the king suggested that the discussion be prorogued until the spring of 1435, when he would send envoys to Bruges.[3] The English had in any case already withdrawn the new system of reckoning tonnage and poundage because it damaged trade with places other than the north.[4]

Not content with forcing the League to accord them equal privileges in the Baltic, English merchants sought at the same time to enlarge fishing and trade with Iceland. In the parliament meeting at Westminster in January 1431 the Commons petitioned for repeal of the statute made in 1428 providing that ships fishing near Iceland should go and come by way of the staple at Bergen.[5] The king answered that ambassadors had been commissioned to treat with the King of Denmark and he was awaiting their report. He had indeed commissioned Dr. William Sprever and John Grymesby to accomplish this task the preceding November. Sprever did not depart until February,[6] but he returned before the year was out, apparently having convinced the Danes that Henry had no intention of repealing the statute of 1428. The following summer the council again considered the state of Anglo-Danish affairs and decided to commission a jurist and a knight to sort out the differences that had arisen between the two countries as a result of the illicit trade between England and Iceland.[7] Dr. William

---

[1] *Regesta*, no. 5669.   [2] Ibid., no. 2334.
[3] C. P. Cooper, *Appendix C to the Report on the Foedera* (London, 1869), no. 12.
[4] Schulz, pp. 80–4.   [5] *Rot. parl.* iv. 378.
[6] Rymer, x. 477, 481; E 404/54/178; E 403/693/m. 4; E 101/322/42. To Sprever's retinue the corporation of King's Lynn added John Salus. John Muriell had already been named to accompany the king's agent (*Hist. MSS. Com. 11th Report*, app., pt. iii, p. 162).
[7] Rymer, x. 520; *Proc. P.C.* iv. 124.

Sprever and Sir Robert Shottesbrook were the envoys chosen.[1] They set out in September and on Christmas Eve concluded an agreement with an embassy composed of the Bishops of Roskilde, Bergen, five knights, and others, by which the English promised to pay for the damages they had caused in Norwegian territory, to return the people they had abducted, and to forbid all trade with Iceland except through the Bergen staple.[2] The English did not get around to issuing orders forbidding intercourse with Iceland contrary to the laws of the King of Denmark until the summer of 1434.[3] By this time conflict between Denmark and the Hanseatic League was drawing to a close. Whatever King Eric had in mind regarding English influence at the Bergen staple, he got no profit from it, since one of the effects of the settlement between Denmark and the League was to confirm the Hanseatic monopolies in Norwegian cities.[4]

To prevent further deterioration of Anglo-Hanseatic relations in the crucial months before Arras, the king appointed John Stokes, Stephen Wilton, and Richard Selling (who were also to see the Duke of Bavaria, Philip of Burgundy, and delegates of the Flemish cities), Richard Bokeland, and Thomas Borowe, a merchant of King's Lynn, to treat with the Grand Master and the Hanseatic League for redress of grievances at Bruges.[5] For all practical purposes this embassy accomplished nothing; it may never have reached the continent, for the diet at Bruges was prorogued in early January. At the end of the year (17 December) Stokes, Richard Woodville, the lieutenant of Calais, Bokeland, Borowe, and Selling received a new commission

---

[1] Rymer, x. 521.

[2] *Diplomatarium Islandicum*, iv. 523–5; Gjerset, p. 46; *The 45th Report of the Deputy Keeper of the Public Records* (London, 1884), app. ii, p. 4 misread Spenser for Sprever. It may be that the Danish envoy to whom the council awarded a silver-gilt cup in July 1433 brought the confirmation of this agreement with him (*Proc. P.C.* iv. 168).

[3] Rymer, x. 578; *Diplomatarium Islandicum*, iv. 541–4.

[4] The wars had forced the Germans to leave Norway, but they were back by 1435 (J. A. Gade, *The Hanseatic Control of Norwegian Commerce during the Late Middle Ages* (Leiden, 1951), p. 100). For Anglo-Norwegian trade relations prior to Henry VI's reign see A. Bugge, 'Handelen mellem England og Norge indtil beygundelaen af det 15de aarhundrede', *Historisk Tidsskrift*, iv (1898), 1–148.

[5] Rymer, x. 604, 605; *Regesta*, no. 6944; *Hanserecesse, 1431–76*, ed. G. von der Ropp (Verein für hansische Geschichte, 1876–92), vol. ii, pt. i, no. 429.

designed to the same end.[1] But the reversal at Arras the previous September had furnished another impediment to the negotiations; the English were now *personae non gratae* in the lands of the Duke of Burgundy, and, in any event, the envoys of the Grand Master had not yet arrived. As a result Henry tried to move the convention to Calais, but the Grand Master still delayed sending his agents.[2] Having frustrated earlier plans by the Lübeckers to hold a diet for discussing relations with England, the Grand Master appointed on 14 February a priest of Thorn, Heinrich Vorrath, Burgomaster of Danzig, and the Grand Master's secretary to treat with the English about the complaints of their merchants and about Hanseatic privileges in England.[3] Thus in March Henry VI commissioned a third embassy composed of Stokes, John Radcliffe, and John Sutton,[4] and to ensure their success the king wrote to the bailiffs and collectors of the customs in Boston to remind them of the Hanseatic League's privileges in England.[5] Yet in April Henry was still trying to persuade the Hanseatic envoys, who had arrived in Bruges, to come to Calais where this third embassy was waiting because of the 'insecurity of Englishmen in Bruges'.[6] The badly damaged instructions dated in the Catalogue of the Cotton Charters between 1434 and 1438 seem to refer to this last embassy.[7] This fragment shows only that the ambassadors were to convey that the king was aware of the reparations owing to the League and that when the injuries to England had been redressed and the king's subjects in

---

[1] Rymer, x. 627; E 404/52/191. Stokes received an advance of £20 for his expenses on 16 Dec. (E 403/721/m. 11). Thomas Burgh, Walter Curzon, and John Bampton of King's Lynn attended these discussions 'to declare oure said soverayn Lordes Ambassiatours and thambassiatours of the Maester of Pruce and of the Duche Hanse the grevaunce . . . and other harmes be the same maiester and his sogettes . . . and to aske restitucioun and reformacioun . . .' (*Hist. MSS. Com. 11th Report*, app., pt. iii, p. 163).

[2] Cooper, *Appendix C*, no. 13.

[3] *Regesta*, no. 7151. At the petition of merchants of Cologne the king allowed a ship called the *Mary knyght* to go from London to Frankfurt with cloth and other goods to carry the envoys. The ship's safe conduct is dated 29 Mar. (*Bronnen tot de geschiedenis van den Handel met Engeland, Schotland en Ierland, 1150–1485*, ed. H. J. Smit (The Hague, 1928), nos. 1076, 1078).

[4] C 76/118/m. 14.

[5] *Geschichte des Stahlhofes zu London*, no. lxxxvii.

[6] Cooper, *Appendix C*, no. 13.   [7] B.M., Cotton Charter X, 20.

Prussia no longer 'hurtid and hermed' by the imposition
of taxes, the English king would undertake to settle his debt.
Stiff-necked instructions of this kind obviously did little
to resolve difficulties, especially since the complaint of the
consuls of Hamburg about two ships taken by some of
the king's subjects from Calais was not mentioned.[1] Because
these talks had no significant results, the merchants themselves arranged a temporary solution; they promised to pay
3,000 Rhenish guilders for the right to enter Prussian
territory.[2]

By this time, however, the English were finding themselves faced with the grim reality of the débâcle at Arras—a
hostile Burgundy. If trade with the Low Countries was
to be cut off, some sort of *rapprochement* with the Hanseatic
cities was mandatory. In the autumn Vorrath, the proconsuls
of Lübeck and Hamburg, and two other envoys came to
England to pick up the threads of the negotiations.[3] This
time the Bishop of Norwich, Ralph Lord Cromwell, and
Tiptoft were among the Englishmen appointed to treat
with Vorrath's party.[4] Most of these talks seem to have
concerned how the English proposed to pay 19,272 nobles
4*s.* 4*d.* owed since Henry IV's reign.[5] As far as the damages
were concerned the English king agreed to pay 50 marks
immediately in return for a quittance of the sum; the next
year the Grand Master would receive a similar sum and
thereafter annual payments of £50 sterling until the debt had
been satisfied. The money was to be raised from the customs
that Prussian and Hanseatic merchants paid. In addition the
English had to provide for speedy justice in cases involving
Hanseatic merchants and to restrict the customs officials
who preyed on German merchants.[6] The final details of the

---

[1] Rymer, x. 623.   [2] Cooper, *Appendix A*, p. 130.
[3] Rymer, x. 666; B.M., Add. MS. 48009, p. 545 contains a résumé of the events
of this diet; Schulz, p. 85.
[4] *Regesta*, no. 7320. Their safe conduct was granted on 26 Oct. (Rymer, x. 656).
Before the treaty was concluded the Bishop of Norwich had been translated to
Lincoln. Henry VI's letter to the pope requesting the translation is dated 24 May
1436 (ibid. 645).
[5] The question of Cologne's trading privileges was also up for consideration
(*Quellen zur Geschichte des Kölner Handels und Verkehrs im Mittelalter*, ed. B.
Kuske (Cologne, 1917–38), no. 908).
[6] Rymer, x. 657.

treaty were not settled until the following spring (1437);
on 18 March Vorrath was given an instalment of £100
and a transcript was made of the relevant financial clauses
in the treaty.[1] When all the arrangements had been completed the ratification of the treaty was drafted on 8 June,
and before Vorrath returned to Prussia he received a further
£233. 6s. 8d.[2]

The commonly accepted interpretation of this treaty is
that it was a great victory, in fact the last, for the English
over the Hanseatic League in that the protocol provided
that merchants and lieges of both parties 'libere . . . in terris
eorum emere et vendere possint'. If the English had won
reciprocal rights in the Baltic, they had been charged almost
20,000 nobles. Furthermore, the German envoys were
perhaps likewise influenced by the conviction that the
League could not have both England and Burgundy as
enemies. Pressured by deteriorating relations with Burgundy
—eighty Germans had been massacred in Flanders in June
1436 because they were suspected of supporting the English[3]
—the ambassadors were led to exceed their power as far as
the Grand Master of the Teutonic Order was concerned.
Consequently, he refused to ratify the agreement, and the
English were poorly placed to complain about this failure to
ratify the treaty, because the next two years were ones of
great famine owing to crop failure. This meant that the
English needed to import corn from Prussia.[4] And finally
England could hope for little support from her Danish ally;
King Eric, unsuccessful in supressing the revolt which broke
out in Sweden, was deposed in 1438, and the weak kings who
followed came more and more under Hanseatic influence.
Thus Henry VI's efforts to shore up his defences in the
north following Arras failed, and the period after the sealing
of the London protocol witnessed a deterioration of relations
between the two parties.

[1] E 403/725/m. 19; E 30/1617.
[2] E 403/721/m. 13; C 47/30/9/16; *Cal. Pat. Rolls, 1436–41*, p. 62; *Regesta,*
no. 7426 is the Grand Master's receipt.
[3] Dollinger, p. 368.
[4] B.M., Cotton Charter XI, 62; *Regesta,* no. 7391, pt. ii, no. 2475; Cooper,
Appendix A, p. 131. There is a similar request for grain to the King of Denmark
(*45th Report of the Deputy Keeper,* app. ii, p. 4).

Symptomatic of the worsening relations was the capture by the English of twelve ships belonging to the Hanseatic League and to the Dutch, which were on their way from Bourgneuf Bay to the north in May 1438. At the end of the next year Henry, at the insistence of English merchants, wrote to the Grand Master complaining that his subjects in Danzig were suffering various impositions in spite of the agreement just concluded with the Grand Master's envoy who had signed the protocol with his initial V.[1] The king's attempt to interest the Grand Master in Eugenius IV's plight apparently came to nothing.[2] A steady stream of complaints flowed from England to the Hanseatic cities during the next few years: Lübeck and other cities ought to pay damages for plundering certain merchants from Lyme Regis and Sandwich and then imprisoning them; the London mercer John Church was to receive letters of marque and reprisal because Hanseatics plundered his ship the *Evangelist*. Then Hanseatics held the messenger bringing royal letters demanding restitution for a £30 ransom. Two merchants from Great Yarmouth had complained that men from Hamburg had seized their ship containing salted fish and cloth from Holland worth more than 200 marks and kept the ship and sailors in Hamburg's service for twenty-six weeks. Still other English merchants presented a bill to the royal council demanding redress of damages done by the Hanseatics and affirming that they did not enjoy the privileges accorded by the Grand Master in his treaty with the king.[3] The council believed that an embassy should be sent and requested the mayors and bailiffs of certain port cities to make inquiries about the actual situation of English merchants in ports belonging to the League, Denmark, and the Order.[4] Apart from a document from the Danzig council, the dating of which is uncertain, however, no evidence has survived to suggest that an embassy was sent at this time. In 1443 the idea of a mission was revived; the treasurer, Lord Cromwell, declared in council that 'the Sprucier and Hansze beth' frer here in Ingland' than the Kyng' subgitt to the loss

---

[1] E 28/63/54 is misdated in Rymer, x. 753.   [2] *Regesta*, no. 7624.
[3] Rymer, x. 755; PSO I/11/552; E 32/67/194; E 30/1288; *Proc. P.C.* v. 167.
[4] *Regesta*, no. 8204.

of the kyng yerely of c^mli';[1] and Henry wrote to the Grand
Master, Konrad von Erlichshausen, about the seizure of
English goods.[2] But no embassy set out. During the spring
of 1447 a Prussian agent arrived in England to discuss the
hindrances and restrictions affecting English trade in the
Baltic, but little was accomplished beyond renewing a protection for the Hanseatic merchants against letters of marque
for three years.[3] It seems likely that the reason for this lack
of initiative was that all England's efforts were trained
towards reaching an agreement with the French.

Meanwhile England was gradually becoming embroiled
with the Danes about illegal trading with Iceland.[4] Not only
had the volume of business increased tremendously but the
Danes from about 1443 had begun to reassert their control
over the Germans running the Bergen staple and were
consequently anxious to reclaim the revenue from the staple
for their own use. In response to a complaint by King
Christopher, Henry had issued an order prohibiting this
trade.[5] Apparently it had little effect. Although the council
deputed John Bek and Richard Leyot in October to discuss
the problem with the Danes, they accomplished little (if
they went at all), for King Christopher died the next year.[6]
Only after a renewal of the war with France in 1448 was
progress made towards a new settlement: John Bek and
Dr. Richard Caunton came to Copenhagen from negotiations in Germany to conclude a truce (17 July 1449) to last
until 1451, a renewal of the prohibition of direct voyages
from England to Iceland, and the requirement for all ships
going to this colony, to Finmark (the extreme northern part
of Norway) or to Heligoland to pass through the Bergen

---

[1] *Proc. P.C.* v. 228.

[2] Ibid. 233–4; *Regesta*, pt. ii, no. 2561.

[3] Schulz places this embassy in the summer rather than the spring of 1447
(Schulz, p. 90). *Proc. P.C.* vi. 61; *Regesta*, nos. 9365, 9366, pt. ii, nos. 2697, 2702.

[4] Dollinger, p. 366; *Diplomatarium Islandicum*, iv. 646–7; Rymer, x. 651;
E 404/60/206. In 1447 Henry requested King Christopher to restore the *Catherine
of Hull* which his subjects had captured (*Hist. MSS. Com. 8th Report* (London,
1881), app., pt. iii, p. 5).

[5] Rymer, xi. 188.

[6] E 101/322/16; E. M. Carus Wilson, 'The Icelandic Trade', *Studies in English
Trade in the Fifteenth Century*, ed. E. Power and M. Postan (London, 1933),
p. 178.

staple. Caunton returned to England in March 1450 and the English confirmed the truce.[1]

The mission to Denmark also had another purpose; the council had decided to put their trade in the north and east on a new footing.[2] Before proceeding to Copenhagen to conclude the Danish truce, the English ambassadors were to make contact with the Prussians, who were at Bremen negotiating with the Dutch. Bek, Sir Robert Shottesbrook, and Caunton received their letters of proxy on 24 July 1448, though they seem not to have departed before September.[3] To secure a favourable hearing the royal council had suspended trade with that country. Although the ambassadors made contact with the Prussians in October and apparently assured them that the English wanted to make peace and that England was prepared to allow the Hanseatic League to continue trading for 'a season' be it oon yer' more or lesse', no agreement was reached;[4] the Germans undoubtedly wished to confer with their colleagues. The English agents, as their instructions authorized, agreed to meet delegates of the League when they had returned from Copenhagen.[5] At a diet in Lübeck the following March the Hanseatics discussed the proposed conversations with the English. Since it was thought that the Grand Master could not be relied upon to stop trade with England if the negotiations failed, the diet empowered its agents only to discuss and clarify complaints raised by both parties. Bek and Caunton returned from preliminary discussion in Copenhagen about the middle of March. Only the Prussians (whose envoys included the Burgomaster of Danzig) and five of the Wendish cities sent delegates to meet the English.[6] As a result the

---

[1] He was complaining that of the £338 the exchequer owed him for the trip 'he resceyved nor myght paiement have into this daie but of c li. oonly wherthrough' he is chearged to divers creditours in grete dettes' (PSO I/16/817a). Rymer, xi. 264; 45th Report of the Deputy Keeper, app. ii, p. 5; Diplomatarium Islandicum iv. 165–7.

[2] G. Schanz, Englische Handelspolitik gegen Ende des Mittelalters, mit besonderer Berücksichtigung des Zeitalters der beiden ersten Tudors, Heinrich VII. und Heinrich VIII. (Leipzig, 1881), i. 27–8.

[3] Hanserecesse, vol. ii, pt. iii, no. 463. Shottesbrook returned to England before the Danish treaty was drawn up (E 404/66/229; E 101/324/17; E 404/66/89; E 364/83, 84).

[4] B.M., Cotton Charter X, 19.   [5] Hanserecesse, vol. ii, pt. iii, no. 563.

[6] Regesta, no. 9850.

English agents' displeasure about the small number of
envoys gave rise to a demand to punish those cities which
had been invited to these talks but had not attended. Consequently, they asked for a list of all the cities belonging to
the Hanseatic League—something the Germans did not know
themselves.[1] Not only would this reveal which cities had
not sent representatives, but it would also give the English
a permanent instrument to be used in preventing non-
Hanseatic cities from importing goods through the Steelyard
and evading the customs. In addition a knowledge of the
names of the Hanseatic cities would allow the English to
approach their overlords so as to apply indirect pressure on
them. For the Hanseatic League to have yielded to this
request would have meant that in future every time a new
city was admitted to the federation fresh negotiations with
England would be necessary. Finally, since Prussia still
refused to ratify the 1437 treaty, the old expedient of calling
a new meeting between the two parties was proposed, but
the English ambassadors departed for Copenhagen (where
on 17 July they concluded a truce with the Danes) without
firmly committing themselves to another meeting.

Likewise in England relations with the League declined
still further during the winter and spring of 1449. Parliament had convened in the early months of the year and
raised the subsidy of tonnage and poundage from $3d.$ to $12d.$
Although the Hanseatic merchants were supposed to have
been exempt from this new levy, customs officials insisted
upon collecting it from them.[2] When the German merchants refused to pay, their goods were confiscated. In
retaliation the Grand Master followed suit.[3] Whether the
decision to seize the huge Hanseatic salt fleet coming from
Bourgneuf Bay through the Channel to the Baltic[4] was

---

[1] Stein, p. 30. This policy is not as new as Stein thought. The English had been
trying to learn the names of the Hanse cities since the late fourteenth century.

[2] *Rot. parl.* v. 147–8; E 28/79/63. At the third session of the 1449 parliament
the poll tax for alien merchants or their factors was set at 6s. 8d.; their clerks paid
1s. 8d. (*Rot. parl.* v. 150–1).   [3] *Regesta*, pt. ii, no. 2791.

[4] On the organization of the Bay Fleet and for the details of its capture in 1449
see A. R. Bridbury, *England and the Salt Trade in the Later Middle Ages* (Oxford,
1955), pp. 90–3. The earlier sections of this book should be supplemented by
W. Fellmann, 'Die Salzproduktion im Hanseraum', *Hansische Studien: Heinrich
Sproemberg zum 70. Geburtstag* (Berlin, 1961), pp. 56–71.

deliberately designed to put an end to the zigzag course of negotiations by resorting to force cannot now be determined, though such an interpretation has something to recommend it. There is no doubt that safe passage for this fleet through the Channel served as a strong motive for the Hanseatic League's keeping good relations with England, for since the decline of salt manufacture at Lüneburg, the Baltic countries depended more and more upon the salt produced in the march between Brittany and Poitou.[1] And if the pirates who captured the fleet did not give the royal council prior warning of their intention, there is little reason to believe that they thought the news would be heard with disfavour. Note that even the pirates thought that after securing their prizes 'it were time for to treat for a final peace as for these parts'.[2] And so it seemed, for despite this colossal affront—of the hundred ships taken sixteen belonged to Lübeck and fourteen to Danzig[3]—the Hanseatic League was in no position to start a war with England. Differences in Prussia between the Order and the cities were on the verge of turning into an open conflict which would end with the Grand Master subjected to the overlordship of Poland, and Hanseatic–Burgundian relations were deteriorating.[4] Furthermore members of the League had a vast quantity of goods stored in London; war would subject them to confiscation and the cost of this might amount to even more than the loss of the fleet. On the English side, renewal of the war with France and worsening relations with Philip of Burgundy as a result of capturing his ships in the Hanseatic fleet made it imperative for the English to carry on relatively peaceful trading with the north.[5] Thus instead of a full-fledged war the customary round of reprisals and counter reprisals began once more. When the news of the fleet's seizure became

[1] One must bear in mind that Bay salt did not become dominant in Scandinavia and the eastern shore of the Baltic until about 1590 (Fellmann, p. 64).

[2] *The Paston Letters, 1422–1509*, ed. J. Gairdner (London, 1900), vol. i, no. 68.

[3] *England und Köln: Beziehungen durch die Jahrhunderte in archivalischen Zeugnissen*, ed. H. Stehkamper (Cologne, 1965), pp. 28–9.

[4] Stein, p. 52; F. Vollbehr, *Die Holländer und die deutsche Hanse* (Pfingstblätter des hansischen Geschichtsvereins, 1938), vol. xxi.

[5] Despite the fact that Burgundian ships were released (for ransom) after their goods had been confiscated, Philip allowed the Hanseatic merchants to seize English goods in his domains.

known in Lübeck, which had lost the greatest number of ships in the raid, English merchants and their goods in that city were placed under arrest. Prussia quickly recouped 41,000 of the 47,776 marks she claimed to have lost by seizing English goods in Danzig and other ports. Although no figures survive, Lübeck does not seem to have been so fortunate.[1] In their turn the English, ignoring the plight of their kinsmen abroad, confiscated goods belonging to Lübeck and Prussian merchants in London and commenced actual hostilities on the high seas.

It was the English, suffering under the strain of the French war and governmental crisis at home, who made the first move towards ending this unprofitable state of affairs. In April 1450 the king confirmed the truce with Denmark. At the end of June while the Hanseatic cities were preparing to meet to decide how to respond to the English threat, the king resolved to send agents to the Grand Master. Since Prussia's losses were less than Lübeck's, the English hoped to exploit the differences between these two parts of the League and thus escape costly reparations. Having arranged to borrow £400 from certain King's Lynn merchants and the clerk of the council,[2] Henry ordered the drafting of letters of proxy for the London merchant John Stocker, Henry Bermyngham of King's Lynn, and Thomas Kent.[3] Bermyngham set out immediately,[4] but Kent and Stocker tarried in London while Kent ransacked the treasury looking for some correspondence from the Grand Master. More than a month passed before Kent found the letters and made arrangements for their transcription;[5] the delay proved costly, for in the meantime the safe conduct from Lübeck had expired.[6] Consequently, when the ship carrying the two envoys was captured by Bergen privateers and taken to Lübeck, the city had a valid excuse for imprisoning the

---

[1] Stein, p. 64.   [2] *Cal. Pat. Rolls, 1452–61*, pp. 119, 419.

[3] Rymer, xi. 272, 274. In fact the decision to send envoys was made earlier in the year, for the safe conduct from Lübeck is dated 25 Feb. (*Regesta*, pt. ii, no. 2786).

[4] E 101/324/18; E 364/86. Bermyngham, who received an advance of £26. 15s. 6d. on 14 June, was awarded a further £92. 4s. 6d. when he returned in 1452 (E 404/68/186). He received the final payment on 22 June 1452 (E 403/793/m. 8).

[5] Palgrave, *Antient Kalendars*, ii. 82.

[6] Stein, p. 67. *Regesta*, no. 11018 wrongly dates the safe conduct 1451.

royal agents and allowing the pirates to confiscate the merchandise in the ship. Not only did this act put an end to English schemes in Prussia, but the valuable goods replaced some of the losses of Lübeck's allies in 1449. The arrest of the king's ambassadors coincided with a meeting of the Hanseatic cities in Lübeck; the chief item on the agenda was the English problem. The best course of action, the cities decided, was to hold a conference with the English early the next year. There only the question of damages would be discussed, since it was generally agreed that the English would attempt to offer to confirm Hanseatic privileges in England, if the amount of damages claimed by the cities was reduced.[1]

In spite of Lübeck's firm refusal to liberate the Englishmen, the king assented to the proposed meeting.[2] In October the English renewed the League's privileges for another year, and in November the English and the Prussians seem to have made some sort of non-binding agreement to meet in Utrecht the following June.[3] The next March notice was posted in England of the forthcoming meeting and merchants were advised to prepare schedules of damages they had sustained in order to present them either personally or through their attorneys at Utrecht. Then Robert Botyll, Prior of the Order of St. John of Jerusalem in England, received letters of protection and a few weeks later was commissioned to treat with Prussia and the Hanseatic League for redress of grievances.[4] Since the English claimed they could not undertake discussions until they had conferred with the imprisoned envoys, the Lübeckers released John Stocker on parole, but retained Kent. However, Kent escaped, made his way to Utrecht, and assumed a place in the English delegation.[5] The representatives of Lübeck were incensed by this behaviour and regarded Kent's inclusion in the English delegation as an act of open hostility; but their effort to have Kent excluded from the meeting failed because the English king had named him in the quorum without whom the envoys could not treat.

[1] Stein, pp. 72–5.   [2] Ibid., p. 76.
[3] Not in 1450 as in Stein, p. 56.   [4] C 76/133/mm. 9, 1.
[5] Stein, pp. 83–4.

When the delegation went a stage further and made the
future progress of the conference rest on Lübeck's formal
liberation of the English envoys, negotiations ground to a
halt.[1] There is little doubt that the League suffered a considerable setback at Utrecht. The English, strengthened by
their recent reconciliation with Burgundy, were in no mood
to pay extensive damages to Lübeck. And having announced
that the quarrel was a personal one, Kent and Botyll sought
to exploit the League's internal rivalries by concluding
arrangements for Cologne and Prussia to resume trade. (In
fact even before the conference opened the Grand Master
had granted a safe conduct to English merchants coming
to the ports of Danzig and Elbing.)[2] At Canterbury on
21 September Henry VI formally exempted the merchants of
Cologne (together with those of her satellites Dortmund,
Münster, and Nimwegen) from confiscation of Hanseatic
goods in London,[3] and on 6 August the Grand Master
signified his assent to a future diet with the English.[4]

Lübeck had foreseen the possibility of such double
dealing in the League, and had approached the impecunious
Christian of Denmark with a view to closing the Sound to
English merchants and their goods. It is true that Christian
had concluded a treaty with England in 1449 and had
accepted Henry VI's ratification of it, but the Danes never
ratified the treaty themselves. Moreover, to compensate himself for the evasion of taxes on Icelandic trade, the Danish
king appropriated the goods from Kent's ship, which had
been taken to Bergen by the pirates, and auctioned the
contents at Copenhagen. Furthermore the proceeds from
English goods captured in the future would serve to offset
the vast outlay occasioned by Christian's war in Sweden.
Unfortunately for Lübeck, this attempt to exclude English
merchandise from the Baltic did not succeed; some merchants

---

[1] 'Sed nil potuit obtinere quia Anglici noluerunt tractare nisi prius oratoribus
integre relaxatis. In quod Lubicenses noluerunt consentire.' (*Hansisches Urkundenbuch*, ed. K. Höhlbaum, K. Kunze, W. Stein (Verein für hansische Geschichte,
1876–1907), vol. viii, no. 47.) There is a similar summary of the Utrecht diet in
B.M., Add. MS. 48009, p. 546.

[2] Cooper, *Appendix C*, p. 131.   [3] *England und Köln*, no. 42.

[4] On 6 Aug. the Grand Master indicated his agreement to a future diet with the
English and presented them with a statement of damages he intended to collect
(*Hansisches Urkundenbuch*, vol. viii, no. 84; Stein, pp. 91–2).

carried cloth with false labels, others shipped it by land. And indiscriminate piracy involved Lübeck in conflict with the Dutch.[1] Nevertheless the English undertook to heal the breach with Denmark. On 15 March Henry wrote to inquire why Christian had sent neither his ratification of their treaty nor his ambassadors,[2] and in April the royal officials at Kingston upon Hull were reminded of the statute forbidding trade with Iceland and Finmark without a licence from the Danish sovereign.[3]

As the months passed Lübeck's frustration and isolation increased. By August 1452 the Grand Master had gained support for calling a meeting with England (at which Lübeck would not be represented) for April 1453 at Utrecht.[4] Henry VI had already signified his willingness to send delegates with sufficient powers to conduct the business.[5] But Lübeck countered by summoning a general diet to meet at the same time where the Hanseatic League's relations with Philip of Burgundy would be discussed instead. Thus checked the Grand Master was forced to accord (in January 1453) the English merchants a safe conduct for a year and to postpone the projected congress.[6] In August the Prussians were in turn granted letters of safe conduct to last until September 1456.[7] Since no solution to the problem of reciprocal privileges appeared at hand, the request lay in abeyance for the time, though in June 1454 Henry exempted certain merchants of the Steelyard from the new levy of tonnage and poundage discussed in the parliament at Reading.[8]

The outbreak of the war between Poland and the Teutonic Order increased the Grand Master's desire for some accommodation with Henry VI's government, while civil war in England and the alternately hot and cold relations with the Low Countries made the English more tractable. Moreover, Lübeck was rapidly becoming aware of the

---

[1] Ibid., pp. 94–104.   [2] Rymer, xi. 307–8.
[3] E 28/82/56. However, Anglo-Danish relations were to remain stormy. On 20 Sept. 1456 Charles VII concluded an aggressive alliance with Denmark against England (P.R.O. 31/8/136).
[4] Stein, pp. 108–9.   [5] Rymer, xi. 311.   [6] *Regesta*, pt. ii, no. 2886.
[7] *Hansisches Urkundenbuch*, vol. viii, nos. 281, 298.
[8] B.M., Cotton Charter X, 5.

dangers of isolation and of the ineffectiveness of her embargo on English goods. In January 1454 she announced the lifting of the ban.[1] And when Heinrich Grevenstein, the Steelyard's clerk, canvassed the Hanseatic League late that same year about obtaining an eight-year truce with England, Lübeck consented.[2] Upon returning to London he put the idea of the truce to the English; it was not until the following October, however, that the English council announced its willingness to make such an agreement, providing certain conditions were met. English prisoners in Lübeck had to be set free and that city had to furnish a statement of its position regarding England.[3] These conditions the Hanseatic city hastened to fulfil and on 1 March 1456 the truce was proclaimed in England.[4] Peace was restored.[5] Although neither side had achieved its goal regarding privileges, England had forced Lübeck to abandon her claims for compensation. Since political conditions both in the Baltic and in England were in turmoil, diplomatic relations between the two parties lost their sense of immediacy. In any event the great days of the Hanseatic League were over. Although trade would revive when Edward IV came to the throne, the importance of the fur trade to England was declining and the Russians were slowly strangling the Hanseatic factory in Novgorod where so much English cloth was sold.[6] Seen in this light, Edward IV's concessions to the League by the Treaty of Utrecht are perhaps not so significant.

In retrospect, it appears that four pivotal events mark the course of Anglo-Hanseatic relations during the late Middle Ages: the Prussian revocation of 1398, the Vorrath treaty of 1437, the English seizure of the great Hanseatic fleet in 1449, and the Treaty of Utrecht negotiated by Edward IV

---

[1] Stein, p. 120.   [2] *Hansisches Urkundenbuch*, vol. viii, no. 380.
[3] Stein, pp. 123–4.   [4] Rymer, xi. 274.
[5] But it should not be supposed that this was the end to English conflict with the Hanseatic merchants during Henry's reign. Just three months after the treaty was proclaimed Casimir of Poland was writing to complain about a Danzig ship captured at King's Lynn (B.M., Cotton Nero B. II, f. 94). Two years later a commission was summoned to Rochester to have the testimony of anyone who knew about the Earl of Warwick's attack on ships from Lübeck (*Cal. Pat. Rolls, 1452–61*, p. 44).
[6] E. M. Veale, *The English Fur Trade in the Later Middle Ages* (Oxford, 1966), pp. 160, 162.

in 1474. It is usual to regard the Vorrath treaty as a victory for the English inasmuch as it provided for the reciprocal trading arrangements the English merchants had so long desired. As we have seen, however, the practical effects of this treaty were minimal, and English frustration in this regard may account in part for the indulgence shown to the pirates who carried out the seizure of the Hanseatic fleet returning from Bourgneuf. Although the Utrecht treaty and its consequences lie outside the bounds of this study, it should be noted that political conditions prevented the treaty's becoming so disadvantageous to the English as has sometimes been supposed.

Finally, the erratic course of Anglo-Hanseatic relations must be understood in the light of three main factors, of which one is long-standing and the others novelties of the period. The constitution of the Hanseatic League had always been a loose one and its members were bound to reject the claims of any one city to exclusive dominance, as Lübeck found to her cost. The two new factors were the weakness of the English government of Henry VI and the disintegration of the Teutonic Order in the face of the Polish threat combined with the revolt of the Prussian cities. In earlier times both the English and the Hanseatics had been able to refer their problems to one single figure of authority: the Plantagenet kings and the Grand Master of the Order respectively. In addition the Hanseatics could call on the emperor to protect them. But imperial authority by the beginning of the fifteenth century had been reduced to a shadow of its former greatness and the Teutonic Order finally gave way to other powers. The English council in its turn had always been accustomed to follow the lead of a powerful monarch. But during the period under discussion the authority of the father-figures, so to speak, was greatly diminished and the committee governments on both sides were thrown back on their own resources. This shift from the monarchical principle of feudal times to a corporate one goes some way in explaining the tangled course of our story.

VI

ENGLAND AND THE EMPIRE

On 1 May 1416 Sigismund, King of the Romans, set sail from Calais bound for Dover. Ostensibly Sigismund undertook this journey to promote a reconciliation between the kings of England and France, but having left Paris in a disgruntled mood—the French took a dim view of Sigismund's licentious behaviour and his insistence upon presiding at the Parlement of Paris—and having suffered 'atrocious treatment' on his journey from Paris to Calais, he was hardly an unbiased arbiter.[1] Perhaps it was not without cause that the French mistrusted him. In any event when Sigismund learned that the Count of Armagnac had defeated plans in the French royal council to co-operate with him in reaching an agreement with England (even to the extent of a three years' truce), he denounced King Charles for his perfidy and promptly made a league with Henry V at Canterbury by which he promised perpetual alliance with the king and with Henry's successor whether he be a son or one of the king's brothers. The motives that lay behind the conclusion of this alliance, as Professor Wylie noted, are numerous. Sigismund, whose grand designs for the pacification of Europe included arbitrating between the Poles and the Knights of the Teutonic Order, between Orléans and Burgundy, as well as between Pope Benedict XIII and the Council of Constance, may have formed this alliance against the French out of spite for their having frustrated part of his plan. It is not inconceivable that the emperor-elect hoped to reassert his claims to certain territories in Languedoc and the Dauphiné, though it seems doubtful that he extended this scheme to the conquest of all France. Furthermore, he hoped to use this alliance to strengthen the bonds of Anglo-German co-operation at Constance. A final consideration—surely not

[1] J. Caro, *Das Bündniss von Canterbury: eine Episode aus der Geschichte des Constanzer Conzils* (Gotha, 1880), p. 32; Wylie and Waugh, *Henry V*, iii. 1–35.

the least pressing for the impecunious monarch—was the necessity of finding some way of exiting gracefully from England. However, if Sigismund hoped to secure English military assistance in the dispute between the Poles and the Teutonic Knights, his judgement of the English king was not very astute.[1]

For Henry V's part there seems little doubt that he intended to extract from this treaty the greatest possible support in terms of soldiers for his armies in France. The following December he dispatched an embassy to Constance with a view to approaching the imperial princes for alliances to bolster the Treaty of Canterbury. And the next year, after he had received Sigismund's letter declining for the present to furnish military support because of the delicate situation at Constance, Henry commissioned his uncle the Bishop of Winchester to repair to Constance with instructions that the English envoys there were to adopt a position of neutrality and thus pave the way for the election of a new pope and the end of King Sigismund's involvement.[2] This move and the concomitant approach to several princes of the empire for a wife for John of Bedford produced no fruit, for by this time Sigismund had withdrawn to Hungary whence he was not to emerge until the end of 1419.[3]

Henry's plans, however, were not so easily thwarted. During the summer of 1419 John Stokes and Hertonk van Klux set out to deliver messages to the Count Palatine, presumably reminding him of his promised military aid;[4] having accomplished this task, they went on to the emperor. In August Stokes returned to Henry with the news that King Wenceslas of Bohemia was dead and that although earlier Sigismund 'sent hem worde that rathe [he] wolde be dede or he wolde susten' hem in yore malesse', he was faced with such turbulence in Bohemia 'that he is lyke to have a grete batell'.[5] To compensate for his failure to provide

---

[1] The English ambassador Sir Hertonk van Klux was sent, however, to help negotiate a truce between the two parties (*Regesta*, pt. i, nos. 3029, 3033).

[2] C. M. D. Crowder, 'Henry V, Sigismund and the Council of Constance, a Re-examination', *Historical Studies*, iv (1963), 104–5.

[3] Wylie and Waugh, *Henry V*, iii. 174.

[4] Finke, *Acta Concilii Constanciensis*, iv. 489–90.

[5] B.M., Cotton Charter XIII, 30 (1).

tangible support Sigismund ratified the Treaty of Canterbury as King of Bohemia on 31 July 1420.[1] At this time
Stokes was back in Germany making sure of imperial
support for the coming campaigns in France. From his
mission he had learned that the king could count on aid
from the Rhine Palatinate; that the Archbishop of Cologne
had declared 'how that he wolde come to ʒow and alwey
schulde be redy to come to do ʒow servise upon hys owne
cost', but he did not have a safe conduct; and that the
King of the Romans was involved in a great rebellion in
Bohemia 'and so mochyll a doo upon on every syde that we can
nowght make ʒow sure nother of his commyng in his owne
persone nother of sendyng by other'.[2] When he had learned
that Sigismund was not going to furnish him troops, Henry
decided to send another embassy with messages couched in
stronger terms. On 17 July 1421 Walter de la Pole and
John Stokes were appointed to remind Sigismund that he
owed Henry certain money for which the Duchy of Luxembourg had been pledged as security. Furthermore, the
English envoys were to sound out the emperor-elect about
ceding his rights to the Dauphiné and lands in Languedoc.[3]
Whatever the exact reply, its general tenor was evasive, for
early the next year Henry commissioned Richard Fleming,
Bishop of Lincoln, to go to Sigismund and remind him once
again of his promise to send armed men to fight in France.[4]
A month later this embassy was strengthened by the
addition of Master Nicholas Bildeston and Walter de la
Pole. This embassy apparently met with even less success
than the last one, for although Bishop Fleming had talks at
Nürnberg about Wycliff's heresy, it seems unlikely that he

---

[1] J. C. Lünig, *Das Teutsche Reichs-Archiv* (Pars Specialis Continuationen I,
1700–14), p. 71.

[2] *Original Letters Illustrative of English History*, ed. H. Ellis, 2nd series (London,
1827), i. 80–2.

[3] Rymer, x. 143; Wylie and Waugh, *Henry V*, iii. 359. Stokes and Walter de la
Pole were additionally commissioned to treat with the Margrave of Baden for the
release of his prisoner the Count of Poitou (*Regesten der Markgrafen von Baden und
Hachberg, 1050–1515*, ed. R. Fester (Innsbruck, 1900–15), no. 3292). In May 1423
De la Pole petitioned the council for payment of £219. 9s. 10d. owed to him for this
and other embassies (*Proc. P.C.* iii. 97).

[4] V. Murdock, 'John Wyclyf and Richard Flemyng, Bishop of Lincoln:
Gleanings from German Sources', *Bulletin of the Institute of Historical Research*,
xxxvii (1964), 239–45.

even saw Sigismund. Henry V, however, never learned the outcome of this mission: he had been dead almost a month when these envoys returned to London. At the time of Henry's death it must have appeared fairly clear to his son's councillors that no substantial military aid would be forthcoming from Germany. This alliance had some value because of the pressure the emperor could bring to bear on the papacy and on the general council and because of the psychological pressure on the French, who would feel surrounded by enemies. But there were no immediate attempts to renew this connection. Perhaps the English thought that the terms of Henry V's treaty obviated the need for Henry VI to reconfirm it. On Sigismund's part, since the league did not work to his material advantage, there was no urgency to renew it, and he was too busy with his crusades against the Hussites and with schemes to ally himself with Aragon without incurring papal enmity, which would shatter his dream of a Roman coronation.[1]

Apart from including letters of recommendation to the German princes in the diplomatic bags of the English agents at Pavia and ordering six choir boys to be chosen as a gift to King Sigismund,[2] the English council sent no major embassy to Germany until the summer of 1424, when Dr. John Stokes set out for the continent. The purpose of this journey, as Sigismund later wrote to Vitold of Lithuania,

---

[1] K. A. Fink, 'König Sigismund und Aragon; Die Bündesverhandlungen vor der Romfahrt', *Deutsches Archiv für Geschichte des Mittelalters*, ii (1938), 149–71. Milan's wars between 1422 and 1454 stood in the way of Sigismund's plans for a coronation journey to Rome. Since he had always been an opponent of Venice, Sigismund had to turn his attention towards ending the enmity between Milan and Alfonso V's Neapolitan party in order that the imperial retinue might have safe passage through the mountain passes of northern Italy. At the same time Sigismund had to avoid alienating the pope, who felt his temporal possessions threatened by Alfonso's intervention in Naples (K. A. Fink, 'Martin V und Aragon', *Historische Studien*, Heft 340 (1938), p. 60).

[2] *Proc. P.C.* iii. 60, 218. Sigismund apparently heard some of the revolutionary trends in English music, which were shortly to enrich singing all over western Europe, when he was in England in 1416 (M. F. Bukofzer, 'English Church Music of the Fifteenth Century', *The New Oxford History of Music*, ed. Dom A. Hughes and G. Abraham, iii (London, 1960), 165–208). Thus did England repay the cultural debt she owed the empire, for there is no doubt that Bohemian influences following Richard II's marriage to Anne of Bohemia at the end of the fourteenth century greatly improved the quality of English painting (M. Rickert, *Painting in Britain : The Middle Ages* (London, 1954), pp. 173, 175).

was to secure his support as well as that of the electors and
other German princes for a new council.[1] The extent of the
support the English received is not known. Sigismund did
write requesting Vitold to assist English agents at the curia;
beyond this he may not have gone, for on 25 February
Alfonso had written that he had by no means encouraged the
English in their hopes for a council.[2] Stokes was back in
England before the end of the next month, and with the
exception of a letter from the King of the Romans on behalf
of the Hanseatic League, Anglo-Imperial relations lapsed
until summer 1427,[3] when Cardinal Beaufort arrived in
Germany as leader of a crusade against the Hussites.

Cardinal Beaufort reached Nürnberg by mid July.[4]
From there he wrote to the Hussites on the theme, 'sed omnes
erravimus et unusquisque declinavit a via Domini', exhorting
them to return to the church.[5] Then he set out to catch up
with the crusading army that he was to lead; but the army,
anticipating his arrival, had invaded Bohemia, only to flee
when it was learned that the Hussite army commanded by
Procop the Great was approaching Tachau. By the time the
cardinal reached his troops it was too late to restore order;
consequently he withdrew to Nürnberg where on 14 August
he summoned a diet to meet in Frankfurt on 14 September.[6]
The diet convened, but owing to the meagre attendance and
the emperor's preference for stopping Philip of Burgundy's
usurpation of imperial land,[7] no definite decisions were
taken about raising more troops to fight the Hussites.[8]
However, the delegates did agree to call a meeting of imperial estates to Frankfurt on 16 November and to fix the
agenda in advance.[9] The cardinal approached the Frankfurt

---

[1] *Deutsche Reichstagakten*, vol. viii, no. 322.   [2] See above, p. 16.

[3] E 403/666/m. 14.

[4] *Die Chroniken der deutschen Städte*, vol. i: *Nürnberg* (Leipzig, 1862), p. 442.

[5] F. Bartoš, 'An English Cardinal and the Hussite Revolution', *Communio
Viatorum*, i (1963), 49.

[6] *Deutsche Reichstagakten*, vol. ix, no. 52.

[7] Hamburg, for example, wrote that difficulties with the King of Denmark
prevented her sending delegates (*Frankfurts Reichs-correspondenz, nebst andern
verwandten Aktenstücken von 1376–1519*, ed. J. Janssen (Freiburg im Breisgau,
1863–72), nos. 648, 652).

[8] *Deutsche Reichstagakten*, ix. 58–9.

[9] Ibid., nos. 58, 59.

diet with the idea of pulling Germany together by launching another crusade, but he met with so little success that the matter was dropped.

From Frankfurt Beaufort proceeded to Cologne in January 1428 to try his hand at patching up the differences that had arisen between Archbishop Dietrich, his entourage, and the Duke of Cleves.[1] No doubt his intention was to smooth out a situation that could distract the Duke of Burgundy from attending to the war in France. Unlike the earlier attempt at mediation by Lewis of the Palatine, Beaufort achieved a small measure of success. Although the cardinal had tried to secure a lasting peace between Archbishop Dietrich, the young Duke Ruprecht of Jülich and Berg, and Gerard of Cleves on the one side and Duke Adolf of Cleves on the other, the most he could arrange was a truce from 11 February until the following Whitsuntide. Then the cardinal returned to England to gather men and supplies for another crusade in Bohemia. Since this army was appropriated by the English for fighting in France, and since the Germans despaired of defeating the Hussites in battle, it was almost four years before another army marched against them.

Before Beaufort returned to England pressure was put on Sigismund to support English demands for a new oecumenical council: on 10 February the University of Paris announced that the deplorable state of the church had prompted them to send envoys to King Sigismund,[2] and in July Henry commissioned the Bishop of London, John Lord Lescrope, Peter Partridge, and John Stokes, who were on their way to meet Alfonso of Aragon in Rome, to call on Sigismund.[3] These talks evidently met with scant success, and Anglo-imperial relations languished for almost ten years, during which time Sigismund endeavoured to reach some sort of settlement with the Bohemians and secured his coronation at Milan.[4]

---

[1] Gert's van der Schüren Chronik von Cleve und Mark, ed. L. Tross (Hamm, 1824), pp. 189, 196; Lacomblet, iv, nos. 180, 184.

[2] Correspondence Bekynton, ii. 124.

[3] Rymer, x. 407; C 81/698/1940, 1941; B.M., Add. MS. 35204, m. 10.

[4] William Wells received a commission to go to Basel and Frankfurt in the spring of 1434 (E 101/322/29). The purpose of his mission seems to be incorporated

But English indignation at the excesses of the Council of Basel and the Duke of Burgundy's defection served to reactivate England's imperial diplomacy. The emperor's messenger Johannes Erkenbroch' arrived in England early in 1437, presumably to report on the situation at Basel.[1] At the diet that met at Cheb the following May the German princes discussed the state of Anglo-Burgundian relations, and the knight Sigismund Otlynger, who had returned in July from Germany with messages from Sigismund, seems to have conveyed Henry VI's dismay at the prospect of a renewal of schism in the church and solicited imperial assistance in compelling the fathers of the council to moderation.[2] Following up this initiative the king wrote a similar letter to Archbishop Dietrich of Cologne and at the end of the year he asked the Duke of Saxony to indicate what measures he deemed necessary to prevent the impending schism.[3] Before these discussions matured Sigismund was dead.[4]

During the next few years England's foreign policy regarding the empire developed at a rapid pace. Not only was it urgent to seek a ratification of the Treaty of Canterbury (which had fallen into abeyance on Sigismund's death) to shore up defences against the new adversary Burgundy, but the Council of Basel's defiance of Pope Eugenius necessitated securing the emperor's support in ending this new schism. Thus Henry's advisers, perhaps even before they learned of Sigismund's death, discussed the advisability of sending envoys to Albrecht, Duke of Austria, with the Garter; at his court the embassy was to raise the possibilities of an alliance with England, backed up by some sort of

in a letter from the king to his envoys at the council; they were instructed to follow the emperor's lead in matters transacted there (*Correspondence Bekynton*, ii. 260). In the summer of the same year John Stokes seems to have gone once again to Germany (*Proc. P.C.* iv. 265; Rymer, x. 593; E 101/322/28; E 403/719/m. 8). In Nov. 1436 the king rewarded Sigismund, a German knight, who had been on the king's behalf to the emperor, with 100 marks (E 403/725/m. 5).

[1] E 404/53/176; E 403/725/m. 11.
[2] *Deutsche Reichstagakten*, xii. 122; E 403/53/325; E 403/727/m. 10; *Correspondence Bekynton*, ii. 83.
[3] Ibid. 86.
[4] Sigismund died on 9 Dec. not in Nov. as in *Chronique de Jean de Stavelot*, p. 383, and O. Odložilík, *The Hussite King* (New Brunswick, 1965), p. 17.

marriage arrangement.[1] Next the king solicited the imperial electors not to choose the new emperor from among the king's enemies and he instructed the council to make plans for holding a memorial service for Sigismund at St. Paul's and to write to each cathedral in the realm 'to preforme exequies for emperor' to be don' solepmelyth' in all goodely haste'.[2] At the same time an embassy was being organized that was to go to the new emperor, but nothing came of these plans immediately.[3] Albrecht of Austria was formally elected emperor on 18 March, but it was not until May that the English council made final plans to send envoys with letters congratulating Albrecht upon his election and presumably, since they took care to examine the letters previously sent to the new emperor, to press for a renewal of the Anglo-imperial alliance.[4] Albrecht's short reign, however, allowed little time for English diplomatic success. Friar Thomas Bird was dispatched from England in October to conduct 'certaines persones' to the King. England's ambassadors seem to have attended the diet meeting at Mainz in May 1439 where the policy of neutrality adopted by the German electors in the dispute between Eugenius IV and Basel was under consideration.[5] And in July Albrecht wrote to Henry complaining about the seizure of goods belonging to merchants from Nürnberg by a Gascon subject of King Henry residing in Barcelona.[6] Otherwise the emperor's attention was distracted by a threatened Turkish invasion of Hungary.

Albrecht died on 27 October and Frederick III was elected on 2 February. Whatever hopes the English might have harboured for an active alliance with the empire were frustrated by this youthful ruler, who was so busy consolidating his position that he rarely bothered to attend the diets where the problems of the church were discussed. Nevertheless the English worked diligently for the next three years to obtain a resolution of papal-conciliar difficulties.

---

[1] *Proc. P.C.* v. 86–7.
[2] Ibid. 86.
[3] Ibid. 88, 91; E 404/54/160, 162; *Correspondence Bekynton*, i. 68. Albrecht, however, was never installed as a member of the Order (Fellowes, *The Knights of the Garter*, p. 58).
[4] *Proc. P.C.* v. 96–8; E 404/55/56, 126.
[5] E 403/733/m. 14.
[6] E 28/62/86.

In April the king had commissioned the Prior of St. John of Jerusalem to attend the imperial diet to be held at Mainz, but the prior secured permission to go instead to Rhodes, which was under attack by the Turks;[1] the next month Henry wrote both to Frederick and the Duke of Saxony assuring them of his good health and apologizing for his failure to send envoys—the way had been too dangerous lately.[2] Six days after composing these letters Hertonk van Klux and William Swan, who were about to set out for Cologne, received a commission to Frederick explaining that the death of Sigismund followed closely by that of Albrecht (as well as the perils of the road) had prevented him from sending ambassadors earlier to express his joy at Frederick's accession.[3] This embassy got no further than Cologne where Swan was turned back for further instructions.

The English government apparently reconsidered its policy and redispatched Swan towards the beginning of July with a letter explaining the delay.[4] Now the embassy concerned not only the renewal of the Treaty of Canterbury but also the effort to get Frederick to abandon his policy of neutrality regarding the schism in the church. Frederick's answer to this embassy is embodied in a credence which he gave to Hertonk van Klux;[5] the tenor of his message was direct: the state of the church grieved him and he had disbursed much money and expended great effort to extirpate the discord. Frederick reminded the English king that the Germans had proposed holding a council to settle the differences between Eugenius and Basel, but the English had sent an evasive reply and dropped the matter. Since the

---

[1] *Correspondence Bekynton*, i. 80.

[2] Ibid. 105, 107; E 404/56/252; E 403/739/mm. 6, 7.

[3] E 28/63/72; Rymer, x. 769; *Correspondence Bekynton*, i. 243.

[4] E 403/739/m. 8. 'Diversis clericis de privato sigillo regis in denariis sibi liberatis in persolucionem v marcarum quas ibidem dominus rex de avisamento et assensu consilii sui eisdem habendas clericis liberare mandavit habendas de dono suo per viam regardi pro diversis scripturis per ipsos factis et specialiter de transcripto convencionum imperatoris—66s. 8d.'; E 404/56/272; *Correspondence Bekynton*, i. 134, 166.

[5] The Germans had discussed sending Hertonk to England as early as Apr. 1439 (*Deutsche Reichstagakten*, vol. xiv, no. 111). B.M., Add. MS. 48001, ff. 291ʳ–294ʳ, is a copy of his credence.

troubles of the church were increasing rather than diminish-
ing, the emperor again proposed to call a general council to
solve the problem and requested Henry's agreement to the
plan. The true purpose of this mission, however, was
embodied in a complaint that the French had invaded the
lands belonging to the empire around Verdun and Metz
without having sent a letter of defiance: there were Englishmen serving among the French troops. The emperor mar-
velled that this should be so, for a flourishing friendship
had grown up between the English and Germans, who
were related not only by blood but by similarity of language.[1]
Therefore Henry ought to recall the Englishmen fighting in
the French army.

Hoping to exploit this opening Henry sent Thomas Bird
to the diet held at Frankfurt the following Michaelmas. In
November Frederick sent a messenger to England with
further instructions regarding the best way to obtain peace
in the church, and the king immediately undertook to send
the Bishop of Rochester with his answer.[2] On Christmas
day Henry again wrote to Frederick that English envoys
were coming to him that a way might be found to ensure
that the church did not founder in a sea of trouble. The
Bishop of Rochester seems never to have left England;
John Bek, who was to travel in his retinue, departed alone in
late January or early February.[3] From London he journeyed
to the diet at Mainz; towards the end of April he left Mainz
for Vienna, which he probably reached before the end of
May. In addition to securing a safe conduct for the English
delegation to a diet called to discuss the state of the church,
the council had instructed Bek to explain that the English
delegation had not yet left because the diet at Nürnberg
had procrastinated for so long that discussions seemed
problematical. Moreover, he was to sound the emperor out
about holding a council independent of Eugenius and Basel
to settle the matter.[4] Frederick received Bek before the

---

[1] 'Et primo quod apud omnes gentes Anglici cum Germanis eadem nacio propter
conformitatem lingue et sermonis reputantur.'

[2] PSO I/13/691; E 404/57/145; Rymer, x. 834; E 404/57/147.

[3] E 404/59/128. For some reason the Bishop of Rochester's mission to Frankfurt
seems to have been called off (E 404/57/164).

[4] *Deutsche Reichstagakten*, xvi. 34–5.

middle of June and wrote to Henry praising his interest in the welfare of the church, but saying nothing of his intentions.[1] Nothing more is known about the course of these negotiations nor of Frederick's reply to Henry.

Henry reminded Frederick on 1 July that the safe conduct he had requested had not yet arrived and that his envoys could not depart without it.[2] Frederick granted the safe conduct on 4 July and Bek departed soon afterwards.[3] So that the emperor would have no cause for complaint the king wrote to him on 1 August certifying that the goods of his subjects seized in Aquitaine would be promptly restored.[4] Final preparations were made during the autumn of 1441 to send an English delegation to the diet to be held at Frankfurt. The Bishop of St. Asaph, the Abbot of St. Peter's Gloucester, Adam Moleyns, and the notary John Foston all received advances on their wages and an order was issued to pay for their shipping.[5] Early the next year Henry wrote to Robert Botyll, the Prior of St. John of Jerusalem, reminding him that he had not attended the diet at Mainz to which he had been commissioned and that now he was to proceed without delay to Frankfurt.[6] This embassy left London about 15 March and at the end of July the council considered strengthening the mission by the addition of the Abbot of St. Albans.[7] But the meeting held at Frankfurt accomplished little beyond an invective against violence in the empire, since the electors moved steadily towards accommodation with Pope Felix. Consequently, the Bishop of St. Asaph and the Abbot of St. Peter's returned to London before 14 August,[8] while Moleyns and the notary set out to see Eugenius at Florence where they concluded

[1] *Deutsche Reichstagakten*, xvi. 72–3.   [2] *Correspondence Bekynton*, ii. 98.
[3] *Deutsche Reichstagakten*, xvi. 73.   [4] E 28/68/51; Rymer, x. 849.
[5] E 403/743/m. 2, 747/m. 3; E 404/58/73, 76, 78, 94; 59/122, 289; E 101/324/2, 5. Moleyn's letter of protection can be found on the treaty roll for 20 Henry VI (C 76/124/m. 22). There are numerous documents relative to Foston's collection of his wages (E 28/73/62; E 404/61/58; E 403/755/m. 10, 759/m. 2, 765/m. 3, 767/m. 4, 769/m. 7, 772/m. 3, 775/mm. 1–10).
[6] *Deutsche Reichstagakten*, xvi. 345. The preceding day he wrote to the same purport to the Grand Master of Rhodes (*Correspondence Bekynton*, i. 87).
[7] There is a letter of protection for the Abbot of St. Albans going to Frankfurt dated 28 July 1442 enrolled on the treaty rolls (C 76/124/m. 8).
[8] They reported to the council on the small success of their mission on 21 Aug. 1442 (*Proc. P.C.* v. 197).

an alliance of friendship between him and the King of England.[1]

With the breakdown of discussions at Frankfurt in 1442 Anglo-imperial relations declined sharply in both importance and interest. Frederick was occupied during the summer of 1444 with the problem of getting rid of the French soldiers laying waste the Rhine valley and in August at the Nürnberg diet the most he could accomplish was a postponement of the decision on whether to support the Council of Basel or Eugenius. It was in fact not until Eugenius lay on his death-bed in February 1447 that the main lines of a papal-imperial settlement were defined, the final concordat with the papacy being published a year later. Only in the middle years of the next decade did conversations between the two realms briefly revive: Frederick tried to interest the English in a campaign against the Turks.[2] By this time, of course, England had problems enough at home and the plea (like later ones from the King of Hungary and from Pius II) fell on deaf ears.

In the course of the foregoing narrative we have noted that England's energy—in terms of money and effort expended—was concentrated on the principalities fringing the eastern border of the French kingdom. Another question, the problem of dealing with the Hussites, must be understood within the larger framework of the pacification of the church. It seems, then, that apart from this ecclesiological problem (which of course engaged the whole of Europe) English attention was focused almost exclusively on what might be termed the western tier of the continental German states. Two motives suffice to explain this concentration of interest: geographical proximity with concomitant trade relations, and the French quarrel.

[1] For the preliminary conversations leading to this league see the fascinating documents in Bishop Brouns's register at Norwich (Norwich Diocesan Registry, REG 5, Book 10, ff. 204^r–206^r).

[2] E 28/85/56; Rymer, xi. 355.

VII

ENGLAND AND THE PAPACY

EDWARD III's statutes of Provisors and Praemunire determined the atmosphere of Anglo-papal diplomacy in which Henry VI's councillors were compelled to work. Despite the legislation of 1351 and 1353, English policy until 1388 normally permitted the pope to bestow provisions; but the system adumbrated in that year and subsequently embodied in the statute of 1390 only allowed (under pain of heavy penalty) a petition to Rome for a provision after the issuance of a royal licence. The result was that the number of papal provisions in England decreased sharply, and their reduction produced a concomitant decline in papal revenue from services and annates.[1] By Martin V's reign, though we cannot precisely determine his revenues from these sources,[2] the situation had become acute enough to warrant serious efforts on the pope's part to secure the revocation of the offending law, which had the added demerit of furnishing the French a pattern for the Gallican liberties. And in fact the question of provisions was to remain the apple of discord in Anglo-papal relations throughout Martin's reign.

In 1419 Martin dispatched an envoy to the king to urge that he ought to 'qualify, suspend or modify' the statute of Provisors.[3] To this request Henry promptly and curtly replied that the war in France kept him too busy to consider

---

[1] On the question of provisions see G. Barraclough, *Papal Provisions* (Oxford, 1935); E. B. Graves, 'The Legal Significance of the Statute of Praemunire of 1353', *Haskins Anniversary Essays* (Cambridge, Mass., 1929), pp. 57–80; W. T. Waugh, 'The Great Statute of Praemunire', *English Historical Review*, xxxvii (1922), 173–205; and W. E. Lunt, 'Financial Relations of the Papacy with England, 1327–1534', *Studies in Anglo-Papal Relations during the Middle Ages* (Cambridge, Mass., 1962), ii. 407–8.

[2] Ibid. 432.

[3] J. Haller, *England und Rom unter Martin V.* (Rome, 1905), p. 9 n. 3. Although this monograph contains in outline part of what follows for Martin V's reign, it fails to exploit manuscript sources available in England.

the matter.[1] Two years later the pope renewed his request. Although the outcome of this attempt is not precisely known, Simon of Teramo, the consistorial lawyer and papal collector in England, could at least report on his return to Rome that Henry did not intend to extend the statute of Provisors into the lands he conquered in France. Further-more, the king had hinted that he might repeal the statute when he returned to England, a specious lure probably advanced to forestall Roman protest against the Treaty of Troyes. At any rate this report deluded the pope into over-estimating his real authority in England; he refused a royal initiative to translate the Bishop of Hereford to London and undertook a major shuffle of English bishops. Next he sent an unannounced envoy to France to negotiate peace,[2] and finally he wrote to the king that he was undertaking pro-ceedings against the English proctor in Rome for disorderly conduct during the celebration of the mass.[3] It is not surprising that Henry became enraged, to such an extent that he apparently forbad his uncle Beaufort's projected journey to Rome.[4] Moreover, the English king surely was not unaware (perhaps it had been his suggestion) that the University of Paris had dispatched an embassy in May 1422 to remind Martin that in accordance with the decree *Frequens* he must shortly call a new general council to reform the church.[5] Only Henry's unexpected death in

---

[1] In addition to the war in France Henry was engaged in a struggle to prevent his uncle Beaufort from accepting Martin's offer to make him a cardinal. (K. B. McFarlane, 'Henry V, Bishop Beaufort and the Red Hat', *English Historical Review*, lx (1945), 316–48).

[2] 'Cum pro nonnullis magnis et arduis negotiis pacem et tranquillitatem Christ-ianissimi Francorum regni ad carissimos in Christo filios nostros Carolum ipsius Francorum et Henricum Anglie regnorum reges ac nobiles viros Carolum dalphi-num Viennen' ipsius regis Francie unigenitum ac Philippum Burgundie ducem tangentibus venerabilem fratrem nostrum Nicolaum . . . destinemus . . . '(B.M., Add. MS. 15380, f. 63ʳ). Martin V's letter to his envoy is printed in N. Valois, *Histoire de la Pragmatique Sanction de Bourges sous Charles VII* (Paris, 1906), no. 8.

[3] J. P. von Ludewig, *Reliquiae manuscriptorum omnis aevi diplomatum ac monu-mentorum ineditorum adhuc* (Frankfurt and Leipzig, 1720–41), vol. v, no. xiii.

[4] Beaufort's signature on council documents concerning diplomacy for late 1423 and early 1424 indicate that he remained in England (E 28/42/49, 43/301, 44/35, 99; *Proc. P.C.* iii. 110, 111, 117).

[5] C. J. von Hefele, *Histoire des conciles*, trans. and ed. by H. Leclerq (Paris, 1916), vol. vii, pt. i, pp. 610–11.

late August 1422 prevented a serious breach in Anglo-papal relations.

The pope's next move was, obviously, to win over a dominant faction in the infant Henry VI's council with a view to restoring the *status quo ante* 1421. The assistance of Henry Beaufort, the Bishop of Winchester, could be confidently expected, for Beaufort and Martin were friends of long standing: Beaufort's support at Constance had been instrumental in obtaining the triple tiara for Martin. The Duke of Gloucester, Beaufort's avowed opponent in the council, could be discounted as a source of trouble so long as his suit for legitimizing his marriage with Jacqueline of Bavaria was pending before the curia. Although Archbishop Chichele always professed obedience, Martin distrusted him, for he suspected that Chichele's advice had induced Henry V to force Beaufort's renunciation of the red hat. But the most ardent support for the papal cause was anticipated from John Duke of Bedford, from whom the pope expected assiduous backing in hope of assistance in harnessing the French clergy to the English cause. Within three months of Henry V's death Martin had launched his campaign. He wrote to the council that Henry's death grieved him deeply, that the members of the council must labour to restore peace in France, and that they must repair the liberties of the church, which the schism had damaged.[1] In December that same year the Cardinal Bishop Louis of Porto, having been appointed legate, departed for France armed with a commission empowering him to pacify the kingdoms of France and England and to inflict ecclesiastical sanctions on those who rebelled.[2]

Pursuing this initiative, in March 1423 Martin dispatched Bishop James of Trieste to England, accompanied by Simon of Teramo, who had been out of the country since 1421.[3] On 24 March Teramo was ordered to pay the bishop four florins per day for the duration of his stay in England from the papal funds in that country. (This,

---

[1] O. Raynaldus, *Annales ecclesiastici . . .*, ed. J. Mansi (Lucca, 1725), *sub anno* 1422, no. xxix.

[2] P.R.O. 31/9/40/f. 107ᵛ; B.M., Add. MS. 15380, f. 66ʳ.

[3] The request for safe conduct is dated 13 Mar. (B.M., Add. MS. 15380, ff. 79ᵛ–80ʳ).

Professor Lunt observed, was more than the bishop would have received had the curia footed the bill.)[1] Teramo reached England on 5 May,[2] and on 13 September the pope wrote to Humphrey Stafford requesting that he obtain the abolition of the statutes against provisions and that he give a favourable reply to the pope's envoys.[3] What followed is not clear. The pope had declared the year 1423 a jubilee and he hoped to use the revenue from the celebration to repair damages to the city of Rome. But Archbishop Chichele had reduced the expectations of substantial revenue by decreeing a jubilee in England in 1420. It may be that James's mission involved no more than inquiring into the truth of the assertion that the Archbishop of Canterbury had proclaimed the year 1420 as a jubilee 'to ensnare simple souls and to extort from them a profane reward', though the actual purpose of the celebration was to recall the two-hundredth anniversary of the translation of Thomas Becket.[4] But James had other powers as well: he was to search out those accused of forging papal documents vilifying the curia, he might commute vows of pilgrimage to go beyond the seas, absolve fornicators, and confer the office of notary.[5] Apparently the pope obtained no satisfaction from this embassy and ultimately dropped the inquiry. The English council may have been awaiting news of the Council of Pavia before replying to the pontiff.

Destitute of excuses for delaying the general council, Martin had issued orders for it to be convened at Pavia. It opened in April 1423. After the king had written to his proctor in Rome to have him inquire what the place of the King of France at this assembly was, he commissioned envoys.[6] Among the English delegates were Bishop Richard Fleming of Lincoln, Nicholas Frome, Abbot of

---

[1] Lunt, ii. 691.

[2] See the warrant dated 8 July granting him 225 marks for taking messages to the pope and remaining abroad from 19 July 1421 until 5 May 1423 (E 404/39/339).

[3] B.M., Cotton Charter XI, 29.   [4] *Cal. Pap. Let., 1417–31*, p. 12.

[5] Ibid., p. 14. To grant plenary indulgences, as was the custom during jubilee, had been forbidden to anyone except the pope (without a special licence) since the end of the schism (R. Foreville, *Le Jubilé de saint Thomas Becket* (Paris, 1958), pp. 63–6; *Chichele*, vol. i, pp. xliv–xlv).

[6] Rymer, x. 269.

Glastonbury, and Henry Percy.[1] Soon after the opening an
outbreak of the plague made it necessary to move to Siena,
where the council reconvened on 21 July. Discovering that
no immediate advance appeared likely towards reconciliation
with the Greek church and that in any case little beyond
confirmation of the decrees promulgated at Constance
against heresy and the Wycliffites could be expected, the
pope had the council secretly dissolved on 7 March 1424
as of 26 February.[2] The ostensible reasons for terminating
this assembly (according to Martin's letter to Henry VI
dated 12 March 1424) were that after nine months only
a few prelates had appeared and of those who had come
many had returned home; and more significantly, that
the bad feeling between the delegates to the council and
the citizens of Siena had reached such a pitch that public
sessions of the assembly could not be held in safety.[3]
Though not stated explicitly, the pope's well-known distaste for conciliar activity and the Aragonese revival of the
question of Benedict XIII, which challenged the validity
of Martin's election, played a large part in the decision to
disperse the council.

In the interim the English seem to have forgotten the
pope's embassy. On 10 June the king ordered the chancellor
to write to John Forster, his clerk at Rome, ordering him to
return to England as fast as possible,[4] and just over a
fortnight later Nicholas Bildeston left London for the curia
with a retinue of six men and seven horses to stall for time

---

[1] On 3 May 1423 the English council ordered letters of protection to be drawn
up for Nicholas, Abbot of Glastonbury, who was about to go to the general council
(E 28/39/66). These letters of protection are printed in Rymer, x. 281. Henry
Percy was paid £606. 12s. 4d. for his expenses while attending the council (E 404/
39/151; F. Devon, ed., *Issues of the Exchequer. Henry III to Henry VI* (London,
1873), pp. 377–8). Furthermore, it seems that Bishop Beaufort was to attend this
assembly, for the king granted a letter of protection to a member of his retinue who
was going to Pavia (Rymer, x. 279). Other proposed members included Philip
Morgan, Bishop of Worcester, Lord Ferrers of Groby, John Tiptoft, Master
Robert Gilbert, Dr. Nicholas Bildeston, and Walter de la Pole (*Proc. P.C.* iii. 42).

[2] Hefele, *Histoire des conciles*, vol. vii, pt. i, p. 622.

[3] Mansi, col. 1075; Hefele, *Histoire des conciles*, vol. vii, pt. i, p. 643.

[4] C 81/681/1189. Forster, who had been arrested by the French in 1419 as he
returned from the curia, had evidently obtained his liberty and made his way to
Rome (E. Jacob, 'To and from the Court of Rome in the Early Fifteenth Century',
*Studies in French Language and Medieval Literature Presented to Professor Mildred
K. Pope* (Manchester, 1939), pp. 167–8).

by discussing things far removed from the problem of
provisions.[1] John Fytton, the Duke of Gloucester's con-
fessor, arrived in England from Rome in the late summer
or early autumn where he had entered an appeal for protection from one Geoffrey Davenport, who had seized
Fytton's church of Stockport.[2] He brought with him a
letter of recommendation from the pope addressed to the
duke. The latter, so it appears from the letter, had instructed
Fytton to complain about the unconscionable amount of
time it was taking to settle the disputed marriage with the
Countess of Hainault; moreover, Gloucester had learned
from a papal envoy (Teramo) that the pope thought Gloucester to be in the right. The pope of course denied this
categorically and asserted that the difficulty of the matter
had prevented a rapid conclusion to the case. Then taking
as his text 'Radix [enim] omnium malorum est cupiditas'[3]
the pope denounced his legate and suggested that Teramo
had hoped to win favours from the duke by telling him
things pleasing to hear.[4] But Martin had only heard part of
the story of his double-dealing envoy. By October the rumour
had spread in England that Teramo had reported to the
pope the English council's willingness to allow papal
provisions in return for a condemnation of Gloucester's
matrimonial alliance. Although no council document survives that might substantiate this rumour, that such an
offer was made is conceivable. What better way could be
found to force the duke to abandon his claims to territory

---

[1] In a letter of 1424 Martin wrote to the king 'verum ipse [Nicholas Bildeston]
nullam earum rerum tractatum aut conclusionem asserens alia quedam exposuit
longe remota ab opinione nostra' (P.R.O. 31/8/40, f. 118ᵛ). Bildeston received an
advance of £16. 13s. 6d. on 8 June; the following 4 Aug. a Lombard merchant
collected £46. 13s. 4d. advance on Bildeston's wages; and on 13 Nov. a further
advance of £48. 13s. 6d. was allowed. On 22 Mar. the next year Bildeston received
£33. 6s. 8d. in settlement of his account (E 403/666/mm. 7, 4; 669/mm. 3, 18;
E 101/222/10). There is no evidence for assigning this embassy to 1422. Haller
(England und Rom, p. 291) unfortunately misled Jacob (Chichele, vol. i, p. xlii)
in this matter.

[2] Chichele, vol. i, p. clxx; iv. 248–9.

[3] 1 Timothy 6: 10.

[4] K. A. Fink, 'Die politische Korrespondenz Martins V. nach den Brevenregis-
tern', Quellen und Forschungen aus italienischen Archiven und Bibliotheken, xxvi
(1935–6), 200–2. See also a similar letter to the Bishop of Trieste and to Simon de
Teram (Cal. Pap. Let., 1417–31, p. 27).

coveted by the Duke of Burgundy, thereby alleviating the strain Gloucester's invasion of the Low Countries placed on the Anglo-Burgundian alliance? Gloucester, when he had heard these tales, burst into a violent rage and promptly fired off a letter to Rome, which contained a threat to arrest Simon and hold him until the pope's pleasure became known. The papal collector, he declared, had not only slandered the duke but also plotted against the Holy See.[1] Despite the fact that the Bishop of London, John Kemp, successfully pleaded Teramo's case before the council, the pope recalled him to Rome almost immediately and appointed Giovanni d'Obizzi, an auditor of the rota, his successor.[2] Despite the new appointment, Anglo-papal relations further deteriorated the next year.

The story of the pope's major diplomatic defeat in England, beginning in the spring of 1426, has often been told. Giuliano Cesarini, an auditor of the camera and future president of the Council of Basel, came to England at the pope's request but received only the stock answers usually offered about revoking the statute: the king could do nothing on such a grave matter without the advice of parliament (an excuse the Aragonese ambassadors received a few years later when the English again wished to play for time), but he would ask the opinion of the parliament when it next met. Upon receiving the report of Cesarini's mission, Martin wrote to the king informing him that even though his using parliament as an excuse for inaction was no more than an evasion,[3] the curia was willing to wait for another parliament, though no pope had ever been used as badly by

---

[1] *Correspondence Bekynton*, i. 279–80. '. . . ipsum similes factiones etiam in injuriam Sanctitatis vestrae ausu nefario et sacrilego praetemptasse . . .'.

[2] See his letters of recommendation and credence to the king, the Bishop of Winchester, and the Archbishop of Canterbury dated 10 Ka. Feb. (23 Jan.) 1425 (*Cal. Pap. Let., 1417–31*, p. 35). His appointment as papal collector in Scotland is dated 14 Sept. 1425 (P.R.O. 31/9/40/ pp. 103–4).

[3] '. . . Quod quamprimum commode possit, parliamentum, sine quo idem nequit aboleri statutum, convocaret, et in eo, quod sibi possibile foret, pro nostrae requisitionis complemento faceret; protestans quod sanctae Romanae ecclesiae sedisque apostolicae juribus ac privilegiis nullo modo detrahere aut derogare intendebat. Quod quam citius commode poteris parliamentum, sine quo (ut inquis) idem aboleri nequit statutum, convenire intendens . . . Sed quoniam sine parliamento id fieri non posse, excusas . . .' (D. Wilkins, *Concilia Magnae Britanniae et Hiberniae* (London, 1788), iii. 479–82).

any nation as Martin had by the English.[1] Next the pope
wrote to the Duke of Bedford admonishing him to labour
zealously for the restoration of the liberties of the church;[2]
he sent Beaufort, who within three months' time was to
receive papal appointment as leader of the Hussite crusade,[3]
a very cordial note commending his efforts on behalf of the
church.[4] Finally he wrote to Archbishop Chichele, whom
Cesarini had inaccurately represented as the soul of opposition to the papacy,[5] requiring under pain of excommunication that he maintain and make generally known papal
reservations in England and that he not be so negligent in
his duties as he had in the past. Because the papal envoy
Obizzi delivered this last letter, he was thrown into the
Tower where he was confined intermittently until about
24 June, the reason for his arrest being 'pro deliberacione
certarum bullarum contra statuta regis etc'.[6] Inasmuch as it
was not usual, to say the least, for papal envoys to be
arrested, Martin felt justified in complaining to the Duke
of Bedford and to the Bishop of Winchester in the strongest
terms, though at the end the pontiff softened his tone by
remarking that such a thing would never have occurred had
the bishop and the duke been in England—an astute
comment on the control of English foreign policy.[7] Nevertheless the pope averred that this outrage could not shake
his resolve. The English council now realized that they had
gone too far and set the collector free; but when parliament
at last assembled on 13 October the only mention made of
this whole affair (though the pope had written on the opening
day to warn the members of parliament of the danger to
their souls if they did not abolish the statute)[8] is a petition

[1] Haller, *England und Rom*, p. 28 n. 1.
[2] Ibid., Beilage 8.
[3] P.R.O. 31/9/61/50. The appointment is dated 16 Feb. 1427.
[4] Haller, *England und Rom*, Beilage 9; *Cal. Pap. Let., 1417–31*, pp. 24–5.
[5] Haller, *England und Rom*, p. 29. Jacob has suggested that Beaufort rather
than Cesarini may be responsible for Archbishop Chichele's bad press in Rome,
but he offers no evidence to support his surmise (E. Jacob, 'Two Lives of Archbishop
Chichele', *Bulletin of the John Rylands Library*, xvi (1932), 449).
[6] *Proc. P.C.* iii. 268.
[7] B.M., Cotton Cleopatra E. III, f. 40ʳ; Cambridge University Library, Mm. I.
45, pp. 7–8; Haller, *England und Rom*, Beilage 11.
[8] Raynaldus, *sub anno* 1427, no. xv.

of the commons to have the king write to the pope or instruct his ambassador in Rome to clear the Archbishop of Canterbury's name of the malicious slanders reported to the Holy See.[1]

Faced with this contumacy only one alternative remained: either to excommunicate the king and council and to place the whole country under interdict, or to abandon the struggle.[2] But the time for such sweeping ecclesiastical sanctions was, as the pope shrewdly recognized, past. Defeated in his long battle with the English nation, Martin retired from the field of combat.

The English soon gave the pope reason for displeasure in another matter. Cardinal Beaufort was reappointed to lead the Hussite crusade on 8 March 1428, his initial mission having failed; he returned to England at the end of August that year and began raising the 259 spears and 2,500 lances he required for the new expedition. The next year, during the summer, the pope's ambassador Master James de Charataneis, who had been in England the previous autumn for an unknown purpose,[3] presented the council with a request to double the number of troops going on the crusade. However, the council refused, alleging that 'the people of this land is lessed' and decreased' of late time by mortalitee werres and in other diverse wyses . . .'.[4] By contrast, the pope's petition that those who went on the crusade be accorded the king's protection was granted.[5] By 1 July, the council, having learned of the defeat at Patay, asked Cardinal Beaufort to turn aside his forces from the crusade that they might fight in France and further asked him to pay these troops with the money he had

---

[1] *Rot. Parl.* iv. 322.

[2] There is some evidence that the council expected the pope to do the former rather than the latter, for as early as 7 May they had decided to send William, Bishop of London, John Lord Lescrope, and John Stokes, the prothonotary, to the pope with a gift of jewels (*Proc. P.C.* iii. 311). This embassy, which also had certain Aragonese matters to discuss, did not depart until 17 July (E 101/322/41). They did not return until 5 Feb. 1429 (E 364/65/f. 9). The warrant for letters of protection and record of an advance on Stokes's wages also survive (PSO I/66/13; E 403/686/m. 14).

[3] *Cal. Close Rolls, 1422–29*, p. 422; Rymer, x. 409 contains a licence for James to take certain silver plate from England free of duty.

[4] *Proc. P.C.* iii. 333.   [5] Ibid. 336; Rymer, x. 419.

raised.[1] To this plea the cardinal assented,[2] and it seems likely that Robert Fitzhugh, the king's proctor in Rome, was selected to bear this unpleasant news to the curia.[3]

Later that same year the council drew up instructions for Dr. Nicholas Bildeston to deliver to the curia, but perhaps remembering that Bildeston had been employed somewhat earlier to deliver an unwelcome letter to Rome, the council entrusted the new letter to a merchant who was to deliver it to Fitzhugh.[4] The instructions, which have survived in somewhat damaged form, nevertheless strike a new note in Anglo-papal relations. No longer does direct bartering between London and the Holy See about provisions occupy the centre of attention, rather negotiations during the rest of Henry's reign revolve chiefly around the pope's function as mediator and peacemaker and as grantor of ecclesiastical privileges. The purpose of these instructions, the last known to have reached Rome before Martin's death in February 1431, was to request that if papal mediators be sent to France, as some princes had suggested, then these mediators ought not to be partisans of the king's adversary and Cardinal Beaufort should also be invited to the meeting.[5]

Why did Martin reap so little benefit from his vigorous efforts? It might be suggested that his preoccupation with the restoration of the papal state and his zealous attempts to avoid another council left him little time to determine how sound the opinions were of those whom he sent to England. It might well be urged that his failure rested on

[1] There seems little doubt that the English government ultimately reimbursed the curia, though at least one contemporary thought they had not. 'Also the seyde seditious personys have caused our seyde sufferen' lorde to spend the godes of our holy fader the pope which were yeffyn' hym' for the defens of Christen feyth of many the godly pepul' disesyd of thys land withowt repayment' to our seyde holy fadyr for the which cause thys land standyth' in grete jeperde of enterdytyng' (B.M., Cotton Charter IV, 61).

[2] Rymer, x. 424.

[3] See the council orders for his letters of protection, since he was about to set out for Rome with a retinue of five, dated 15 July (*Proc. P.C.* iii. 347).

[4] Ibid. iv. 12–15. Strangely enough Bildeston seems to have gone to Rome anyway; see the order for his advance in E 404/46/172.

[5] But note the unexplained order witnessed by Gloucester that if Beaufort was called to Rome through the machinations of the king's enemies, no English subject was to accompany him (Rymer, x. 472; *Cal. Pat. Rolls, 1422–29*, p. 429).

his lack of understanding of English psychology and the misrepresentation to him of their attitude, and in one case it seems clear that his envoy treacherously betrayed his confidence. In other words, the pope had not learned the lesson of the Investiture Conflict: the English passionately believed it necessary for the king and private patrons to be able to provide deserving clerks with benefices in return for good services, and because they believed this so strongly they embodied it in a statute not likely to be renounced. Moreover, with the decline of papal prestige the English had little to gain by giving way.

Hardly had the papal tiara settled on the head of the austere Eugenius IV when the Council of Basel was inaugurated (23 July 1431). The history of this turbulent council, of the English delegation to it, and of its attempt to reconcile Henry VI and Charles VII is well known.[1] Since the main facts have been recounted many times a cursory summary will provide a sufficient link between Anglo-papal relations at the beginning of the reign and those at the end. The strategy of the English at the great ecclesiastical councils of the fifteenth century, Professor Jacob has argued,[2] was largely determined by their attitude towards papal finance and foreign policy, though the former factor played a diminished role after 1428. Thus once the papacy had abandoned the struggle over provisions, it was unlikely that the English would undertake with much enthusiasm any discussion leading to the abolition of annates. English foreign policy, as far as it concerned the church and the councils, centred chiefly on the creation of a system of alliances in which Rome served as a foil to the Franco-Avignonese *entente* and later to the Franco-Basel friendship. In the realm of *Realpolitik*, the English were unscrupulous

[1] J. Haller, *Concilium Basiliense, Studien und Quellen zur Geschichte des Concils von Basel* (Basle, 1896–1904), vols. i–v; A. Zellfelder, *England und das Basler Konzil* (Berlin, 1913); J. Toussaint, *Les Relations diplomatiques de Philippe le Bon avec le concile de Bâle* (Louvain, 1942); Dickinson, *Arras*; A. N. E. D. Schofield, 'The First English Delegation to the Council of Basel', *Journal of Ecclesiastical History*, xii (1961), 167–205; id., 'England, the Pope, and the Council of Basel, 1435–1449', *Church History*, xxxiii (1964), 248–78.

[2] E. F. Jacob, 'Englishmen and the General Councils', *Essays in the Conciliar Epoch*, 2nd edn. (Manchester, 1953), pp. 44–56.

enough to threaten to send envoys to the Conciliarists so as to produce a more tractable attitude at the Holy See. As regards the reform of the church *in capite*, the English showed little concern as a body, though there were some individuals with a deep interest in the matter. Although the English envoys helped Martin V break up the Council of Siena when it threatened to act, in 1425 they tried to use the threat of reform to compel the pope to stop pressing for the revocation of the statute of Provisors. At the Council of Basel (whose purpose was to define orthodoxy, to bring peace to Europe, and to reform morals),[1] the English ignored reform, spending much time in complaint about Charles VII's French delegates having a vote;[2] and through inept foreign policy the English envoys allowed the council and the pope to do everything possible to bring Burgundy and France together, thereby paving the way for the diplomatic débâcle at Arras in 1435.

It was in fact largely by reminding the English of their threat to use secular power to reform the church that Bishop Landriani of Lodi, Basel's envoy to Henry VI's court in the summer of 1432, secured a favourable reply to his request for an English embassy to the council.[3] However, English support was lukewarm at best. The English council had heard that Sigismund might not be as well disposed to the ecclesiastical assembly as he had been initially, and wishing their policy to accord with his, as it had at Constance,[4] many of the king's advisers wanted to wait for future development before acting. That Henry actually sent the promised embassy seems due to the influence of the Duke of Gloucester, who perhaps hoped to equal the role Beaufort had played at Constance or at least

---

[1] Toussaint, *Les Relations diplomatiques*, p. viii.

[2] *Proc. P.C.* iv. 297.

[3] Schofield, 'The First English Delegation to the Council of Basel', p. 170. The king gave this embassy £86. 13s. 4d. as a reward for their efforts (E 403/703/m. 14). It is interesting to note in the royal response to Landriani the rejection of Basel's offer to mediate in the struggle with France because the king had accepted the advances of the papal legate Albergati (Mansi, vol. xxx, coll. 133–4). The letter instructing Albergati to act as mediator is dated 1431 (Raynaldus, *sub anno* 1431, no. xiv).

[4] C. M. D. Crowder, 'Henry V, Sigismund and the Council of Constance, a Re-examination', *Historical Studies*, iv (1963), 93–110.

to forestall a similar performance.[1] Moreover, once the decision to send envoys was finally taken,[2] Henry went so far as to write to the pope (2 July 1432) saying that he intended to send his ambassadors to Basel,[3] but if it was the pope's will they would be sent to Bologna instead, to which the pope had ordered the council to be removed on 18 December.[4] Hardly had the envoys to Basel (instructed first to deal with the Hussites and secondly to see what could be made of the council's offer of mediation with France) departed when the king wrote telling them that if required to take the oath of incorporation, they were to withdraw towards Cologne or elsewhere nearer England to await further instructions.[5] After the failure of the embassy, Landriani returned to England and secured the promise of a large delegation, which was incorporated in 1434. But the English never got along very well with the council. In addition to their delayed arrival, one member of the delegation (William Sprever) presented a treatise on the authority of the council in which it took second place to the pope except in cases of schism or papal heresy. Then there were quarrels with the Castilians about precedence. It is not surprising that even after the papal legate Albergati's failure at Corbeil in 1432, the council did not succeed in accomplishing much in the pacification of England and

---

[1] An alternative explanation, advanced by Schofield (p. 175 n. 6) turns on Gloucester's possession of a collection of council documents (B.M., Cotton Nero E.V), which affords grounds for assuming that he was personally interested in the council. While the presence of a single item in the rich library of a bibliophile is not in itself a convincing argument, Schofield buttresses his contention by citing evidence that Gloucester hoped to use the council to extradite the English heretic Peter Payne. The Duke of Gloucester's letter to the council promising his support is printed in Mansi, vol. xxx, coll. 165–6. Despite his support, the council did not turn Payne over to Gloucester, and as late as 1440 Henry VI was trying to purchase Payne from his captor John Burian (*Correspondence Bekynton*, i. 187). On Payne see the *Register of Oxford*, iii. 1440–3.

[2] The king's answer to Landriani can be found in Mansi, vol. xxxi, coll. 133–4.

[3] This news was known at Basel by Sept. (Haller, *Concilium Basiliense*, i. 60).

[4] Mansi, vol. xxxi, col. 132; Schofield, 'The First English Delegation to the Council of Basel', p. 202 n. 4.

[5] '. . . et vobis mandamus quod, protestacionibus congruis nostro regnorum ac dominiorum subditorumque et ligeorum nostrorum nomine per vos discrete emissis, ab ipso loco Basilien' recedatis apud Coloniam vel alibi versus Angliam moraturi donec de nostra voluntate aliter fueritis informati' (S.C. I/57/70).

France.[1] And the English embassy, following the papal success at Arras, withdrew from Basel in November 1435. That they sent no further embassy to the council was largely due to the papal envoy, Pietro del Monte, who fostered the idea that the conciliar legate had neglected English interests at Arras.

The formal withdrawal of the English embassy did not end contact between the two parties. The Bishop of Dax and an English cleric remained at the council for a while. In May 1438 envoys from Basel came to England in an effort to secure support. Though they had no success, they made repeated attempts at Mainz and at Calais the next year. Notwithstanding one last effort by Felix V, the English position remained firm, and they joined with the French and Germans in securing the anti-pope's abdication.

Meanwhile the Anglo-papal *status quo* was maintained with no apparent difficulty. Henry had dispatched Nicholas Rixton with a knight John Colville in his retinue to Eugenius at the end of December 1431, presumably to congratulate the new pope upon his elevation, though the phrase *pro secretis negociis* coupled with the fact that Colville's account reveals that he did not return until the following October make the lack of further evidence particularly bothersome.[2] The next year the pope sent a safe conduct for the Bishop of London,[3] who was also to serve at Basel, to come to Rome with a retinue of thirty men, and the king allowed John Milez, his advocate at the curia, fifty marks annually.[4] But discord was soon to raise its head again over the matter of confirmation of episcopal elections. The schism had given local ecclesiastical authorities the opportunity to regain this right, but from Martin V's election a phase of papal reaction set in. The principle of free election soon disappeared. Now the conflict focused not so much upon

---

[1] As early as May 1433 Piccolomini had recorded in a letter to Siena the extreme animosity existing between France and England. '. . . concordia inter Gallos et Anglicos desperata est . . .' (*Der Briefwechsel des Eneas Silvius Piccolomini*, ed. R. Wolkan (Fontes rerum Austriacarum, 1909–18), Bd. 61, p. 119). Waurin notes even earlier that 'ne polt il riens concorder quant a paix' (Waurin, iv. 21).

[2] E 101/322/18.   [3] B.M., Add. MS. 15380, ff. 244ʳ–245ᵛ.

[4] *Proc. P.C.* iv. 111.

the king against the pope as the struggle within the English council about whom to appoint.[1] In October 1434 the king wrote to Andrew Holes, the future keeper of the privy seal, 'and to al the curtezeins English in the courte of Rome' that they permit no one to be provided to the see of Rochester 'nor to noon other than shal voide fro this tyme forwarde in oure reaum of Englande or lordship of Hirlande . . .' until they had learned the king's recommendation.[2] What happened when an Englishman allowed himself to be so provided, and what had prompted the preceding letter, the missive to the Dean of Salisbury, Thomas Brouns, quite clearly reveals. The king had heard, he wrote to Brouns, that Eugenius had granted him the bishopric of Worcester (vacant since the death of Thomas Polton on 23 August 1433), 'which as ye knowe wel ye mown not accepte . . . without oure assent furst had therepon' and thenkeyfully that it was nevere is nor shal be our' entente that ye shal have our assent to that chirch no noon other while ye laboure as we been enformed that ye do ayenst our wille in this matter'.[3] Furthermore, the king charged the dean to signify to the pope that the church could not be accepted without the king's consent. When he had done this, the king was to be so informed.[4] In fact the pope acceded to the king's request and provided Brouns with Rochester on 21 February 1435; Bourgchier, though elected to the see of Worcester in December 1433, did not receive papal provision until 9 March 1435.

[1] 'Under Henry VI bishops were recommended not so much by the king as by the lords who dominated his council. Not unnaturally these preferred to bestow benefices on their kinsmen and chaplains rather than on "civil servants" whom they were less likely to know' (R. J. Knecht, 'The Episcopate and the Wars of the Roses', *University of Birmingham Historical Journal*, vi (1958), 110). L.-R. Betcherman, 'The Making of Bishops in the Lancastrian Period', *Speculum*, xli (1966), 397–419, has proposed a naïve and inaccurate expansion of this thesis.

[2] *Proc. P.C.* iv. 281. The see of Rochester was vacant from 30 Sept. 1434.

[3] B.M., Cotton Cleopatra E. III, f. 67. In 1429 the king had informed the pope that Brouns would be an acceptable occupant of the see of Chichester, but nothing came of this suggestion (Rymer, x. 433). On this problem see A. Hamilton Thompson, *The English Clergy and their Organisation in the Later Middle Ages* (Oxford, 1947), pp. 19–20, and E. F. Jacob, 'Thomas Brouns, Bishop of Norwich, 1436–45', *Essays in British History Presented to Sir Keith Feiling*, ed. H. R. Trevor-Roper (London, 1964), pp. 61–83.

[4] However, the king wrote to the pope at the same time certifying that Brouns would be acceptable for the church at Rochester if Thomas Bourgchier were appointed to the see of Worcester (B.M., Cotton Cleopatra E. III, f. 68).

In April 1435 Eugenius appointed collector in England[1] the Venetian Pietro del Monte,[2] who was later to dedicate some philosophical tracts to the Duke of Gloucester.[3] In June Henry informed Eugenius that John Ely had delivered the pope's letter and that the king would send envoys to Arras to treat for peace with France as the pope had urged.[4] Following this letter came an assurance from the pope that no prince had asked for or received any release from oaths made either to Henry VI or his father.[5] About Christmas-time, despite the outcome of Arras, the council granted the pope's nephew, Paolo Barbo, a licence to hold English benefices worth 1,200 gold ducats per year.[6]

Yet behind this relatively amicable front matters were not so congenial. Whether with Eugenius's connivance or not (the documents do not say), Albergati, the pope's legate at Arras, dispatched his secretary, the future Pius II, to Scotland for the ostensible purpose of restoring some prelate to James I's favour; however, Campano, author of the *Vita Pii II*,[7] states that it was to stir up trouble for the English. In view of the failure of the English to offer proposals which could serve as a reasonable basis for serious peace negotiations at Arras, the suspicion that this trip aroused,[8] the refusal of the English to grant the secretary a safe conduct, and his assumption of an elaborate disguise when returning from Scotland via England give every reason for belief that Campano was recording the truth.[9] Furthermore, the moment for stirring up trouble was opportune: Anglo-Scottish relations had deteriorated badly and by this time James seems to have already agreed to

---

[1] A. Zanelli, 'Pietro del Monte', *Archivio storico lombardo*, ser. 4a viii (1907), 92.
[2] Ibid. vii (1907), 320.
[3] L. Einstein, *The Italian Renaissance in England* (New York, 1902), p. 5.
[4] Rymer, x. 610.   [5] Ibid. 620.
[6] C 81/701/3153.
[7] L. A. Muratori, *Rerum Italicarum scriptores* (Milan, 1731), vol. iii, pt. ii, p. 967.
[8] Pius II, *Commentaries*, ed. F. A. Gragg and L. C. Gabel (Smith College Studies in History, xxv, 1937), p. 16.
[9] Balfour-Melville, *James I*, pp. 235-7, sees no reason to disbelieve in the political significance of this mission. Likewise Dunlop believes that the purpose of the mission was to increase England's isolation and thereby hasten the pacification of France (A. I. Dunlop, *The Life and Times of James Kennedy, Bishop of St. Andrews* (St. Andrews University Publications, 1950), p. 16). But *contra* see Dickinson, *Arras*, p. 130.

send his daughter to France and to let the negotiations with the English lapse.[1]

The outlines of the narrative for the next few years are comparatively vague. In early June 1437 the pope wrote to Henry from Bologna exhorting him to select ambassadors to the oecumenical council that had been called for reconciling the Greek and Latin churches.[2] The king's reply, which the monk John O'Heyne may have delivered after carrying letters to the emperor and to the Council of Basel,[3] is unknown. It must in fact have been favourable, for in May 1438 the royal council decided to send ambassadors to the emperor and to the pope;[4] these ambassadors were to treat first with the emperor about making peace between the pope and Basel and then they might 'go to the tretie of the reduccion of the Greekes'. At the same royal council meeting it was decided to send the Bishop of Rochester and either the Bishop of Worcester or the Bishop of St. Asaph as envoys to Basel, the emperor, and the pope. Sigismund, Father Gill noted, had hoped to draw enough members away from Basel to Ferrara and thus end the Council of Basel.[5] That he was unable to do so perhaps invalidated the second part of the English envoy's instructions. Thus, these envoys seem never to have reached the pope. Despite the efforts of the pope's faithful collector, who by this time was publicly proclaiming that 'nothing holy, upright or honest' would ever result from the council meeting at Basel,[6] and writing about the dissension between pope and council,[7] Eugenius got no support for the Council of Florence from the English, apart from Master Giovanni d'Obizzi who went to Ferrara in the summer of 1438 on the

---

[1] Balfour-Melville, *James I*, p. 236.

[2] *Epistolae pontificiae ad concilium Florentinum spectantes*, ed. G. Hofmann (Rome, 1940), pt. i, pp. 72–3.

[3] *Proc. P.C.* v. 82; E 404/54/144; J. Gill, *The Council of Florence* (Cambridge, 1961), p. 132.

[4] *Proc. P.C.* v. 96–7.   [5] Gill, *The Council of Florence*, p. 131.

[6] His letter dated 12 Dec. 1437 expressed in mild terms his attitude towards Basel: 'mihi vero, ut testis est Dominus, nunquam persuaderi potuit, ex ipsa Basiliensi synodo iustum aliquid sanctum, rectum, aut honestum prodire ullatenus posse' (G. Hofmann, 'Briefe eines päpstlichen Nuntius in London über das Konzil von Florenz', *Orientalia Christiana Periodica*, v (1939), 411).

[7] V. Guden, *Sylloge variorum diplomatariorum res Germanicas in primis moguntinas illustrantium* (Frankfurt, 1728), i. 677.

king's business.[1] The pope's pertinacity did not flag. He wrote to Henry again in the summer of 1439 about the union of the Greek and Latin Churches.[2] This letter, written at about the time Basel's ambassadors were in England trying to arrange peace between England and France and to slander the pope as well,[3] likewise fell on deaf ears, though the Archbishop of Canterbury made it clear to the Baselers that the English backed the pope and wondered how the council, which was quarrelling so violently with Eugenius, could advise peace for England. Even though the English had lent him no assistance, in the late autumn the pope had letters of indulgence that had been drawn up on the occasion of the ending of the schism sent to Henry VI.[4]

The urgency of Anglo-papal relations diminished further in the next few years. As the position of the English in France grew more exposed and their demands were revealed as increasingly unrealistic, hopes for successful papal mediation melted away. Heretofore grounds had existed for sending envoys to expound the English position to the curia with the aim of gathering support, but now messengers were only dispatched with requests, generally of an ecclesiastical nature, and the pope followed in due course with a reply. Symptomatic of the slackening of Anglo-papal conversations is the fact that apparently not one English source bears on the quarrel arising between the Archbishops of Canterbury and York in January 1440 over precedence,[5] though the momentous decision ran that York (a cardinal)

---

[1] On 24 July he received £100 from the exchequer (E 403/731/m. 15).

[2] *Epistolae pontificiae*, pt. ii, p. 85.

[3] '. . . in sanctitatem vestram egerant linguas eorum blasfemas atque maledicas convertentes . . .' (P.R.O. 31/9/62/273).

[4] *Epistolae pontificiae*, pt. ii, p. 142. The messenger had been paid by 5 Sept. 1439: 'Pro uno cursore transmisso [cum brevibus et bullis decreti unionis Grecorum] ad dominum ducem et alios prelatos Burgundiae, necnon ad serenissimum dominum regem, reverendissimum dominum cardinalem et alios prelatos Anglie florenos xxv' (N. Jorga, *Notes et extraits pour servir à l'histoire des croisades au xve siècle* (Paris, 1899), p. 14).

[5] It is possible that either William Swan, who, according to the warrant ordering £40 paid to him, went 'in a certaine message of ours into the tother parties of the see', or Richard Chester took letters to the curia on this matter (E 404/56/265, 325; 57/41). Instead they may well have taken Henry's letters thanking Eugenius for raising Archbishop Kemp to the cardinalate (*Correspondence Bekynton*, i. 50).

took precedence over the Archbishop of Canterbury because cardinals were *contigua membra* of the pope in his jurisdictional aspect.[1] The king's expenses at the curia for 1442–3 likewise give some idea of the types of conversations between the two courts: the king's 'solicitor' Richard Caunton took £30 for his unspecified troubles during the preceding year; Adam Moleyns secured the services (in return for a stipend) of Francesco Condulmari, Cardinal Priest of S. Clemente, and Branda di Castiglione, Cardinal Bishop of Sta. Sabina, in response to the king's instructions to secure eminent clergymen to represent him at the court of Rome;[2] and an unnamed official received 200 ducats for expediting a bull concerning the king's college at Eton,[3] while only six ducats were spent for writing letters, and two Flemish messengers charged the king thirty ducats for a journey from Bruges to London.[4] Although as early as June 1443 the emperor, having grown tired of the conflict between the clergy still left at Basel and the pope, wrote to the King of England that the quickest way to heal this wound was to hold another general council,[5] surviving English sources methodically and monotonously do no more than tick off payments for messengers: to the Abbot of Gloucester going to Rome in August 1444 as the king's proctor £100,[6] to Henry Verbondeswyk for going to the

[1] W. Ullmann, 'Eugenius IV, Kemp and Chichele', *Medieval Studies presented to Aubrey Gwynn, S.J.*, ed. J. A. Watt et al. (Dublin, 1964), pp. 359–83.

[2] The notarial instruments whereby Moleyns certifies that the Cardinals of S. Clemente and Sta. Sabina have accepted the king's offer in return for 100 marks annually to each are preserved in the Public Record Office. There is also a quittance for fifty marks advanced to Cardinal Castiglione (E 30/425, 1436, 1285).

[3] The bull for the foundation of Eton bears the date 28 Jan. 1441 (*Correspondence Bekynton*, ii. 270).

[4] The lack of business notwithstanding, English officials in Rome spent £145. 12s. 0d. that year (E 404/59/121). The Dean of Salisbury's mission 'foedus seu confoederationem et alligantiam reciprocae dilectionis et amicitiae contrahere, inire et firmare' in the spring of 1442 and the effort to secure the canonization of King Alfred may account for some of this expense (Rymer, xi. 3; *Correspondence Bekynton*, i. 118).

[5] *Der Briefwechsel des Eneas Silvius Piccolomini*, Bd. 61, p. 157.

[6] But it seems the abbot did not go to Rome after all. 'Thabbot of Gloucestre whom at that tyme we appointed' for to goo to the courte of Rome and to be oure oratour' and proctour' general there ye shulde pay unto him of oure yift . . . c li. the which . . . after the receyvyng by you of oure said lettres he had and receyved of us by assignement and made him and his servant' redy in ryght' honest wise for our worship to goo theder by force and vertu of oure said appoyntement to his

pope and returning with certain letters touching Eton College £10,[1] to the papal ambassador who returned to Rome in June 1445 with answers to his instructions £40,[2] and to the Marquis of Suffolk in repayment of the sum he gave 'to a man to oure holy fadre the pope for a licence to have been married en the tyme of Lent if the comyng of oure moost dere and bestbeloved wyfe the queen had so fallen'.[3] On 24 June the next year, just a few months before his death, Eugenius IV wrote that he was sending his chamberlain Lodovico de Cardona to collect the papal tenth for a crusade against the Turks that the Bishop of Concordia had refrained from gathering the previous year.[4] Cardona (bearing a golden rose as a gift from Eugenius to Henry)[5] arrived in September to collect the tax, but he met with no success.[6] Although the king was willing for the clergy to give 6,000 gold florins, convocation proclaimed that the church in England was not able to bear so great an exaction. And Cardona departed empty-handed, saving a reward from the king, in February 1447.[7]

Eugenius's death the following February and the elevation of Nicholas V, better known for his schemes to rebuild St. Peter's than for his astute diplomacy in northern Europe, produced little change in the understanding between Rome and London. Late in the summer of 1447, the Bishop of Norwich, Robert Botyll, Prior of St. John of Jerusalem, and a lawyer Thomas Candour set out for France and Rome by way of Florence at the king's request.[8] At

---

grether cost', charg' and expenses than the said c li. . . . for as moch' as he yede not unto the said courte to be oure oratour . . . we willed by oure said' lettres that he shuld' have of our yift . . . the said c li. and after oure said appointment we desired willed and appointed hym to be and abyde in this our reaume of Englande and not to goo to the said courte . . .' (E 404/63/5).

[1] E 404/61/191.   [2] E 404/61/246.   [3] E 404/61/267.
[4] Mansi, vol. xxxii, coll. 33–6.   [5] E 403/765/m. 14.
[6] E. F. Jacob, 'Archbishop John Stafford', *Transactions of the Royal Historical Society*, 5th ser. xii (1962), 18–22. Both these envoys had previously been to England. Cardona was arrested at Calais early in 1445 and searched to see that he was taking no money to Rome (B.M., Cotton Charter XXIV, 6). Concordia was paid a reward on 25 June as he was about to return to the pope (E 404/61/242).
[7] E 403/765/m. 14.
[8] E 403/767/m. 13; E 101/324/13; E 404/63/162. On 31 July the exchequer had been ordered to advance him six months' wages (£336) (E 404/63/135). He actually received the money seven days earlier (E 403/767/m. 13).

Lyons the Bishop of Norwich and Botyll, were joined by Vicent Clement, an Aragonese ecclesiastic.[1] These envoys were instructed to meet with representatives of the Germans, the French, and Duke Louis of Savoy to secure the abdication of Felix V. The English envoys, however, did not arrive until the talks had been adjourned to Geneva, where they were invited despite the presence of Clement, whose Aragonese allegiance (the French felt) might prejudice the pope's cause. The talks at Geneva ended in a stalemate early in December and the English envoys returned to Bourges with their French colleagues to report the outcome of the mission.[2] Botyll and Clement, at least, seem to have accompanied the French embassy that arrived in Rome on 10 July 1448; from there they went to Lausanne[3] where on 4 April 1449 they guaranteed the promise of the papal envoy regarding bulls safeguarding Felix V's followers after his abdication.[4] While the prior was abroad the king and pope exchanged several letters: in April 1448 both the king and the queen wrote to Nicholas asking that William Booth be translated to the bishopric of Coventry and Lichfield,[5] and the pope sent a letter urging that Archbishop Kemp's nephew Thomas, as the king seemed to have forgotten an earlier request, be given the bishopric of London,[6] and that the Bishop of Carlisle, whom Henry had designated for the

---

[1] A. Grunzweig, *Correspondance de la filiale de Bruges des Medici* (Commission royale d'histoire de Belgique, 1931), p. 10. On 24 July 1447 Clement received £168 from the exchequer for his services; the following Feb. he received a further £133. 6s. 8d. and Botyll got £244 (E 403/767/m. 13; 769/mm. 12, 13).

[2] *Procès-verbal des conférences tenues en 1447 à Lyon et à Genève pour mettre fin au schisme de Bâle*, ed. G. Pérouse (*Concilium Basiliense*, 1936), Bd. 8, pp. 253–428. G. Pérouse, *Le Cardinal Louis Aleman et la fin du grand schisme* (Paris, 1904), pp. 446–55. R. H. Trame, *Rodrigo Sánchez de Arévalo, 1404–1407* (Catholic University of America Studies in Medieval History, 1958), pp. 64–75 has a rather garbled version of this embassy.

[3] In Feb. 1449 the king wrote to the exchequer that Botyll had spent the money initially advanced to him and also wages for four additional months, now he needed another advance on his wages for nine months (E 404/65/102). On 27 May 1450 he was granted £100 arrears on his wages (C 81/762/9207; *Cal. Pat. Rolls, 1446–52*, pp. 376–7).

[4] The original document is in the Basel Universitätsbibliothek, E. I, 4, f. 127 (Pérouse, *Louis Aleman*, p. 458).

[5] Corpus Christi College, Cambridge, MS. 170, pp. 211, 212.

[6] He received the temporalities of the see on 6 Feb. 1450 even though he had been provided in Aug. 1448.

see of London, would be promoted when a vacancy occurred.[1]
Furthermore, Nicholas signified to the king that his proctor
William Gray had not made this arrangement, but the pope
himself had done it, as he had informed the king in an
earlier letter, to please the king and to favour the cardinal.[2]
Nicholas went even further: he wrote to the Duke of Somerset thanking him for his recommendation of the Bishop of
Carlisle, Marmaduke Lumley, but the pope affirmed that
the appointment to London had been made and could not
be reconsidered; there were no other positions in England
suitable for the Bishop of Carlisle.[3]

   As the political situation worsened in England and Henry
VI's dotage became more marked, correspondence between
Rome and London declined still further in bulk and in
importance.[4] Although the papal embassy to France in
1451–2, led by Guillaume d'Estouteville, ostensibly was to
attempt once again the pacification of France and England,
the cardinal's primary concern was an altogether different
matter.[5] In July 1452 the pope granted the Archbishop
of Canterbury power to absolve the rebels who had followed
the Duke of York.[6] This letter was followed by another on
the same subject.[7] In the spring the council wrote to John
Laxe, one of the king's agents in Rome, 'to putte in your ful
devour and halp and assiste' John Langstrother of the hospital of St. John of Jerusalem, who was coming to Rome to

[1] *Correspondence Bekynton*, i. 155.   [2] Ibid. 157.

[3] Ibid. 158. It seems that these letters reached England in late Feb. or early
Mar. 1449. See the writs ordering payment to Master Mighet Amici coming from
the pope with letters of credence and to Master John Simonis de Lotharingia coming
with messages from the court of Rome (E 404/65/113).

[4] Processions were ordered in the province of York because of the king's frequent
illness and trouble in the country; they may provide the chief reason for this
decline (Wilkins, *Concilia*, iii. 560–2, 564).

[5] Franco-papal relations now resembled Anglo-papal conversations during
Martin V's pontificate; that is, Nicholas V wanted the pragmatic sanction abolished.
It may have been this desire that prompted a promise to reopen the trial of Joan of
Arc, though lack of papal success against the pragmatic sanction probably explains
why nothing definite was undertaken until the next pontificate (R. Aubenas
and R. Ricard, *L'Église et la Renaissance* in *Histoire de l'Église*, ed. A. Fliche and
V. Martin (Paris, 1951), pp. 26–7).

[6] G. G. Leibnitz, *Codex juris gentium diplomaticus* (Hanover, 1693), i. 405.

[7] 'Convellit Pontifex eas subreptitias literas, ac pronuntiat Richardum ducem
et alios conjuratos sacramento fidei Henrico Regi praestito obstrictos teneri'
(Raynaldus, *sub anno* 1453, no. xxi).

request the pope 'to graunte annum jubileum in lenton' next comyng in such place or places withinne this lande of Irlande as shawe thought good to the prior of the said order in England'.[1] This unedifying state of affairs continued from Nicholas V's pontificate throughout that of his successor Calixtus III and into the reign of Pius II.

With the loss of their territory abroad and the sporadic outbreaks of civil war at home, the English heard pleas from the pope (as well as those from the Kingdom of Hungary)[2] for aid against the Turks and support of the general Diet of Mantua with little sympathy. The English, like the Burgundians,[3] made preparations to offer their obedience to Pius in 1458. In return Pius sent Francesco Coppini, Bishop of Terni, to England to solicit aid against the Turkish infidels, to secure the promise of an English embassy to Mantua, and to pacify the country.[4] As a result of Coppini's entreaties, Henry VI did commission a small embassy to Mantua. On 16 May he appointed John Tiptoft, Earl of Worcester, the king's chaplain and Dean of Lincoln, Robert Fleming, Master Henry Sharp, and Master Richard Bole.[5] Anticipating that Tiptoft, who was travelling in Italy, might be unable to take up the commission, the king issued a similar letter which omitted the earl's name.[6] In July the king, goaded by Coppini's insistence, decided to appoint a larger embassy, which included the Bishop of Worcester, the Abbot of Peterborough, Lord Dudley, Sir Philip Wentworth, John Laxe, and others.[7] It may be, as the pope later heard, that these men

---

[1] E 28/85/8, 11. Letters to the pope on the same subject, to the cardinals, and letters of credence to the cardinals also survive in the same file (E 28/85/7, 10, 9; Rymer, xi. 351).

[2] Whethamstede, i. 268.   [3] Waurin, iv. 390.

[4] Whethamstede, i. 333–5.   [5] Rymer, xi. 422.

[6] Ibid. Considerable confusion exists about the final make-up of the English embassy to Mantua. R. J. Mitchell describes an embassy, commissioned in July likewise, composed of Tiptoft, Fleming, Henry Sharp, and Richard Bole, which she distinguishes from an embassy commissioned to congratulate Pius II upon his elevation. She does not reveal the sources upon which she builds these constructions (R. J. Mitchell, *John Tiptoft, 1427–1470* (London, 1938), p. 74). Mitchell offers an abbreviated and slightly different account of this embassy in *The Laurels and the Tiara, Pope Pius II, 1458–1464* (London, 1962). It is nevertheless inaccurate.

[7] *Proc. P.C.* iv. 302.

simply refused to obey the king, or perhaps, as Abbot Whethamstede reported, the outbreak of civil war hindered the dispatch of this larger embassy.[1] Furthermore, it seems certain that the Earl of Worcester never attended the Diet at Mantua.[2] It is likely that Robert Fleming, the king's proctor in Rome since 1455,[3] was already in Italy since he had recently received an order to tender the king's obedience to the late Calixtus III.[4] Bole may have been with Tiptoft.[5] Henry Sharp did attend the pope's council, for one of Pius II's letters dated September 1459 mentions Sharp's presence.[6] Thus it seems to have been the king's proctor at the curia and his prothonotary whose insignificance and improper credentials the pope so despised that he refused to admit them to his presence.[7]

To secure more favourable action on papal requests Coppini's status was enhanced by appointment as papal legate to England to transact certain arduous business.[8] But Henry neglected, or was unable to heed the legate's request for the pacification of the kingdom.[9] Consequently Coppini, despairing of success, decided to leave for Rome. At Calais he met the Earl of Warwick and agreed to accompany him and his troops to England, perhaps in return for

---

[1] Whethamstede, i. 33.

[2] Mitchell states (relying upon another undisclosed source) that Tiptoft took up his commission in the spring or early summer of 1461 when he set out for Rome (Mitchell, *John Tiptoft, 1427–1470*, p. 75). But Pius II had abandoned the Diet of Mantua in Jan. 1460.

[3] *Cal. Pat. Rolls, 1452–61*, p. 227.

[4] Ibid., p. 424. On 21 June 1458 a warrant was issued ordering the exchequer to pay him for this assignment (E 404/71/2/72).

[5] Mitchell, *John Tiptoft, 1427–1470*, p. 75. But again she does not exhibit her evidence.

[6] *Cal. Pap. Let., 1455–64*, pp. 556–7. In the records of the deliberations of the royal council on 7 May 1459 there is a note that Henry Sharp, who was going to the pope, was to receive an advance on his wages, and the same day that note was transformed into a warrant for issue. On 9 May Sharp withdrew £112 from the exchequer (E 28/88/46; E 404/71/3/74; E 403/819/m. 3). I can find no evidence for Miss Mitchell's assertion that Sharp was appointed the king's proctor at the court of Rome in Sept. 1459 (Mitchell, *John Tiptoft, 1427–1470*, p. 202 n. 25).

[7] Pius II, *Commentaries*, xxv. 269.

[8] 'Pro quibusdam arduis universalem ecclesiam orthodoxamque fidem, nostrum et apostolice sedis statum et honorem concernentibus negociis, nostrum et apostolice sedis nuncium et commissarium cum plena potestate legati de latere auctoritate apostolica tenore presencium facimus . . .' (B.M., Add. MS. 15384, ff. 34ʳ–41ʳʳ *Cal. Pap. Let., 1455–64*, p. 398). [9] P.R.O. 31/9/62/ ff. 301ʳ–307ʳ.

Warwick's suggestion that the legate be elevated to the rank of cardinal. Moreover, Coppini went so far as to raise the banner of the church in Warwick's army and to grant plenary remission to those who served in it;[1] his aim, so we learn from his correspondence with the Duke of Milan, was to raise up the Yorkists, who had intimated that they would launch an attack on France shortly—a project as dear to the legate's patron Francesco Sforza as to the Duke of Burgundy and to the disgruntled dauphin.[2] Although the Bishop of Terni eventually lost his see for this high-handed action, Pius II seems to have been pleased initially, for hardly had Edward IV seized the throne when the pope's letters of congratulation arrived. And Coppini, for his aid to the Yorkist cause, was rewarded with the post of king's proctor at the curia.[3]

These last episodes, interesting as they are, remain marginal to the main theme of Anglo-papal relations in the reign of Henry VI. Reviewing the course of these relations in general terms, it appears that the most active phase occurred during the pontificate of Martin V. With respect to England this pope's policies revolved entirely around the question of a redress of grievances in the matter of provisions. This was of particular importance to Martin, for after the long neglect of the papal states funds were urgently needed to put them in order. After the collapse of Martin's project, papal pressure on England greatly diminished. The English, for their part, once they had put their foot down, assumed a benevolent attitude towards the papacy. They sought to avert the schism developing in the late 1430s at the Council of Basel and to reaffirm the legitimacy of the pope's position. The English backed the papacy both with respect to the monarchical as against the conciliar principle and with respect to the rights of the Roman

---

[1] Pius II, *Commentaries*, xxv. 270; Basin, ii. 13.

[2] *Calendar of State Papers and Manuscripts existing in the Archives and Collections of Milan, 1385–1618*, ed. A. B. Hinds (London, 1912), pp. 29–30; C. L. Scofield, *The Life and Reign of Edward the Fourth* (London, 1923), i. 145. For two popular accounts of this embassy see P. M. Kendall, *Warwick the Kingmaker* (London, 1957), p. 64 *et passim*; J. R. Lander, *The Wars of the Roses* (London, 1965), pp. 102–3.

[3] Rymer, xi. 489.

incumbent as against the pretentions of the anti-pope Felix V. In this matter the French problem seems to have been uppermost in the minds of the English. If they could secure the support or at least the neutrality of other powers, their position would be correspondingly strengthened.

VIII

LAW AND PRACTICE IN
FIFTEENTH-CENTURY DIPLOMACY

MORE than fifty years have passed since J. N. Figgis propounded a maxim of medieval political theory that has now become a commonplace: 'in the Middle Ages the omnipotent territorial State, treated as a person, was non-existent'.[1] Historians of diplomacy in the later Middle Ages, while paying lip-service to this concept, have largely overlooked its significance. In theory, if not always in fact, the church presided over by the pope constituted the only authentic state in western Europe; secular governors served simply as the police arm of the state. Thus, disagreements between pope and emperor, seen in their proper context, were no more than quarrels between officers of the same institution. The laws of the Roman Empire, which was still regarded as a living entity,[2] were the foundation-stone of this state. Since the *corpus juris civilis*, amended by the accretions of time and by the industry of the glossators, furnished the primary governmental principles of Christendom, one might expect to find in this code the basic rules for settling differences between secular rulers.[3]

Adherence to rules such as these may have appertained in theoretical treatises—and for a brief period in fact—but universal agreement to work within this juristic framework

---

[1] J. N. Figgis, *Political Thought from Gerson to Grotius, 1414–1625* (repr. New York, 1960), p. 17.

[2] See, for example, F. Schneider, *Rom und Romgedanke im Mittelalter* (Munich, 1926); E. Dupré Theseider, *L'idea imperiale di Roma nella tradizione del Medioevo* (Milan, 1942); R. Folz, *L'Idée d'empire en Occident du Ve au XIVe siècle* (Paris, 1953).

[3] See especially the works of W. Ullmann, *The Growth of Papal Government in the Middle Ages* (London, 1955); *Principles of Government and Politics in the Middle Ages* (London, 1961); 'The Bible and Principles of Government in the Middle Ages', *La Bibbia nell'alto Medioevo* (Spoleto, 1963), pp. 181–227; and 'The Papacy as an Institution of Government in the Middle Ages', *Studies in Church History*, ii, ed. C. J. Cuming (London, 1965), pp. 78–101.

did not survive the early Middle Ages. The final destruction
of the sovereign power of the papacy over Christendom
during the Reformation furnished the immediate impetus
for the development of a new international law; the origins of
this radical change, however, stretch back several centuries.

No one has yet determined the exact implications of the
decline in respect for the papacy on the regulation of diplomatic conduct. Just as when Figgis's book appeared in
1900, the copious sources remain untapped in many areas.
It is true that Dr. Keen's monograph *The Laws of War in the
Late Middle Ages* deals with this problem, but his attention
is primarily focused on the rules governing sieges, the conditions necessary for a just war, and ransoms. Messrs. Chaplais
and Keen, and to a lesser extent Professors Cuttino and Post,
have fairly conclusively established that Roman private law
as adopted by the church furnished the frame of reference
for the settlement of differences between princes.[1] And
abundant proof exists from the fifteenth century to show
that diplomats owned, if they did not read and study,
treatises on Roman law.[2] But quite early in medieval

---

[1] P. Chaplais, 'Some Documents Regarding the Fulfilment and Interpretation
of the Treaty of Brétigny (1361–1369)', *Camden Miscellany Vol. XIX*, 3rd ser.
lxxx (1952), 51–84; M. H. Keen, *The Laws of War in the Late Middle Ages*
(London, 1965); G. P. Cuttino, *English Diplomatic Administration, 1259–1339*,
2nd edn. (Oxford, 1971); G. Post, *Studies in Medieval Legal Thought* (Princeton,
1964).

[2] No more than a cursory look through the *Register of Oxford* shows that men
such as Richard Andrew, the king's secretary, possessed copies of the *Digest*,
Innocent IV on the Decretals, the *Canones et decretales conciliorum xii seculi*, the
Sext, and the *Clementines* (i. 35), and Thomas Kent, clerk of the council, at one
time had such works as Baldus on the Decretals and on the *usus feudorum*, along
with two other works explaining the Decretals and a copy of the *Digest* (ii. 1038). In
addition to chronicles and Vegetius, the inventory of Sir John Fastolf's library
mentions a copy of the *Institutes (Hist. MSS. Com. 8th Report* (London, 1881), p. 267).
Henry VI had to write to Thomas Beckington, who had a treatise on reprisals
by Bartolus of Sassoferrato copied into one of his collections of diplomatic documents (B.M., Harley MS. 861, ff. 212ʳ–213ʳ), to return the royal copy of Hostiensis
so that someone else who worked as an envoy might use it (E 404/58/127); in addition the 'royal library' contained legal commentaries by Jacobus de Bello Visu and
Jacobus de Ravenna (PSO I/8/404). On the continent Alfonso V could boast of his
Vegetius and *De auctoritate conciliorum secundum grecos* (T. de Marinis, *La biblioteca napoletana dei re d'Aragona* (Milan, 1952), i. 9–10), the Counts of Angoulême
and of Dunois of a *Songe du vergier* (B.M., Add. Charter 8121), and Charles of
Orléans of his volumes of Christine de Pisan, Honoré Bonet, the *Institutes*, and the
English Dr. Sprever's *De summorum pontificum potestate* (P. Champion, 'La librairie
de Charles d'Orléans', *Bibliothèque du xvᵉ siècle*, vol. xi, 1910).

England the relationship between the forms provided by
Roman law and actual practice began to diverge appreciably.
Despite Bartolus's warning that such was the case, historians
have tended to disregard this asymmetry. As a result undue
emphasis has been placed on the normative value of established juristic traditions in the actual conduct of diplomacy.
Thus, the purpose of this chapter is first to examine the
influence of Roman law and the lawyers on the hierarchy of
diplomatic personnel; then to see how closely the legal
terminology embodied in letters, credences, and proxies
restricted the authority of diplomatic agents. Finally we
shall survey the factors alleged to invalidate a treaty, such
as the one concluded at Troyes in 1420.

The truth is that the political events noted above cost
the papacy an incalculable loss in prestige; consequently,
willingness to accept papal arbitration is tantamount (in
fifteenth-century England at least) to an acknowledgement
of weakness. The verbal jousts before Arras between the
pope and the Council of Basel, who were vying for the
prize of Franco-Burgundian reconciliation, if England could
not be brought into line, must account in part at least
for her indifference to papal pleas for ambassadors to the
Council of Florence and the Diet of Mantua and for the
fact that the English apparently never again considered
papal arbitration as a means of bringing the French wars
to a close.

In addition to the general background of disillusionment
created by papal behaviour, a detailed examination of the
foreign affairs of Henry VI's reign suffices to bring the
elaborate structure of a diplomatic *cursus honorum* tumbling
like a house of cards about the heads of its principal archi-
tects Miss Behrens and Professor Queller.[1] Despite the

---

[1] B. Behrens, 'Treatises on the Ambassador Written in the Fifteenth and Early
Sixteenth Centuries', *English Historical Review*, li (1936), 616–27; D. E. Queller,
'The Thirteenth-Century Diplomatic Envoys: Nuncii et Procuratores', *Speculum*,
xxv (1960), 196–213. Queller has recently enlarged and modified his views on
the hierarchy of diplomatic officials (*The Office of Ambassador in the Middle
Ages*, Princeton, 1967). His structure, now founded on evolutionary principles, includes the *nuncius*, the proctor, and the ambassador. The earliest of the
medieval diplomats, the *nuncius*, served as a speaking letter; he had no discretionary
authority, acting not according to his own volition, but following explicitly the
instructions of his master. With the rediscovery of Roman law and the expanding

complex notion of a diplomatic hierarchy that emerges from a reading of the canonists and civilians, in practice the theoretical distinction between *ambassiatores, oratores, legati, procuratores*, and *nuncii solempnes* does not obtain. In England at least, there were—so far as the meagre evidence admits a generalization—no more than two kinds of envoys: one was a messenger; the other had the power to negotiate. The variety of names assigned to these diplomats by their contemporaries had only an honorific function.

Although the hierarchy of diplomatic agents in medieval Europe (the proponents of this concept assert) did not become fixed until the end of the fifteenth or the beginning of the sixteenth century, its rudimentary forms are held to be present, especially in England, as early as the mid thirteenth century, for by that time the use of agents having full powers was common.[1] Briefly stated, this theory places the *legatus*—originally a general term for all agents but restricted by the thirteenth century to the papal *legatus a latere*, who was to see (according to Gregory VII) 'ut propriam faciem nostram seu nostrae viva vocis oracula . . .'[2]

diplomatic entanglements of the high Middle Ages, a new agent appears, the proctor. Roman law and its medieval commentators divided the office of proctor into several species, each with narrowly prescribed duties. Some of these Queller designates as diplomats. Finally, in the later Middle Ages, a super-*nuncius* appears, called an ambassador; ordinarily he had no discretionary authority. But his distinction between types of agents, as I have argued below, still seems over-subtle. Medieval minds trained in the sophistication of the scholastic method might have appreciated the difference between a bishop called *nuncius* and another called ambassador, between a *nuncius* with letters of proxy and a proctor with letters of credence, between an ambassador with full powers and an earl appointed proctor, but it seems more likely that the lawyers' admission of inconsistency should be taken literally. And how can one feel confident in such a structure where Frederick Barbarossa's agents at the Peace of Constance are 'mere *nuncii*' on p. 17, 'so-called *nuncii*' on p. 29, and 'proctors' on p. 47 ? The elegance of simplicity is a formula to be recommended to historians as well as scientists. See also the review by P. Chaplais in *History*, liii (1968), 403–4.

[1] In addition to the works cited above H. S. Lucas ('The Machinery of Diplomatic Intercourse', *The English Government at Work*, ed. J. F. Willard and W. A. Morris (Cambridge, Mass., 1940), i. 300–31), G. Cuttino (*Diplomatic Administration*, pp. 127–31), G. Mattingly (*Renaissance Diplomacy* (London, 1955), p. 33), and F.-L. Ganshof (*Le Moyen Âge* (Histoire des relations internationales, 1953), pp. 266–70) all adopt variants of this theory.

[2] 'Chronicle of Cosmas' in the *Monumenta Germaniae Historica* cited by F. Wasner, 'Fifteenth-Century Texts on the Ceremonial of the Papal Legatus a latere', *Traditio*, xiv (1958), 300.

—in the first position. Below the legate was the ambassador, rarely employed as a secular agent before the fifteenth century, when only princes and independent communes had the right to his services. The *procurator* held the next lower post. His functions were divided, according to Roman law, into that of an attorney for the case (*procurator litis*)—who was not really a diplomat—and an administrator (*procurator negotiorum*), who in turn was designated as either general or special. If general, he could not make peace, neither receive or take an oath, nor negotiate alone; if special, he was entitled by right of his *plena potestas* and *mandatum speciale* to treat for and commit irrevocably, within the terms of the grant, his constituent. The *nuncius*, if mere messengers (*cursores*) are excluded, occupied the lowest rank in this system. He might either negotiate an agreement or conclude it—not both; he could do anything the king could do by letter. The proctor had the power to use his own discretion and exercise his will while the *nuncius* simply related the will of his principal. Such, then, are the broad outlines of the hierarchical theory propounded by modern scholars.

Evidence for a hierarchy of diplomatic personnel existing at Rome (if nowhere else) has been seen in the quarrel that broke out between the English proctor at Rome, Thomas Polton, the Bishop of Chichester, and the King of Castile's ambassador, the Archbishop of Santiago de Compostela, in 1422.[1] In April of that year Pope Martin V wrote to King Henry, lest he should be astonished by gossip from the curia, that proceedings were to be instituted against the two bishops, who had begun brawling (*rixa*) at the altar during the celebration of the Easter mass.[2] Henry V, weighed down by the responsibility of the renewed war in France, responded quickly and bluntly to this distasteful news. With his own hand he wrote to the pope avowing his astonishment at the abuse his royal dignity suffered at the curia. The fact that the king himself wrote prompted Martin to reply speedily offering further explanation. The

[1] B. Behrens, 'The Office of English Resident Ambassador', *Transactions of the Royal Historical Society*, 4th ser. xiv (1933), 161–92; id. 'Origins of the Office of the English Resident Ambassador in Rome', *English Historical Review*, xlix (1934), 640–58.

[2] Haller, *England und Rom*, Beilage 5.

origin of the quarrel, it seems, lay in Polton's being accorded a less honourable place than the Castilian envoy at a public consistory. The reason, Martin proffered, was that at the time of the consistory Polton was not an ambassador but a proctor ('. . . usque tunc prefatus episcopus apud nos communi Romane curie opinione versabatur non ut orator, sed tantummodo procurator sublimitatis tue').[1] In fact, Polton had been the king's lawyer at the curia since 1414.[2]

The truth or falsity of the papal statement need not concern us. The matter should probably be taken as another episode in the series of acrimonious disputes between Spaniards and Englishmen over precedence which began at Constance and continued at Basel.[3] In this context the significant fact is the distinction drawn between *orator* and *procurator*. If one recalls that since the thirteenth century English monarchs had been accustomed to appoint lawyers to represent them at Rome and at the Parlement of Paris, a custom that persisted until the outbreak of the Hundred Years' War, then the distinction the pope wished to make becomes clearer. What he intended the king to understand was not that the Bishop of Chichester held an ambassadorial status inferior to the Archbishop of Compostela's, but that Polton had been ranked as a lawyer, one of the 'promoters of his nacione, as alle other Cristen kynges had in the courte of Rome',[4] and the Castilian as a diplomatic agent. Despite the confusion of terms in the pope's two letters, *nuncius* and *orator* are clearly employed to denote diplomats and *procurator* is never linked with either of these terms. Moreover, in Henry VI's reign, at least, when the king's proctor at Rome was entrusted to execute a diplomatic function he received a special letter of proxy. Although Robert Fleming, Henry's chaplain, received his appointment as the king's

---

[1] Moreover, he wrote, '. . . multum interest inter oratoris et procuratoris officia' (Haller, *England und Rom*, Beilage 6).

[2] Rymer, ix. 138.

[3] An interesting parallel to these disputes over precedence is one involving east-west relations. The Council of Florence almost broke up because the emperor refused to kiss the pope's foot and genuflect, and because Eugenius wished his throne to be placed in the middle of the church as if he were a mediator (D. J. Geanakoplos, *Byzantine East and Latin West: Two Worlds of Christendom in Middle Ages and Renaissance* (Oxford, 1966), pp. 97–8).

[4] Stevenson, *Wars*, ii. 442.

proctor at the curia in 1455, he accepted a special commission in 1458 to offer the king's obedience to Calixtus III
and further letters in 1459 empowering him to represent
the king at Mantua.[1] Finally, the term *procurator* is the
customary way to describe other lawyers at the curia,
representatives of both secular and ecclesiastical magnates;
and it has never been alleged that these men belonged to the
English diplomatic hierarchy.

In practice, as noted above, there were only two types of
envoy, whatever the names given to them in the documents.
The first of these agents can be designated the *nuncius* or
nuncius simplex, and the feature defining such an agent is his
letters of credence (*littere credencie, littere de credencia*). Letters
of credence are not letters of appointment, for they contain
no contract requiring the person designated in them to
carry out any specific task or to keep secret the business of
the king. Rather they served to identify the bearer as a seal
impression or a letter—the antecedents of letters of credence
—had done in Anglo-Saxon England,[2] or as a knight's
shield of arms, and to certify his trustworthiness. Writing in
1457 the Abbot of St. Albans put it in another way. Certain
priests from Hungary came to Henry VI's court that year
bearing letters testifying that they were telling the truth
about the advance of the Turks.[3] An agent with letters of
credence recited the instructions or credences (as they are
indifferently called) entrusted to him just as if the king himself were speaking, that is 'dar ferma fe e creença como si
nos personalment las vos deziamos'.[4] But he had no authority
to say anything more than the message he had been given.
To venture some private opinion that in no way obligated
his principal was possible. Pierre de Fontenay returned
from Navarre in 1421 with Don Carlos's outrageous
demands of the counties of Champagne and Brie as the
price of his adherence to the Treaty of Troyes. Rejecting
these claims, Henry V asked Fontenay what reasonable
compensation the King of Navarre would accept; the envoy

[1] *Cal. Pat. Rolls, 1452-61*, pp. 227, 424, 487; Rymer, xi. 422.
[2] P. Chaplais, 'The Anglo-Saxon Chancery: From Diploma to Writ', *Journal of the Society of Archivists*, iii (1966), 168-9.
[3] Whethamstede, i. 268.   [4] A.C.A., Registro 2689, f. 31ᵛ.

replied *ne de sa sceue mais le dist seulement par supposicion*; in other words, he told the king what *il ymaginoit et pensoit*.[1] Additionally, a number of accounts mention envoys going to explain why *nuncii solempnes*, that is envoys armed with full powers, had not been sent as requested. In 1425, for example, the Duke of Brabant sent an envoy *cum litera credencie* to Pope Martin to explain that plenipotentiaries had not arrived in Rome because the duke awaited the outcome of Bedford's and Burgundy's mediation:[2] the envoy's mission was to explain to the pope, not wring concessions from him.

At this point the temptation is to see sixteenth-century practice as a continuation from the late Middle Ages, for by then there could be no diplomatic status at all without letters of credence. Or, as Chief Justice Coke put it, 'At this day [*temp*. Eliz. I] there could be no Ambassadour without letters of credence of his sovereign . . . .[3]' Unfortunately, in the fifteenth century letters of credence were sealed with one of the lesser seals, and the originals and their copies, partly because of the fire at Whitehall which destroyed the signet archives, but chiefly because of the ephemeral nature of documents drafted under smaller seals, have almost entirely disappeared. But there is one small piece of evidence that survives from this period, a letter to the Duke of Milan from his agent in France.[4] 'I have no letter of credence,' he wrote, 'and it does not seem decent to me to base one's operations upon mere words without the guarantee of letters.' Surely this is simply another way of saying that one might not be recognized as an envoy without letters of credence.

If letters of credence, as the argument from silence and the future use to which that document was put lead one to believe, comprise the essential factor in determining who is and who is not an envoy, then it is important to know who could issue such letters. In fact anyone could. The Bishop of Tournai sent his nephew to the Medici factor at Bruges 'pour vous

---

[1] B.N., MS. Dupuy 223, ff. 224ᵛ–225ʳ.   [2] Dynter, iii. 453–4.
[3] E. Coke, *The Fourth Part of the Institutes of the Laws of England* . . ., 6th edn. (London, 1681), p. 153.
[4] *Cal. State Pap. Milan*, p. 99.

dire et exposer aucunes choses qui grandement me touchent';[1]
Richard, Duke of York, received from his son a request 'to
yeve ful faith and credence' to what his envoy related about
the evil-doing of Richard Croft and his brother;[2] and in
1460 the Abbot of St. Albans found nothing strange in
receiving Lord Sudley's *nuncius* with information about
selling the reversion of the manor of More.[3] Thus in the
late Middle Ages little attention was paid to the lawyers'
dictum that only sovereign powers, independent communes,
and perhaps great princes could employ ambassadors;
instead the rule was that much-quoted maxim: 'Quicumque
ab alio mittitur legatus dici potest . . . '.[4]

Letters of credence, drawn up and issued as letters close,
varied considerably in form and content; however, their
form (in the fifteenth century) resembles that which Professor
Cuttino observed for the fourteenth century.[5] The first
clause addressed either an individual or a group. To the
supreme pontiff, the emperor, or a prince of equal status the
address opened (just as in ordinary letters) with the name
and style of the recipient followed by the name of the
English king and his style;[6] in letters to inferiors the formula
was reversed. Deviation from this practice indicated an
insult, and perhaps the approach of war.[7] In the letters of
defiance that the King of Scotland sent to England in 1456,
for example, the traditional formula is reversed.[8] And
Shakespeare illuminates the rupture of Anglo-Burgundian
relations in 1435 by having Gloucester comment on a
change in the way Burgundy customarily addressed the
king:[9]

---

[1] Grunzweig, *Correspondence Medici*, pp. 4–5.

[2] *Original Letters Illustrative of English History*, ed. H. Ellis, 2nd ser. (London, 1827), vol. i, no. v.

[3] Whethamstede, i. 357–60.

[4] Hrabar, *De Legatis et Legationibus tractatus varii* (Dorpat, 1905), p. 32.

[5] Cuttino, *Diplomatic Administration*, p. 157.

[6] Henry VI's royal style was invariably *Henricus rex Anglie et Francie et dominus Hibernie* on letters originating in the English chancery; letters drawn up for the administration of the French government reversed the position of *Anglie* and *Francie*.

[7] The Byzantine emperor balked at accepting the Decree of Union in 1439 because it began with the pope's name, not his (Geanokoplos, *Byzantine East and Latin West*, p. 107).

[8] *Correspondence Bekynton*, ii. 139–41.

[9] *1 Henry VI*, IV, i.

What means his Grace, that he hath chang'd his style?
No more, but plain and bluntly, 'To the King'.
Hath he forgot he is his sovereign?
Or doth this churlish superscription
Pretend some alterations in good will?

Although a putative letter from the Sultan beginning
'Johannes Soldanus, quondam Christianus . . . Christiano-
rum inimicus et desolator . . . magno Sacerdoti Romanorum'
apparently went unchallenged in Rome,[1] when the King of
Portugal's cousin failed to accord Pius II his correct style,
torrents of abuse poured down on the young man's head.
'We pardon you your youth', Pius wrote, 'you do not yet
know in what terms the majesty of the supreme bishop
should be addressed. Because you are of royal blood, do you
scorn Christ's Vicar? Christ's rank is far loftier than yours.'[2]
Finally, the English rightly judged the Flemings' attitude
to be hostile when they received a schedule containing
articles about a truce in which was found 'une peisant et
odiouse parole, cest assavoir celly que se dit roy Dengleterre'.[3]

After the address, the king notified the recipient that the
bearer of the letter was authorized to speak for his master.
Then the subject of the mission was often inserted, but
rarely with any details. The supplication, which asked that
the person to whom the envoy had been sent believe what
was told him, was followed by a dating clause, giving the
place, the day, and the month. Customarily, privy seal clerks
drew up these letters in Latin and affixed the privy seal on to
the tag used to close the letters. However, letters of credence
in both French and Latin were issued under the signet.[4]

The powers of the simple *nuncius* could be increased by
giving him letters of proxy (*littere procurationis, potestates,
procuratoria*), which allowed him to confer and to make
agreements on behalf of his principal; letters of proxy
established the authority of the envoy as the personal representative of his sovereign with the power to commit the
sovereign, with the exception of certain cases noted below,

[1] Whethamstede, i. 269.
[2] Pius II, *Commentaries*, p. 128.
[3] B.M., Add. Charter 1397.
[4] *Proc. P.C.* iv. 137–8; *Correspondence Bekynton*, i. 86.

to ratify the acts of his agent. Armed with such powers the simple *nuncius* became the *nuncius solempnis*. By the fifteenth century the solemn *nuncii*, previously called *procuratores*, *legati*, and *oratores*, were usually designated *ambaxiatores*: 'ambaxiatorum nomen modernum est.'[1] Of this diplomatic agent the lawyers have much to say. The ambassador like the papal legate was under the special protection of the pope; those who molested an ambassador committed the sin of sacrilege whose punishment was excommunication. Moreover, the guilty party was to be handed over to the country whose ambassador he had molested, and in the fifteenth century (so the lawyers stated) the punishment for abducting an ambassador on his mission was death. There were, however, certain limits to ambassadorial immunity. The pope apparently thought ambassadors at the curia who were clerks came under the normal provisions of canon law. By extension the prince to whom an ambassador was sent could attempt to punish a foreign agent for such crimes as murder, treason, and conspiracy just as if he were that prince's subject. But, as Conradus Brunus remarked,[2] such immunities were often violated with impunity.

Although the nature of the mission and the importance of the court at which the mission was executed determined in large part the ambassador's social position, there were certain general characteristics all ambassadors were expected to possess. In addition to having the reputation of a paragon of virtue, the envoy should be middle-aged so that neither the violent passions of youth nor the slowness of mind and body that accompanies old age was apparent. An ambassador should be a competent orator, moderate, humble, intelligent, not given to avarice, and a good spy.

In practice medieval rulers looked for similar traits when they selected their diplomatic agents. Louis XI required that his ambassadors to the English court be distinguished, learned, discreet, confident, and dependable to carry out the business at hand.[3] The chronicler Waurin, noting the places

---

[1] Hrabar, *De Legatis*, p. 33.

[2] Conradus Brunus, *De Immunitate legatorum* (Lyons, 1541), pp. 150–2.

[3] *Lettres de Louis XI, roi de France*, ed. É. Charavay *et al.* (Société de l'histoire de France, 1883–1909), viii. 32.

the Duke of Cleves passed on his way to Mantua, recalled that the local populace received him with honour as much because of his personal eminence as the fact that he was the Duke of Burgundy's envoy.[1] Christine de Pisan echoes a similar sentiment, '. . . send suche ambaxadours that be moost nygh thy noble person . . . in whom thou most trusteth'.[2] And numerous English council documents testify the concern for selecting ambassadors of suitable character, though Commynes thought that the English lost skirmishes at the conference table because they were unable to select suitable envoys.[3] Furthermore, as the English learned at Mantua,[4] if persons of unsuitable rank were chosen, they might not be received or the king might be subjected to a scathing rebuke like the one Pope Pius II hurled at the Emperor Frederick III: 'You however have neither come nor sent ambassadors worthy of such an occasion [the Diet of Mantua] or of yourself. Those who observe this think that you are either stingy and are trying to economise or careless for the defence of the faith. . . . If you cannot do this [i.e. come in person], at least send ambassadors of distinguished rank and prestige and do not let the Church of God perish through this indifference (or must we say avarice?) of yours.'[5]

The solemn envoy's letters of proxy furnish convincing evidence of the decaying influence of Roman law on diplomatic conduct. The form of letters of proxy drawn up for the solemn *nuncius* was that of a letter patent under the great seal. The first clause was the protocol customary for letters patent. The clause of constitution, occasionally beginning with a solemn proem stating the reasons the king was impelled to negotiate,[6] recorded that certain persons named therein had been made, deputed, and constituted envoys of the king. The third clause usually

[1] Waurin, iv. 114–15.

[2] Christine de Pisan, *The Book of Fayttes of Armes and of Chyvalrye*, ed. A. T. P. Byles (*Early English Text Society*, 1932), pp. 73–4.

[3] Commynes, i. 276.   [4] See above, pp. 142–3.

[5] Pius II, *Commentaries*, p. 205.

[6] These reasons, generally pious, were mostly derived from quotations or paraphrases of the Scripture—Genesis 1: 26 being alleged as a reason for matrimony (Rymer, xi. 7).

included a grant of *plena potestas* and *mandatum generale et speciale*, stated the requirements for a minimum quorum to conclude a binding agreement, and noted the reason for undertaking the embassy. In the clause of *ratihabitio* the king promised in advance for himself and his heirs to abide by the agreement concluded by his envoys, even if no more than the minimum quorum had agreed to it. The clause of corroboration (*corroboracio*) was followed by the date. Unlike normal letters patent a full place date—*in palacio nostro Westm'* instead of *apud Westm'*[1]—and the year of the incarnation as well as the regnal year were generally given. *Per ipsum regem*, the usual note of warranty both before and after Henry VI's reign, gave way while he occupied the throne to *per breve de privato sigillo* (more rarely to *per concilium* or *per regem et concilium*). The great seal in white wax was appended on a tag.

It is commonly agreed that this letter of proxy, 'the envoy's most important letter', gave him the power to act. It bestowed negotiatory authority. The first stage of full-scale meetings between ambassadors, the examination of proxies, bears witness to the function of this document. Alfonso V's envoys at Bayonne in 1431 decided to seek additional instructions before negotiating with the English because they believed that a minor was unable to grant letters of proxy.[2] At the Anglo-French conference at Bonport during the summer of 1449, the French envoy Jean L'Enfant, when he learned that the English had not brought their letters of procuration to the conference table, declared that he and his colleagues laboured in vain with men who had no power.[3] Treaties with the Count of Mark and with the Bishop of Münster were not ratified because the powers of the envoys had not been sufficient.[4] And at the Congress of Arras the English, on the one hand, insisted that the French obtain new full powers because the number of ambassadors was unclear and Henry VI had only been

[1] H. C. Maxwell-Lyte, *Historical Notes on the Use of the Great Seal of England* (London, 1926), p. 237.

[2] Appendix II, no. 3.

[3] *Narratives of the Expulsion of the English from Normandy*, ed. J. Stevenson (Rolls Series, 1863), p. 495.

[4] See above, p. 61.

styled *rex Anglie;* the French, on the other hand, persisted in their demand for new proxies from the English, the old ones having omitted the year of the incarnation and referred to the King of France as *Karolus de Valoys* instead of *adversarius noster* as was their custom.[1] Finally, in a letter dated 27 February 1459 the pope, noting the arrival of the Castilian envoys at Mantua, thanked their king for sending sealed letters (*procuratorium*) empowering the envoys to act for him.[2] Two hundred years later the French ambassadors at Münster succinctly summed up the reason for such careful scrutiny of these letters: 'Ces commissaires n'ont en effect dessin que d'entrer en conference pour ecoutir et fair raport avant que rien resoudre . . . '.[3]

That the procuration conferred power to treat on behalf of the grantor has given rise to the assumption that it also defined the limits within which decisions could be made. The phrasing of these letters, which borrows words having precise, technical meanings in both civil and canon law and which are couched in terms of a contract, buttressed this assumption substantially. In these letters the duly constituted envoy was often styled *nuncius, procurator, orator,* and even *negociorum gestio,* that is a *voluntarius procurator.* He had *plena potestas* and *mandatum speciale* (a term whose precise interpretation is still vexed by conflated passages in the *Digest*)[4] to carry out the king's business, even though, as one scholar has argued, the result was contrary to the king's will.[5] And the king promised *bona fide et verbo regio* to ratify whatever his envoy did.

This attractive theory cannot be substantiated by the realities of English diplomatic practice in the fifteenth century. Although the *littere procuracionis* delegated authority to act, it was the *instrucciones* or *credencie* that defined the extent of the envoy's discretion. The form of these documents has considerable interest. Until the end of Edward III's

---

[1] *Proc. P.C.* v. 343–4, cited in Dickinson, *Arras,* p. 134.

[2] Trame, *Rodrigo Sánchez de Arévalo,* p. 98.

[3] Cited in J. Mervyn Jones, *Full Powers and Ratifications* (Cambridge, 1946), p. 7.

[4] A. Watson, *Contract of Mandate in Roman Law* (Oxford, 1961), p. 40; W. Buckland, *The Main Institutions of Roman Private Law* (Cambridge, 1931), p. 51. See also Watson, *The Law of Obligations in the Later Roman Republic* (Oxford, 1965).

[5] Watson, *Contract of Mandate,* pp. 38–9, 60.

reign instructions were drafted as bipartite chirographs, sealed from about 1340. That is to say, the king's wishes were set out in duplicate on a piece of parchment that was then cut in half, separating the two recitals; one was to be kept in England, the other was presumably presented upon demand at the destination of the embassy. In the late fourteenth century the diplomatic of these documents changed; instructions were drawn up to which the great seal, the privy seal, and the signet were appended on tags.[1] That the external appearance of credences had changed by the beginning of the fifteenth century, is of no particular consequence in itself. (Letters of credence, issued under the great seal in the mid fourteenth century, had come to be issued under the smaller seals and of their enrolment no trace has yet come to light.) But if one recalls that the diplomatic of the royal testament changed at precisely the same time and in the same way as the form of instructions, then the change is of considerable interest.[2]

Royal wills before Edward III's time took the form of bipartite chirographs. Professor Hazeltine has argued, and Father M. Sheehan confirmed, that testaments are a type of contract in which one person agrees in the presence of witnesses to make certain *donaciones post obitum* to a beneficiary or beneficiaries.[3] Record of this contract, which in Anglo-Saxon England at least was made orally, was often embodied in a chirograph; that is, the chirograph itself was not a contract, but evidence of it. Transferring this argument to diplomacy, an envoy's instructions become the record of an oral contract between him and the king, probably made in the presence of the council, obligating the envoy to carry

---

[1] E 39/102/3 is a surviving original with all three seals intact. There are variant forms of instructions. From time to time instructions carried only the great and the privy seals (Stevenson, *Wars*, iii. 431–3), the privy seal and signet (*Proc. P.C.* i. 323–37), only the privy seal (*Le Cotton MS. Galba B. I*, ed. E. Scott and L. Gilliodts-van Severen (Brussels, 1896), p. 346). The precise significance of these variants, if they are more than a matter of convenience, has eluded me.

[2] P. Chaplais, 'English Diplomatic Documents to the End of Edward III's Reign', *The Study of Medieval Records, Essays in honour of Kathleen Major*, ed. D. A. Bullough and R. L. Storey (Oxford, 1971), p. 37. This idea is to be discussed at greater length in the author's forthcoming introduction to the Treaty Rolls.

[3] *Anglo-Saxon Wills*, ed. D. Whitelock (Cambridge, 1930), pp. xxi–xxvi; M. M. Sheehan, *The Will in Medieval England* (Toronto, 1963), pp. 19–66.

out certain business for the king. In return—and reciprocity is essential for any contract—the agent received his expenses, though this is not mentioned in the credence. Since written evidence was not necessary to certify the validity of such a contract, some instructions, particularly those that were better kept secret, were apparently never written down. Witnesses to the contract between the king and his representative would assure faithful execution of the commission. In any case after 1390 the change in diplomatic meant that only one authenticated copy of the instructions, unless the drafts were systematically filed or enrolled, was drawn up, and it seems to have served chiefly as an *aide-mémoire* for the envoy.

If instructions outweigh full powers in circumscribing the envoy's activity, one ought to find evidence corroborating this hypothesis in cases where ambassadors violated the contract they had made with the king. The notorious case of William de la Pole, Duke of Suffolk, who was charged with promising the county of Maine to Charles VII in return for a truce,[1] appears to be the only fifteenth-century trial for which substantial evidence exists.

William de la Pole, the grandson of the Yorkshire merchant who had established the family's fortune in Edward III's reign, had succeeded to the earldom of Suffolk on the deaths of his father and eldest brother at Agincourt and Harfleur. Between 1417 and 1430 he was fighting in France (except for the period spent as the Count of Dunois's prisoner), becoming commander of the English forces not long before they withdrew from the siege of Orléans. Afterwards Suffolk concentrated his attention on politics in England. In November 1431 Henry VI's council admitted him to membership, where he took up the cause of peace which his Beaufort relatives championed. Apart from a temporary setback when the peace negotiations at Arras failed and the council's war party gained the ascendancy, his influence steadily increased. In 1440 his party overrode the Duke of Gloucester's plea not to liberate Charles of Orléans and subsequently squelched Humphrey's scheme

---

[1] *D.N.B.* xlvi. 50–6; *Complete Peerage*, xi, pt. i, 433–48.

for an Armagnac wedding, fostering instead a marriage alliance with Margaret of Anjou. Although he protested against being sent to conclude this arrangement because of his French connections (in addition to making friends with his captor Dunois he had been Orléans' warden), the king appointed him. When the negotiations had been completed, Henry sent him and his wife to fetch Margaret from France. The story of the fruitless Anglo-French negotiations leading up to a renewal of the war after the sack of Fougères need not be pursued here. It is sufficient to note that the rapid loss of Normandy in 1449–50 put parliament in a bad mood, and they began to look for a scapegoat. Suffolk was the obvious choice. Following the deaths of Gloucester— which some attributed to him—and of Beaufort, Suffolk virtually governed the kingdom, bypassing the council and conducting business directly through the king. If the charge that he helped himself to money in the exchequer cannot be proved, the accusations that he had impoverished the king by obtaining an excessive number of lucrative grants and that he had perverted royal justice could. Thus—shortly after his chief opponent, Lord Cromwell, was assaulted (28 November 1449) by one of Suffolk's henchmen, William Tailboys, who managed to avoid arrest and arraignment— the Commons presented the king with a list of accusations against the marquis, by then duke. Mr. C. L. Kingsford's account of this whole incident largely ignored, as we shall, the charges of financial peculation, perversion of justice, and the like to concentrate on the allegation that Suffolk was responsible for the English losing Maine and Le Mans to Charles VII. Without further evidence, however, neither the duke's guilt nor innocence can be positively established. Although in view of the years that passed between the act and the charge Mr. Kingsford exculpated Suffolk, we have seen that there are equally good reasons why either the duke or his henchman Adam Moleyns would have made such a promise. Be that as it may, it is the charge itself that is of interest.

The Commons meeting on 7 February 1450 declared that the king had commissioned the Earl of Suffolk, 'being next and grettest of your counceill', to obtain a treaty of

peace with Charles VII.[1] Suffolk of course knew what
discussions had preceded this decision to send an embassy
to France, what conclusions had been reached and what
'power and auctorite committed to all your [the king's]
ambassiatours sent in this behalf'. While in France, the
Commons claimed, he 'hath deceyvably and traiterously, by
his letters and messages, discovered and opened to your
seid grete ennemye Charles, callyng hymself kyng of
Fraunce, all instructions and informations geven to your
seid ambassiatours afore their commyng into Fraunce'. As a
result efforts to secure a peace treaty came to naught and the
English had to sue for a truce. Furthermore, he personally
promised to have Maine and Le Mans returned to the
French. King Henry dismissed the case, but the Commons renewed their onslaught in March and the duke was
banished for five years. Pirates lying in wait for his
Channel crossing intercepted his boat and murdered him.

Modern scholars (as noted above) writing on the subject,
with the single exception of Dr. Chaplais, apparently believe
that full powers defined the scope of an embassy. Now this
embassy received two letters of procuration: one (dated at
the royal manor at Sheen on 11 February 1443) gave as its
purpose the concluding of perpetual peace;[2] the other,
bearing the same date, contained authority to conclude
'good, firm and stable truces on land and sea' that would
last as long as the ambassadors thought suitable, and to
appoint conservators of the truce, whose duty was to ensure
its effectiveness by correcting infractions.[3] Yet note, nothing
in either of these letters prevented Suffolk from offering to
restore Le Mans, Maine, indeed all of Lancastrian France,
if this would bring peace. As the duke himself is reputed to
have remarked, 'his said power was large and sufficiant
discharge for him to have reasonably departed the kynge's
title'.[4] Extending one's powers to the uttermost, to borrow
Hall's phrase,[5] was no crime, though it might be dangerous. To break contract with the king by exceeding his
instructions, which would contain the specific limits beyond

[1] *Rot. parl.*, v. 178.   [2] Rymer, xi. 60–1.   [3] Rymer, xi. 62–3.
[4] *Hist. MSS. Com. 3rd Report* (London, 1872), Appendix, p. 280.
[5] Hall, p. 203.

which the ambassador could not make concession—if it could be proved—was a crime. Violating the oath of the royal councillor not to reveal the king's secrets not only constituted treason,[1] but imperilled the soul's salvation.[2]

In theory the pope guaranteed the immunity of an ambassador from ordinary arrest. Yet in fact fifteenth-century ambassadorial privilege and immunity existed in a very primitive form; neither the credentials of an ambassador nor the herald's coat of arms provided a talisman assuring the bearer freedom from arrest. If the dignity of the office had included freedom from arrest, then acquisition of letters of safe conduct would have been gratuitous, and letters such as the English king received from his envoy to Rome, the Bishop of Chichester, complaining of the dangers inherent in crossing Brabant without a safe conduct, unintelligible.[3] In 1456 Sigismundo Malatesta wantonly attacked the retinue of Sánchez de Arévalo, the King of Castile's envoy to the pope, and stole some mules, which Sigismundo refused to give up despite Calixtus III's intervention.[4] Christine de Pisan might as well have spoken to the wind when she asserted that 'theyre thynges shall be sure and sauffe'.[5] And as late as 1538 French envoys on their way to the Sublime Porte to conclude an alliance against the Emperor Charles V were murdered by the emperor's soldiers when they crossed into territory belonging to Milan.[6] No redress was offered. Likewise Honoré Bonet averred that 'according to the written law ambassadors and legates pass in security through a country . . . [and] no man may hinder or disturb or injure them'.[7] But Guillaume Cousinot, a French ambassador to Scotland in 1455, remained in prison for three years after he was shipwrecked on the English coast, and Charles VII had to increase the salt tax in Normandy to underwrite his ransom.[8] The

[1] J. F. Baldwin, *The King's Council in England during the Middle Ages* (Oxford, 1913, reissue 1969), pp. 345 ff.
[2] Christine de Pisan, pp. 239–40.   [3] B.M., Add. MS. 24062, f. 169ʳ.
[4] Trame, *Rodrigo Sánchez de Arévalo*, p. 85.
[5] Christine de Pisan, p. 324.
[6] G. R. Elton, *Reformation Europe, 1517–1559* (London, 1963), p. 240.
[7] H. Bonet, *The Tree of Battles*, ed. and trans. G. W. Coopland (Liverpool, 1949), p. 186.   [8] *Chronique de la pucelle, pièces justificatives*, pp. 76–80.

ostensible reason for Cousinot's arrest, and no doubt for the Florentine ambassador's to Charles VI who spent the years between 1406 and 1408 in a French gaol,[1] was that they were 'annemis et malveillans'.

Princes not at war might uphold the lawyers' dicta: the Duke of Burgundy released two Englishmen captured in Brabant because (Waurin heard) the Duke of Burgundy had not exchanged letters of defiance with Henry at that time.[2] Martin V's reminder that even the Saracens and Turks honoured envoys was intended as a rebuke to the English who had imprisoned the papal agent Obizzi.[3]

Envoys who had safe conducts were a different matter. For arresting such an agent from Scotland, the English were properly excoriated as 'evil islanders, who are born with tails'.[4] The English king regarded murder and assault of an ambassador to his court, not as a violation of the envoy's immunity, but as an infringement of his letters of safe conduct, and violation of letters of safe conduct was treason. Although the outcome of the case is unknown, the tavern keeper who attacked a member of Sancho de Roxas' party for taking liberties with the barmaid was hauled away to the Tower for breaking the king's safe conduct. Earlier, in the third year of Richard II's reign, two citizens of London had been attainted of high treason for the murder of the Genoese envoy, John Imperial, who was in England under Richard's safe conduct.[5] Murder like this was a *justi belli causa*. This fact the English were not slow to appreciate when Charles V declared war because some ambassadors sent to the Duke of Lancaster 'were slayn in that journey or waye'.[6]

In short, the concept of ambassadorial immunity and extraterritoriality meant little in fifteenth-century Europe. An envoy might reasonably expect to travel freely and safely

[1] L. Mirot, 'Un Conflit diplomatique au xve siècle: l'arrestation des ambassadeurs florentins en France (1406–1408)', *Bibliothèque de l'École des Chartes*, xcv (1934), 74–115.

[2] Waurin, iv. 114–15.

[3] Haller, *England und Rom*, pp. 51–9.

[4] *Cal. State Pap. Milan*, p. 16.

[5] Coke, *Institutes*, p. 56.

[6] Christine de Pisan, p. 17.

through countries with whom his prince was on friendly
terms, but this was a courtesy accorded to merchants as
well. What mattered was whether the envoy had a safe conduct or not; without such security he was no better than a
spy and, if caught, could expect corresponding treatment.
Not until Queen Elizabeth's time did extraterritoriality
catch on because a prince's failure to accord this right 'may
at another time return the like disadvantage of his own
agents and ambassadors . . . '.[1]

One other official whose duties sometimes included
diplomatic ones must be mentioned, for the herald as envoy
has been little studied.[2] By Edward I's death the office of
King of Arms, ultimately derived from the minstrels, had
been functioning for some years. In addition to serving as
ambassadors and king's messengers, heralds proclaimed,
prohibited, and adjudicated tournaments and assisted the
marshal (to whom they were responsible) at coronations.
Military and diplomatic tasks had been added to the
herald's duties by the beginning of Edward III's reign.
(In 1333 Dundee Herald was sent to ask for a parley, and
Hereford Herald had been sent in 1376 to Flanders 'in
secretis negociis regis'.) Yet, in spite of the scanty fourteenth-
century evidence and the plentiful material from the fifteenth
century, it has been affirmed that the herald was a true
ambassador only when he went to a place to which one would
not ordinarily send an accredited ambassador and that even
then he had no powers, instructions, or letters of credence.[3]
Even the lawyers do not countenance this belief. Nicholas
Upton, Duke Humphrey's servant, clearly states that the
function of a herald is to initiate negotiations for peace and
for matrimonial alliances between princes and to report
faithfully his mission.[4] In fact, the role of the herald in
late medieval diplomacy seems rather underestimated. At
Barnet in 1471 a herald was used to ask for negotiations

---

[1] M. Hale, *Historia placitorum coronae; The History of the Pleas of the Crown*
(London, 1736), i. 98–9.

[2] A. R. Wagner, *Heralds and Heraldry in the Middle Ages*, 2nd edn. (London,
1960); N. Denholm-Young, *History and Heraldry 1254–1310* (Oxford, 1965).

[3] R. de Maulde, 'Les Instructions diplomatiques au Moyen-Âge', *Revue d'histoire
diplomatique*, vi (1892), 433.

[4] N. Upton, *De Studio militari*, ed. E. Bysshe (London, 1654), pp. 20–1.

and stated his party's terms.[1] A draft of letters of credence for Garter King of Arms dated 2 December 1432 survives and has been printed; instructions exist for a herald going to the King of Scotland to remonstrate with him about not paying his ransom.[2] Before he crossed the Somme in 1475 Edward IV sent a herald to declare war on Louis XI and at the same time this herald 'took occasion to tell him [Louis XI] either of his own head or from some private instruction that if he had any proposal to make he must apply to the Lords Howard and Stanley . . .'.[3] But undoubtedly messenger service was the herald's most common duty: the royal council appointed Aquitaine King of Arms to take letters to the emperor and to the council of Constance, and Gloucester Herald to take letters to the kings of Castile, Portugal, Aragon, and Navarre in February 1416.[4] In 1430 the king appointed a herald to bring back news from France; five years later French heralds were sent from Arras to publish news of the treaty throughout France.[5] A more ordinary message involved no more than a request for safe conducts, or delivering ratification of agreements to the opposed side. The herald's coat of arms may have served as a sufficient safe conduct for him, but this was not invariably the case. The English council recorded an instance in which a herald who, sent to France for letters of safe conduct, was imprisoned.[6]

If the king's safe conduct provided safety for an individual from a foreign country, his truce provided the same security for those it covered. Like the safe conduct the truce was a royal security recording the king's protection of persons and goods for the specified period in which the war was in abeyance. Moreover, it furnished 'hope of peace', for during the truces ways and means to reconcile the opposing parties were to be sought. That is, a truce was a temporary peace at whose conclusion the agreeing parties (unless it had been prolonged by further agreements) found themselves again at war; and like instructions and credences the form

[1] P. M. Kendall, *Warwick the Kingmaker* (London, 1957), p. 357.
[2] *Proc. P.C.* iii. 259; iv. 137–8.
[3] *Chronicles of the White Rose of York*, ed. J. Giles (London, 1845), p. 164.
[4] *Proc. P.C.* iii. 192.
[5] Rymer, x. 505; Dickinson, *Arras*, p. 106.   [6] *Proc. P.C.* i. 103.

8218400   N

it took was that of a legal bond or contract by which two parties bound themselves to do or to cease doing something for their common benefit. The right to conclude a truce, although it could be delegated, was the prerogative of a sovereign prince.[1] Thus in addition to the innumerable royal peaces and truces that mark intervals in the French wars, a number of local agreements, made presumably without the king's special knowledge, survive. The treaty marking the capitulation of Vitry and other fortresses in 1424 concluded between the emissaries of the Duke of Bedford and La Hire is one convenient example.[2] Without delegated authority such activity was treasonable.

The point that diplomacy is essentially *negocium regis* has been overworked. However, the tendency to read history backwards and talk about treaties between the French and English nations in the Middle Ages as if these peoples formed self-conscious entities and had some part in making decisions about foreign policy may justify this repetition. In diplomacy, France and England between 1422 and 1461 are merely their kings writ large.

Treaties to which England was a party in the mid fifteenth century usually had their origin in a protocol. When the ambassadors deputed by the king had reached a satisfactory agreement with the representatives of the opposite party, the articles were drawn up in duplicate. Beginning with the names of the responsible parties, that is those properly accredited as envoys, the document concluded with their seals on tags, and increasingly often signatures of the envoys. Treated like a sealed chirograph except for the differences in the address, signature, and seals, the copy signed and sealed by the English was delivered to the other party while the copy the English received went technically to the king, but more likely to his advisers for scrutiny and deliberation. Having taken the decision to ratify the agreement, the king ordered the drafting, sometimes in both Latin and French and occasionally in English as well. The form the ratification took resembles that of the *inspeximus*.

[1] M. Keen, 'Treason Trials under the Law of Arms', *Transactions of the Royal Historical Society*, 5th ser. xii (1963), 97–8.

[2] Archives Nationales, J. 643.

It was issued under the great seal in white wax if the agreement had a time limit, in green (like grants of land) if the agreement was a perpetual peace.[1] Beginning with a clause stating that the king had read and approved the agreement, a verbatim repetition of the envoy's protocol followed, and the document concluded with the king's promise to ratify, the corroboration, and the date.

Since a truce (or peace for that matter) was a royal contract, it could be broken only with good cause. For when a king broke his agreement, as Henry VI did with the Count of Armagnac, he left himself open to the malevolence of fate, according to the *Brut*.[2] Consequently, it was a capital offence for one of the king's subjects to break a truce, and if Hostiensis's theory worked in practice, the violator could also be excommunicated.[3] During Lent in 1440, for instance, a group of pirates set upon foreign ships, which had come to provision London with food, murdered the men aboard and threw their bodies into the Thames. Two of the pirates, having been caught, tried, and convicted 'þat they break the kynges trewes and pease', were hanged with 'cheynes and colers of Iron, till they be wasted and spent'.[4] So highly prized was the sanctity of truces that Henry V promulgated a statute making it high treason to break a truce or peace, but in the middle of his son's reign it was suspended for seven years and finally the treason clause was expunged.

Since the corner-stone of Henry VI's foreign policy rested on the treaty made at Troyes in 1420, its validity formed the chief bone of contention between England and France.[5] From the first, since they had had a similar experience with the Treaty of Brétigny in 1360, French lawyers and propagandists left no stone unturned in the task of discovering the treaty's flaws, and at the crucial moment in 1435 a doctor from Bologna was empressed to add the *coup de*

---

[1] Chaplais, 'Paleography and Sigillography', p. 48.
[2] *Brut*, pt. 2, pp. 511–12.
[3] Hostiensis, *Aurea Summa* (Cologne, 1612), Lib. I, rub. 6.
[4] *Brut*, pt. 2, pp. 475–6.
[5] What follows will be covered more thoroughly in a future edition of the legal documents upon which Edward III and Henry V based their claim to the French crown.

grâce.[1] (Although some Englishmen doubtless rebutted these arguments, apparently none of their efforts have come to light.) Nevertheless, the reasons alleged for the treaty's validity can be adduced, for fifteenth-century lawyers proceeded in the manner of Peter Lombard's *Sic et Non*, reciting both the pros and the contras of the argument.

The dauphin's flight from Paris in 1418 gave the signal for French lawyers to muster their intellectual equipment for battle.[2] By 1420 when the seals were affixed to the Treaty of Troyes these men were ready for the struggle: where the carcass is the vultures gather. Not Roman law alone, but customary, feudal, canon, and fundamental laws comprised the weapons. For a contract to exist in Roman law, the parties must be competent to make the agreement and its nature, the people concerned and the subject-matter must be suitable. That is, inability to reason, or to know one's own mind as well as constraint, whether resulting from overt force or fear, invalidated the contract if it appertained to either part. Charles VI's insanity was common knowledge, averred the Bolognese doctor Garsiis at Arras in 1435, and the government should have fallen to his next of kin. Equally

[1] The best-known and most extensive rebuttal of the Treaty of Troyes is by Louis de Garsiis (Plancher, *Histoire de Bourgogne*, vol. iv, *preuves* no. cxxii). A partial copy of this document survives in Bodley MS. 885, ff. 69ʳ–71ᵛ. There are at least two English translations from this copy (Bodley MS. 710, ff. 73ʳ–77ᵛ and B.M., Lansdowne MS. 223, ff. 35ᵛ–37ʳ). Bodley MS. 885, ff. 30ʳ–31ʳ, also contains an undated fragment (translated in Bodley MS. 710, ff. 32ʳ–33ᵛ and B.M., Lansdowne MS. 223, ff. 73ʳ–78ᵛ) that apparently concerns this problem. The opinion of the Count of Foix's lawyer on the Treaty of Troyes is in B.N., Coll. Doat, vol. 214, ff. 53ʳ–78ᵛ. Propaganda such as the note in B.M., Add. MS. 13961, ff. 94ʳ–96ᵛ and the longer treatise in G. W. Leibnitz, *Mantissa codicis juris gentium diplomatici* (Hanover, 1700), pp. 63–96, rely to some extent on legal arguments. Of this latter work B.M., MS. 36541 contains a copy. See also B.M., Add. MS. 48005, ff. 92ᵛ–96ʳ. On fifteenth-century propaganda see A. Bossuat, 'La littérature de propagande au xvᵉ siècle: le mémoire de Jean de Rinel, secrétaire du roy d'Angleterre, contre le duc de Bourgogne (1435)', *Cahiers d'histoire*, i (1956), 131–46; J. McKenna, 'Henry VI of England and the Dual Monarchy: Aspects of Royal Political Propaganda, 1422–1432', *Journal of the Warburg and Courtauld Institutes*, xxviii (1965), 145–62; P. S. Lewis, 'Two Pieces of Fifteenth-Century Political Iconography', ibid. xxvi (1964), 317–20; id., 'War Propaganda and Historiography in Fifteenth-Century France and England', *Transactions of the Royal Historical Society*, 5th ser. xv (1965), 1–21.

[2] R. E. Giesey, 'The Juristic Basis of Dynastic Right to the French Throne', *Transactions of the American Philosophical Society*, new ser. li (1961), 3–47. The same author's *The Royal Funeral Ceremony in Renaissance France* (Travaux d'humanisme et Renaissance, 1960) adds nothing new to his arguments.

well known, Garsiis continued, was the fact that the enemy held King Charles. If he did not consent to the treaty under physical duress, then fear forced his agreement. Imprisoned and deprived of good advice, the French monarch had no alternative to submission to Henry's command. Positive proof of these contentions is given by the treaty: no one willingly disinherits his son in favour of his mortal enemy.

From customary law, the civilians devised rules of succession based on the distinction between public and private property, in other words, a distinction in what can be disposed of in a will and what cannot. The crown of Aragon, on the one hand, was a hereditary monarchy; as a result that king could leave his crown to whom he pleased. The crown of France, on the other hand, fell into the realm of public property, of which the king could not dispose. Furthermore, the right of the paterfamilias in Roman law to disown his son had no force with regard to the crown of France.

Amalgamating and refining customary law produced fundamental law, the French equivalent of the British constitution, or the principles by which France's government functioned. According to these precepts the crown of France was inalienable—an idea often stressed during the sixteenth century—and the king had to promise at his coronation to do nothing that would diminish his royal dignity. Moreover, royal dignity did not pass from father to son by inheritance, but by birthright—the right of blood. As stated by Jean Juvenal des Ursins 'le roy n'a guerre maniere d'administration et usage pour en jouïr sa vie durant tant seulement'.[1] Only an act of treason, an exception not admitted in customary law, empowered the king to disinherit his eldest son. And the civilians maintained that although the king lost his throne, his son was his only legitimate successor.

Feudal laws provided less sophisticated weapons, but they were more easily comprehended. Of these laws primogeniture was far and away the most important. Professor Giesey intimates a wider adhesion to this principle, established in France by 1270, than customarily accepted. None the less, kings could find Biblical references to substantiate

---

[1] Cited by Giesey, 'Dynastic Right', p. 17 n. 53.

this tenet, though the English did not fail to remark on the opposite conclusion to be drawn from the setting aside of Joseph's elder brothers and David's choice of Solomon as his heir. To disinherit a son in this legal system was possible; it was not the father's prerogative, however, but his superior's. Where kings were concerned, the pope made the decision, and in 1420 Martin V certainly had not disinherited the dauphin. In England, where the theory of primogeniture did not command so much interest as the practice, Lancastrian apologists chose to ignore it by arguing first that the French monarchy was hereditary and the heir could be named in advance. Like contracts of vassalage, the efficacy of treaties, safe conducts, and similar instruments terminated at the death of one of the parties. Consequently, Henry VI had not the slightest right to succeed to the French throne. Circumstances made it impossible for English diplomats to affirm this principle; their actions, however—like the attempts to have the 1416 Treaty of Canterbury reconfirmed—prove their belief in it. Similarly, unilateral violation of the contract released the other party from obligation. Since the English had violated the Treaty of Troyes by using the royal style before Charles VI had died, the contract was 'nul, void and of no effect'. From this it followed that the Anglo-Burgundian agreement to hasten and certify the execution of the May 1420 agreement was also invalid.

Despite the immense number of technicalities, canon law ultimately aimed at the creation of a reasonable facsimile of heaven on earth. Between Christian states the existence of peace was important, and provisions were made for dealing with sowers of discord. The Treaty of Troyes, in the eyes of pro-French canonists, contained wicked and impious elements that imperilled the subscriber's salvation. Henry VI's refusal to make peace at Arras in spite of the entreaties of Duke Philip made a mockery of Henry V's claim that his treaty's purpose was to establish peace between England and France. War not peace prevailed, as anyone travelling in France could see. The clause prohibiting reconciliation between the dauphin and his father before fufilling elaborate conditions contravened the principle of charity, as did the restrictions on Burgundy's relations with Charles VI's son.

For these numerous and manifest reasons the French, Burgundian, papal, and conciliar representatives at Arras in 1435 deemed the treaty and the arrangements between Henry V and Burgundy for implementing it invalid. Because of the evils that would result from carrying this treaty out, the oath in which Burgundy swore to uphold Henry V's French settlement placed his chances of eternal salvation in jeopardy and ought to be repudiated. And the cardinals at Arras stood ready to perform this act.

Thus although Burgundy may have decided long before 1435 to shed his English alliance, the weight of opinion against the validity of the Treaty of Troyes may have furnished, as the opinions of Richard of Saliceto and John of Legnano against Edward III's claims may have served Charles V,[1] the justification for joining with Charles VII to drive the English from France.

Although the sources for fifteenth-century diplomatic history appear saturated by the spirit of Roman law, on closer inspection, however, some of these Romanisms emerge as mere ornamental survivals from a hallowed past. Formal diplomatic documents of course abound in technical terms borrowed from civil as well as canon law. Yet comprehension of the precise meaning of these terms was not essential for an agent to fulfil his mission, and in fact not all envoys possessed the background that would be required to interpret the terms adequately. Moreover, the hypothetical organization of the *corps diplomatique*, postulated by medieval lawyers and seemingly substantiated by the labours of modern erudition, existed more as an ideal prototype than as a description of reality. Then, too, the envoy's personal safety did not attain the recognition envisaged by scholars in the seclusion of the study.

Local rules that had been assimilated into customary law rather than those of a more universal application furnished the framework within which differences arising from truces were adjudicated and settled.[2] Despite vast changes in

---

[1] Chaplais, *Brétigny*, pp. 51–84.

[2] W. Nicholls, *Leges marcharum* . . . (London, 1747); P. Chaplais, 'Règlement des conflits internationaux franco-anglais au xive siècle (1293–1337)', *Le Moyen Âge*, lvii (1951), 269–302.

social organization, the impressive legal edifice of late antiquity retained enormous prestige. Fifteenth-century diplomats read the laws assiduously and devotedly. Although the French selected a Bolognese doctor to furnish propaganda to swing Burgundy to the French side, native efforts (witness the unpublished fragment preserved in Bodley MS. 885) reveal the competence of the French to deal with the subject themselves.

CONCLUSION

FEW modern historians would seriously contest the assertion that 'feebleness of mind and self-will'—a phrase which certain Englishmen applied to their king in 1440—accurately characterize Henry VI's reign. Yet in diplomacy at least the factual basis for such a generalization has been fragmentary and unsubstantial. The standard work on fifteenth-century England, for example, contains no mention of diplomatic relations with the Count Palatine or with the King of Aragon during the years between 1422 and 1461, although the count received about £10,000 to ensure his friendship and the Aragonese twice tried to arrange the English king's marriage. The primary purpose of this study, then, has been to work out what happened in this period so as to establish the essential fabric of England's relations with the continent.

The approach to what happened in medieval history does not admit of as many sophisticated methods as the question why things happened, for in the former one tends to adopt the method of Nennius and make a heap of all one knows. The raw materials for this book have necessarily been drawn from quite varied sources. Not only are the state archives of western European powers as important for this study as those of England, but mercantile correspondence often reveals as much as letters of diplomats. The footnotes and appendices convey some notion of the wealth of continental material that relates to England.

Perhaps the most significant conclusions to emerge from this effort to enlarge our knowledge of English foreign policy at the end of the Hundred Years' War concerns the pattern of decision making. In connection with the Treaty of Troyes, historians of the period have rightly stressed the detailed provisions for separating the governments of France and England, though they failed to realize that this principle of bipartition extended into the realm of diplomacy. Although the expulsion of the English from France stems from many causes, the fact that the Regent of France and his brother

Gloucester pursued mutually antagonistic foreign policies
has been generally underestimated or ignored. Moreover, the
policy-making role of those who controlled the English
economy deserves greater attention than it has previously
received.

More specifically, in order to clarify the issues involved,
this work focuses on a number of main areas of English
diplomatic activity.

1. An examination of Anglo-German relations has shown
the efforts of the English council to reanimate the system
of money fiefs previously established by Edward III in
Germany as a buffer against a hostile France. The intran-
sigence of Burgundy after 1435 gave further impetus to
this policy.

2. With regard to the papacy, England's steadfast
refusal to annul or to mitigate the statute of Provisors and
her indifference to the plight of Constantinople determined
the background for the frequent, but largely inconsequential
exchanges between London and the Holy See.

3. England's frustration at the Council of Basel and her
failure to send noteworthy delegates either to Florence or to
Mantua explain why the conciliar movement, so important
to fifteenth-century European history in general, was largely
neglected in the island's diplomacy after Henry VI's
accession.

4. Economic considerations account for the minor role
played by the Italian city-states in this study: the substitu-
tion of the wool for the cloth trade decreased the number of
Italian merchants willing to lend money to the English king.

5. Conversely, diplomatic relations with the Hanseatic
cities loomed larger as the English came to depend on them
for salt and for grain in years when the harvest was bad. A
re-examination of the actual course of events has permitted
a revision of the traditional interpretation of the Anglo-
Hanseatic treaties.

6. In the Iberian peninsula the war between England and
France was only marginally significant because of the special
political situation there. Alfonso V of Aragon courted the
English only when they seemed about to make an alliance
with his enemies in Castile, and although he proposed a

marriage alliance linking Aragon, England, and Navarre, the conditions he offered were such that the English would not accept them. Alfonso's dream of a Mediterranean empire left no room for involvement in the Anglo-French war. England would have liked an alliance with the Castilians, but her support of the Trastámaras's rivals, as well as her flirtation with the Aragonese, and her Portuguese link made such an *entente* unlikely. The peculiar relationship with Portugal gave England little comfort apart from generally friendly trade connections. The attempt to strengthen the alliance through a marriage tie was inopportune, for at the time the English felt impelled to offer their king to a French wife in return for an end to the war.

The discussion of these main themes has, hopefully, provided a composite picture of English diplomatic history in the reign of Henry VI. As a necessary corollary a last chapter describing the legal framework of later medieval diplomacy was added. While the overriding importance of Roman law as a factor governing relations between states in the Middle Ages has always been affirmed, the significant deviations have generally been underestimated. It would not be an exaggeration to say that the study of the practical workings of Roman law in the diplomatic field represents another aspect of the recurring problem set for the modern medievalist: to distinguish theory from reality. Thus, despite its specious attractiveness, the diplomatic *cursus honorum* outlined by fifteenth- and sixteenth-century lawyers is little more than an intellectual phantasy.

All told, Henry VI's diplomacy was not so much inept as it was unoriginal. In a period of economic regression, continued application of policies, some of which Edward I had inaugurated, was inevitably less efficacious than two centuries earlier. Impelled along a zigzag course by the various contending factions in the English council and by the Duke of Bedford in France, English foreign policy during Henry VI's reign could only achieve the negative success of mitigating adversity.

APPENDIX I. LISTS OF ENVOYS

I. ENGLISH ENVOYS TREATING WITH FRANCE

Note: An asterisk before an entry indicates strong doubt that the mission was fulfilled. Bibliographical references have been shortened, but not, it is hoped, beyond recognition.

AISCOUGH, William, Bishop of Salisbury: (25 Aug. 1443), order to pay for going to France, E 404/59/231; *Register of Oxford*, i. 15–16.

ALNWICK, William, Bishop of Norwich: (9 July–17 [Sept.] 1435), account for going to Arras, E 101/322/2; (6 Nov. 1436), full powers to treat with France, Rymer, x. 643; (8 May 1439), order to pay for going abroad for one half year, E 404/55/274; *D.N.B.* i. 343; *Register of Cambridge*, p. 11.

ANDREW, Richard, secretary: (9 Feb.–27 June 1444), payment for going to France, E 403/755/m. 6; P.S.O. I/15/764; E 404/60/224; (13 Aug. 1445), prorogation of truce with France, Rymer, xi. 97; *Register of Oxford*, i. 34–6.

ASSHEBY, George, signet clerk: (19 June 1439), order to pay for going to Calais, E 404/55/301; Otway-Ruthven, p. 185.

BEAUFORT, Henry, Bishop of Winchester: (12 May 1427), order to pay for his shipping to France, E 404/43/317; (summer 1435), Arras, Dickinson, *Arras*, p. 34 *et passim*; (20 June 1436), full powers to treat with Burgundian ambassadors, Rymer, x. 619; (23 May 1439), full powers to treat and conclude a treaty with France, Rymer, x. 732; L. B. Radford, *Henry Beaufort* (London, 1908); *Register of Oxford*, i. 139–42.

BEAUMONT, John, Viscount: (12 Nov. 1445), full powers to treat with the French, Rymer, xi. 106.

BECKINGTON, Thomas, Bishop of Bath and Wells: (15 Sept.–30 Dec. 1432), account of mission to France, E 101/322/19; (24 June–9 Oct. 1439), order to pay for going to Calais, E 404/56/38; (28 May 1442–20 Feb. 1443), account of mission to Gascony, E 101/324/7; *Register of Oxford*, i. 157–9.

BILDESTON, Nicholas, Dr.: ([18] 23 June–9 Oct. 1439), account of mission to Calais [E 404/56/39] E 101/323/8; *Register of Oxford*, i. 187–8.

BIRD, Thomas, Fr.: (8 Feb.–16 July 1444), order to pay for going to France, E 404/60/115, 235; *Register of Oxford*, i. 191.

BLUEMANTLE Pursuivant: (7 May 1448), order to pay for taking letters to the English envoys in France, E 404/64/206; ? *College of Arms*, pp. 77–8, 121, 132.

BONNEAVENTURE Pursuivant: (3 Dec. 1448), payment for taking letters to the Parlement of Paris, E 403/773/m. 8.

BOTELER, Ralph, Lord Sudeley: (9 Sept. 1442), full power to select a place to treat with France, Rymer, xi. 13; (25 Jan. 1443), order to pay for going to the Duke of Orléans, E 404/59/130; (20 July, 12 Nov. 1445), full power to treat with the French envoys, Rymer, xi. 94, 106; *Complete Peerage*, xii, pt. 1, 419–21.

BOTYLL, Robert, Prior of St. John of Jerusalem in England: (23 Aug. 1446–5 June 1449), mission to Lyons, the pope, and the King of France, E 403/767/m. 13, E 404/64/22, E 101/324/15; E. J. King, *The Grand Priory of the Order of the Hospital of St. John of Jerusalem in England* (London, 1924), pp. 50–2.

BOULERS, Reginald, Abbot of St. Peter's Gloucester: (30 Jan. 1448), full powers to treat with the French, Rymer, x. 642; *Register of Oxford*, i. 228–9.

BOURCHIER, Henry, Lord Bourchier: (7 June–7 Oct. 1439), account of mission to Calais, E 101/323/12; (3 Dec. 1445), payment for treating with the king's adversary, E 403/759/m. 9; *Complete Peerage*, ii. 248–9.

BOWET, Henry, Archdeacon of Richmond: (summer 1435), in the retinue of John Kemp at Arras, Dickinson, *Arras*, p. 40 n. 5.

BRADFIELD, Henry: (27 Mar. 1449), mentioned, a servant who accompanied Adam Moleyns abroad, E 28/78/74.

BROUNS, Thomas, Bishop of Norwich: (9 June–[5] 15 Oct. 1439), account of mission to Calais [P.S.O. I/11/576]; E 101/323/16; *Register of Oxford*, i. 281–2; E. Jacob, 'Thomas Brouns, Bishop of Norwich, 1436–45', *Essays in British History Presented to Sir Keith Feiling*, ed. H. R. Trevor-Roper (London, 1964), pp. 61–83.

CAUCHON, Pierre, Bishop of Lisieux: (summer 1435), Arras, Dickinson, *Arras*, p. 46; (30 May 1439), powers to treat with France, Rymer, x. 728; (9 Sept. 1442) power to select a place to treat with France, Rymer, xi. 13; P. Champion, *Jeanne d'Arc*, ii. 336–7.

CHESTER Herald: (11 July 1444), order to pay for going to Paris, E 404/60/228; (28 Jan. 1448), order to pay for attending Moleyns, Botyll, and Clement, the king's ambassadors in France, E 404/64/13.

CHILTERN, Edward, notary: (20 Feb. 1444), payment for going to France, E 403/753/m. 6.

CLEMENT, Vicent, Dr.: (27 July 1447), payment for going to the King of France, E 403/767/m. 14; *Register of Oxford*, i. 432–3.

COLLAR Pursuivant: (20 Feb. 1444), payment for going to France with the Earl of Suffolk, E 403/753/m. 6; (10 July–9 Nov. 1445), payment for going to France, E 403/757/m. 8, 759/m. 2; (20 Feb. 1446), payment for going to France with the French ambassadors, E 403/759/m. 13; (11 May 1447), order to pay for taking letters to the English ambassadors in France, E 403/767/m. 13; (24 July 1447), payment for going to France, E 403/767/m. 14; ? *College of Arms*, p. 105.

DERANT, William: (4 June 1444–9 Apr. 1445), account of mission to France, E 101/324/11.

DUDLEY, Robert: (23 Aug. 1447–5 June 1449), account for a journey to France and to the pope, E 101/324/15.

DUREMONT, Gilles de, Abbot of Fécamp: * (summer 1435), Arras, Dickinson, *Arras*, p. 48; (17 Mar. 1438), full powers to treat with the French, Rymer, x. 638; (30 May 1439), full powers to treat with the French, Rymer, x. 728; (9 Sept. 1442), full powers to select a place to treat with the French, Rymer, xi. 13; *Gallia Christiana*, xi. 892; P. Champion, *Jeanne d'Arc*, ii. 328–9.

ERARD, Guillaume, Dr.: (summer 1435), Arras, Dickinson, *Arras*, p. 47; P. Champion, *Jeanne d'Arc*, ii. 330–1.

FASTOLF, John, knight: (1 Dec. 1432), full powers to treat with Charles de Valois, Rymer, x. 527; (20 May 1436), order to draw up a proxy for, C 81/703/3334A; *D.N.B.* xviii. 235–40.

FAUCONBERG, Thomas, Lord: (9 Sept. 1442), full power to select a place to treat with France, Rymer, xi. 13; *D.N.B.* xviii. 240.

FRAILLON, Nicholas, Archdeacon of Paris: * (summer 1435), Arras, Dickinson, *Arras*, p. 48; Aubert, *Le Parlement de Paris*, p. 345.

GARTER King of Arms: (12 July 1428), order to pay for going to Calais, E 28/50; (Easter 1438), payment for going to France in the retinue of the Earl of Warwick, E 405/2/39/1rb; (5 Nov. 1440–10 Apr. 1441), order to pay for going abroad with the Duke of Orléans, E 404/51/110; (25 Aug. 1443), order to pay for going to France, E 404/59/291; (4 Feb. 1444), order to pay for going to France, E 28/72/17; (6 Apr. 1445), order to pay for two trips to the Kings of France and Sicily, E 404/61/162; (12 July–2 Dec. 1445), payment for going to France with letters and instructions, E 403/ 757/m. 8, 759/m. 9; (13 July 1446), payment for going to France, E 403/ 762/m. 9; (23 July 1447), order to pay for going to the dauphin, E 404/63/ 163; (27 Jan. 1448), order to pay for going to the King of France, E 404/ 64/110; (26 June 1448), payment for taking messages to English ambassadors in France, E 403/772/m. 8; (27 Nov. 1448), payment for taking letters to the King of France, E 403/773/m. 1; (19 Feb. 1449), payment for going to France, E 403/773/m. 13; (15 July 1457), payment for going to Calais, E 403/810/m. 11; *College of Arms*, pp. 40–1.

GOGH, Matthew, esquire: (15 Mar. 1448), protestation to the King of France, Rymer, xi. 204.

GREENFIELD, Thomas: (1430), request for protection for, B.M., Cotton MS. Vespasian F. XIII, f. 34.

GRIMESTON, Edward: (20 Feb.–5 June 1449), payment for taking letters and instructions to the King of France, E 403/773/m. 16, 775/m. 5.

HARINGTON, Richard, bailiff of Caen: (17 Mar., 28 July 1438), full powers to treat, to conclude a truce with France, Rymer, x. 183, 208; (9 Sept. 1442), full powers to select a place to treat with France, Rymer, xi. 13; Wedgwood, *History of Parliament: Biographies*, p. 425.

HOLLAND, John, Earl of Huntingdon: (summer 1435), Arras, Dickinson, *Arras*, p. 35 *et passim*; (20 May 1436), full powers to treat with France, Rymer, x. 643; *Complete Peerage*, v. 205–11.

Hoo, Thomas, knight: (9 Sept. 1444), full power to select a place to treat with France, Rymer, xi. 13, E 101/304/12; (22 Feb.–27 June 1444), order to pay for journey to France, E 404/60/233; (22 Aug. 1444–11 Apr. 1445), account of a mission to France, E 101/324/12; Wedgwood, *History of Parliament: Biographies,* pp. 466–7.

Hull, Edward: (21 July 1442–16 May 1443), order to pay for going to Gascony, E 404/59/231; Wedgwood, *History of Parliament: Biographies,* pp. 481–2.

Hungerford, Walter, Baron: (11 July–18 Sept. 1435), Arras, E 101/322/34, Dickinson, *Arras,* p. 43; (20 May 1436), full power to treat with the French for a marriage alliance, Rymer, x. 643; (11 June–8 Oct. 1439), order to pay for going to Calais, E 404/56/40; (20 Feb.–6 July 1440), account of mission to Calais, E 101/323/20; *D.N.B.* x. 258; *Complete Peerage,* vi. 613–18.

Ireland King of Arms: (17 Oct. 1447), payment for a trip to Paris, E 403/769/m. 1; ? *College of Arms,* p. 268.

Issak, Thomas, esquire: (22 May 1441), full power to treat with France, Rymer, x. 847.

Jeune, Robert le: (summer 1435), Arras, Dickinson, *Arras,* p. 47.

Kemp, John, Bishop of London, Archbishop of York: ([1421–5]), payment for going to France, E 405/2/38/7vb; (summer 1435), Arras, Dickinson, *Arras,* p. 40; (20 May 1436), full power to treat with France, Rymer, x. 643; (20 Nov. 1438–26 Feb. 1439), account of a mission to Calais, E 101/323/7; (27 May–8 Oct. 1439), order to pay for a mission to Calais, E 404/56/49; (20 July 1445), power to treat with the French ambassadors in England, Rymer, xi. 94; *Register of Oxford,* ii. 1031–2.

Kent, Thomas, Dr.: (24 July 1447–17 Apr. 1448), payment for a trip to the king's uncle [Charles VII] of France, E 403/767/m. 13; *Register of Oxford,* ii. 1037–8.

Kyriell, Thomas, knight: (24 Apr., 2 May 1440), full power to treat for peace, for a truce, Rymer, x. 767, 769; (3 Nov. 1440), full power to treat with France, Rymer, x. 826; (21 May 1441), full power to treat with France, Rymer, x. 840; Wedgwood, *History of Parliament: Biographies,* pp. 521–2.

Langdon, John, Bishop of Rochester: (15 Sept. 1432–30 July 1433), account of mission to France, E 101/322/21; *Register of Oxford,* ii. 1093–4.

Langport, Richard, privy seal clerk: (6 Apr. 1448), order to pay for going abroad with Adam Moleyns, E 404/64/156.

Lion d'or Pursuivant: (13 July 1446), payment for going to France, E 403/762/m. 9; ? *College of Arms,* p. 271.

Luxembourg, Louis de, Bishop of Thérouanne, Archbishop of Rouen: (20 May 1436), full power to treat with the French about a marriage alliance, Rymer, x. 643; (9 Sept. 1442), power to select a place to treat with the French, Rymer, xi. 13; P. Champion, *Jeanne d'Arc,* ii. 419–20; *Gallia Christiana,* xi. 89.

LYHERT, Walter, Bishop of Norwich: (31 July 1447), order to pay for going
to the king's uncle of France, E 404/63/137; (7 Feb. 1448), order to pay
his shipping to Calais, E 404/64/119; *Register of Oxford*, ii. 1187–8.

LYNDWOOD, William, Dr.: (summer 1435), Arras, Dickinson, *Arras*, p. 44;
Register of Oxford, ii. 1191–3.

MAILLY, Nicholas de: (summer 1435), Arras, Dickinson, *Arras*, p. 47; P.
Champion, *Jeanne d'Arc*, ii. 336–7.

MEREDITH, Louis de, bailiff of Mantes: (18 Aug. 1444), order to pay for
taking a message to Queen Margaret, Stevenson, *Wars*, i. 461.

MESSANGER, John: (27 Nov. 1444), order to pay his passage to France,
E 404/60/113.

MOLEYNS, Adam, Bishop of Chichester: (19 Feb.–27 June 1444), account of
journey to France, E 101/324/10; (3 Aug. 1445), power to prorogue
truce with France, Rymer, xi. 97; (18 Nov. 1445), order to pay for going
to France, E 404/62/77; (20 July 1446), order to pay for going to France,
Proc. P.C. vi. 52; (1 July 1447), full power to treat with the French,
Rymer, xi. 175, 176; (6 Apr. 1448), order to pay for his shipping to
France, E 404/64/160; *Register of Oxford*, ii. 1289–91.

MONTGOMERY, John, knight: (9 Sept. 1442), full power to select a place to
treat with France, Rymer, xi. 13; Wedgwood, *History of Parliament:
Biographies*, p. 604.

MORHIR, Simon, knight: (28 July 1438), full power to conclude a truce with
France, Rymer, x. 708.

MOWBRAY, John, Duke of Norfolk: (8, 21 May 1439), order to pay for going
abroad for one half year, E 404/55/273; instructions, Rymer, x. 724;
Complete Peerage, ix. 608–9.

NEVILL, Richard, Earl of Salisbury: (20 May 1430), full power to treat with
France, Rymer, x. 642; (20 May 1436), order to draw up proxy for,
C 81/703/3334A; *Complete Peerage*, xi. 395–8.

OGARD, Andrew, knight: (17 Mar. 1438), full power to treat with the
French, Rymer, x. 683; (28 July 1438), full power to conclude a truce
with France, Rymer, x. 708; (9 Sept. 1442), power to select a place
to treat with France, Rymer, xi. 13; Wedgwood, *History of Parliament:
Biographies*, pp. 644–5.

PARIS, Michel de, French secretary: (22 July 1446), order to pay for going to
France, E 404/62/225; (11 Mar. 1449), order to pay for going to France
with Adam Moleyns and Lord Dudley, E 404/65/118.

PLANTAGENET, Richard, Duke of York: (20 May 1436), order to draw up
a proxy for, C 81/703/3334A; (9 Sept. 1442), full power to select a place
to treat with France, Rymer, xi. 13; *Complete Peerage*, xii, pt. 2, 905–9.

POLE, William de la, Earl of Suffolk: (15 July–15 Sept. 1435), Arras, E 101/
322/34, Dickinson, *Arras*, p. 42; (20 May 1436), full power to treat with
France, Rymer, x. 643; (11 June–8 Oct. 1439), order to pay for going to
Calais, E 404/56/40; (25 Aug. 1443), order to pay for going to France,

E 404/59/293; (20 Feb. 1444), order to execute instructions, Rymer, xi. 53; (20 July, 12 Nov. 1445), power to treat with the French ambassadors, Rymer xi. 94, 106; (1 July 1447), power to treat with the French, Rymer, xi. 175–6; *D.N.B.* xvi. 51; *Complete Peerage*, viii. 305.

POPHAM, John, knight: (13 July–10 Sept. 1435), Arras, E 101/322/38, Dickinson, *Arras*, p. 44; (28 July 1438), power to conclude a truce with France, Rymer, x. 708; (15 May–8 Aug. 1439), order to pay for going to Calais, E 404/56/44; Wedgwood, *History of Parliament: Biographies*, pp. 692–3.

PURCHASE Pursuivant: (6 Apr. 1441), order to pay for going to France, E 404/57/186; (17 June 1441), payment for going with letters and safe conducts to the Duke of Alençon, E 403/741/m. 9.

PURSUIVANT: (20 July 1446), order to pay for going to France, *Proc. P.C.* vi. 53.

PYRTON, William, esquire: (22 May 1441), commission to treat with the French, Rymer, x. 847.

RADCLIFFE, John, knight: (23 June–15 Sept. 1435), Arras, E 101/322/37, Dickinson, *Arras*, p. 44; *Complete Peerage*, v. 484 n. g, 585, n. a.

RAYMOND, William, clerk: (15 Dec. 1453), payment for accompanying Hull and Roos to Gascony, E 403/795/m. 9.

RINEL, Jean de, French secretary: (summer 1435), Arras, Dickinson, *Arras*, p. 47; (17 Mar. 1438), power to treat with the French, Rymer, x. 683; (30 May 1439), power to treat with the French, Rymer, x. 728; (9 Sept. 1442), full power to select a place to treat with the French, Rymer, xi. 13; Otway-Ruthven, pp. 91–3.

ROCHE GUYON, Guidon VIII, seigneur de la: * (summer 1435), Arras, Dickinson, *Arras*, p. 48; Anselme, *Histoire généalogique et chronologique de la maison royale de France*, viii. 620.

RODBURN, Thomas, Bishop of St. David's: (9 July–20 Sept. 1435), Arras, E 101/322/32, 33; (11 June–10 Oct. 1439), order to pay for going to Calais, E 404/56/45; *Register of Oxford*, iii. 1582–3.

Roos, Robert, knight: (4 Nov. 1440–29 Apr. 1441), account of a mission to Normandy, E 101/323/25; (30 June 1441–14 Apr. 1442), account of a mission to France, Normandy, and Gascony, E 101/323/27; (11 June 1442–14 Feb. 1443), account of a journey to Gascony, E 101/324/8; (22 Feb.–27 June 1444), account of mission to France, E 101/324/9; (22 Aug. 1444–11 Apr. 1445), account of a journey to France, E 101/324/13; (29 Jan. 1448), order to pay for going to the King of France, E 404/64/116; (11 June 1448), order to pay for going to the King of France and the Duke of Burgundy, E 404/64/259; (15 Dec. 1458), mentioned, E 403/795/m. 9.

ROUSSEL, Raoul, Dr.: * (summer 1435), Arras, Dickinson, *Arras*, p. 48; (28 July 1438), power to conclude a truce with France, Rymer, x. 708; P. Champion, *Jeanne d'Arc*, ii. 330–1.

SAGE, Raoul le, knight: (20 May 1436), full power to treat with France, Rymer, x. 642.

SALISBURY, John de, knight: (1430), request for protection for, B.M., Cotton MS. Vespasian F. XIII, f. 34.

SAY, John: (19 Feb. 1444), payment for going abroad in the retinue of the Earl of Suffolk, E 403/751/m. 5.

SCALES, Thomas, Lord: (17 Mar. 1438), full power to treat with the French, Rymer, x. 683; (9 Sept. 1442), power to select a place to treat with the French, Rymer, xi. 13; *Complete Peerage*, xi. 504–7.

SHOTTESBROOK, Robert, knight: (summer 1435), Arras, Dickinson, *Arras*, p. 44; Wedgwood, *History of Parliament: Biographies*, pp. 766–7.

SPREVER, William, Dr.: (15 July–? Sept. 1435), Arras, E 101/322/40; (27 May–7 Oct. 1439), account of mission to Calais, E 101/323/17; (24 Apr. 1440), full power to treat with the French, Rymer, x. 767; (29 Apr.– 8 Dec. 1445), order to pay for going to Calais, E 404/62/93; *Register of Oxford*, iii. 1745–6.

STAFFORD, Humphrey, Earl of Stafford: (4 June–6 Oct. 1439), account of mission to Calais, E 101/323/12; (20 July 1445), full power to treat with the French, Rymer, xi. 94; (1 July 1447), full power to treat with France, Rymer, xi. 175, 176; *Complete Peerage*, ii. 388–9.

STAFFORD, John, Bishop of Bath and Wells: (27 Mar.–8 Sept. 1430), account of mission to France, E 101/322/16, 17; *Register of Oxford*, iii. 1750–2.

STANLEY, John: (28 July 1438), full power to conclude a truce with France, Rymer, x. 709; ? Wedgwood, *History of Parliament: Biographies*, pp. 797–9.

STOURTON, John, knight: (8 May 1439), order to pay for going abroad one half year, E 404/55/280; (25 Nov. 1444), payment for taking the Duke of Orléans to Calais, E 403/755/m. 7; Wedgwood, *History of Parliament: Biographies*, pp. 818–19; *Complete Peerage*, xii, pt. 1, 301–2.

SUFFOLK Herald: (15 Mar.–15 Dec. 1441), order to pay for going to the Duke of Orléans, E 404/58/167; (18 Feb. 1444), order to pay for going to France, E 404/60/121; (18–28 Feb. 1445), order to pay for going to France, E 28/74/59; ? *College of Arms*, pp. 298–9.

SUTTON, John, Lord Dudley: (27 Apr.–14 Sept. 1440), account of mission to Calais, E 101/323/19; (22 May 1441), full power to treat with France, Rymer, x. 847; (10 Feb.–28 June 1442), account of journey to Calais, E 101/323/28; (19 Feb. 1444), payment for going to France, E 403/753/ m. 5; (20 July 1446), full power to treat with the French envoys, Rymer, xi. 138; (1 July 1447), full power to treat with France, Rymer, xi. 175, 176; *Complete Peerage*, iv. 479–80.

TALBOT, John, Earl of Shrewsbury: (9 Sept. 1442), full power to select a place to treat with France, Rymer, xi. 13; *Complete Peerage*, xi. 698–702.

THISANT, Jean de: (1448), mentioned, *Chronique des Pays-Bas*, iii. 426.

TOLY, William, clerk: (25 Aug. 1443), order to pay for going to France, E 404/59/293; Otway-Ruthven, p. 184.

VALIS Herald: (8 Aug. 1442), payment of a reward to the Duke of Orléans's herald, E 403/705/m. 13.

VAVASOUR, Henry: (1 Mar. 1447), order to pay for going to Calais, E 404/63/27.

VERE, John, Earl of Oxford: (5 June–8 Oct. 1439), account of mission to Calais, E 101/323/11; *Complete Peerage*, x. 236–9.

VULRE, Gervase le, French secretary: (9 Sept. 1442), full power to select a place to treat with the French, Rymer, xi. 13; (4 Feb. 1444), order to pay for taking letters about Burgundy to the Duke of York, E 404/60/113; Otway-Ruthven, pp. 95–6.

WELLS, William, Bishop of Rochester: (27 Apr.–9 Dec. 1440), account of mission to Calais, E 101/323/22.

WENLOCK, John, esquire: (30 June–2 Dec. 1441, 20 Dec. 1441–29 May 1442), order to pay for going to France, Brittany, and Alençon, E 404/58/102; (9 Sept. 1442), full power to select a place to treat with France, Rymer, xi. 13; (10 Sept. 1442–26 June 1443), order to pay for going to France, E 404/60/22; (27 Feb. 1444), order to pay for going to France, E 28/72/72; (13 Aug. 1445), prorogation of the truce with France, Rymer, xi. 97; Wedgwood, *History of Parliament: Biographies*, pp. 931–2.

WHITTINGHAM, Robert, esquire: (30 May 1439), full power to treat with France, Rymer, x. 728; (24 Apr., 2 May, 3 Nov. 1440), full power to treat for peace, or for a truce, with France, Rymer, x. 767, 769, 827; (22 May 1441), full power to treat with France, Rymer, x. 847; Wedgwood, *History of Parliament: Biographies*, pp. 943–4.

WILTON, Stephen, Dr.: ([15 May] 31 Aug.–7 [8] Oct. 1439), account of a journey to Calais, E 101/323/9, [E 404/56/152]; (20 Feb.–6 July 1440), account of mission to Calais, E 101/620/27; (5 Nov. 1440–2 Apr. 1441), account of mission to France, E 101/323/24; *Register of Oxford*, iii. 2053–4.

WOODVILLE, Richard, knight: (11 Feb. 1427), order to pay for taking messages to Calais; *Complete Peerage*, xi. 19–22.

2. ENVOYS FROM FRANCE TO ENGLAND

BATUTE, Jean, master: (24 Apr. –21 July 1442), order to pay an English servant for waiting on, E 404/59/281.

BEAUVAU, Bertrand de, Lord of Precigny: (13 July 1445), payment of a reward to, E 403/757/m. 8; (15 July 1447), payment of a reward to, E 403/767/m. 9.

BOAFAULT, Aucogne de: (31 Jan. 1424), request for safe conduct for, E 28/43/70.

BOURBON, Charles I de, Duke of Bourbon: (23 Dec. 1433), order to draw up a safe conduct for, C 81/696/2615.

BOURBON, Louis de, Count of Vendôme: (13 July 1445), payment of a reward to, E 403/757/m. 8.

CASTILLION, Charles de, clerk: (2 July 1445), order to pay a reward to, E 404/60/251.

CHAPERNON, Almeric, knight: (19 June 1445), ambassador from King René in the retinue of the queen, payment to, E 403/757/m. 6.

CHARTIER, Étienne, trompette of the Count of Vendôme: (2 July 1445), order to pay a reward for coming to England with the French ambassadors, E 404/61/270.

CHEVALIER, Étienne: (July 1445), mentioned, Beaucourt, *Charles VII*, iv. 145.

CLEPE, Oudart, Dr.: (23 Dec. 1433), order to draw up a safe conduct for, C 81/696/2651.

COLUMBIERS Pursuivant: (1 Feb. 1447), payment of a reward, E 403/765/m. 14; (26 Nov. 1448), order to pay for bringing letters, E 404/65/72.

COUSINOT, Guillaume: (31 Jan. 1424), request for safe conduct for, E 28/43/70; (13 July 1445), mentioned, E 403/757/m. 8; (20 Dec. 1445), order to pay a reward for 44 days in England, E 404/62/98; (1 Feb. 1447), payment for expenses in England, E 403/765/m. 14; (15 July 1447), order to pay a reward to, E 403/767/m. 2; G. Dupont-Ferrier, *Bibliothèque de l'École des chartes*, xcvii (1936), 50.

DAUPHIN DE VIENNE Pursuivant: (18 July 1444), order to pay a reward to, E 404/60/241.

ELE Pursuivant: (17 May 1442), order to pay a reward to, E 404/58/157.

FOLKET: (7 June 1448), order to pay a reward to, E 404/64/215.

GAUCOURT, Lord of: (July 1445), mentioned, Beaucourt, *Charles VII*, iv. 145.

GESTER, messenger: (10 June 1449), mentioned, E 404/65/185.

GOSNE, Charles de: (31 Jan. 1424), request for safe conduct for, E 28/43/70.

HAVART, Jean, esquire: (20 Dec. 1445), order to pay a reward for 44 days in England, E 404/63/98; (5 July 1446), mentioned, E 404/64/99; (1 Feb. 1447), payment of his expenses in England, E 404/765/m. 14; (15 July 1447), payment of a reward to, E 403/767/m. 9; (7 June 1448), order to pay a reward to, E 404/64/215; (21 July 1449), order to pay a reward to, E 404/62/98.

HERALD: (24 July 1447), payment of a reward to, E 403/767/m. 13.

JURET, Jean, pursuivant: (23 Oct. 1445), payment of a reward to, E 403/795/m. 2.

JUVENAL DES URSINS, Jean, Archbishop of Reims: (13 July 1445), payment of a reward to, E 403/757/m. 8; P. L. Péchenard, *Jean Juvénal des Ursins, historien de Charles VI, évêque de Beauvais et de Laon, archevêque duc de Reims* (Paris, 1876).

LAVAL, Guy XIV, Count of: (13 July 1445), payment of a reward to, E 403/757/m. 8.

L'HÔPITAL, François de: (31 Jan. 1424), request for safe conduct for, E 28/43/70.

LORYALL, Thomas: (21 July 1449), payment of a reward to, E 403/775/m. 8.

MORGAN, Colin, pursuivant: (12 Aug. 1445), order to pay a reward to, for coming from the Count of Vendôme with the French ambassadors, E 404/60/95; (23 Feb. 1446), payment of a reward to, E 403/756/m. 15.

MOUSAY, Alardin: (6 Nov. 1444), order to pay a reward to: E 404/61/100.

ORLÉANS, Jean, Count of Dunois: (14 July 1447), payment of a reward to, E 403/767/m. 9.

PANETERIE, Jean de la: (21 June 1445), order to pay a reward to, for coming from King René, E 404/61/243.

PURSUIVANT: (2 Dec. 1445), payment of a reward to, E 403/795/m. 9; (20 July 1446), mentioned, E 404/62/205; (24 July 1447), payment of a reward to, E 403/767/m. 13; (28 Oct. 1447), order to pay a reward to two pursuivants from France, E 404/64/63.

PURSUIVANT of the King of Sicily: (18 July 1444), order to pay a reward to, E 404/60/241; (27 June 1446), payment of a reward to, E 403/762/m. 4.

REBOURGET, Nicholas de: (6 Nov. 1444), order to pay a reward to, E 404/61/100.

SAINT-AVIT, Bertrand de: (23 Dec. 1433), order to draw up a safe conduct for, C 81/696/2615.

SAINT-LOUVIER-DE-BLOIS, Abbot of: (31 Jan. 1424), request for safe conduct for, E 28/43/70.

SAUVAGE, Pierre, master: (31 Jan. 1424), request for safe conduct for, E 28/43/70.

SCALE, Antoine de la, esquire: (19 June 1445), payment for a reward for coming from King René, E 403/757/m. 6.

SCOT, Monnypenny: (28 Oct. 1447), order to pay a reward to, E 404/64/63.

VALOIS Herald: (1 Feb. 1447), payment of a reward to, E 403/765/m. 14; (7 June 1448), order to pay a reward for coming with Jean Havart, E 404/64/215; (18 Oct. 1448), order to pay for bringing letters and returning with answers, E 404/65/44; (10 June 1449), mentioned, E 404/65/185.

3. ENGLISH ENVOYS TREATING WITH BURGUNDY

ALNWICK, William, Bishop of Norwich: (20 July 1427), mentioned as having been to Arras about the Duchess of Holland, *Proc. P.C.* iii. 276; *Register of Cambridge*, p. 11; *D.N.B.* i. 343.

BEAUFORT, Henry, Bishop of Winchester: (8–10 Mar. 1428), Burgundy's expenses for entertaining, Lille, *Arch. du Nord*, B 3396; (14 Jan. 1429), payment of £1,000 for going to the duke, E 403/692/m. 14; (27 Jan. 1430),

Beaufort at Burgundy's wedding, *Brut*, ii, pt. 2, 37–8; L. B. Radford, *Henry Beaufort* (London, 1908).

BECKINGTON, Thomas, Bishop of Bath and Wells: (18 Dec. 1439), full powers to prorogue truce with Flanders, Lille, *Arch. du Nord*, B 572; (24 June–9 Oct. 1440), account for going to Calais, E 101/323/21; *Register of Oxford*, i. 157–9.

BOKELAND, Richard: (1428–9), full power to redress grievances with Flanders, C 81/700/3042; (9 Mar. 1430), order to pay for delivering gold to Burgundy, E 404/46/345.

BONNEAVENTURE Pursuivant: (29 July 1449), order to pay for going to the Duchess of Burgundy with letters, E 404/65/213; (18 May 1450), payment for taking messages to the duchess, E 403/799/m. 3.

BONREPORT Pursuivant: (9 May 1450), order to pay for going to the duchess, E 28/80/40.

BOTYLL, Robert, Prior of St. John of Jerusalem in England: (20 July 1453), order to pay for passage to Calais to redress grievances, E 404/69/196; E. J. King, *The Grand Priory of the Order of the Hospital of St. John of Jerusalem in England* (London, 1924), pp. 50–2.

BROWN, William: (18 Feb. 1446), power to redress grievances with Holland, Zeeland, and Flanders, E 28/76/19.

BURTON, Thomas: (18 Feb. 1446), full power to redress grievances with Holland, Zeeland, and Flanders, E 28/76/19; ? Wedgwood, *History of Parliament: Biographies*, pp. 140, 141.

CAUNTON, Richard, master: (21 Mar. 1453), order to pay for going to Calais with Robert Botyll, E 404/69/104.

CHALTON, Thomas: (16 May 1435), full powers to redress grievances with Flanders and Burgundy, C 81/700/3024; (18 Feb. 1446), full power to redress grievances with Holland, Zeeland, and Flanders, E 28/76/19.

CHESTER Herald: (24 July 1447), payment for attending Burgundian ambassadors in England, E 403/767/m. 13; (10 June 1449), mentioned, E 404/65/185; (5 July 1449), payment for going to the duchess, E 403/775/m. 5.

COLLAR Pursuivant: (17 July 1440), payment for taking letters to the English ambassadors at Calais and to the Duchess of Burgundy, E 403/739/m. 14; (25 Oct. 1440), payment for taking letters to the Duchess of Burgundy, E 403/740/m. 2; (13 July 1445), payment for going to the duchess for a safe conduct for the Bishop of Rochester, E 403/757/m. 8; ? *College of Arms*, p. 105.

COTESBROOK, William, London merchant: (4 July 1444), full powers to redress grievances with Zeeland and Holland, C 61/132/m. 8; Wedgwood, *History of Parliament: Biographies*, p. 227.

DERBY, John, Dr.: (28 May 1447), order to pay for going to Calais, E 28/80/36; (3 Feb. 1451), payment for going to Calais to treat for redress of grievances, E 403/781/m. 5; (20 July 1458), full power to redress infractions of the truce with Burgundy, Rymer, xi. 414.

DRAGON Pursuivant: (6 July 1434), payment for going to the Duke of Burgundy, E 403/715/m. 12.

DRAYTON, John: (5 June 1449), payment for going to Calais, E 403/775/m. 5.

DUDLEY, John: (27 Apr.–14 Sept. 1440), account of a mission to Calais, E 101/323/19.

EASELEY, Robert, Dr.: (12 Nov. 1458), order to pay for going to the Duke of Burgundy, E 404/71/6/14.

ESTCOURT, John, master: (6 Aug.–10 Oct. 1426), account for going to the Duke of Burgundy, E 101/322/14.

ESTFIELD, William, knight: (4 July 1441), power to negotiate with Holland and Zeeland, Rymer, x. 848.

FIELD, John: (28 July 1449), full power to treat with Burgundy, Rymer, xi. 233.

FROWICK, Henry: (18 Feb. 1446), full power to redress grievances with Holland, Zeeland, and Flanders, E 28/76/19; Wedgwood, *History of Parliament: Biographies*, p. 357.

GALET, Louis: (22 Nov. 1454), payment for going to Flanders, E 403/800/m. 8.

GARE, Thomas, Jr.: (14 Feb. 1435), full power to treat with Flanders, Rymer, x. 605.

GARTER King of Arms: (22 July 1424), payment for going to the Dukes of Bedford, Brittany, and Burgundy, E 403/666/m. 12; (15 Jan. 1425), payment for going to the Duke of Gloucester in Hainault, E 403/669/m. 12; (7 May 1425), payment for taking letters concerning secret matters to the Duke of Burgundy in Flanders, E 403/671/m. 1; (2 Aug. 1425), payment for going to the Dukes of Burgundy and Bedford, E 403/671/m. 15; (4 Dec. 1427), payment for mission to Flanders in the retinue of Estcourt and Oldhall, E 403/683/m. 8; (4 Oct. 1429), payment for going to the Dukes of Bedford and Burgundy, E 403/692/m. 1; (18 Feb. 1429), payment for going to the duke, E 403/688/m. 12; (8 Oct. 1431), order to pay for a mission to the Duke of Burgundy, B.M., Add. Charter 11736; (1433), mentioned in letter to the Duke of Burgundy, *Proc. P.C.* iv. 150; (19 May 1440), order to pay for going to the Duchess of Burgundy, E 404/56/267; (19 Nov. 1450), mentioned, E 404/67/91; (11 Dec. 1451), payment for going to the duchess, E 403/786/m. 6; *College of Arms*, pp. 40–1.

GRIMESTON, Edward: (19 Feb.–25 Nov. 1441), order to pay for going to the Duchess of Burgundy and the Duke of Orléans, E 404/56/88, 57/177; (23 Feb. 1446–19 May 1447), order to pay for going to Calais to communicate with the ambassadors of Hainault, Holland, and Zeeland, E 404/62/122, 176; (17 Mar. 1449), order to pay for going to the Duchess of Burgundy with letters and instructions, E 404/65/120; (28 May, 28 July 1449), full power to treat with Burgundian ambassadors, Rymer, x. 229, 233.

GUYENNE Herald: (30 Mar. 1450), payment for going to the duchess, E 403/778/m. 4; (12 July 1456), payment for going to the duchess, E 403/807/m. 8; ? *College of Arms*, pp. 40–1, 263.

HALL, Robert, master: (14 May 1457), power to treat with the Duke of Burgundy, Rymer, xi. 410.

HARLEY, Nicholas, clerk: (5 July–20 Oct. 1426), account for going to the Duke of Burgundy, E 101/322/14.

HARTON, William, esquire: (16 July 1426), order to pay for going to the Duke of Burgundy, *Proc. P.C.* iii. 202.

HERBERT, William, esquire: (6 Nov. 1453), mentioned, E 403/795/m. 3.

HORNE, Robert: (28 July 1449), full power to treat with Burgundy, Rymer, xi. 233.

HUNT, Roger: (14 July 1441), full power to treat with Holland, Rymer, x. 848.

HYSSHAM, Nicholas, merchant: (28 May, 8 Dec. 1439), full power to treat with Holland and Zeeland, Rymer, x. 733, 739.

KEMP, John, Archbishop of York: (23 Nov. 1438), full power to negotiate with the Flemings, Rymer, x. 713; (23 May 1439), full power to treat with the Flemings, Rymer, x. 730; *Register of Oxford*, ii. 1031–2.

KENT, Thomas, Dr.: (13 July 1444), order to pay for going to redress grievances with Holland and Zeeland, E 404/60/234; (13 Mar. 1445), order to pay for going to redress grievances at Bruges, E 404/61/146; (24 Feb. 1446–17 May 1447), order to pay for going to Calais to redress grievances with Holland, Zeeland, and Flanders, E 404/62/127, 176; (29 July 1449), order to pay for going to Burgundy, E 404/65/214; (9 May 1450), order to pay for going to Burgundy and Cologne, E 404/66/166; (20 July 1453), order to pay for passage to Calais to redress grievances, E 404/69/196; (13 Mar. 1456), order to pay for going to Bruges, E 28/86/15; *Register of Oxford*, xx. 1037–8.

KNYGHT, Roger: (14 Feb. 1435), power to treat with Flanders, Rymer, x. 605.

KYRIELL, Thomas, knight: (6 Feb., 12 July 1440), full power to treat with the Flemings, Rymer, x. 760, confirmation of truce with the Duchess of Burgundy, Rymer, x. 791; Wedgwood, *History of Parliament: Biographies*, pp. 521–2.

LANGPORT, Richard, clerk: (14 Feb. 1445), order to pay for going to redress grievances with Holland and Zeeland, E 404/61/131.

LESCROPE, Henry, Lord Scrope (of Bolton): (14 May 1458), power to treat with the Burgundians, Rymer, xi. 410; *Complete Peerage*, xi. 543.

LUDLOW, William: (6 Feb. 1440), full power to treat with Flanders, Rymer, x. 761; (22 May 1441), full power to treat with Flanders, Rymer, x. 847.

LYNDWOOD, William, Dr.: (12 May 1427), order to pay for going to Holland, E 404/43/305; (11 May 1430), order to pay for going to Arras, E 28/63/73; (24 Dec. 1439), power to prorogue the truce with Flanders, Rymer, x. 750; (14 July 1441), power to treat with Holland, Zeeland and Friesland, Rymer, x. 848; *Register of Oxford*, ii. 1191–3.

MALET, Edmund: (3 Apr. 1451), order to pay for going to the duchess for a safe conduct, E 404/67/127.

MARENEY, John, knight: (25 Oct. 1448), full power to treat with the Burgundian ambassadors, Rymer, xi. 218; (28 May 1449), full power to treat with the Burgundian ambassadors, Rymer, xi. 229.

MITCHELL, John: (16 Aug.–22 Oct. 1426), account for 67 days redressing grievances with Burgundy, E 101/47/35; (14 Feb. 1435), full powers to treat with Flanders, Rymer, x. 605; (16 May 1435), full power to redress grievances with Flanders and Burgundy, C 81/700/3024; ? Wedgwood, *History of Parliament: Biographies*, p. 596.

MOREYS, John: (18 Feb. 1446), full power to redress grievances with Holland, Zeeland, and Flanders, E 28/76/19; ? Wedgwood, *History of Parliament: Biographies*, p. 613.

MULSCO, Edmund, knight: (24 July 1454), order to pay for going to Flanders, E 404/70/1/83; Wedgwood, *History of Parliament: Biographies*, p. 618.

NANFAN, John: (3 Apr. 1451), order to pay for going to the Duchess of Burgundy, E 404/67/129; (10 Nov. 1453), mentioned, E 403/795/m. 3; Wedgwood, *History of Parliament: Biographies*, p. 621.

NEVILL, John, knight: (14 May 1458), full power to treat with Burgundy, Rymer, xi. 410; ? Wedgwood, *History of Parliament: Biographies*, p. 627.

NEVILL, Thomas, Sr., knight: (14 May 1458), full power to treat with Burgundy, Rymer, xi. 410.

OARE, Thomas: (16 May 1435), full power to redress grievances with Flanders and Burgundy, C 81/700/3042.

OBERY, William, merchant: (14 May 1458), full power to treat with Burgundy, Rymer, xi. 410; (20 Aug. 1458), full powers to treat with the Flemings at Bruges, Rymer, xi. 414.

OLDHALL, William, knight: (1 Aug.–10 Oct. 1426), account for going to treat with the Burgundians, E 101/322/14; Wedgwood, *History of Parliament: Biographies*, pp. 647–8.

PLANTAGENET, Richard, Duke of York: (23 Apr. 1443), truce with the Duchess of Burgundy, Rymer, xi. 24; *Complete Peerage*, xii, pt. 2, 905–9.

POPHAM, John, knight: (23 May 1439), full power to treat with the Flemings, Rymer, x. 730; Wedgwood, *History of Parliament: Biographies*, pp. 692–3.

PULTER, John, Jr.: (28 July 1449), full power to treat with Burgundy, Rymer, xi. 233.

PURCHASE Pursuivant: (12 July 1440), payment for taking letters to the duchess at Saint-Omer, E 403/739/m. 10.

PURSUIVANT: (17 May 1447), order to pay for going to Flanders, E 404/62/176.

PYRTON, William, esquire: (4 July 1444), full powers to redress grievances with Zeeland and Holland, C 61/132/m. 8; (1 Apr. 1445), full power to treat with Burgundy, Rymer, xi. 82; (25 Oct. 1448), full power to treat with the Burgundian ambassadors, Rymer, xi. 218; (28 May 1449), full power to treat with the Burgundian ambassadors at Calais, Rymer, xi. 229;

(14 May 1458), full powers to treat with the Burgundian ambassadors, Rymer, xi. 410.

REMPSTON, Thomas, knight: (23 Nov. 1438), full power to treat with Hainault, Holland, and Zeeland, Rymer, x. 714.

RINWELL, John, merchant: (23 Nov. 1438), full power to treat with the Low Countries, Rymer, x. 713, 714.

RODBURN, Thomas, Bishop of St. David's: (23 May 1439), full power to treat with the Flemings, Rymer, x. 730; *Register of Oxford*, iii. 1582–3.

Roos, Robert, knight: (11 June 1448), order to pay for going to the King of France and to the Duke of Burgundy, E 404/64/259.

RUBIN, Guillaume, knight: (9 Dec. 1429), payment for taking letters to the Duke of Burgundy, E 403/692/m. 10.

SALMAN, Thomas, esquire: (Easter 1425), payment for going to the Duke of Burgundy, E 405/2/38/2rb.

SELLING, Richard, esquire: (14 Feb. 1435), full power to treat with Flanders, Rymer, x. 605: (16 May 1435), full power to redress grievances with Flanders and Burgundy, C 81/700/3024.

SHARP, Henry, Dr.: (7 Feb.–17 Mar. 1459), order to pay for going to Bruges, E 28/88/56.

SHARP, John: (28 Aug. 1449), paid for going to the Duchess of Burgundy, E 403/775/m. 11.

SHOTTESBROOK, Robert, knight: (16 May 1435), full power to redress grievances with Flanders and Burgundy, C 81/700/3042; Wedgwood, *History of Parliament: Biographies*, pp. 766–7.

SPREVER, William, Dr.: (23 Nov. 1438), full power to treat with the Low Countries, Rymer, x. 713, 714; (23, 29 May 1439), full power to treat with the Low Countries, Rymer, x. 728, 733; E 101/323/17 (29 Apr.–8 Dec. 1440), account for going to Calais to treat with the Duke of Burgundy, E 101/323/17; (14 July 1441), full power to treat with Hainault, Holland, and Zeeland, Rymer, x. 848; (20 July 1458), full power to redress infractions of the truce with Burgundy, Rymer, xi. 414; *Register of Oxford*, iii. 1745–6.

STACEY, Thomas: (4 Mar. 1448), order to pay for going to Flanders with messages, E 404/64/135.

STAFFORD, Humphrey, Earl of Stafford: (4 July 1444), full power to treat with the Low Countries, Rymer, xi. 67; (25 Oct. 1448), full power to treat with the Burgundian ambassadors, Rymer, xi. 218; *Complete Peerage*, ii. 388–9.

STILLINGTON, Robert, Dr.: (25 Oct. 1448), full power to treat with the Burgundian ambassadors, Rymer, xi. 218; *Register of Oxford*, iii. 1777–9.

STOKES, John, Dr.: (26 Dec. 1430), account of jewels he was to take to Holland, E 101/355/28; (21 Feb. 1435–Mar. 1436), payment for going to Calais, Bruges, and to the Duke of Bavaria, E 403/717/m. 1, E 404/52/218; (29 Dec. 1439–3 May 1440), account for going to Holland, E 364/75/F, G; (14 July 1441), full power to negotiate a commercial alliance with Holland, Zeeland, and Friesland, Rymer, x. 848; *Register of Oxford*, iii. 1781–3.

STOKTON, William: (28 July 1449), full power to treat with Burgundy, Rymer, xi. 233; Wedgwood, *History of Parliament: Biographies*, p. 811.

STOPINGDON, John: (18 Dec. 1439), full power to prorogue a truce with Flanders, Lille, *Arch. du Nord*, B 572.

STRATTON, Bartholomew, merchant: (8 Dec. 1439), full power to treat with Holland and Zeeland, Rymer, x. 739.

STRATTON, John, master: (14 May 1457), full power to treat with Burgundy, Rymer, xi. 410; ? *Register of Oxford*, iii. 1850.

SUFFOLK Herald: (16 July 1434), payment for going to Flanders with letters for the Duke of Burgundy, E 403/715/m. 11, *College of Arms*, p. 299.

SUTTON, Hamond: (1428–9), full powers to redress grievances with Flanders and Burgundy, C 81/700/3042; (14 Feb. 1435), Rymer, x. 605; (18 Feb. 1446), full power to redress grievances with Holland, Zeeland, and Flanders, E 28/76/19; Wedgwood, *History of Parliament: Biographies*, pp. 828–9.

SUTTON, John, Lord Dudley: (29 July 1449), order to pay for going to Burgundy, E 404/65/214; E 403/775/m. 8; *Complete Peerage*, iv. 479–80.

THRYSK, John: (18 Feb. 1446), full power to redress grievances with Holland, Zeeland, and Flanders, E 28/76/19; Wedgwood, *History of Parliament: Biographies*, pp. 845–6.

THURLAND, Thomas: (18 Feb. 1446), power to redress grievances with Holland, Zeeland, and Flanders, E 28/76/19; (28 July 1449), power to treat with Burgundy, Rymer, xi. 233; Wedgwood, *History of Parliament: Biographies*, pp. 853–4.

TIPTOFT, John, Lord: (20 July 1427), mentioned as having been to Arras about the Duchess of Holland, *Proc. P.C.* iii. 276; *Register of Oxford*, ii. 1191–3.

TOLY, William, master: (25 July 1453), payment for going to Calais to communicate about redress of grievances, E 403/793/m. 14; Otway-Ruthven, p. 184.

TULYOT, William: (25 July 1445), full power to treat with Burgundy, Rymer, xi. 233.

TYRELL, John, esquire: (12 May 1427), order to pay for going to Holland, E 404/43/305.

VAUGHAN, Thomas, esquire: (23 Nov. 1457), order to pay for going to the Duchess of Burgundy, E 404/71/33; Wedgwood, *History of Parliament: Biographies*, pp. 902–3.

WATER, Richard: (16 May 1435), full power to redress grievances with Flanders and Burgundy, C 81/711/3024; (28 July 1449), full power to treat with Burgundy, Rymer, xi. 233.

WENLOCK, John, esquire: (14 May 1458), full power to treat with Burgundy, Rymer, xi. 410; Wedgwood, *History of Parliament: Biographies*, pp. 903–4.

WHITE, Robert: (18 Feb. 1446), full power to redress grievances with Holland, Zeeland, and Flanders, E 28/76/19; (28 July 1449), full power to treat with Burgundy, Rymer, xi. 233.

WHITEHILL, Richard: (14 May 1458), full power to treat with Burgundy, Rymer, xi. 410.

WHITTINGHAM, Robert: (23 Nov. 1438), full power to treat with the Low Countries, Rymer, x. 713, 714; (18 Dec. 1439), full power to prorogue the truce with Flanders, Lille, *Arch. du Nord*, B 572; (14 July 1441), power to treat with Hainault, Holland, and Zeeland, Rymer, x. 848; Wedgwood, *History of Parliament: Biographies*, pp. 931–2.

WILLIAMSON, John: (28 July 1449), full power to treat with Burgundy, Rymer, xi. 233; (14 May 1458), full power to treat with Burgundy, Rymer, xi. 410.

WILTON, Stephen, Dr.: (21 Mar.–23 May 1435), account of mission to Calais and Bruges, E 101/322/31; (23 Nov. 1438), full power to treat with the Low Countries, Rymer, x. 713, 714; (18 Dec. 1439), full powers to prorogue the truce with Flanders, Lille, *Arch. du Nord*, B 572; (12 July 1440), confirmation of truce with Duchess of Burgundy, Rymer, x. 791, E 101/323/20; (25 Nov. 1441), order to pay for going to the Duchess of Burgundy and to the Duke of Orléans, E 404/58/89; *Register of Oxford*, iii. 2053–4.

WOODHOUSE, John, esquire: (25 Oct. 1448), full power to treat with the Burgundian ambassadors, Rymer, xi. 218; (28 May 1449), power to treat with the Burgundian ambassadors, Rymer, xi. 229; (14 May 1458), power to treat with the Burgundian ambassadors, Rymer, xi. 410.

WOODVILLE, Richard, knight: (18 July–10 Oct. 1426), account of mission to the Duke of Burgundy, E 101/322/14, 15; (1428–9), full power to redress grievances with Flanders and Burgundy, C 81/700/3024; (9 Mar. 1430), order to pay for delivering gold to Burgundy, E 404/46/345; (14 Feb. 1435), full power to treat with Flanders, Rymer, x. 605; (18 July 1446), order to pay for two trips to Calais, E 404/62/220; *Complete Peerage*, xi. 19–22.

WOTTON, Richard, master: (12 Oct. 1448), order to pay for going to Calais, E 404/65/33; ? *Register of Oxford*, iii. 2092.

WRIXWORTH, John, chamber messenger: (3 Dec. 1440), payment for going to the Duchess of Burgundy, E 403/740/m. 9; *College of Arms*, pp. 263–4.

4. ENVOYS FROM BURGUNDY TO ENGLAND

ALBRIGHTSON, James: (17 July 1430), payment for taking letters to the King of Scotland, E 403/695/m. 17.

ALVERS, João, esquire: (3 Oct. 1449), order to reward for coming with letters of the Duchess of Burgundy, E 404/67/99; (6 Dec. 1450), payment of a reward to, E 403/67/99.

ARCHEMBAUD: (3 Feb. 1447), payment for coming from the duchess, E 403/ 765/m. 14.

ARTOIS King of Arms: (25 Aug. 1450), order to pay a reward to, *Proc. P.C.* vi. 100.

AUDRINET, Phillibert: (7 May–24 July 1426), in England to negotiate a truce for the Flemings, Lannoy, *Lannoy*, p. 82.

BAROENS, Corneille: (1442), mentioned, Marle, *pièce justif.* no. xxxi.

BRABANT, Gautier de: (21 July 1453), order to pay for bringing messages from the Duke of Cleves, E 404/69/207.

COILLE, Jean: (18 July 1453), mentioned as returning to the Duchess of Burgundy via Calais, E 38/83/4.

COPIN: (21 Feb. 1435), payment for bringing letters from Flanders to the king, E 403/717/m. 13.

CREVECOUER, Lord of: (4 June 1435), order to pay a reward to, *Proc. P.C.* iv. 301.

ETEN, Barthélemy van: (1442), mentioned, Marle, *pièce justif.* no. xxxi.

FOURMELLES, Simon de: (7 May–24 July 1426), in England to negotiate a truce for the Flemings, Lannoy, *Lannoy*, p. 82.

GENT, Arnaud de: (11 July 1427), payment of a reward to the envoys from the Duchess of Holland, E 403/680/m. 8.

GODBY, Colard: (16 July 1451), payment to, E 403/784/m. 7.

GUIDECHON, Marc: (14 July 1426), order to pay a reward to, E 404/42/292.

HERALD: (23 Nov. 1435), pay Thomas Pound, a messenger of the king, for going to Dover to receive letters from a Burgundian herald, E 403/721/ m. 5; (21 Feb. 1448), payment to, E 403/769/m. 15.

HORNES, Jean de, Lord of Boussagines: (14 July 1426), order to pay a reward to, E 404/42/292.

LANNOY, Guillebert de: (5 Nov. 1423), payment to, E 403/663/m 4.

LANNOY, Hugues de, Lord of Santes: (7 May–24 July 1426), in England to negotiate a truce for the Flemings, Lannoy, *Lannoy*, p. 82; (1 Feb. 1427), payment to the keeper of the wardrobe for Lannoy's expenses in England, E 403/678/m. 1; (21 Dec. 1429), order to pay a reward to, E 404/46/168; (4 June 1435), order to pay a reward to, *Proc. P.C.* iv. 301; (31 May 1439), permission to export cloth and grain, *Cal. Close Rolls, 1435–41*, p. 196.

MENART, Quentin de, master: (7 May–24 July 1426), in England to negotiate truce for the Flemings, Lannoy, *Lannoy*, p. 82; (21 Dec. 1429), order to pay a reward to, E 404/46/168; (14 June 1434), payment of a reward to, E 403/715/m. 9; (20 July 1435), payment of a reward to, E 403/719/ m. 11.

MONTFORT, Louis de: (11 July 1427), payment of a reward to the envoys of the Duchess of Holland, E 403/480/m. 8.

PIERS, servant of the Bishop of Liège: (5 July 1449), order to pay the expenses of, E 404/65/196.

SCRIVELE, Adrian: (29 May 1451), mentioned, E 404/67/167.

SECAR', Evon' de: (28 Oct. 1456), payment for coming to the king with letters, E 403/809/m. 3.

TALENT Pursuivant: (20 July 1435), payment of a reward to, E 403/719/m. 12.

TOISON D'OR King of Arms: (4 June 1435), order to pay a reward to, *Proc. P.C.* v. 301; (16 Oct. 1448), payment to, E 403/773/m. 1.

VAULX, Robinet, messenger: (29 July 1441), sent with messages to the Burgundian ambassadors in England, Beaucourt, *Charles VII*, iii. 202, n. 4.

VOCIER Pursuivant: (16 July 1442), payment of a reward to, E 403/745/m. 10.

5. ENGLISH ENVOYS TREATING WITH BRITTANY

BEAUCHAMP, Richard, Earl of Warwick: (Jan. 1438), minutes concerning an embassy to Brittany, *Proc. P.C.* v. 86; *Complete Peerage*, xii, pt. 2, 385–92.

BECKINGTON, Thomas, Bishop of Bath and Wells: (21 Mar. 1433), full power to redress grievances with Brittany, Rymer, x. 546; *Register of Oxford*, i. 157–9.

COLLAR Pursuivant: (2 Dec. 1440), order to pay for carrying letters, E 403/740/m. 8; (11 July 1442), payment for taking letters to the duke, E 403/745/m. 9; ? *College of Arms*, p. 105.

DUREMONT, Gilles de, Abbot of Fécamp: (30 June 1438), receipt for expenses he incurred while on a mission to Brittany, Stevenson, *Wars*, ii. 294.

ESTFIELD, William, knight: (24 Mar. 1433), full power to redress grievances, Rymer, x. 546.

GARTER King of Arms: (22 July 1424), payment for going to the Dukes of Bedford, Burgundy, and Brittany, E 403/666/m. 12; (28 June 1425), order to pay for going to the Dukes of Bedford and Brittany, E 404/41/342; (18 Feb. 1433), instructions, Rymer, x. 545; (18 July 1442), payment for going to the Dukes of Brittany and Orléans, E 403/745/m. 12; (19 July 1443), payment for going with letters and instructions to the Duke of Brittany, E 404/59/299; *College of Arms*, pp. 40–1.

KENTWOOD, Reginald, Dean of St. Paul's: (24 Mar. 1433), full power to redress grievances with the Bretons, Rymer, x. 546.

LOWIS, John, esquire: (Jan. 1438), minutes concerning an embassy to Brittany, *Proc. P.C.* v. 86.

LYNDWOOD, William, Dr.: (24 Mar. 1433), power to redress grievances with the Bretons, Rymer, x. 546; *Register of Oxford*, ii. 1191–3.

MAUGER, Jean: (1425), payment of an advance for going to the Duke of Brittany, B.N., MS. français 4491, f. 18^r.

MERLIN, William: (9 Nov. 1444), order to pay for going to Brittany with messages, E 404/61/104; (27 June 1445), order to pay for going to Brittany with messages, E 404/61/247.

MONTFERRAND, Bernard de, knight: (24 Feb. 1440), payment for going to Brittany, E 403/736/m. 16.

MORE, Philip: (20 Dec. 1436–29 Mar. 1437), account of mission to the Duke of Brittany, E 101/323/4.

POLE, Walter de la, knight: (c. 10–24 May 1432), mentioned, E 101/322/38; (21 Mar. 1433), power to redress grievances with the Bretons, Rymer, x. 543.

POPHAM, John, knight: (23 June–20 Oct. 1438), account of a trip to Normandy and Brittany, E 101/323/5, 6; Wedgwood, *History of Parliament: Biographies*, pp. 692–3.

ROOS, Robert, knight: (11 June–30 Dec. 1451), order to pay Roos's executors for his mission to Brittany, E 404/68/89.

STOKES, John, Dr.: (10–24 May 1432), account of mission to the duke, E 101/328/38; (21 Mar. 1433), full power to redress grievances with Brittany, Rymer, x. 543. *Register of Oxford*, iii. 1781–3.

TYRELL, William, esquire: (17 Apr. 1444), order for attending Gilles of Brittany for 48 days he was out of court, E 404/60/143; Wedgwood, *History of Parliament: Biographies*, pp. 891–2.

VULRE, Gervaise le, master: (4 July 1443), order to pay an advance on his wages for going to Brittany, *Proc. P.C.* v. 297.

6. ENVOYS FROM BRITTANY TO ENGLAND

BRETAIGNE Herald: (9 Mar. 1443), payment of a reward to, E 403/747/m. 13.

BRUN, Jean de: (9 July 1423), mentioned, C 81/679/831.

CHARDOWNE, servant of Gilles of Brittany: (12 Dec. 1447), mentioned, E 404/64/99.

ERMINE Herald: (8 Aug. 1442), pay a reward to, E 403/745/m. 13.

GODART, Jacques, secretary of the Duke of Brittany: (12 Nov. 1433), payment of a reward for having come to redress grievances, E 403/712/m. 3; (21 June 1445), order to pay a reward to, E 404/61/243.

GOLDYN, Reginald, master: (8 Aug. 1442), payment to, E 403/745/m. 13; (1 Feb. 1447), payment to, E 403/765/m. 14.

GRIVYNE Pursuivant: (21 June 1445), order to pay a reward to, E 404/61/243.

GUÉMÉNÉ, Seigneur de: (13 July 1445), mentioned, E 403/757/m. 9.

HUSY, Nicholas, esquire: (26 Jan. 1444), payment for going abroad with Gilles of Brittany, E 404/60/109.

L'ABBÉ (LAWE), Alan: (2 Dec. 1443), pay a reward to, E 403/751/m. 3; *Proc. P.C.* vi. 17.

L'HOSTEL, Jean de, master: (13 July 1445), mentioned, E 403/757/m. 9.

MALESTROIT, Guillaume, Bishop of Nantes: (19 July 1432), payment of a reward to, E 403/703/m. 14; (13 July 1445), payment of a reward to, E 403/757/m. 9.

PASEN, Jean, servant of Gilles of Brittany: (12 Dec. 1447), mentioned, E 404/64/99.

PEGER, Jean, servant of Gilles of Brittany: (12 Dec. 1447), mentioned, E404/64/99.

PREGENT, Jean, Dr.: (12 Nov. 1433), payment of a reward to, for having come to redress grievances, E 403/712/m. 3.

PURSUIVANT: (24 July 1447), payment of a reward to, E 403/775/m. 2.

TROMPETTE, Pierre, pursuivant: (24 Nov. 1445), order to pay a reward, E 404/62/83.

VILLEBLANCHE, Henri de la: (13 July 1445), mentioned, E 403/757/m. 9.

7. ENGLISH ENVOYS TREATING WITH CASTILE

ALNWICK, William, Bishop of Norwich: (8 Nov. 1430), one-year truce with Castile, Rymer, x. 473; *Register of Cambridge*, p. 11.

AVISA, Pedro de, Regent of Portugal: (9 Aug. 1445), full powers to treat for a truce with Castile, Rymer, xi. 96.

CROMWELL, Ralph, Lord Cromwell: (8 Nov. 1430), one-year truce with Castile, Rymer, x. 473; *Complete Peerage*, iii. 552.

DUDLEY, John (19 Aug.–24 Sept. 1447) account for going to Aquitaine and places in Spain, Rymer, v. 182 (Hague edn.).

KENT, Thomas, Dr.: (Aug. 1447–Sept. 1448), full powers to treat for redress of grievances, C 61/135/m. 3; *Register of Oxford*, ii, 1037–8.

LYNDWOOD, William, Dr.: (8 Nov. 1430), one-year truce with Castile, Rymer, x. 473; *Register of Oxford*, ii. 1191–3.

MONBRUN, Sampson de: (15 Oct. 1429), order to pay for taking messages to Castile, E 404/46/122.

SAINT-PEY, Jean de: (7 Nov. 1432), payment for negotiating with the King of Castile, E 403/707/m. 5.

SUTTON, John, Lord Dudley: (19 Aug. 1447–24 Sept. 1448), account of mission to Castile, E 101/324/4; *Complete Peerage*, iv. 479–80.

8. ENVOYS FROM CASTILE TO ENGLAND

ASTURIAS Herald: (24 Nov. 1445), order to pay, and payment of a reward to, E 404/62/82, E 403/759/m. 5.

BISCAY Pursuivant: (30 July 1447), order to pay, and payment of a reward to, E 404/63/115, E 403/767/m. 13.

BURGOS, Alfonso de: (20 Nov. 1430), safe conduct for, C 76/113/m. 19.

CURRALLI, Juan de, Fr.: (8 Mar. 1430), safe conduct for, Rymer, x. 452; (8 Nov. 1430), one-year truce with England, Rymer, x. 473.

CURRILLO, Pedro, knight: (14 June 1430), full powers, which are misdated in Rymer, to treat with the English, Rymer, x. 468; E 30/436.

ESQUERRA, Sancho: (12 June 1428), safe conduct for, C 76/110/m. 14; (21 Nov. 1429), safe conduct for, Rymer, x. 411.

FRU', Guidani: (2 Dec. 1430), payment for coming from the King of Castile, E 403/696/m. 9.

MARTÍN, Francisco: (30 July 1447), order to pay a sum of money owed the Spanish, E 404/63/134.

ROXAS, Sancho de, Bishop of Astorga: (14 June 1430), full powers, which are misdated in Rymer, to treat with the English, Rymer, x. 468; E 30/436.

TORRES, Juan de: (22 Jan. 1433), order to draw up safe conduct for, C 81/696/2621.

9. ENGLISH ENVOYS TREATING WITH ARAGON

BLODWELL, John, master: (1 Mar. 1424), full powers to treat for an alliance with Alfonso V, Rymer, x. 319; *Register of Oxford*, i. 202–3.

BORDE, Guillaume Arnaud de la, Bishop of Bayonne: (16 Nov. 1430), full powers to treat with the Aragonese and Navarrese at Bayonne, Rymer, x. 477; *Gallia Christiana*, vol. i, coll. 1317–18.

BOTYLL, Robert, Prior of the Order of St. John of Jerusalem in England: (29 Apr. 1451), order to pay for going to Utrecht, the pope, and Alfonso V, E 404/67/141; E. J. King, *The Grand Priory of the Order of the Hospital of St. John of Jerusalem in England* (London, 1924), pp. 50–2.

BRETON, Guillaume, master: (*c.* Jan. 1423), instructions for negotiations with Alfonso V, B.N., MS. Dupuy 223, f. 232ʳ.

BRUTAILS, Louis de: (14 July 1459), mentioned in letter from Joan II to Henry VI, A.C.A., Registro 3408, f. 24ᵛ.

BURTON, Thomas, Mayor of Bayonne: (16 Nov. 1430), full powers to treat with the envoys from Aragon and Navarre, Rymer, x. 477; (16 Feb. 1432), full powers to treat with envoys from Aragon and Navarre, Rymer, x. 499.

CLARENCEAU King of Arms: (27 June 1452), order to pay for taking the Garter to Alfonso V and the King of Poland, E 404/68/188; ? *College of Arms*, pp. 75–7.

CLEMENT, Vicent, Dr.: (26 Jan. 1423), order to pay for going to the pope and Alfonso V, E 404/59/132; *Register of Oxford*, i. 432–3.

COMITON', Henry: (1 Feb. 1451), order to pay for taking letters to Aragon, E 404/67/112.

EIMERI, Guillaume, master: (*c.* Jan. 1423), instructions for treating with Alfonso V, B.N., MS. Dupuy 223, f. 232ʳ.

FITZHUGH, Robert, master: (16 July 1429), full powers to treat with the King of Aragon, Rymer, x. 433; *Register of Oxford*, ii. 689–90.

GENTILL, John, Dr.: (28 July 1424–15 Mar. 1425), account of mission to the Spanish kingdoms, E 101/322/8; (16 Nov. 1430), full powers to treat with envoys from Aragon and Navarre, Rymer, x. 477; *Register of Oxford*, ii. 755.

GRAY, William, Bishop of London: (13 July 1428), full powers to treat with Alfonso V and Sigismund, Rymer, x. 407; *Register of Oxford*, ii. 808–9.

HERBURG, Henry: (16 July 1429), full powers to treat with Aragon, Rymer, x. 433.

HOLES, Andrew, master: (16 July 1429), full powers to treat with Aragon, Rymer, x. 433; *Register of Oxford*, ii. 949–50.

LESCROPE, John, Lord: (13 July 1428), full powers to treat for an alliance with Alfonso V, Rymer, x. 407; *Complete Peerage*, xi. 566–8.

MONTFERRAND, Bernard de, knight: (*c*. Jan. 1423), instructions for negotiating with Alfonso V, B.N., MS. Dupuy 223, f. 232^r.

NEWPORT, John, esquire: (27 June 1452), order to pay for taking the Garter to Alfonso V and the King of Poland, E 404/68/188; Wedgwood, *History of Parliament: Biographies*, pp. 630–1.

PARTRIDGE, Peter, master: (13 July 1428), full powers to treat with Alfonso V and Sigismund, Rymer, x. 407; *Register of Oxford*, iii. 1430–1.

PLANCHE, Bernard de la, Bishop of Dax: (16 Feb. 1432), full powers to treat with envoys from Aragon and Navarre, Rymer, x. 499; *Gallia Christiana*, i. 1055.

POLE, Walter de la, knight: (1 Mar. 1424), full powers to treat for an alliance with Alfonso V, Rymer, x. 319; Roskell, *Parliament of 1422*, pp. 172–4.

SALBURY, William, Abbot of Beaulieu: (1 Mar. 1424), full powers to treat with the King of Aragon, Rymer, x. 319.

SPOFFORD, Thomas, Bishop of Hereford: (16 July 1429), full powers to treat with the King of Aragon, Rymer, x. 433; *Reg. Spofford*, pp. i–v.

STOKES, John, master: (13 July 1428), full powers to treat with Alfonso V and Sigismund, Rymer, x. 407; *Register of Oxford*, iii. 1781–3.

VESCOMTAU, Pierre Arnaud deu: (16 Feb. 1432), full powers to treat with envoys from Aragon and Navarre, Rymer, x. 499.

10. ENVOYS FROM ARAGON TO ENGLAND

BOYL, Felip, knight: (18 Oct. 1445), order to pay for bringing letters and instructions from Alfonso, E 404/62/46; (16 Aug. 1449), order to pay a reward to, E 403/775/m. 9; (2 July 1450), payment of a reward to, E 403/779/m. 19.

CATALUNYA, Joan Colonie de: (19 Feb. 1449), payment for coming to see the king, E 403/773/m. 13.

Fal, Andreu: (2 Nov. 1450), mentioned in a letter from Alfonso V to Henry VI, A.C.A., Registro 2655, f. 97ᵛ.

Falcs, Lluís de: (10 Mar. 1423), order to pay for bringing messages from Alfonso V, E 403/658/m. 14; (summer–Oct. 1430), in London negotiating with the English, A.C.A., Registro 2692, f. 41ʳ; (15 Nov. 1430), full powers to treat with the English at Bayonne, A.C.A., Registro 2692, f. 117ʳ⁻ᵛ.

Fanosse, Dalmanu: (2 Nov. 1450), mentioned in a letter from Alfonso V to Henry VI, A.C.A., Registro 2655, f. 97ᵛ.

Ferrer, Andreu: (2 Nov. 1450), mentioned in a letter from Alfonso V to Henry VI, A.C.A., Registro 2655, f. 97ᵛ.

Grau, Pere: (27 Aug. 1436), letters of credence for, Archivo Histórico de la Ciudad de Barcelona, Lletres Closes, 1436–8, f. 43ʳ.

Herald: (22 Aug. 1443), order to pay a reward to, E 404/71/2/5; (3 July 1445), payment of a reward to, E 403/757/m. 7; (21 Nov. 1452), payment of a reward to, E 403/791/m. 3.

Jofre, Pere: (23 Aug. 1436), letters of credence for, Archivo Histórico de la Ciudad de Barcelona, Lletres Closes, 1436–8, f. 43ʳ.

Mill' Pursuivant: (17 Oct. 1442), order to pay a reward to, E/404/59/66.

Pellegrini, Jaume: (summer–Oct. 1430), in London negotiating with the English, A.C.A., Registro 2692, f. 41ʳ; (15 Nov. 1430), full powers to treat with the English at Bayonne, A.C.A., Registro 2692, f. 117ʳ⁻ᵛ.

Pujades, Mateu: (15 Nov. 1430), full powers to treat with the English at Bayonne, A.C.A., Registro 2692, f. 117ʳ⁻ᵛ.

Pursuivant: (17 July 1454), payment of a reward to, E 403/798/m. 17.

Sicily King of Arms: (28 Apr. 1456), order to pay, and payment for coming to England with letters, E 404/70/3/67, E 403/807/m. 1.

Stiparlo Herald: (28 Apr. 1449), payment of a reward to, E 403/775/m. 11.

Urries, Hugo de, knight: (24 Mar. 1448), order to pay a reward for bringing letters and credences, E 404/65/125, E 28/78/3.

Villafranca (Willefrance), Joan: (10 Sept. 1443), order to pay a reward to for bringing letters and returning, E 404/60/14.

II. ENVOYS FROM NAVARRE TO ENGLAND

Aibar, Peyron Ruiz de: (11 Mar. 1426), payment to, A.G.N., Cajón 125, no. 9 (iii).

Beaumont, Charles de: (c. Jan. 1431), payment for going to England, A.G.N., Compto del tesorero, t. 398, f. 123ᵛ.

Beaumont, Luis de: (10 Sept. 1426), payment to, A.G.N., Cajón 139, no. 30.

Bonnefoi Pursuivant: (9 Dec. 1430), payment for going to Bayonne, A.G.N., Compto del tesorero, t. 398, f. 124ʳ.

DAGNERR', Johanicot, servant of Charles de Beaumont: (11 July 1427), payment for bringing letters to England, E 403/680/m. 2.

DEZPELETE, Juan, knight: (*c.* Jan. 1431), payment for going to Bayonne to treat with the English, A.G.N., Compto del tesorero, t. 402, f. 110^r.

GALLINDO, Juan, prior of Santa Maria de Roncesvalles: (*c.* Jan. 1431), payment for going to Bayonne to treat with the English, A.G.N., Compto del tesorero, t. 403, f. 79^r.

LONDRES, Juan de: (15 Sept. 1436), payment to, A.G.N., Compto del tesorero, t. 427, f. 101^r; Cajón 139, no. 30.

MONTREAL, Gracián de: (1430), payment for going to England, A.G.N., Compto del tesorero, t. 398, f. 123^v.

PAMPLONA Herald: (*c.* Jan. 1431), payment for going to the English at Bayonne, A.G.N., Compto del tesorero, t. 403, f. 77^v.

UXIZ, Martín de: (11 Dec. 1441), payment for going to Bayonne and Bordeaux, A.G.N., Cajón 151, no. 29.

12. ENGLISH ENVOYS TREATING WITH FOIX

BARRY, Guillaume, French secretary: (5 Mar. 1423), order payment of expenses in London after having come from Foix, E 404/39/155.

GUIRAUD, Pierre, master: (22 Mar. 1423), order to pay for going to Foix, E 404/39/168; (22 July 1424), payment for going to Foix, E 403/666/m. 12.

LEBRET, Raymond Arnaud de: (Sept. 1422), mentioned, B.N., MS. Dupuy 223, f. 230^r.

LESCAR, Guillaume Raymond, viscount of: (Sept. 1422), mentioned, B.N., MS. Dupuy 223, f. 230^r.

13. ENVOYS FROM FOIX TO ENGLAND

LOBYE, Raymond Arnaud de: (22 Mar. 1423), order to pay a reward to, E 404/39/17.

SAINT-JEAN, Guillaume Raymond de: (22 Mar. 1423), order to pay a reward to, E 404/39/17.

14. ENGLISH ENVOYS TREATING WITH PORTUGAL

CAREW, Thomas, baron: (3 Mar.–14 Sept. 1422), mentioned, E 101/322/1, 2.

GARTER King of Arms: (8 June 1437), payment for going to Portugal, E 403/727/m. 5; *College of Arms*, pp. 40–1.

GENTILL, John, Dr.: (28 July 1424–15 Mar. 1425), account of mission to the Spanish kingdoms, E 101/322/8; *Register of Oxford*, ii. 755.

GLOUCESTER Herald: (24 May 1427), payment for taking livery of the Garter to the Duke of Coimbra, E 403/727/m. 5.

LYNDWOOD, William, Dr.: (3 Mar.–14 Sept. 1422), account for going to the King of Portugal, E 101/322/1, 2.

SETPLACE, John, esquire: (4 Nov. 1457), order to pay for taking the livery of the Garter to Portugal, E 404/71/2/24.

15. ENVOYS FROM PORTUGAL TO ENGLAND

ALGARVE King of Arms: (9 July 1448), order to pay a reward to, E 404/64/ 229.

ALMADA, Rolando Alvaro Vaz de, knight: (20 May 1449), order to pay a reward to, E 404/65/176.

BALENCE Pursuivant: (18 July 1442), payment of a reward to, E 403/745/ m. 12; (22 Oct. 1443), order to pay a reward to, E 404/60/64.

CASTRO, Fernando de: (15 July 1455), mentioned and payment of a reward for coming to redress grievances, B.M., Cotton MS. Nero B.I, f. 52; E 403/801/m. 7.

CUNHA, Alvaro de: (8, 23 Feb. 1440), orders to pay a reward to, E 404/56/ 167, 176.

DAZENEDE, Luiz: (4 Apr. 1436), payment of a reward to for coming to the king and to the council, E 403/721/m. 18.

FALERO, Pedro de: (6 Aug. 1455), order to pay a reward to, E 404/70/2/95.

HERALD: (27 June 1446), order to pay a reward to, E 403/772/m. 4; (29 Aug. 1449), order to pay a reward to, *Proc. P.C.* v. 209.

LISBON Herald: (4 June 1452), order to pay the Earl of Shrewsbury who paid a reward to, E 404/68/132.

MONS MAJOR Herald: (20 July 1438), order to pay a reward to, E 404/809/ m. 2.

MYNDEE, Rothomagus, knight: (10 Mar. 1424), payment of a reward to, E 403/658/m. 14.

OLEXIRA, knight: (21 Oct. 1456), payment of a reward to, E 403/52/322.

PORTUGAL King of Arms: (15 July 1455), payment of a reward to, E 403/ 801/m. 2.

PYRIS, Alvaro, clerk: (22 July 1440), payment of a reward to, E 403/739/ m. 16.

VASQUEZ, Rolando: (18 July 1442), payment for bringing answers to messages previously sent to Portugal, E 403/745/m. 2.

WILTSHIRE (WILTES), John, knight: (28 Oct. 1456), payment of a reward to, E 403/809/m. 3; (7 Feb. 1457), order to pay for bringing letters from Portugal, E 404/71/1/53.

16. ENGLISH ENVOYS TREATING WITH COLOGNE, MARK, AND MÜNSTER

BONREPORT, pursuivant: (9 May 1450), payment for going to Cologne with Thomas Kent, E 403/779/m. 3.

CARSTER, Janyn, from Valencia: (16 May 1442), payment for going to Cologne, E 403/745/m. 4.

CLEMENT, Vicent, Dr.: (18 Aug. 1441), mentioned as going to the Archbishop of Cologne with secret instructions, *Correspondence Bekynton*, i. 131; *Register of Oxford*, i. 432–3.

CLIFTON, Robert, knight: (16 Dec. 1435), payment for going to the emperor and to the Archbishop of Cologne, E 403/721/m. 11; Wedgwood, *History of Parliament: Biographies*, pp. 195–6.

HULL, Edward: (? Oct. 1441), mentioned as going to Cologne with secret instructions, *Correspondence Bekynton*, i. 167; Wedgwood, *History of Parliament: Biographies*, pp. 481–2.

KENT, Thomas, Dr.: (9 May 1450), order to pay for going to Cologne, *Proc. P.C.* vi. 92; *Register of Oxford*, ii. 1037–8.

KLUX, Hertonk van, knight: (13 May 1440), letters of credence to the Archbishop of Cologne, *Correspondence Bekynton*, i. 85.

LESCROPE, John, Lord: (4 Feb. 1439), full powers to treat with the Archbishop of Cologne, C 76/121/m. 16; (12 Dec. 1439), treaty between the Count of Mark and England, Urkunde Kleve-Mark, 1603; *Complete Peerage*, xi. 566–8.

LYNDWOOD, William, Dr.: (12 Dec. 1439), treaty between the Count of Mark and England, Urkunde Kleve-Mark, 1603; *Register of Oxford*, ii. 1191–3.

MOLEYNS, Adam, Dr.: (23 Aug. 1440), treaty between Cologne and England, Rymer, x. 834–40; *Register of Oxford*, ii. 1289–91.

RODBURN, Thomas, Bishop of St. David's: (4 Feb. 1439), full powers to treat with the Archbishop of Cologne, C 76/121/m. 16; *Register of Oxford*, iii. 1582–3.

SIGISMUND, a knight, from Germany: (17 Mar. 1438), payment of a reward to, E 403/729/m. 15.

STOPINGDON, John: (23 Aug. 1440), treaty between Cologne and England, Rymer, x. 834–40.

STORTHWAYT, John: (12 Dec. 1439), treaty between the Count of Mark and England, Urkunde Kleve-Mark, 1603; (23 Aug. 1440), treaty between Cologne and England, Rymer, x. 834–40.

SWAN, William: (23 Aug. 1440), treaty between Cologne and England, Rymer, x. 834–40; *Register of Oxford*, iii. 1829–30.

TALBOT, John, knight: (4 Feb. 1439), full powers to treat with the Archbishop of Cologne, C 76/121/m. 16; *Complete Peerage*, xi. 698–702.

TIPTOFT, John, Lord: (23 Aug. 1440), treaty between Cologne and England, Rymer, x. 834–40; *Complete Peerage*, xii, pt. ii, 746–9.

WILTON, Stephen, Dr.: (27 Dec. 1435–24 May 1436), account for going to the emperor and to the Archbishop of Cologne, E 403/721/m. 11, E 101/323/3; *Register of Oxford*, iii. 2053–4.

WYPENORD, Johannes von, *alias* Rosencrans: (Feb. 1443) payment for going to Cologne, Rymer, xi 19.

17. ENVOYS FROM COLOGNE, MARK, AND MUÑSTER TO ENGLAND

ARDENBURY, John, pursuivant: (12 Dec. 1449), payment of a reward for coming with letters, E 403/778/m. 7.

ARNSBERGHE': (25 June 1449), mentioned, Urkunde Kleve-Mark, 2216.

BOCHOLDIA, Simon de: (18 Nov. 1439), mentioned as having brought letters to England, *Correspondence Bekynton*, i. 75.

BREMPT, Arnold de: (4 Mar. 1437), payment of a reward to, E 403/735/ m. 11; (21 May 1439), credence to deliver to the Archbishop of Cologne, Lacomblet, vol. iv, no. 231; (5 Nov. 1439), mentioned, *Correspondence Bekynton*, i. 73.

BYLLESTRAYNE, Gerard, herald: (8 Apr. 1450), order to pay a reward to, E 28/80/30.

COELFELDA, Johannes, clerk: (4 Mar. 1437), payment of a reward to, E 403/ 725/m. 11.

DOWLER, Johannes: (27 Apr. 1438), full powers to negotiate an alliance with England, E 30/449.

DUBIO, Johannes de, master: (30 Feb.–24 Mar. 1449), payment of a reward to, E 403/773/m. 14, E 404/65/124.

FROWENBERGH, Johannes de: (20 Feb. 1441), order to pay a reward to, E 404/57/176; (7 Nov. 1441), payment of a reward for bringing letters and returning to Cologne with answers, E 403/743/m. 3.

LINS', Theolman de, provost of St. Florian, Koblenz: (22 July–2 Sept. 1440), payment of a reward to and treaty between the Count of Mark and England, E 403/734/m. 17; Urkunde Kleve-Mark, 1974.

MERWYCK, Isbrand de: (12 Dec. 1439–3 Feb. 1440), treaty between England and Cologne, Urkunde Kleve-Mark, 1603; *Correspondence Bekynton*, i. 77; (Oct. 1451–29 Nov. 1452), order to pay a reward to, E 404/68/61, 69/72; (28 Feb. 1454), payment of a reward to, E 403/759/m. 13.

NURNAI, Gumbrecht de, Lord of Alpen: (22 July–2 Sept. 1440), payment of a reward to and treaty between Cologne and England, E 403/739/m. 17; Rymer, x. 834–40; Urkunde Kleve-Mark, 1974.

PASTEUR, Simon, de Herpell': (14 Nov. 1439), payment of a reward to, E 404/56/137.

PETERSSON, Dauker: (17 July 1438), mentioned as having brought letters from Cologne to England, *Correspondence Bekynton*, i. 131.

PURSUIVANT: (10 May 1449), payment of a reward to, E 403/775/m. 2.

ROULANDZWERDE, Johannes: (20 Feb.–24 Mar. 1449), payment of a reward to, E 403/773/m. 14, E 404/54/124.

UPINGRAVE, Johannes, clerk: (4 Mar. 1437), payment of a reward to, E 403/ 725/m. 11.

18. ENVOYS FROM ITALY TO ENGLAND

EMONG', Roberto, esquire: (19 Apr. 1448), payment for coming from Mantua with messages, E 403/772/m. 1.

HERKYN', Reynaldo: (5 July 1446), payment for bringing messages from the Duke of Milan to the king, E 403/762/m. 5.

MINSTRELS: (18 June 1445), payment for coming to see and report the coronation of the queen for the Duke of Milan, E 403/757/m. 5.

19. ENGLISH ENVOYS TREATING WITH PRUSSIA AND THE HANSEATIC LEAGUE

ALNETO, Gilbert de, knight: (24 Dec. [1442]), mentioned, *Regesta*, vol. i, no. 8632.

ALNWICK, William, Bishop of Lincoln: (6 Nov. 1436), full powers to treat with envoys from the Hansa, Rymer, x. 659; *Register of Cambridge*, p. 11.

BAMPTON, John: (4 Apr. 1435), envoy from King's Lynn to treat with the Prussians at Bruges, *Hist. MSS. Com. 11th Report*, app., pt. 3, p. 163.

BEK, John, knight: (24 July 1448), letters of proxy to redress injuries with the Hanseatic League, Rymer, xi. 217–8.

BERMYNGHAM, Henry: (28 June 1450–14 June 1452), account of mission to Prussia and the Hansa towns, E 101/324/18; Wedgwood, *History of Parliament: Biographies*, p. 79.

BOKELAND, Richard: (17 Dec. 1435), letters of proxy to redress injuries with the Hanseatic League, Rymer, x. 627–8.

BOROWE, Thomas: (17 Dec. 1435), letters of proxy to redress injuries with the Hanseatic League, Rymer, x. 627–8.

BOTYLL, Robert, Prior of the Order of St. John of Jerusalem in England: (17 Apr. 1451), letters of attorney for, C 76/133/m. 9; E. J. King, *The Grand Priory of the Order of the Hospital of St John of Jerusalem in England* (London, 1924), pp. 50–2.

BURGH, Thomas: (4 Apr. 1435), envoy from King's Lynn to treat with the Prussians at Bruges, *Hist. MSS. Com. 11th Report*, app., pt. 3, p. 163; Wedgwood, *History of Parliament: Biographies*, p. 135.

CAUNTON, Richard, Dr.: (17 Dec. 1435), letters of proxy to redress grievances with the Hanseatic League, Rymer, x. 657; (24 July 1448), letters of proxy to redress injuries with the Hansa, Rymer, xi. 217–18; (4 Sept. 1450), order to pay for a mission abroad, E 404/67/7; *Register of Oxford*, i. 373–4.

CROMWELL, Ralph, Lord Cromwell: (6 Nov. 1436), full powers to treat with envoys from the Hanseatic League; Rymer, x. 657; *Complete Peerage*, iii. 552.

CROUCH, Thomas, merchant: (10 July 1450), letters of protection for, in the retinue of Thomas Kent, Rymer, xi. 274.

CURZON, Walter: (4 Apr. 1450), envoy from King's Lynn to treat with the Prussians at Bruges, *Hist. MSS. Com. 11th Report*, app., pt. 3, p. 163; Wedgwood, *History of Parliament: Biographies*, p. 246.

FROWICK, Henry: (2 Feb. 1438), mentioned, E 28/63/54; Wedgwood, *History of Parliament: Biographies*, p. 357.

GOSSELYN, John: (June 1450), letters of protection, going abroad in the retinue of Thomas Kent, C 76/132/m. 4; (5 May 1451), letters of protection for, going abroad in the retinue of Robert Botyll, C 76/133/m. 9.

HEYWORTH, William, Bishop of Coventry and Lichfield: (2 Feb. 1439), mentioned, E 28/63/54; *Register of Oxford*, ii. 929.

KENT, Thomas, Dr.: (23 Sept. 1449), letters of proxy to redress grievances with Prussia, Rymer, xi. 241; (June 1450–11 Dec. 1451), mission to the Hansa and Prussia, Cooper, *Appendix C*, p. 8; (3 Nov., 2 Dec. 1452), payments for mission to Prussia and the Hansa, E 403/791/mm. 2, 5; *Register of Oxford*, ii. 1037–8.

LYNDWOOD, William, Dr.: (2 Feb. 1439), mentioned, E 28/63/54; *Register of Oxford*, ii. 1191–3.

RADCLIFFE, John, knight: (9 Mar. 1436), full powers to treat with Prussia and the Hansa, C 76/118/m. 14; *Complete Peerage*, v. 584, n. g., 585, n. a.

SELLING, Richard: (17 Dec. 1435), letters of proxy to redress injuries with the Hanseatic League, Rymer, x. 627–8.

SHOTTESBROOK, Robert, knight: (9 Sept. 1432–8 May 1433), account of a mission to Denmark and the Hansa, E 101/322/23; (24 July 1448), letters of proxy to redress injuries with the Hanseatic League, Rymer, xi. 217–18; Wedgwood, *History of Parliament: Biographies*, pp. 766–7.

SPREVER, William, Dr.: (6 Nov. 1436), full powers to treat with envoys from the Hansa, Rymer, x. 657; (2 Feb. 1439), mentioned, E 28/63/54; *Register of Oxford*, iii. 1745–6.

STOCKER, John: (16 July 1450–14 June 1452), mentioned in Bermyngham's account, E 364/86.

STOCKHARD, Robert: (20 June 1442), mentioned, *Regesta*, vol. i, no. 8149.

STOKES, John, Dr.: (16 Dec. 1435), payment for going to Bruges to treat with the Prussians, E 403/721/m. 11; (6 Nov. 1436), letters of proxy to redress grievances with the Hansa, Rymer, x. 657; (2 Feb. 1439), mentioned, E 28/63/54; *Register of Oxford*, iii. 1781–2.

SUTTON, John, Lord Dudley: (9 Mar. 1436), full powers to treat with Prussians and the Hansa, C 76/118/m. 14; (23 Sept. 1449), letters of proxy to redress infractions of the truce with Prussia, Rymer, xi. 241; *Complete Peerage*, ix. 479–80.

TIPTOFT, John, Lord: (6 Nov. 1436), full powers to treat with envoys from the Hansa, Rymer, x. 657; *Complete Peerage*, xii, pt. 2, 946–9.

WILTON, Stephen, Dr.: (14 Feb. 1435), full powers to treat with Prussia and the Hansa to restore the former treaty, *Regesta*, vol. i, no. 6977; *Register of Oxford*, iii. 2053–4.

WITHAM, William: (5 May 1451), full power to treat with Prussia and the Hansa, C 76/133/m. 9.

WOODVILLE, Richard, knight: (17 Dec. 1435), full powers to redress injuries with the Hansa, Rymer, x. 627–8; *Complete Peerage*, xi. 19–22.

20. ENVOYS FROM PRUSSIA AND THE HANSEATIC LEAGUE TO ENGLAND

AST, Johannes von, priest of Alt-Thorn: (7 Aug. 1447), report on negotiations with the English, *Regesta*, vol. i, no. 9375; (12 June 1451), peace articles between England and Prussia, *Regesta*, pt. 2, no. 2820.

CALVEN, Wilhelm von: (12 June 1451), peace articles between England and Prussia, *Regesta*, pt. 2, no. 2820.

DANNENBERG, Hildebrand: (11 Feb. 1436), full powers to negotiate with the English, *Regesta*, vol. i, no. 7151.

DISTRETES, Heinrich: (2 Feb. 1439), mentioned, E 28/63/54.

GREVENSTEIN, Heinrich: (12 June 1454), mentioned, *Hansische Urkundenbuch*, vol. viii, no. 380.

HARDENURST, Eberhard: (12 Feb. 1435), mentioned, Cooper, *Appendix C*, p. 6.

HERTZE, Johannes: (2 Feb. 1439), mentioned, E 28/63/54.

HOIGER, Heinrich: (12 Feb. 1435), mentioned, Cooper, *Appendix C*, p. 6.

HOUE, Viko vam: (2 Feb. 1439), mentioned, E 28/63/54.

KEDDEKON, Fauk: (2 Feb. 1439), mentioned, E 28/63/54.

KLINGENBERG, Johannes: (12 Feb. 1435), mentioned, Cooper, *Appendix C*, p. 6.

MEYDEBURG, Johannes: (23 Apr. 1451), full powers to negotiate a treaty between England and Prussia, *Regesta*, vol. i, no. 10695.

MINDEN, Gerhard von: (12 June 1451), peace articles between England and Prussia, *Regesta*, pt. 2, no. 2820.

ROWBER, Georg: (23 Apr. 1451), full powers to treat with England, *Regesta*, vol. i, no. 10695.

SOBBE, Johann, priest of Thorn: (14 Feb. 1436), full powers to negotiate with the English, *Regesta*, no. 7151.

VORRATH, Heinrich: (12 Feb. 1435), mentioned, Cooper, *Appendix C*, p. 6; (14 Feb. 1436), full powers to negotiate with the English, *Regesta*, vol. i, no. 7151; (25 July 1435–18 Mar. 1437), payment of money owed to the Hansa, E 403/725/m. 19; (18 Mar. 1438), receipt for 500 marks paid to the Hansa, *Regesta*, vol. i, no. 7426; (2 Feb. 1439), mentioned, E 28/63/54.

21. ENGLISH ENVOYS TREATING WITH DENMARK

BEK, John, knight: (28 Oct. 1447–1 Mar. 1450), order to pay for a mission to Denmark, E 404/65/192, E 101/324/16; (30 Nov. 1453), payment for a mission to Denmark, E 403/795/m. 6.

CAUNTON, Richard, Dr.: (Sept. 1448–22 Mar. 1450), order to pay for a mission to Denmark, PSO I/16/817a; *Register of Oxford*, i. 373–4; (*Deputy Keeper's 45th Report*, app. ii, p. 5, mistakenly records his Christian name as John).

LEYOT, Richard, Dean of Salisbury: (25 Oct. 1447), letters of protection for, Rymer, xi. 188; *Register of Oxford*, iii. 2189–90.

MURIELL, John: (2 Jan. 1431), mentioned, *Hist. MSS. Com. 11th Report*, app., pt. 3, p. 162.

NORTON, John, Dr.: (4 Aug. 1424–28 Feb. 1425), account of mission to Poland and Denmark, E 101/322/9; (14 May 1441), order to pay, E 404/58/77; *Register of Oxford*, ii. 1373–4.

ROLLESTON', Avery: (28 June 1449), mentioned as having brought a message from the English ambassador in Denmark, E 404/65/192.

SALUS, John: (3 Jan. 1431), to travel in the retinue of the ambassador John Muriell, *Hist. MSS. Com. 11th Report*, app., pt. 3, p. 162.

SHOTTESBROOK, Robert, knight: (9 Sept. 1432–8 May 1433), account of mission to Denmark and the Hansa, E 101/322/23; (6 Sept. 1448–24 May 1449), account of mission to Denmark, E 101/324/17; Wedgwood, *History of Parliament: Biographies*, pp. 766–7.

SPREVER, William, Dr.: (6 Feb.–23 Dec. 1431), account of mission to Denmark, E 101/322/42; (21 July 1432), letters of proxy to treat with the King of Denmark, Rymer, x. 521; (7 July 1437), order to pay, E 404/54/178; *Register of Oxford*, iii. 1745–6.

22. ENVOYS FROM DENMARK TO ENGLAND

DENMARK Herald: (28 Feb. 1454), payment of a reward to, E 403/795/m. 14; (9 Aug. 1456), order to pay a reward to, E 404/71/1/42.

HAWSENORE, George, de Bavoir': (28 May 1444), order to pay for bringing letters and returning with answers, E 404/60/206.

TRINISAM, Andrew: (3 Aug. 1459), safe conduct for, Rymer, xi. 425.

TRINISAM, Gremiman, knight: (18 July 1456), safe conduct for, C 76/132/m. 6; (22 July 1459), safe conduct for, Rymer, xi. 425.

23. ENGLISH ENVOYS TREATING WITH POLAND

CLARENCEAU King of Arms: (27 June 1452), order to pay for taking the Garter to the King of Poland, E 404/68/188; ? *College of Arms*, pp. 75–7.

NEWPORT, John, esquire: (27 June 1452), order to pay for taking the Garter to the King of Poland, E 404/68/188; Wedgwood, *History of Parliament: Biographies*, pp. 630–1.

NORTON, John, Dr.: (4 Aug. 1424–28 Feb. 1425), account of a mission to Poland and Denmark, E 101/322/9; (14 May 1441), order to pay a reward to, E 404/58/77; *Register of Oxford*, ii. 1373–4.

24. ENVOY FROM POLAND TO ENGLAND

BALALANEZ, James de, knight: (3 Feb. 1428), order to pay for a gold collar given to this knight, Rymer, x. 386.

25. ENGLISH ENVOYS TREATING WITH THE EMPIRE, AUSTRIA, BRUNSWICK, AND SAXONY

BEAUFORT, Henry, Bishop of Winchester: * (20 Feb. 1433), letters of protection for, C 76/115/m. 10; *Register of Oxford*, i. 139–42.

BEK, John, knight: (29 Jan.–16 June 1441), order to pay for going to the diet at Mainz and returning with letters from the emperor, E 404/57/164, *Correspondence Bekynton*, ii. 100.

BILDESTON, Nicholas, Dr.: (3 Mar.–27 Sept. 1422), account of mission to the princes of Almain, E 101/321/39; *Register of Oxford*, i. 187–8.

BIRD, Thomas, Fr.: (10 Nov. 1438), order to pay for going to Germany, E 404/55/126; (12 Sept. 1440–21 June 1441), order to pay for going to Germany, E 404/57/277; (26 Mar. 1442), order to pay, PSO I/13/691; (14 July 1449), order to pay for going abroad, E 28/78/219; *Register of Oxford*, i. 191.

BLATON, John de: (13 Feb. 1438), order to pay for going to the Duke of Austria, E 404/54/160.

BODULGATE, Thomas: (25 Feb. 1433), letters of protection for, C 76/115/m. 10; Wedgwood, *History of Parliament: Biographies*, pp. 87–8.

BOULERS, Reginald, Abbot of St. Peter's Gloucester: (13 Mar.–14 Aug. 1442), account of a mission to Frankfurt, E 101/324/2; *Register of Oxford*, i. 228–9.

CLIFTON, Robert, knight: (16 Dec. 1435), payment for going to the emperor and to the Archbishop of Cologne, E 403/721/m. 11; Wedgwood, *History of Parliament: Biographies*, pp. 195–6.

DUCHEMAN', Hanse: (1438), payment of a reward to, E 405/39/2rb.

FLEMING, Richard, Bishop of Lincoln: (23 Feb.–27 Sept. 1422), account of a mission to Germany, E 101/321/40; *Register of Oxford*, ii. 697–9.

FOSTON, John, clerk: ([Mar.–Aug.] 1442), payment for accompanying Adam Moleyns, E 403/755/m. 10.

GRAY, William, Bishop of London: (13 July 1428), full powers to treat with Sigismund, Rymer, x. 407; *Register of Oxford*, ii. 808–9.

GRENEVILL, John: (3 Dec. 1440), payment for going to the emperor, E 403/740/m. 8.

HOLLAND, John, Earl of Huntingdon: * (20 Feb. 1433), letters of protection for, C 76/115/m. 10; *Complete Peerage*, v. 205–11.

HULL, Edward: (13 July 1441), payment for going to Germany, E 403/741/ m. 8; Wedgwood, *History of Parliament: Biographies*, pp. 481–2.

KLUX, Hertonk van: (1438), payment of a reward to, E 405/2/39/2rb; (11 May 1440), full powers to renew the treaty with the emperor, *Deutsche Reichstagakten*, vol. xv, no. 138.

LESCROPE, John, Lord: (13 July 1428), full powers to negotiate a league with King Sigismund, Rymer, x. 407; *Complete Peerage*, xi. 543.

LOWE, John, Bishop of St. Asaph: (15 Mar.–14 Aug. 1442), account of a mission to Frankfurt, E 101/324/5; *Register of Oxford*, ii. 68–9.

MAKDOUNCHID, Magon, master: (30 Apr.–4 June 1440), order to pay and payment of a reward to, E 404/56/252, E 403/739/m. 7.

MOLEYNS, Adam, master: (16 May 1442), payment to, E 403/745/m. 4; *Register of Oxford*, ii. 1289–91.

NOSTWICH', George: (13 May 1438), order to pay a reward to, E 404/54/290.

PARTRIDGE, Peter: (13 July 1428), full powers to negotiate a league with King Sigismund, Rymer, x. 407; *Register of Oxford*, iii. 1430–1.

POLE, Walter de la: (3 Mar.–25 Sept. 1422), order to pay for a mission abroad, *Proc. P.C.* iii. 29–30; Roskell, *Parliament of 1422*, pp. 172–4.

SIGISMUND, a German knight: (15 Nov. 1436), order to pay for going to the emperor, E 404/53/137.

STOKE, John, Abbot of St. Albans: (7 May 1433), letters of protection for, C 76/115/m. 7; *V.C.H., Hertford*, iv. 402–4; *Register of Oxford*, iii. 1780.

STOKES, John, Dr.: (22 July–29 Nov. 1422), account of a mission to Germany, E 364/56; (2 Aug. 1424–20 Mar. 1425), account of a mission, E 364/58; (13 July 1428), full powers to negotiate a league with King Sigismund, Rymer, x. 407; (12 July 1434–7 July 1435), account of a mission, E 101/322/28; *Register of Oxford*, iii. 1781–2.

SWAN, William, master: (27 Nov. 1430), order to pay for taking letters to the emperor, Rymer, x. 481; (11 May–Dec. 1440), full powers to renew the treaty with the emperor, Rymer, x. 769, E 403/740/m. 8; *Register of Oxford*, iii. 1829–30.

WELLS, William, Bishop of Rochester: (24 May 1434–27 Dec. 1435), account of a mission to Basel and Frankfurt, E 101/322/29; (18 June 1443), payment for going to Frankfurt, E 403/749/m. 8.

26. ENVOYS FROM THE EMPIRE, AUSTRIA, BRUNSWICK, AND SAXONY TO ENGLAND

BARCHELONE Herald: (17 July 1454), order to pay a reward for bringing letters from the emperor, E 28/85/40.

CONRAD, a secretary: (20 Dec. 1452), order to pay a reward to, E 404/68/61.

CZUCHE, Deryk de: (12 July 1458), order to pay a reward for bringing letters, E 404/71/2/74.

ERKENBROCH', Johannes: (8 Mar. 1437), order to pay for bringing messages from the emperor and returning, E 404/53/178.

GUIDO, Antonius: (5 Dec. 1427), payment of a reward to, E 403/683/m. 10.

MORSYN', Martin, esquire: (31 Mar. 1450), payment of a reward to, E 403/778/m. 17.

OSTRINGG', nuncius: (28 Nov. 1440–16 Jan. 1441), order to pay and payment of a reward to, E 28/65/56, E 403/740/m. 10.

OTLYNGER, Sigismund, knight: (28 Aug.–9 Nov. 1436), E 403/732/m. 12; E 404/53/137; (17 July 1437), payment for going to the emperor and returning, E 403/721/m. 10; (10 June 1439), order to pay a reward to, E 404/55/300.

PISIS, Bartholomew de, Dr.: (5 Dec. 1427), payment of a reward to, E 403/683/m. 10.

PUSLYK, Otto de: (2 May–4 June 1440), order to pay and payment of a reward to, Correspondence Bekynton, i. 108; E 403/739/mm. 6–7.

STYRAND Herald: (21 July 1449), payment of a reward to, E 403/775/m. 8.

TEROM, Johannes von: (3 Oct. 1443), payment for bringing letters and returning with answers, E 403/751/m. 1.

WALDENCOTE, Heinrich de, knight: (2 July 1440), safe conduct for, C 76/122/m. 10.

ZINGELL, Stephen: (13 Feb. 1438), order to pay for returning to the Duke of Austria, E 404/54/162.

27. ENVOYS FROM THE RHINE PALATINATE TO ENGLAND

BAYER, Stephan, knight: (4 Dec. 1442), payment of the count's annuity, E 403/747/m. 7.

BERENFRAS, Johannes: (19 Nov. 1436), mentioned, Rymer, x. 659.

CRESZ, Bernard: (11 Apr.–17 May 1423), payment of the count's annuity, E 403/660/m. 5.

DANS, Johannes: * (13 Nov. 1424), mentioned, E 403/747/m. 4.

ENCZBEARK, Johannes de: (12 Dec. 1440), mentioned, Correspondence Bekynton, i. 182.

HOGGE, Hermann van der: (29 Oct.–16 Nov. 1439), payment of the costs and expenses he has incurred in England, E 404/56/132, E 403/736/m. 5.

KETWICH, Wilhelm: (19 Nov. 1436), mentioned, Rymer, x. 659.

LABANUM, Johannes: (15 Jan. 1423), payment of the count's annuity, E 403/658/m. 7.

LAPIDE, Otto de: (11 Apr.–17 May 1423), payment of the count's annuity, E 30/428 A, E 403/660/m. 5; (6 Oct.–25 Nov. 1427), receipt for 2,000 marks, Rymer, x. 379, 383; (30 Sept. 1434), full powers to receive 1,000 marks from the English, E 30/1427; (22 Feb. 1435), payment of a gift to, E 403/717/m. 14.

MITRA, Friedrich de: (14 Jan.–29 Aug. 1426), full powers to collect and a receipt for the count's annuity, E 30/1246 (2), (1); (6 Oct.–25 Nov. 1427), receipt for 2,000 marks, Rymer, x. 379, 383; (8 Oct. 1428–18 Feb. 1429), full powers to collect and a receipt for the count's annuity, E 30/1347, 1411; (30 Sept. 1434), full powers to collect the count's annuity, E 30/1427; (21 Feb. 1435), payment of a gift to, E 403/717/m. 14.

ONESTEBERG, Tylmann: (19 Nov. 1436), mentioned, Rymer, x. 659.

PETRA, Otto de, Dr.: (6 July 1434), payment of a reward to, E 403/715/ m. 12.

POTT(E), Johannes: (13 Nov. 1424), mentioned, E 403/649/m. 4; (19 Nov. 1436), mentioned, Rymer, x. 659.

ROISS, Conrad: (19 Nov. 1436), mentioned, Rymer, x. 659.

RUBETO, Hermann de: (5 Nov. 1439), mentioned, *Correspondence Bekynton*, i. 183; (3 Oct.–4 Dec. 1442), payment for coming to collect money, E 403/747/mm. 1, 7; (20 July 1444), order to pay for collecting the count's annuity, E 404/60/231.

RUSCHELMAN, Gerard: (19 Nov. 1436), mentioned, Rymer, x. 659.

RYNK, Johannes: (13 Nov. 1424), payment of the count's annuity, E 403/ 669/m. 4; (19 Nov. 1436), mentioned, Rymer, x. 659.

RYNK, Rotgerus: (19 Nov. 1436), mentioned, Rymer, x. 659.

SPEGYN, Tydemann: (13 Nov. 1424), payment of the count's annuity, E 403/ 669/m. 4.

STOCKDALE (STOCKEDE), Johannes: (13 Jan. 1423), payment of a reward to, E 403/658/m. 7; (19 Nov. 1436), mentioned, Rymer, x. 659.

SWERT, Ertiner: * (13 Nov. 1424), mentioned, E 403/669/m. 4.

VINGENFELS, Bernard Cresz (Cresser) de, knight: (11 Apr.–17 May 1423), payment of the count's annuity, E 30/428 A, E 403/660/m. 5.

WACHENHEIM, Nicholas de: (12 Dec. 1440), mentioned, *Correspondence Bekynton*, i. 182; (20 July 1444), payment of the count's annuity, E 30/ 482, E 404/60/231; (9 Apr. 1445), payment of the count's stipend, E 403/757/m. 1, E 30/428 A.

WYPENORD, Johannes von, *alias* Rosencrans: (1 Mar. 1436), mentioned as taking letters to the count, Rymer, x. 633.

28. ENGLISH ENVOYS TREATING WITH ENVOYS FROM THE RHINE PALATINATE

SELLING, Richard: (14 Feb. 1435), full powers to treat with the count about money due to him, C 76/117/m. 7.

STOKES, John, Dr.: (16 Sept.–25 Nov. 1435), account of a mission to Calais, Bruges, and to the Duke of Bavaria, E 364/71 F; *Register of Oxford*, iii. 1781–2.

WILTON, Stephen, Dr.: (21 Feb. 1435), payment for going to the Duke of Bavaria, E 403/717/m. 13; *Register of Oxford*, iii. 2053–4.

29. ENVOYS FROM SILESIA TO ENGLAND

LUNGEBERGE, Hanze: (12 Dec. 1447), order to pay a reward to, E 404/64/96.

MENSER, Hanze: (12 Dec. 1447), order to pay a reward to, E 404/64/96.

PHOEWZIT, Philip, priest: (20 May 1443), order to pay for bringing letters, *Proc. P.C.* v. 275.

RECHENBERG, Melchior: (17 July 1452), mentioned, E 28/82/44.

30. ENVOY FROM BRIG TO ENGLAND

PURSUIVANT: (21 July 1432), order to pay a reward to, *Proc. P.C.* iv. 125.

31. ENGLISH ENVOYS TO THE POPES AND TO THE COUNCILS

BABINGTON, William, Abbot of Bury St. Edmunds: (13 Mar. 1449), appointed the king's proctor in Rome, Rymer, xi. 227; *Register of Oxford*, i. 86.

BEAUFORT, Edmund, Count of Mortain: (4 May 1434), payment for going to Basel in the king's service, E 403/715/m. 3; *Complete Peerage*, xii, pt. 1, 49–53.

BEAUFORT, Henry, Bishop of Winchester: * (22 Feb. 1423), order to draw up letters of proxy for, to go to Pavia, *Proc., P.C.* iii. 42; * (16 Feb. 1433), licence to take £20,000 worth of goods to Basel, C 81/696/2655; *Register of Oxford*, i. 139–42; L. B. Radford, *Henry Beaufort*, (London, 1908).

BERKLEY, James, Lord Ferrers of Groby: (22 Feb. 1423), order to draw up letters of proxy for, to go to Pavia, *Proc. P.C.* iii. 42; *Complete Peerage*, v. 357–8.

BILDESTON, Nicholas, Dr.: (22 Feb. 1423), order to draw up letters of proxy for going to Pavia, *Proc. P.C.* iii. 42; (27 June 1424–7 Jan. 1425), payment for going to the curia, E 101/322/10, E 403/666/m. 7, 669/m. 18; (23 Jan. 1430), order to pay for going to Rome, E 404/46/172; *Register of Oxford*, i. 187–8.

BLODWELL, John, master: (1 May 1425), mentioned as in Rome to secure a reduction of the time till the next council, B.M., Cotton MS. Cleopatra C. IV, f. 177ᵛ; *Register of Oxford*, i. 202–3.

BOLE, Richard, master: (16 May 1459), letters of proxy to offer the king's obedience to Pius II, Rymer, xi. 422; *Register of Oxford*, i. 213–14.

BOTYLL, Robert, Prior of St. John of Jerusalem in England: (23 Aug. 1446–5 June 1449), account for going to France and to the pope, E 101/324/15; E. J. King, *The Grand Priory of the Order of the Hospital of St. John of Jerusalem in England* (London, 1924), pp. 50–2.

BROMFLETE, Henry, knight: (4 May 1434), payment for going to the Council of Basel, E 403/715/m. 3.

BROUNS, Thomas, Dean of Salisbury: (4 Dec. 1432), payment for going to the Council of Basel, E 403/707/m. 13; (12 Feb. 1435), account for having spent two years and 36 days in the king's service at the Council of Basel, E 101/320/24; *Register of Oxford*, i. 281-2; E. Jacob, 'Thomas Brouns, Bishop of Norwich, 1436-45', *Essays in British History Presented to Sir Keith Feiling*, ed. H. R. Trevor-Roper (London, 1964), pp. 61-83.

CANDOUR, Thomas: (20 Aug. 1447), order to pay for going to the pope in the retinue of Robert Botyll, E 404/63/162.

CHAPMAN, Thomas, master: (27 Aug. 1442), mentioned, *Proc. P.C.* v. 203; *Register of Oxford*, i. 389.

CHESTER, Richard, clerk: (1433), at Basel in the retinue of the Bishop of London, Rymer, x. 550-1; (23 July 1440), order to pay for going to the curia, E 404/56/325; (14 Feb. 1441), payment for going to the pope, E 403/740/m. 12; *Register of Oxford*, i. 407-8.

CLEMENT, Vicent: (9 Mar., 6 July 1443), payments for going to the pope and to the King of Aragon, E 403/747/m. 13, 749/m. 11; (24 Aug. 1447-5 June 1449), order to pay for conducting arduous business with the pope, E 28/81/173; (7 Nov. 1454), appointed the king's proctor at Rome, Rymer, xi. 359; (19 Apr. 1456), petition to take goods to Rome without hindrance, E 28/87/18; (17 Nov. 1460), reappointed the king's proctor in Rome, *Cal. Pat. Rolls, 1452-61*, p. 644; *Register of Oxford*, i. 432-3.

COLVILLE, John, knight: (14 Dec. 1431-22 Oct. 1432), account of mission to curia, E 101/322/18; (25 Apr.-27 May 1433, 1 May-11 Nov. 1434), account of two missions to the Council of Basel, E 101/322/26.

CORDON, Richard: (1 May 1425), mentioned as in Rome to secure a reduction of the time till the next council, B.M., Cotton MS. Cleopatra C. IV, f. 177ᵛ; *Register of Oxford*, i. 486-7.

DUDLEY, Robert: (23 Aug. 1447-5 June 1449), account for a journey to France and to the pope, E 101/324/15.

FERRERS, Edmund, Lord Ferrers: (22 Feb. 1423), order to draw up letters of proxy for, to go to Pavia, *Proc. P.C.* iii. 42; *Complete Peerage*, v. 317-9.

FITZHUGH, Robert, Bishop of London: (20 June 1429), decision to appoint Fitzhugh the king's proctor in Rome, *Proc. P.C.* iii. 339; (4 May 1434), payment for going to Basel for a year, E 403/715/m. 3; *Register of Oxford*, ii. 689-90.

FLEMING, Richard, Bishop of Lincoln: (24 Feb. 1423), order to draw up full powers for, to go to Pavia, *Proc. P.C.* iii. 43; *Register of Oxford*, ii. 697-9.

FLEMING, Robert: (18 Mar. 1455), appointed the king's proctor in Rome, *Cal. Pat. Rolls, 1452-61*, p. 227; (4 Feb. 1457), reappointed the king's proctor in Rome, *Cal. Pat. Rolls, 1452-61*, p. 366; (5 Aug. 1457), commission to render the king's obedience to Calixtus III, *Cal. Pat. Rolls, 1452-61*, p. 362; (8 June 1458), the preceding commission renewed, *Cal. Pat. Rolls, 1452-61*, p. 426; (16 May 1459), commission to offer the king's obedience to Pius II, Rymer, xi. 422; *Register of Oxford*, ii. 699-700.

FORSTER, John, clerk: (10 June 1424), order for him to return from Rome, C 81/681/1189; *Register of Oxford*, ii. 708-9.

FROME, Nicholas, Abbot of Glastonbury: (3 May 1423), mentioned as going to Pavia, C 76/107/m. 16; *Register of Oxford*, ii. 730.

GILBERT, Robert, master: (22 Feb. 1423), order to draw up letters of proxy for going to Pavia, *Proc. P.C.* iii. 42; *Register of Oxford*, ii. 766–7.

GOLDENER, Johannes, Bishop of Acre: (22 Oct. 1434), payment of travel expenses to Basel, E 403/717/m. 1.

GRAY, William, Bishop of London: (17 Aug. 1428–5 Feb. 1429), payment for a mission to Rome, E 403/703/m. 10; *Register of Oxford*, ii. 808–9.

GRAY, William: (15 Oct. 1450), letters of protection for going to Rome, C 76/133/m. 9; (12 May 1452), letters of protection for going to Rome, C 76/134/m. 7; *Register of Oxford*, ii. 809–14.

HOLES, Andrew: (27 Feb. 1437), licence to appear as the king's proctor in Rome, C 76/119/m. 6; (17 Oct. 1447), payment for duties as king's proctor between 27 Feb. 1437 and 29 Dec. 1444, E 403/769/m. 1; *Register of Oxford*, ii. 949–50.

HOLLAND, John, Earl of Huntingdon: * (19 July 1432), council determines wages for going to Basel, *Proc. P.C.* iv. 123; *Complete Peerage*, v. 205–11.

KEMP, John, Archbishop of York: (17 Mar. 1433), payment for transportation to Basel, E 403/707/m. 21 [but see Schofield, *Journal of Ecclesiastical History*, xi (1961), 184]; *Register of Oxford*, ii. 1031–2.

LANGDON, John, Bishop of Rochester: (19 July 1432), payment for going to Basel, E 403/703/m. 14 [but see Schofield, *Journal of Ecclesiastical History*, xii (1961), 184]; (4 May 1434), payment for going to Basel for a year, E 403/715/m. 3; *Register of Oxford*, ii. 1093–4.

LAXE, John: (13 Dec. 1456), described as *procurator fidelis* at Rome, Rymer, xi. 384; (9 Jan. 1460), protection for three years for going to Rome on the king's business, *Cal. Pat. Rolls, 1452–61*, p. 549; *Register of Oxford*, ii. 1113–4.

LESCROPE, John, Lord: (17 Aug. 1428–5 Feb. 1429), account for a mission to the pope and elsewhere, E 101/322/41; *Complete Peerage*, xi. 566–8.

LYHERT, Walter, Bishop of Norwich: (24 July 1447), payment for going to France and to the pope for six months, E 403/767/m. 13; *Register of Oxford*, ii. 1187–8.

MOLEYNS, Adam: (7 July 1435), payment for going to the pope, E 403/719/ m. 8; (16 Dec. 1435), payment for going to Basel and to the pope, E 403/ 721/m. 12; (27 July–3 Aug. 1442), in Florence on the king's ecclesiastical business, C 47/425, 1436; *Register of Oxford*, ii. 1289–91.

MORGAN, Philip, Bishop of Worcester: (22 Feb. 1423), order to draw up letters of proxy for, to go to the Council of Pavia, *Proc. P.C.* iii. 42; *Register of Oxford*, ii. 1312–13.

MOWBRAY, John, Duke of Norfolk; (21 Oct. 1446), licence to go to Rome, C 76/129/m. 20; *Complete Peerage*, ix. 608–9.

O'HEYNE, John, Fr.: (11 Nov. 1437), payment for going to Basel, E 403/ 729/m. 2; (7 Dec. 1437, 11 Feb. 1438), payments for setting out to Basel, the pope, and the emperor, E 403/729/mm. 8, 11.

PARTRIDGE, Peter, Dr.: (18 Feb. 1429), payment for going to the pope, E 403/688/m. 12; *Register of Oxford*, iii. 1430–1.

PERCY, Henry, Earl of Northumberland: (4 Mar. 1423), payment for going to the Council of Pavia, Devon, *Issues of the Exchequer*, pp. 377–8; *Complete Peerage*, ix. 715–16.

PETERSSON, Dauker: (10 Feb. 1438), order to pay for going to Cologne and to the pope with messages, E 404/54/158.

PLANCHE, Bernard de la, Bishop of Dax: (21 Feb. 1433), payment for going to the Council of Basel, E 403/715/m. 3; *Gallia Christiana*, i. 1055.

PLANHEA, Bernard, Prior of Soulac: (4 Mar. 1423), commission to discover the place of the King of France at the next general council, C 76/107/m. 17.

POLE, Walter de la: (22 Feb. 1423), order to draw up letters of proxy for, to go to Pavia, *Proc. P.C.* iii. 42; (20 July 1425–24 Feb. 1426), account of wages and expenses for going to the pope, E 101/322/11; Roskell, *Parliament of 1422*, 172–4.

POLTON, Thomas, Bishop of Chichester: (15 Feb. 1423), reappointed the king's proctor in Rome, Rymer, x. 266; (4 Mar. 1423), commission to discover the place of the King of France at the next general council, C 76/107/m. 17; (7 Nov. 1432), payment for going to Basel, E 403/707/m. 2; *Register of Oxford*, iii. 1494–5.

PRINCE, Hans van: (21 May 1425), payment for going with the king's messages to the pope, E 403/671/m. 3.

RIXTON, Nicholas: (14 Dec. 1431–22 Oct. 1432), mentioned, E 101/322/26.

SALBURY, William, Abbot of Beaulieu: (20 July 1425–24 Feb. 1426), account of a mission to Rome, E 101/322/11.

SHARP, Henry, master: (16 May 1459), letters of proxy to offer the king's obedience to Pius II, Rymer, xi. 422.

SHOTTESBROOK, Robert, knight: * (late Feb. 1433), at the Council of Basel, Schofield, *Journal of Ecclesiastical History*, xii (1961), 184; Wedgwood, *History of Parliament: Biographies*, pp. 766–7.

SPARROW, Alexander, Archdeacon of Berkshire: (late Feb. 1433), at the Council of Basel, Schofield, *Journal of Ecclesiastical History*, xii (1961), 178. *Register of Oxford*, iii. 1739–40.

SPREVER, William, Dr.: (1433), at the Council of Basel, Schofield, *Journal of Ecclesiastical History*, xii (1961), 178; *Register of Oxford*, iii. 1745–6.

STOKES, John, Dr.: (17 Aug. 1428–5 Feb. 1429), account for going to the pope and elsewhere, E 364/65 E; *Register of Oxford*, iii. 1781–3.

SUTTON, Robert, master: (1 May 1425), mentioned as in Rome to secure a reduction of the time until the next general council, B.M., Cotton MS. Cleopatra C. IV, f. 177ᵛ; *Register of Oxford*, iii. 1823–4.

SWAN, William, master: (1 May 1425), mentioned as in Rome to secure a reduction of the time until the next general council, B.M., Cotton MS. Cleopatra C. IV, f. 177ᵛ; *Register of Oxford*, iii. 1829–30.

SYMONDSBURGH, John, Archdeacon of Wiltshire: (late Feb. 1433), at the Council of Basel, Schofield, *Journal of Ecclesiastical History*, xii (1961), 178; *Register of Oxford*, iii. 1842.

TIPTOFT, John, Earl of Worcester: (5 Aug. 1457), commission to render the king's obedience to Calixtus III, *Cal. Pat. Rolls, 1452–61*, p. 362; (16 May 1459), commission to render the king's obedience to Pius II, Rymer, xi. 422; R. J. Mitchell, *John Tiptoft, 1427–70* (London, 1938); *Register of Oxford*, iii. 1877–9.

TIPTOFT, John, Lord: (23 Feb. 1423), order to draw up letters of proxy for, to go to the Council of Pavia, *Proc. P.C.* iii. 42; *Complete Peerage*, xii, pt. ii, 946–9.

VERBONDESWYK, Henry: (21 Sept. 1444), order to pay for going to the pope and returning with messages about Eton, E 404/61/19.

WALSSH, Nicholas, Fr.: (8 Feb. 1449), payment for going with messages to the pope, E 403/773/m. 11.

WELLS, William, Abbot of St. Mary's, York, Bishop of Rochester: (3 June 1434), letters of proxy for negotiations at Basel, *Cal. Pat. Rolls, 1429–36*, p. 342; (before 13 Jan. 1443), he has returned from Basel, E 101/322/29, 30; *Register of Oxford*, iii. 2012.

WENTWORTH, Philip: (5 Aug. 1457), commission to render the king's obedience to Calixtus III, *Cal. Pat. Rolls, 1452–61*, p. 362.

WEST, Reginald, knight: (13 Dec. 1447), licence to go to Rome, C 76/25/m. 17.

WORSTED, William, Prior of Norwich: (3 June 1434), letters of proxy for negotiations at Basel, *Cal. Pat. Rolls, 1429–36*, p. 342; *Register of Oxford*, iii. 2089–90.

32. ENVOYS FROM THE POPES AND THE COUNCILS TO ENGLAND

AMICI, Mighet, master: (20 Feb. 1443), payment for coming with letters and credences from the pope, E 403/773/m. 14; (6 Mar. 1449), order to pay a reward to, E 404/65/113.

ATRO, Peter de: (10 Feb. 1433), council orders letter of free passage for this envoy from Basel, E 28/54/68.

AURO, Rucellus de, knight of Bologna: (July 1432), Henry VI's response to, Mansi, *Sacrorum Conciliorum collectio*, vol. xxxi, coll. 133–4.

BALARDI, Jaume de, Bishop of Trieste: (13 Mar. 1423), request for safe conduct for, B.M., Add. MS. 15380, ff. 79^r–80^r; (25 Dec. 1427), letters of proxy for, P.R.O. 31/9/40, f. 107^r; *Italia sacra*, vol. v, coll. 506–7.

BALDERONIBUS, Fr. John, master: (13 July 1445), payment for coming from the pope and returning, E 403/757/mm. 10–11; (14 Aug. 1446), order to pay a reward to, E 404/61/272.

CARDONA, Lodovico de, master: (10 Feb. 1445), mentioned as having recently been in England, B.M., Cotton Charter XXIV 6; (Sept. 1446–3 Feb. 1447), in England to obtain money for a crusade and to bring the king a mystic rose, E 403/765/m. 14; Jacob, *Transactions of the Royal Historical Society*, 5th ser. xii (1962), 19.

CARMENYCLA, Dominic: (15 Nov. 1458), payment of a reward to, for coming from the pope, E 403/817/m. 3.

CAVALCANTIBUS, Robert de: (16 May 1438), payment for having brought letters and returning with others to the pope, E 403/731/m. 2.

CESARINI, Giuliano: (17 July 1425), letters of proxy for, P.R.O. 31/9/40, f. 131.

CHARATANEIS, James de, master: (29 Dec. 1428), order to let pass Dover without paying customs, *Cal. Close Rolls, 1422–9*, p. 422; (7 July 1429), mentioned, *Proc. P.C.* iii. 330–8.

CLAND, James: * (1 May–21 July 1438), envoy from the Council of Basel in England, Schofield, *Church History*, xxxiii (1964), 262.

CONDULMARI, Francesco, Cardinal: (13 July 1442), payment to, E 403/772/ m. 11; (12 Dec. 1447), order to pay, E 404/64/98; (6 Mar. 1449), order to pay, E 404/65/114.

COPPINI, Francesco, Bishop of Terni: (7 Jan. 1459), letters of credence for, to Henry VI, Rymer, xi. 419; *Italia sacra*, vol. i, col. 761.

CRUCE, Louis de: (21 Feb. 1452), order to pay for bringing letters from Cardinal Nicholas of Cusa, E 404/68/93.

ELY, John: (2 Mar. 1433), payment for coming to England, Lunt, p. 69; (20 June 1435), mentioned, Rymer, x. 610; (3 Oct. 1442), payment for coming with letters from the pope, E 403/747/m. 1.

FLAMOCHET, Guy, Prior of Chambéry: (July 1432), Henry VI's response to, Mansi, *Sacrorum Conciliorum collectio*, vol. xxxi, coll. 133–4.

GATTOLA, Angelo: (22 June 1441), recommendation for, because he had brought the red hat to the Archbishop of York, *Correspondence Bekynton*, i. 37.

LANDRIANI, Gerardo, Bishop of Lodi: (July 1432), Henry VI's response to, Mansi, *Sacrorum Conciliorum collectio*, vols. xxxi, coll. 133–4; *Italia sacra*, vol. iv, col. 681.

LEGNAME, Baptista, Bishop of Concordia: (25 June 1445), order to pay for returning to the pope with letters, E 404/61/246; (12 Mar. 1446), in England on a mission from the pope, Jacob, *Transactions of the Royal Historical Society*, 5th ser. xii (1962), 18; *Italia sacra*, vol. v, col. 363.

LOISELEUR, Nicholas: (1 May–21 July 1438), envoy from the Council of Basel in England, Schofield, *Church History*, xxxiii (1964), 262.

MARQUETUS, John, Fr.: (5 Dec. 1447), payment for coming with credences from Rome, E 403/769/m. 7.

MERA, Peter de: (10 July 1432), payment of a reward to, E 403/703/m. 10.

NERICUS, Abbot of Bonmont: (1 May–21 July 1438), envoy from the Council of Basel in England, Schofield, *Church History*, xxxiii (1964), 262.

OBIZZI, Giovanni: (24 July 1438), payment for going to Ferrara for the king, E 403/731/m. 15.

ORSINI (URSINUS), Marino, Bishop of Tarento: (16 Dec. 1451), order to pay for coming from the pope, E 404/68/60; *Italia sacra*, vol. ix, coll. 142–3.

PETROBONOLLA, John de, Fr.: (5 July 1446), payment for coming with letters and credences from the pope, E 403/762/m. 5.

PULLAM, William, master: (16 June 1426), request for a safe conduct for, B.M., Add. MS. 15380, ff. 79ʳ–80ʳ.

ROCCA, Antonio, Prior: (6 Aug. 1455), order to pay for coming with messages from the pope, E 404/70/2/96.

ROVERELLA, Sismundo (*sic*), Archbishop of Ravenna: (22 Nov. 1454), order to pay Garter King of Arms for going to meet, E 404/70/2/36.

SERUOPULUS, Franculus, knight of Greece: (21 Oct. 1456), payment of a reward to for coming from the pope, E 403/809/m. 2; (27 Feb. 1459), payment for bringing letters from the pope, E 403/817/m. 9.

SIMONIS, John de, of Lotharingia: (20 Feb. 1449), payment for coming with messages from the curia, E 403/773/m. 14.

TERAMO, Simon de: (8 July 1423), order to pay for going with messages to the pope on 19 July 1421 and staying there until 5 May 1423, E 404/39/339.

VAZEIMES, William de: (11 June 1447), order to pay for coming with letters from the pope, E 404/63/125.

APPENDIX II. DOCUMENTS

1. *Instructions for the ambassadors of the Duke of Bedford to the King of Aragon. Circa January 1423. [B.N., MS. Dupuy 223, ff. 232ʳ⁻ᵛ. Contemporary copy.]*

[*f. 232ʳ*] Instrucciones Arragonie

Instrucciones ex parte domini nostri Francorum et Anglie regis ac domini regentis regnum Francie pro domino Bernardo de Monferrant milite, magistris Guillermo Britonis in jure canonico licenciato archidiacono Pravinensi[1] in ecclesia Senon'[2] et Guillermo in theologia doctori decano Remen'[3] consiliariis domini[4] nostri regis et embassatoribus destinandis ad serenissimum principem regem Arragonie et ejusdem regis principes.[5]

Primo ante ingressum regem Arragonie litteras securitatis et salvi conductus ab habentibus dandi[6] potestatem peti facient[7] que si denegate[8] fuerunt erunt de utiliori profeccione dehonorati.

Item illis habitis incedent caute et secrete de regimine regni et inclinacione regnicolarum[9] secrete inquirendo.

Item presentatis[10] litteris regi, regine et dominis quibus diriguntur postulabunt audiri publice, quod si negatum fuerit, petant[11] audiri sicut voluerint. Si vero negata fuerit omnis audiencia revertentur. Proponent [ut] sequitur.

Primo collaudatis ambobus[12] regnis Francie et Arragonie dicent regiam[13] celsitudinem non immemoriter tenere que dudum bella inter regnum Francie et Anglie fuerunt, que inde mala quam impia facinora secuta sint atque ? temp' intra viscera regni Francie bella plusquam[14] civilia exorta. Pro quibus pacificandis inclite memorie Karolus sextus et Henricus[15] Francie et Anglie reges perhennem finalis pacis tractatum iniverunt et juramentis propriis ac suorum subditorum[16] firmaverunt. Et quod eamdem pacem ineundam[17] multum attulit mors crudelissima piissime memorie Johannis ducis Burgundie per illum Karolum

---

[1] Provins, France, *dép.* Seine-et-Marne.   [2] Sens, France, *dép.* Yonne.
[3] Reims, France, *dép.* Marne.
[4] This word is followed by *reg* struck through.
[5] MS., *pricipes.*   [6] MS., *danti.*   [7] MS., ? *favent.*
[8] MS., *denegati.*   [9] MS., *regnicularum.*   [10] MS., *presentis.*
[11] MS., *patent.*   [12] MS., ? *ambobis.*   [13] MS., *regina.*
[14] MS., *plusque*   [15] This word is followed by a blank in the text.
[16] MS., *subdictorum.*   [17] Expunged by mistake in MS.

qui se dicebat Delphinum tam proditorie[1] quam execrabiliter perpe-
trata que omnia per embassatores dictorum principum fuerunt sibi
reserata anno xx°.

Item quod post decessum dictorum principum dominus noster rex eis
jure successit in illis duobus regnis habens Deo favente majorem
obedienciam in illis regnis et maxime in regno Francie quam a tractatu
pacis finalis habuerint predicti sui predecessores. Et ibi poterunt
ostendere quomodo dominus noster rex in obediencia fere[2] omnis
pars[3] aut pariatus Francie domini nostri regis et quomodo jure
proximitatis dominus dux Bedfordie patruus[4] est regens Francie.

[*f. 232ᵛ*] Item et quod prefatus dominus noster rex ac dominus regens
considerantes proximitatem sanguinis qua regi Arragonie conjunguntur,
rememorantes preterea confederaciones ligas et amicicias inter progenitores suos quondam contractas et[5] observatas[6] attendentes insuper
bonum et securitatem toti Christianitati multipliciter redundare si hec
tria regna pace bona et sincera concordia convenerint illud bonum
federis conciperunt[7] et suos imitando[8] predecessores eadem benivola
vota complexi sunt.

Item et quod licet post decessum regum[9] prefatorum illa longe potentissima nobilissima et maxima pars Francie que eis obediebat in sincera
manserit obediencia domini nostri regis sine ulla divisione aut alienacione.[10] Nichilominus obstantibus occupacionibus hec sancta et bona
voluntas non potuerit[11] pro desiderio regis[12] et regi et regno Arragonie
intimari[13] multa Dei dona in triumphis victoriis et subjugacione
hostium dominus noster rex et regens prefati adepti sunt que occupaciones predictas pro majori subtraxerunt et vias ambassiatorum
apparuerunt.

Item idcirco tandem illis occupacionibus et impedimentis in potissima
parte amputatis missi sunt ad hec exponenda et requirenda quod dictus
rex Arragonie federa ligas et amicicias inire velit et facere cum[14]
predictis domino nostro rege et regente Francie sicut hactenus inter
predecessores partis utriusque fuerunt contracte et observate.

Item quod prefato Karolo nullum prestet auxilium contra regem aut
dominum regentem quinymo si aliquos auxiliatores[15] eidem destinaverit seu in aliqui de regno suo aut terris sibi subditis in auxilium ejus
profecti sunt eos revocare et contramandare velit.

---

[1] MS., *preditorie.* [2] MS., *sero.* [3] MS., *paris.* [4] *Sic* in MS.
[5] *Dieu* expunged. [6] This word is followed by a false start.
[7] MS., *cociperunt.* [8] MS., *initando.* [9] MS., *regnum.*
[10] MS., *alternacione.* [11] This word is followed by *de* struck through.
[12] MS., *? regi.* [13] This word is followed by *tamen* struck through.
[14] This word is followed by *d* struck through. [15] MS., *auxiliares.*

Item et ut regni Francie rebelles ad domini nostri regis obedienciam cicius et facilius reducantur armatos per mare et per terram si opus sit quando requisitus fuerit qua majori numero fieri poterit in subsidium regis transmittere.

Item quod in casu quo dictus rex differre vellet contrahere dicta federa ligas et amicicias ipsi ambassiatores tractabunt quod velit mittere suos ambaxiatores ad dominum nostrum regem et dominum regentem in Francia quam[1] cicius fieri poterit ad eis notifficandum suam bonam voluntatem.

Item et quod interim[2] nullum per se aut suos adversariis domini nostri regis ac domini regentis prestet auxilium aut succursum et precipue[3] illi qui[4] se pro Delphino gerebat si quos jam ei[5] [in] auxilium ejus misit revocet.

Item quod super omnibus premissis et eorum dependenciis dicti ambassiatores procedant[6] secundum casuum emergenciam prout melius poterunt quantum Deus eorum discrecionibus dignabitur inmittere.[7]

2. *Fragment of the draft instructions for the English envoys treating with Aragon and Navarre. Spring 1431.* [*B.M., Cotton MS.* [*f. 175ʳ*] *Vespasian C. XII, f. 175ʳ. Draft.*]

Quod si dicti ambaxiatores Arragonum et Navarre in dictis alliganciis contrahendis omnino desideraverint succursum gencium absque quo noluerint concludere alligancias ullo modo[8] ambaxiatores[9] domini nostri regis habent eosdem assecurare quod per regiam celsitudinem eis non denegabitur succursus talis qui inter ambaxiatores ? parcium poterit concordari. Sed quidem[10] materia succursus est materia[11] satis[12] ponderosa et talis que de sui natura requirit noticiam et concensum omnium dominorum et magnatum[13] regni sui Anglie[14], dominusque[15] noster rex[16] jam reversus[17] in hoc inclitum regnum suum Anglie[18]

---

[1] MS., *quem*.   [2] MS., *iterim*.   [3] MS., *principue*.
[4] This word is followed by *p* struck through.
[5] MS., *et*.   [6] MS., *procedent*.   [7] *Sic* in MS.
[8] *Nichilominus* interlined, *ambaxiatores domini nostri regis intimare eisdem quod* struck through.
[9] *Ambaxiatores . . . poterit concordari* added from margin.
[10] *Sed quidem* interlined.   [11] *Permaxima et* struck through.
[12] *Satis* interlined.
[13] *Ac trium statuum regni in parliamento congregatorum propter unam causam in speciali inter alia* struck through.
[14] *Regni sui Anglie* interlined.   [15] *-que* interlined.
[16] *Statim post decessum suum* struck through.
[17] *Jam reversus* interlined.   [18] *Fecit* struck through.

parliamentum suum[1] in civitate sua London' erga[2] xij diem mensis maii proximo[3] futurum disposuit convocari super qualitate modo et forma[4] ejusdem.[5] In[6] quo super succursu hujusmodi tractabitur cum effectu. Petant igitur ambassatores supradicti quatenus dicti reges Arragonum et Navarre erga illud tempus[7] vel aliud, secundum quod eis videbitur expedire pro responsione super (ubi[8] efficacius et conveniencius possit tractari super qualitate modo et forma numero vadiis ac de ? quibus regnis seu patriis[9] dabitur succursus[10] aliisque circumstanciis ejusdem[11] in quibus omnibus talis etc') succursu habendo[12] suos nuncios seu ambassatores ad presenciam regie[13] celsitudinis[14] velint[15] destinare quibus talis dabitur responsio de qua merito debeant contentari.

Item quod sub eisdem modo et forma quibus cavetur de tractando et procedendo cum commissariis regis Arragonum, tractetur procedatur et concludatur cum commissariis regis et regine regni Navarre.

Item si de matrimonio inter dominum nostrum regem et filiam dictorum regis et regine Navarre de quo per ambaxiatores ipsorum regis et regine nuper motum extitit et locutum sermo fiat seu repetatur, commissarii domini nostri respondebunt quod postquam de hujusmodi matrimonio fuerat per dictos ambaxiatores prefato illustri principi domino duci Gloucestr' et consilio locutum, iidem dux et consilium cum omni diligencia curaverunt domino nostro regi et dominis de

[1] ? *Suum summoniri convocandi* struck through; *disposuit* interlined, but struck through.
[2] *Erga* interlined.
[3] *Incepturi ubi post maturam communicacionem et deliberacionem ? predictorum magnatum ac trium statuum regni super* struck through; *super succursu hujusmodi* interlined, struck through.
[4] *Numero vadiis ac de quibus regnis seu patriis gentes stipendiarii extraducentur aliis circumstanciis dicti succursus graciam* struck through.
[5] *Ejusdem* interlined; *si dictorum regis Arragonum ac regis et regine Navarre serenitatibus erit visum eorum ambaxiatores in premissa materia succursus sufficienti potestate fulcitos ad presenciam domini nostri regis jam in dicto regno suo Anglie personaliter residentis transmittere; talis per Dei graciam eisdem dabitur responsio in premissis de qua* [MS. quo] *de racione debeant contentari eorum serenitates; in quo eciam parliamento quia alias pro parte dictorum ambaxiatorum Arragonum et Navarre contra potestatem ambaxiatorum domini nostri regis ex eo quod* (idem interlined) *dominus noster rex in pupillari est constitutus etate obiciebatur; providebitur gracia divina optulante quod omnia concordanda seu concludenda in materiis alliganciarum confederacionum seu succursus predicti confirmabuntur ejusdem parliamenti auctoritate* struck through.
[6] *In . . . debeant contentari* added from below.
[7] *Vel ullo* struck through.   [8] *Ubi . . . talis etc'* added from margin.
[9] *Gentes stipendiarii extra ducentur* struck through.
[10] *Dabitur succursus* interlined.   [11] *Dicti succursus* struck through.
[12] MS., *habenda*.   [13] *M* struck through.
[14] *Transmittere* struck through.   [15] *Velint* interlined.

sanguine suo¹ regio ad latus sibi assistentibus hoc intimare et quod ab
eisdem dominis de sanguine regio receperunt in responsis quod in
matrimonio quod semel legitime contractum dissolvi non poterit;
opus est utriusque contrahencium maturo deliberatoque consensu et
quod idcirco visum est eis exspectandum in hac re tempus maturioris
etatis ipsius domini nostri regis quo tempore sibi super hoc consulere
valeat et consentire ne quod absit matrimonium quod ex eorum
eleccione sibi placiturum speraretur in displicenciam sibi veniat in
futurum.

H. Gloucestre   H. Cantaur'   ? J. Norwic'   P. Elien'   J. Roffen'
Suffol'   W.² Lincoln'   J. Huntyngton'

3. *Letter from Alfonso V of Aragon to his ambassadors treating
with the English at Bayonne. 17 May 1431. [A.C.A.,
Registro 2692, ff. 140ᵛ–141ʳ. Contemporary copy.]*

[*f. 140ᵛ*] Lo rey

Embaxadors vostra letra de set del present mes havem reebuda e vist
per nos e en nostre consell lo contengut en aquella ensemps ab la
cedula que per part dels embaxadors del rey de Anglaterra vos fon
offerta sobre la manera de liga entre nos e ell fahedora, ensemps
ab lo tollat de lur poder o procuracio. Vos responem que en lo dit
nostre consell es stat vist que jatsia considerada la menor edat distant
de pubertat en la qual es constituhit lo dit rey de Anglaterra no valla
per dret³ comu la dita sua procuracio soub auctoritat e ferm de tudor e
curador seu ni de jutge majorment en affers de tanta gravitat o
importancia com son los que aqui tractats. Empero si a vosaltres
consta que lo rey et regne de Anglaterra se regeixen solament⁴ per
drets e leys municipals, e que sia axi per dret de aquella patria quel dit
rey constituhit en pupillar edat regeixia tots ses regnes e faca e ferme
tots e qualsevol contracts e obligacions a sola ordinacio e disposicio
dels dotze hommes elets per los tres stats o almenys per los sis de
aquells segons se diu e es contengut en vostra letra e que a vosaltres
autenticament consta de la tal ley municipal, e que en lo tal acte de
procuracio se trobe la signatura dels dits xij o sis. Entenem que lo dit
poder o procuracio sia assats sufficient en tal cas. E que [*f. 141ʳ*] pus
segons dit es consta a vosaltres del dit poder en la prop dita forma nul
dejats pus difficultat ou intricat. Quant al altre cap empero de la dita
vostra letra tocant lo queus es⁵ stat respost sobre lo fet del soccors o

---

¹ *Suo* interlined.   ² *D.* expunged.
³ This word is followed by *per dret* struck through.
⁴ MS., corrected from *solaments*.   ⁵ This word is interlined.

ajuda a nos fahedora per lo dit rey Danglaterra juxta forma de les vostres instruccions, nos par que considerat que la raho e causa principal queus mou a contractar de la dita liga es lo soccors que dell speram, e que per aquesta raho volrem quel dit rey de Anglaterra fos tengut dar lo dit soccors a nos primer que nos a ell. E que los dits embaxadors dien que de aquest cap no han manera de finar e cloure mas solament de tractar e apuntar ab vosaltres, e que apres ho reportaran al consell de Anglaterra e que lo mayre tornara ab poder bastant segons lo dit consell haura deiliberat etc'. Nos par los dejats dir que pus axi es la hora sobre tots les caps condicions e qualitats de la dita liga segons en vostres instruccions es mencionada ells hauran plenera comissio e poder sufficient del dit rey de Anglaterra de tractar, apuntar e firmar la dita liga. Vosaltres seren contents de entendre en dar conclusio e fi sobre los dits affers. En tals sobre la forma de la dita liga en quant tota que no consentriem ne permetriem nostres subdits a son o stipendi o seus aquell anar o passar en servey o ajuda de algu contra lo dit rey Danglaterra, vos responem que segons les leys e drets de la patria nos aço non poriem prohibir en nostres regnes senyaladament en aquest principatni en regne de Valenc'[1] com tots barons, cavallers, gentils e altres hommes hajan facultat de anar servir e soccorrer fora lo regne a qui e on los plaura. Pero som contents que aquesta clausula sia modificada per aquestes peraules 'nisi si et in quantum per constituciones jura foros et privilegia patrie eis licitum foret'. E mes encara nos plau que aquells tals que axi contra nostre voler hi volguessen tentar no[2] pusquessen haver de nos offici ni benefici ni haver gracia o merce alguna o soccors de nostra casa. En tals tocant lo fet del matrimoni atesa lur resposta nos par que daquianant non dejats pus parlar. E si veets que donada per vosaltres resposta als dits caps los dits embaxadors sen volran anar en Anglaterra sots color de consultar o en altra manera fets altretal per guisa que lo dit tracta sia vist romandre en sospes e sens demonstracio de rompiment algu. Dada en la nostra torre de Valldaura[3] sots nostre segell secret a xvij dies de maig de any mil cccc xxxj. Rex Alf[onsus].

E som contents que passe la reservacio dels princeps e comunitats segons se diu en vostra letre per part del rey de Anglaterra pus les altres coses passen segons es dit dessus e juxta vostres instruccions. Johannes Olzina secretarius.

Dominus rex mandavit mihi Johanni Olzina prothonotario.

[1] Valencia, Spain.
[2] This word is followed by *pusquen* struck through.
[3] Hunting lodge now in Sardaynola near Sabadell, *prov*. Barcelona.

4. *Fragment of the draft instructions for the English envoys treating with Aragon and Navarre. Winter 1432. [B.M., Cotton MS. Vespasian C. XII, f. 172ʳ. Draft.]*

[*f. 172ʳ*] Et in eventum quo se referant dicti commissarii ad modum alliganciarum ipsarum ab ambassiatoribus dictorum regum et regine in scriptis ministratum aut in modo alliganciarum per eos apperiendo velint alligancias reales et perpetuas cum succursu iterum iniri tractando juxta quod verisimiliter creditur ipsos petituros. Consideratis scripturis per ambaxiatores dictorum regum et regine super hoc ? prius datis responderi poterit quod ex parte domini nostri regis non defuit affectus et inclinacio contrahendi amicicias bonas et firmas cum dictis regibus et regina; nichilominus non videtur regie celsitudini facile appunctuare succursum gencium suarum dandum propter multa: tum propter varias et multiplices guerras quibus occupatur de presenti in quibus eget obsequio subditorum suorum eatenus quod rebus sic sedentibus non comode poterit eos a se dimittere vel eorum obsequio carere; tum propter multiplices et varias difficultates que incidere possent tam super modo et quantitate stipendiorum gencium hujusmodi mittendarum ad succursum ac capitaneorum ac alias nonnullas circumstancias in ea parte necessario appunctuatas, super quibus non sunt iidem commissarii pro parte regie celsitudinis instructi. Etenim ? et cum hoc eis exponant quod in amiciciis contrahendis ad eorum . . . expedit talem ponere modum qui commode observari poterit hinc inde et quod amiciciarum natura non exposcit quod amicus amico faciat vel impendat ? quidquid possit ymmo secundum Philipum[1] . . . eth' ? ibi sufficit ut in modico ? consulatur amico, aperiendo dictis commissariis modum alliganciarum nacionabilem circa succursum gencium talem qui sequitur: videlicet quod dominus noster rex ex omni corde suo diliget et amabit prefatum regem Arragonum eritque eidem regi bonus, fidelis et perpetuus amicus et non procurabit, inferet nec quantum in eo erit ullo unquam tempore inferri consenciet eidem regi regnis terris dominiis ligeis seu vassallis suis dampnum aliquod in persona vel rebus, et presertim et in specie quod non consenciet nec quantum in eo erit permittet subditos suos eciam ad vadia seu stipendia cujusque seu sine stipendiis transire in obsequium vel auxilium cujusque persone adversus seu contra prefatum regem Arragonum regna terras seu dominia sua, et quod si quis subditorum suorum contrafecerit, puniet eum tamquam sibi rebellem et inobedientem et quod si quid dampni vel prejudicii noverit seu intellexerit avisari sive proponi contra predictum regem

[1] ? Philippe de Greve. See F. Überweg, *Grundriss der Geschichte der Philosophie,* 11th edn. (Berlin, 1928), ii. 363.

Arragonum honorem sive statum suum[1] cum omni diligencia quam
cicius[2] commode[3] poterit eidem regi Arragonum[4] hoc intimari faciet
et procurabit quodque omnes et singuli ligei sive subditi dicti regis
Arragonum quecumque regna terras dominia, portus et loca dicto
domino nostro regi obediencia subdita et subjecta libere et licite
ingredi poterunt et intrare et illic cum subditis domini nostri regis
tam in mercandisis quam alias communicare et conversari, solvendo
videlicet custumas et deveria debita et consueta, proviso semper quod[5]
hiis alliganciis non obstantibus possit et valeat idem dominus noster
rex juvare dominum summum pontificem et sanctam Romanam
ecclesiam ac reges et principes illos et eorum regna dominia ac com-
munitates quibus idem dominus noster rex vigore alliganciarum et
amiciciarum realium et perpetuarum per inclite recordacionis nobiles
progenitores suos initarum et firmatarum ad hoc astringitur et ob-
ligatur, quibus quidem alliganciis seu amiciciis sic per nobiles progenitores suos factis et firmatis dominus noster rex nec potest[6] nec vult
quoquomodo derogare per presentes.

Et modo consimili idem rex Arragonum ex omni corde suo diliget et
amabit prefatum regem Anglie etc' eritque eidem regi bonus fidelis et
perpetuus amicus et non procurabit inferet nec quantum in eo erit
ullo unquam tempore inferri consenciet eidem regi Anglie etc' regnis
terris dominiis ligeis seu vassallis suis dampnum aliquod in personis
seu rebus, et presertim et in specie quod non consenciet nec quantum
in eo erit permittet subditos suos eciam ad vadia seu stipendia cujusque
seu sine stipendiis transire in obsequium vel auxilium cujuscumque
persone adversus seu contra prefatum regem Anglie etc' regna terras
seu dominia sua et quod si quis subditorum suorum contrafecerit,
puniet eum tanquam sibi rebellem et inobedientem et quod si quid
dampni vel prejudicii noverit seu intellexerit avisari sive proponi
contra predictum regem Anglie etc' honorem sive statum suum cum
omni diligencia quam cicius[7] commode[8] poterit eidem regi Anglie
etc' hoc intimari faciet et procurabit quodque omnes et singuli ligei
sive subditi dicti regis Anglie etc' quecumque regna terras dominia
portus et loca dicto regi Arragonum obediencia subdita et subjecta
libere et licite ingredi poterunt et intrare et illic cum subditis dicti
regis Arragonum tam in mercandisis quam alias communicare et conversari solvendo videlicet custumas ac[9] deveria debita et consueta etc'.

---

[1] This word is followed by *fuerit* struck through.
[2] This word is followed by *quaquamodo* struck through.
[3] This word is interlined.   [4] MS., *Argonum*.
[5] This word is followed by *pl* struck through.
[6] This word is followed by *ita* struck through.
[7] This word is followed by *quaquamodo* struck through.
[8] MS., *commodo* interlined.   [9] This word is interlined.

5. *Aide-mémoire for the Duke of Bedford's ambassadors to the King of Navarre. Circa January 1423.* [*B.N., MS. Dupuy 223, ff. 223ᵛ–225ᵛ. Contemporary copy.*]

[*f. 223ᵛ*] Memoire pour le roy de Navarre duc de Nemox

Il est vray que le roy Charles de France et le roy Henri Dengleterre heritier et regent de France derreinerement¹ trespassez, dont Dieux ait les ames, lan mil iiijᶜ et vint envoierent en embaxade au royaume de Nauvare pardevers le roy dicellui royaume de Navarre messʳ Perre de Fontenay sʳ de Reuer² et maistre Pierre de Venisse conseiller et aumosnier du dit roy de Navarre et aussi conseiller du roy.

Item que entre les autres poirs de lembaxade furent chargez iceulx embaxadeurs ? des les ditz roys de France et³ Angleterre de dire et exposer au dit roy de Navarre les traictiez et paix final faiz et concluz entre les dits roiz et royaume⁴ de France et Engleterre. Item que ces choses exposees au dit roy de Navarre lui requissent de par les ditz deux roys qui se voulsissent adherer a eulx et a ceste paix et icelle tenir et jurer et semblablement la faire jurer par tous ceulx son royaume et avec ce solliciter et amonnester le conte de Foix et autres ses amis et aliez denviron son royaume de Navarre a eulx adherer a icelle paix et aux traictez faiz entre les deux roys et royaumes dessus ditz.

[*f. 224ʳ*] Item que les dits embaxadeurs requieissent au dit roy de Navarre quil voulsist fere savoir et enquerir par devers le roy de Castelle sil⁵ se vouldroit adherer aus ditz paix et traictez et avec⁶ iceulx deulx roys.

Item que ilz requeissent le dit roy de Navarre quil voulist envoyer en France pardevers les dits roys de France et Dangleterre le conte de Courtes⁷ son filz acompaigne de cent hommes darmes et cent hommes de trait et iceulx deulx roys les feroient paier et deffraier et pour faire leur voyage leur seroit delivre argent a Bourdeaulx⁸ ? ou ailleurs ainsi quil seroit advise et se plus en vouloit envoier plus,⁹ prenroit on.

Item quilz lui requeissent de par le roy regent quilz se voulissent alier et confederer a lui et ses freres.

Item que ces choses exposes au dit roy de Navarre par les¹⁰ ditz embaxadeurs, envoyez tantost apres lexposicion et seue dicelles choses pour

---

¹ MS., *derreinement.*
² La Reure, France, *dép.* Saône-et-Loire, *arr.* La Chapelle-Saint-Sauveur.
³ This word is followed by a false start.
⁴ *Sic* in MS.   ⁵ MS. repeats *sil.*
⁶ This word is followed by one or two words struck through.
⁷ Cortes, Spain, *prov.* Navarra.   ⁸ Bordeaux, France, *dép.* Gironde.
⁹ This word is followed by *en* struck through.   ¹⁰ MS., *le.*

les causes dessus dites une moult grosse embaxade par devers le roy de
Chastelle et aussi envoya incontinent par devers le conte de Foix pour
icelles causes le quel vint tantost incontinent par devers le dit roy de
Navarre.

Item que aussi le dit roy de Navarre manda et fist asemblez tous les[1]
trois estaz de son royaume pour leur monstrer et[2] exposer ces choses.

Item que ces choses ansi[3] faictes le dit roy de Navarre respondi aus dits
embaxadeurs que mais que on lui voulist rendre les contes de Champaigne et Brie a lui appartenans de son propre heritaige il feroit tout
ce que les dits embaxadeurs lui requeroient et avoient requis comme
on a peu et pouroit on encores savoir par la response qui en fu faicte
et baillee par escript au dit feu roy regent et aussi a mons[r] le chancellier
et autres du grant conseil de France.

Les quelles choses ainsi relatees lan mil iiij[c] vint et ung au roy Dengleterre, lui estant a Ruitel[4] pres de Meaulx,[5] icellui roy regent respondi
que le dit roy de Navarre demandoit grans choses et que ce ne pouroit
il faire pour ce quil avoit son serement [*f. 224[v]*] a conserver aug-
menter et non diminuer les droiz de la couronne de France, a la quelle
les dits contez de Champagne et Birie[6] sont venues et annexees
en disant au dit aumosnier quil se voulsist contenter de moins et
quil advisast autres quil vouldroit demander et que sil vouloit estre
content xvj ou de xx[m] livres de terre comprinses en ce les terres de
son dit duchie, le dit roy de Navarre le trouveroit ami en disant
quil avoir moult grant affection et volente davoir le dit roy de Navarre
de son aliance.

Item que depuis et assez longue[7] espace de temps apres ces choses le
dit roy regent, estant logie a Saint Pharon[8] devant la ville de[9] Meaulx
ou il avoit mis le siege, manda le dit aumousnier aler par devers lui.
Au quel liu venu par devers le dit roy regent icellui roy regent pria
bien acertes et avecques ce commanda quil escriveist au dit roy de
Navarre ? y vouloit entendre, il feroit tant que le dit roy de Navarre le
trouveroit ami et quil seroit bien content de lui et lui encharga avecques tresexpressement qui envoyast par devers le dit roy de Navarre
pour ceste cause, et quil lui escriveist[10] et feist savoir ces choses a grant

---

[1] This word is followed by *m* struck through.
[2] This word is followed by *employer* struck through.   [3] ? MS. *ainsi*.
[4] Rutel, France, *dép.* Seine-et-Marne, *arr.* Meaux, *c.* Tancrou. Expunged by
mistake in MS.
[5] Meaux, France, *dép.* Seine-et-Marne.   [6] *Sic* in MS.
[7] This word is followed by *lle* struck through.
[8] Saint-Faron, France, *dép.* Seine-et-Marne, *arr.* Meaux, *c.* Coulommes.
[9] This word is followed by *mau* struck through.
[10] The reading of this word is doubtful.

deligence en priant au dit aumosnier que lui mesmes advisast a aucunes choses dont le roy de Navarre se pouroit contraicter[1] et que de cellui escriveist.

Item que le dit aumosnier voyant et cognoissant la grant affection et volente que le dit roy regent avoit a ceste matiere se adverti de une chose quil dist au dit roy regent dont il ymaginoit et pensoit que le dit roy de Navarre pouroit estre content se la lui vouloit faire et acomplir. La quelle est telle.

Cest assavoir que[2] pour et en recompensacion daucunes choses deues par le roy de nostre dit s^r au dit roy de Navarre et dont le dit roy de Navarre avoit et a droit de faire action et demande au roy nostre dit s^r des quelles la declaracion est cy[3] apres escripte. Le roy lui voulloit bailler et asseoir pres du duchie de Nemox[4] et mesmement de la ville de Nemoux, qui est le chief et lieu cappital dudit duchie, [ƒ. 225^r] xxv^m livres de terre et de rentes et heritaige par chascun[5] an comprises en ce les terres dudit duchie; le dit roy de Navarre seroit content comme il sembloit au dit aumousnier et non pas quil le deist en riens de par le dit roy de Navarre ne de sa sceue mais le dist seulement par supposicion des quelles choses dont le dit roy de Navarra povoit et peut demander recompensacion et faire demande au roy nostre s^r la declaracion ensuit.

Cest assavoir de iiij^m livres de terre et rentes[6] et heritaiges et plus qui restoient et restent a lui asseoir de xij^m livres tourn' de rente et heritaige a quoy devoient monter les terres et revenues que on lui devoit bailler pour son dit duchie dont il ? not oncques quil valist viij^m livres tourn' par an.

Item des[7] arreraiges des dit iiij^m livres tourn' de terre ou rentes qui montoient lors a lxviij^m livres tourn' et plus, ce qui a present montoient a plus de iiij^{xx}m.

Item des dommaiges et interes que le dit roy de Navarre avoit et a euz et soubstenuz pour ce que len lui avoit baille plusieurs terres et seigneuries tenues et mouvans en fief dautres seigneurs que du roy come les chastellenies de Nogent[8] et Bray sur Saine[9] qui sont tenues en fief lune de larcevesque de Sens[10] et lautre de labbe de Saint[11] Denis[12]

---

[1] Read ? *contenter*.   [2] This word is followed by *ce* crossed out.
[3] This word is followed by *dessus* struck through.
[4] Nemours, France, *dép*. Seine-et-Marne, *arr*. Fontainebleau.
[5] MS., *chun*.   [6] MS., *rententes*.
[7] This word is followed by *h* struck through.
[8] Nogent-sur-Seine, France, *dép*. Aube.
[9] Bray-sur-Seine, France, *dép*. Seine-et-Marne, *arr*. Provins.
[10] Sens, France, *dép*. Yonne.
[11] This word is followed by *de* struck through.
[12] Saint-Denis, France, *dép*. Seine.

en France, ce que on ne devoit point fere, mais lui devoit on bailler toutes ses terres tenues nuement et sans moyen a une seule foy et foy et hommaige du roy nostre s^r et non dautre par quoi le dit roy de Navarre a este endommaige de bien et xv^c livres et plus.

Item de ij^m livres de rente qui furent bailles a heritaige a la royne Blanche et ses hoirs et aians cause par eschange pour et en lieu de deux mil livres de rente heritaige que la dite royne prenoit[1] et avoit droit de prendre de son propre heritaige a tousjours sur le tresor du roy nostre s^r a Paris[2] qui lui furent assises sur les terres quelle tenoit en douaire dont feu mess^r Perre de Navarre frere du dit roy de Navarre du quel icellui roy de Navarre[3] depuis le trespas de la dite royne Blanche ne le roy de Navarre depuis le trespas de son dit feu frere pour lempeschement torconnier que les gens du roy y ont mis combien [*f. 225^v*] que icelles ij^m livres de rente appartenoissent au dit feu mess' Pierre de Navarre ce[4] depuis au dit roy de Navarre.

Item des arrerages de celles ij^m livres de rente qui montent pour ce qui en compete au dit roy de Navarre a xxxviij^m livres tourn' et mieulx.

Item de m livres de terre et rente qui pieca furent baillees a la contesse de Foix en mariage sur les terres de Montesqueu[5] dont le dit feu messire Perre de Navarre joissoit et jouy jusques a son trespas, dont le dit roy de Navarre ne jouix[6] ne peu jouir[7] depuis le trespas de son dit feu frere dont il est heritier pour lempeschement que sans cause raisonnable les gens du roy y ont mis.

Item des arrerages dicelles m livres de rente qui monte a xij^m livres et mieulx, toutes les quelles choses montent a vij^m livres de rente a heritaige et a perpetuite et a vi^{xx}xj^{m}v^c livres pour une foiz et plus en quoy le roy nostre sire est tenu au[8] dit roy de Navarre comme dit est.

Les quelles choses ouyes[9] et sceues par[10] le dit roy regent dist au dit aumosnier qui les lui baillast par escript et la ville de Meaulx prise la quelle le fu lendemain que ces choses furent dictes au dit roy regent, il meneroit le dit feu roy Charles et la royne de France ces beaux pere et mere a Senliz[11] en commandant au dit aumosnier que lui retourne de la[12] alast par devers lui au Bois de Vincennes[13] pour parler

---

[1] MS., *prnoit.*   [2] Paris, France, *dép.* Seine.

[3] This word is followed by *depuis le trespas de son dit feu frere* struck through.

[4] Read ? *et.*

[5] Montesquieu-Volvestre, France, *dép.* Haute-Garonne, *arr.* Muret.

[6] MS., *joux.*   [7] MS., *jour.*   [8] MS., *du.*

[9] The reading of this word is doubtful.   [10] MS., *per.*

[11] Senlis, France, *dép.* Oise.

[12] This word is followed by *ast* struck through.

[13] Bois de Vincennes, France, *dép.* Seine, *arr.* Sceaux.

de ceste matiere pour ce quil voiloit renvoyer devers le dit roy de
Navare pour ceste cause et lui commanda aussi quil en escriveist a
icellui roy de Navarre comme dit est, mais en retournant du dit lieu de
Senliz laccident de la maladie du dit roy regent le prist dont il trespassa
comme il est notoire pour quoy[1] la chose demoura et est demoure en
cest estat.

6. Instructions for the ambassadors of the Duke of Bedford to the King of Navarre. Circa January 1423. [B.N., MS. Dupuy 223, ff. 225ᵛ–229ʳ. Contemporary copy.]

[*f. 225ᵛ*] Nouvelle Instruccion de Navarre

Instruccion baillee a messire de Monferant chivaler seigneur etc', a
maistre Guillaume le Breton archediacre de Sens[2] et a maistre Guillaume Eimery maistre en theologie et doyen de Reins[3] conseillers du
roy nostre sʳ pour aler de par le roy nostre sʳ et monsʳ le regent le
royaume de France duc de Bedford devers le roy de Navarre.

Premierement porteront lettres destat et de creance depar le roy
nostre sʳ e depar mon dit seigneur regent le royaume de France duc
de Bedford et feront les salutacions appartenant.

Item diront comment le roy de France derrein[4] trespasse ayeul du
roy nostre dit sʳ japieca envoya pardevers le roy de Navarre par ladvis
et deliberacion du roy Dangleterre derrein[4] trespasse pere [*f. 226ʳ*]
du roy nostre dit sʳ dont Dieu ait les ames pour signifier au dit roy de
Navarre comme a son treschier cousin et parent prochain vassal et
alie lestat[5] de lui et de son royaume.

Item que apres le trespassement des ditz roys le Henri[6] nostre dit sʳ
qui a present est filz des deux roys dessus ditz est venu aux deux
couronnes de France et Dangleterre et par la[7] grace de Dieu comme
seul filz et heritier est vray roy de France et Dangleterre.

Item et est vray que toute la partie que obeissoit au dit feu roy de
France au temps de son trespassement a depuis le dit trespas tousjours
loyaulment obey au roy nostre dit sʳ et a monsʳ le duc de Bedfort
oncle du dit roy de France et Dangleterre qui par le droit proximite
est regent le dit royaume de France.

Item et aussi apres le dit trespas lobeissance est augmente au roy
nostre dit sʳ et se sont plusieurs places reduites et remises a son

---

1 The MS. adds *la quoy* following this word.
2 Sens, France, *dép.* Yonne.   3 Reims, France, *dép.* Marne.
4 MS., *derr'*.   5 MS., *lesta*.
6 *Sic* in MS.
7 This word is followed by *qu* struck through.

obeissance, les aucuns de leur bon gre, et les autres[1] par force tant es pais de Champaigne et de Brie et de Picardie comme dailleurs.

Item et par le bon gouvernement de mon dit s[r] le regent et de ces cappitaines avecques la grace de Dieu le roy nostre dit s[r] a eu la victoire de plusieurs grosses batailles rencontres et assaulx alencontre de ses ennemis et adversaires, et telement que par la grace de Dieu ses ditz ennemis sont tres fort affeblis[2] et sont les afferes du roy nostre dit s[r] en tres grant essaucement et grant esperance[3] pour venir a bonne et briefve conclusion.

Item et pour ce que a cause du trespassement des ditz roys plusieurs afferes sont survenuz lon na peu se tost entendre a envoyer pardevers le dit roy de Navarre comme la bonne affeccion y estoit et est mais maintenant les ditz afferes sont[4] tres fort amaindris et diminiuez comme dessus est dit.

Item et pour ce que le temps oportun est venu le roy nostre dit s[r] qui a pareille bonne affeccion et amitie que les ditz ayeul et pere avoient envers le dit roy de Navarre comme a son treschier cousin parent prouchein[5] et vassal envoye presentement par ladvis et deliberacion de mon dit s[r] le regent ses ditz embaxadeurs pour vacquer et entendre pardevers le dit roy de Navarre ad ce que aucune bonne conclusion soit[6] prise sur les ditz amictie et entretenement dicell' au bien des ditz roys et royaumes de France et de Navarre.

Item en lui priant en requerant que comme il ait eu tousjours singuliere amour, affeccion et bonne volente au bien et prouffit du royaume de France, que pour tel bien cest maintes fois emploie et entremis et a tousjours este avec son dit feu aieul et pere et avec celux de sa partie il comme son parent et vassal en continuant sa bonne amour, volente et affeccion [*f. 226[v]*] se tiengue tousjours avec lui et ceulx de sa partie.

Item et que laccord et[7] paix final qui a este faicte entre les ditz feux roys de France et Dangleterre il veulle avoir agreable a icelle adherer et jurer et de ce bailler ses lettres patents comme son bon cousin, parent, ami et vassal.

Item et que par lettres et autrement ainsi quil avisera estre pour le mieulx il exhorte et induise les royz de Castelle et Darragon et les seigneurs et barons des ditz royaumes autres quil verra estre expedient

---

[1] This word is followed by *et remises a son obeisance* struck through.
[2] MS., *afflebis*. [3] MS., *espante*.
[4] This word is followed by *et* struck through. [5] MS., *prouch*.
[6] This word is followed by *s* struck through.
[7] This word is followed by *f* struck through.

et ad ce quilz soient avec le roy et quilz se desistent[1] de favoriser et aidier cellui qui se disoit Daulphin tenu et repute[2] a juste cause ennemi cappital et adversaire du roy et du royaume et de toute la chose publicque dicellui, et que tous ceulx qui le comforteront ayderont et soustendront le roy les reputera ses ennemis et adversaires.

Item que le dit roy de Navarre tiengne maniere devers le conte de Foix et le veille induire et exorter quil acomplice de sa part tout se quil a promis par lui et ses embaxadeurs aus ditz feux roy de France et Dangleterre derrein[3] trespassez dont lui pouroit declairer les accords et promesses.

Item et pour ce que environ lan cccc xx par les embaxadeurs des ditz roys furent faictes autres teles ou semblables requestes auquelles le dit roy de Navarre respondit par escript[4] signe de son seign manuel comme len dit encore. Il pourroit respondre semblablement; les ditz embaxadeurs pourront dire[5] et respondre aux requestes et demandes du dit roy de Navarre lors faictes par les manieres que sensuivent[6] et par autre que sauront bien aviser ou cas toutesfoiz que le dit roy en feroit mencion ou demande.

Item et premierement a la requeste qui fut faicte depar le dit roy de France au dit roy de Navarre, cest assavoir que laccord et[7] paix final qui fut faicte entre les feux roys de France et Dangleterre, ilz voulissent avoir agreable ratifier et a icelle adherer[8] et jurer et faire jurer par les estaz de son royaume, de ce bailler ses lettres patentes aux embaxadeurs lors envoyez par devers lui. A quoy le dit roy de Navarre ait repondu par escript et dit que toute sa vie il a ame le dit royaume de France de tout son cueur et a tous diz obey comme vray et loyal parent et naturel du royaume a tout ce quil a pleu au roy lui commander pour le bien et honneur du dit roy et royaume de France ou tresgrant prejudice de lui et de son royaulme de Navarre. Toutesvoyes en esperance[9] que le roy de France et les autres seigneurs de son sang eussent consideracion aux tresgrans services et obeissance et a la grant amour et affeccion quil a eu au roy et a son dit royaume comme dit est et aussi a la prochainete du sang et lignaige dont lui et ses antecessours attengnent [f. 227[r]] au roy et a la couronne de France, car il est issu de la lignee du roy Loys ne na aucune collateral lignee qui ne viengne de France jusques a present, cest assavoir de bisaieul, dayeul et dayeule, de pere et de mere lui feussent favorables et gracieux en lui rendant et gardant sans rigueur ce qui appartient et vient de

ses antecesseurs, cest assavoir du comte[1] Devreux[2] jadis filz du roy
Philippe filz du roy Saint Loys son bisaieul de son ayeul filz du dit
conte Devreux de son ayeulle seule fille du roy Loys de France de par
son pere du roy Philippe le Bel et roy de Navarre conte de Champaigne
et de Brie et de par sa femme du dit roy Philippe de Bel et seule fille
du dit roy de Navarre, conte de Champaigne et de Brie desquelles
seigneuries de Champaigne et de Brie et autres la dite damme estant
maindre daus fu privee et desheritee et ses successeurs sans cause
raisonnable et encore sont de present ou tresgrant prejudice du dit
roy et royaume de Navarre.

Item semble soubz correccion a messeigneurs du conseil que sur ce
lon peut dire au dit roy de Navarre que quoy que ce soit de ce que
dit est toutesvoies de son bon gre il pour lui, ses[3] hoirs et successeurs
et aians cause de lui tout le droit et accion quil avoit et povoit demander
et avoir et qui lui povoient competer et appartenir a cause de la hoirrie
ou succession de feu le roy de Navarre son pere et de feue la royne de
Navarre sa mere ou dautres, et autrement en quelque[4] maniere et par
quelque tiltre[5] couleur ou condicion que ce fust ou peust faire tant
en la conte de Champaigne et ses appartenances comme en plusieurs
autres conte, ceitez, villes, chasteaulx et terres designees es lettres sur[6]
ce faictes avecques[7] la clause general, cest assavoir et generalement en
toutes les autres terres, signories, possessions, biens, meubles et autres
choses quelconques quil avoit et povoit avoir et qui a cause des dites[8]
successions des ditz feux pere et mere et autrement pour quelque[9]
tiltre[5] ou cause ou occasion que ce fust lui competoient et apparte-
noient ou povoient compter et appartenir en quelque lieu ou partie que
se feust ou dit royaume de France parmi certain transport qui par le
dit roy de France Charles vj[e] fu fait au dit roy de Navarre pour lui,
ses hoirs, successeurs de xij[m] livres tourn' de terre, rentes et revenues
qui se devoient asseoir sur plusieurs chasteaux, villes et chastellenies
qui ont este adjoinctes a la ville, chasteau et chastellenie de Nemox,
dont a este erige le duchie de Nemoulx comme plus a plain [*f. 227*]
est contenu es lettres sur ses faictes passees par grant et meu[r] deliberacion de conseil le quel duchie de Nemoux avecques plusieurs grans
noblesses et prerogatives le dit roy de Navarre tient et posside par
vertu du dit transport a lassiete seulement de viij[m] livres tourn' par an

---

[1] MS., *contre*.
[2] This word is followed by *de son ayeulle seule fille du roy* struck through.
[3] This word is followed by *biens* struck through.
[4] MS., *quelquel*.   [5] MS., *tltre*.
[6] This word is followed by *lan m cccc° xx* struck through.
[7] This word is followed by *de* struck through.
[8] This word is followed by *susse* struck through.
[9] This word is followed by *que* struck through.

comme il dit. Et pour ce que il restoit encore de la dit somme de xij^m
livres tourn', iiij^m livres pour suppleer la dit rente de iiij^m livres tourn'
le dit feu roy de France a baille au dit roy de Navarre les chasteaulx
et chastellenies de Courtenay,[1] de Ruy[2] et de Nemour[3] par telle
maniere que se les ditz chasteaux et terres avecques les autres chasteaulx et terres du dit duchie de Nemoux baillez pour les xij^m livres
tourn' de rente ne valoient pour lors quilz furent baille[4] les ditz xij^m
livres tourn' le roy de France le parferoit et se plus valoient le roy de
France prendroit le surplus a quoy le dit roy de Navarre a aquiesce et
sest y descendu et par ainsi de raison il ne peut autre chose demander.

Item et a la requeste qui fut faicte au dit roy de Navarre que les estas
du royaume de Navarre jurassent la dite paix et accord come le roy
mesmes a quoy le dit roy de Navarre ait fait responce que apres ce
que les dites requestes des ditz embaxadeurs ont este[5] exposees aux
estas du dit royaume eue grant deliberacion de conseil et aussi consideracion de la situacion du dit royaume de Navarre. Lequel est
assez pres et joignans de deux grans royaumes, cest assavoir Castelle
et Arragon le quel royaume de Chastelle est alie du roy de France
et a son aisne filz; et sil estoit ainsi que le dit roy de Navarre et les
estas de son royaume jurassent tenir la dite paix et accord, le roy de
Castelle feroit guerre au royaume de Navarre a cause des dites[6]
aliances laquelle chose seroit ou grant domaige dicellui royaume, sans
aucun proffit, et ne le pouroient bonnement soustenir mais non
obstant ce ou cas quil plairoit au roy de France rendre et restituer au
roy et royaume de Navarre ce que de droit naturel et civil lui appartient et par especial les contes de Champaigne et de Brie, ilz se accor-
deront aux requestes a eulx faictes par les ditz embaxadeurs et jurerent
la dite paix et adhereront a la part du dit roy de France. Il semble a
mes ditz seigneurs du conseil soubz correction que veu ce que dit est
cy dessus la demande du dit roy de Navarre et des trois estaz des ditz
contez de Champaigne et de Brie nest pas raisonnable, mais se doivent
arrester au traictee dessus dit. Et quant est de ce que le dit roy de
Navarre demande ce [f. 228^r] que de droit naturel et civil lui appartient, il semble au dit conseil quon ne lui doit point refuser, et pour ce
que le dit roy de Navarre se doubte que guerre ne fust faicte en son
dit pais le roy de Castelle se il juroit la dite paix. Il semble que ou cas
dessus dit le roy nostre dit s^r et mon dit s^r le regent le devoient aider
et comforter le mieulx quilz pouroient et que ce on doit offrir au dit

---

1 Courtenay, France, *dép*. Loret, *arr*. Montargis.
2 Le Ruy, France, ? *dép*. Yonne, *arr*. Monsols.
3 MS., *dennemoyre*. Nemours, France, *dép*. Seine-et-Marne, *arr*. Fontainebleau.
4 MS., *baill*.   5 This word is followed by *ex* struck through.
6 This word is followed by *alai* struck through.

roy de Navarre par bonnes qualities et manieres. Il semble aussi que se les ditz trois estas ne vouloient faire le serement dessus dit on devroit estre assez contens si le dit roy de Navarre les fasoit tant seulement et quil en baillast ses lettres de la quelle chose on le doit fer requerir et somer attendu quil est duc de Nemoux et quil le tient en parrie de France le quel duchie est de la vraye obeissance du roy nostre dit s^r.

Item et ad ce que le dit roy de Navarre a la request des ditz embaxadeurs envoya en Castelle pour savoir se le roy et royaume de Castelle vouldroient adherer et estre comprins en la dit paix et accord par le moyen de lenfant Don Jehan son filz et aussi pour rompre larmee qui ja estoit ordonne pour aider a icellui qui se disoit Daulphin et pareillement aux contes Darmignac et de Foiz ses filz. Il semble au dit conseil que on len doibt bien mercier et lui prier que en continuant en[1] la dite bonne volente il veulle ad ce exhorter et induire les ditz seigneurs et y tenir les meilleurs moyens quil pourra devers les quelz le roy nostre dit s^r et mon dit s^r le regent[2] envoyent pour la dite cause, et pourront dire les ditz embaxadeurs au dit roy de Navarre toute la charge quilz[3] devers le conte de Foix en quoi faisant le roy nostre dit s^r et mon dit s^r le regent lui feront toutes les plus grans faveurs quilz purront et tellement quil en devra estre content.

Item et quant ad ce que le dit roy de Navarre et les ditz trois estas de son royaume requirent que les perres[4] de France qui furent presens ou dit traictie de paix de France et Dangleterre et aussi la court de parlement envoyent leurs lettres soubz leurs[5] seaulx par les quelles leur appere quilz ont este presents et consentantz[6] a dit accord pour le bien et utilite de la chose publique du dit royaume et conseillent au dit roy de Navarre quil ratiffient loue et aprouve et veulle adherer a icellui.

Item et se le dit roy de Navarre demandoit[7] ij^m livres de rente qui furent baillees a heritaige a la royne Blanche et a ses hoirs et ayans cause par eschange pour et en lieu de ij^m livres de rente a heritaige que la dite royne prenoit et avoit droit de prendre a tousjours sur le tresor du roy nostre s^r a Paris qui lui furent assises sur les terres quelles tenoit en [*f. 228^v*] douaire, qui par[8] le trespas de la dit royne et depuis par le trespas de feu mess^r Pierre de Navarre frere du dit roy de Navarre doyent apartenir au dit roy de Navarre. Il semble que par la generale renonciacion faicte par le dit roy de Navarre dont dessus est faicte mencion il en peut aucune chose demander par raison mais doit tout appartenir et appartient au roy nostre dit s^r.

---

[1] This word is followed by *o* struck through.
[2] MS. *gent.*
[3] *Sic* in MS.
[4] MS., *partes.*
[5] This word is followed by an ? *l* struck through.
[6] MS., *consent.*
[7] This word is followed by an *i* struck through.
[8] MS., corrected from *puis.*

Item et pareillement peut on respondre se le dit roy de Navarre demande mil livres de terre et rente qui pieca furent baillees Agnes contesse de Foix en mariaige sur les terres de Montequieu[1] dont[2] le dit feu mess[r] Pierre de Navarre joissoit[3] et joit jusques a son trespas, la quelle rente apres son dit trespas a este mise et est la main du roy nostre dit s[r].

Item et non obstant toutes choses, il semble au dit conseil que veu le temps qui est le roy nostre dit s[r] et mon dit s[r] le regent feront bien de adviser a faire quelque liberalite de trois ou de quatre mil livres de rente ou autre au dit roy de Navarre, et que par ce moyen il en sera plus enclin au bien du roy nostre dit s[r] et de mon dit s[r] le regent.

Item et aussi semble que mon dit s[r] le regent fera bien de fere demander et retenir[4] aliances avec lui se on la treuve de bonne volente.

Par lettres royaux en las de soye donnes a Tours[5] x de decembre iiij[c] viij narratives de chasteaulx, terres et lieux bailliez par avant par le roy de Navarre pour xij[m] livres tourn' et que les dites terres ne revenoient pour lors quelles lui furent baillees a viij[m] livres tourn' par quoy lui en restoyt[6] iiij[m] et plus le roy des lors lui transporta Courtenay,[7] Piffons[8] et Chantecoq[9] qui sont de la chastellenie et duchie[10] de Nemour[11] a les tenir avec les dites autres terres a une seule foy, hommaige et en perrie ou duchie de Nemoux sur ce qui restoit a parfaire des dits xij[m] livres tourn' de terre par telle condicion qui ce plus avoit le dit roy de Navarre, il le reprendroit et se pou avoit le roy le parferoit reservees les gardes des eglises,[12] cathedraux, les eglises de fondation[13] royal en la garde du roy et autres privillegiees quelles ne puissent estre mise ? hors de la couronne saucunes en y avoit.

Regina Blanchia quictavit et quictat dominum regem de appreciacione et deliberacione xj[m] v[c] lxxviij l' quas sibi tradere debebat apud Pontifi[14] et in Normannia pro parte dotis sue. Item et de deux mil[15] l' [*f. 229^r*] ad heriditatem[15] quas dicta regina cappiebat[15] super thesaurum hoc mediante quod dominus rex quictat eam de hoc quod ab ea peti posset

---

[1] Montesquieu-Volvestre, France, *dép.* Haute-Garonne, *arr.* Muret.
[2] MS. repeats *dont*.   [3] MS., *jassoit*.   [4] Read ? *recevoir*.
[5] Tours, France, *dép*. Indre-et-Loire.
[6] This word is followed by *qu* struck through.
[7] Courtenay, France, *dép*. Loret, *arr*. Montargis.
[8] Piffonds, France, *dép*. Loret, *arr*. Montargis, *c*. Mezieres-sous-Bellegarde.
[9] Chantecoq, France, *dép*. Loret, *arr*. Montargis, *c*. Courtenay.
[10] The reading of this word is uncertain.
[11] MS., *dennemour*.
[12] This word is followed by *casti si* struck through.   [13] MS., *fondacon*.
[14] Ponthieu, France.   [15] *Sic* in MS.

eo quod sine conclusione dicte appreciacionis tenuit et tenet terras sibi pro predictis tradictas prout hec et alia continentur lacius in litteris ejusdem regine datis a Neauffle[1] xxvj° marcii m ccc iiij^{xx} xv redditis magistro Girardo de Monte Acuto ad reponendum et custodiendum in registro cartarum regis super margine cujus scribitur sic dictam ? quietanciam[2] recipi. G. de Montagu.

Sciatur in thesauro regis quibus medio et titulo dicte ij^m libre ad hereditatem spectabant regine Blanche anno iiij^{xx} et antea.

Item in quo medio sine titulo Anges de Navarra capiebat mille libras terre super thesaurum ad hereditatem per cartam factam x marcii[3] m ccc xlix.

7. *Instructions for the ambassadors of the Duke of Bedford to the Count of Foix. Circa January 1423.* [*B.N., MS. Dupuy 223, ff. 229^r–230^r. Contemporary copy.*]

[*f. 229^r*] Instruccion de Foix

Instruccion de par le roy nostre s^r a messrs' les conte de Longueville et capita[u] de Buch,[4] Jehan de Raclif[5] senechal de Guienne, mess' Bernard[6] de Montferrant, mess' Menault de Favas chivalers, chambellans, maistres Guillem Eim[e]ri docteur en theologie et doyen de Reins,[7] Guillem[8] Breton licencie en droit canon archediarcre de Sens[9] conseilliers du roy nostre s^r sur ce quilz ont a dire, exposer et faire de par le roy[10] nostre dit s^r et ce envers mons' Jehan conte de Foix.

Premierement apres les salutacions faictes baillont ou feront[11] bailler les lettres closes de par le roy nostre dit s^r au dit conte de Foix.

Item et apres ce lui exposeront la grande et bonne affeccion que feux treshaulx[12] princes et noz tresredoutez seigneurs les roys de France et Dengleterre derrein trespassez dont Dieu ait les aimes ont eue en leur vivant au dit conte et aussi la bonne et vraye amour et affeccion que le dit conte a eue aus ditz roys et mesmement en ce que icellui conte a fait faire par ses procureurs souffisaument fondez le xiij^e jour de mars lan [de] grace mil cccc xxj et ou nom de lui comme vray et loyal subget du dit royaume de France le serement de la paix

---

[1] Neaufles-Saint-Martin, France, *dép.* Eure, *arr.* Gisors.
[2] MS., *qui'ctam.* [3] MS., *marci.* [4] MS., *Unch'.*
[5] This word is followed by an *s* struck through.
[6] MS., *Berault.* [7] Reims, France, *dép.* Marne.
[8] This word is followed by *Brt* struck through.
[9] Sens, France, *dép.* Yonne.
[10] This word is followed by *d* struck through. [11] MS., *seront.*
[12] This word is followed by *et* struck through.

final faicte entre iceulx feux roys; leurs royaumes et subgetz et
accorde plusieurs articles touchant le bien et honneur des ditz feux
roys et du royaume de France.

[*f. 229ᵛ*] Item et que apres le dit serement ainsi fait les ditz roys
envoierent tresdiligemment faire et acomplir tout ce que leur ? coste
devoit faire et faire delivrer xijᵐ vijᶜ[1] escuiz ou la valeur a Bertrand
de Domaison, mestre Jehan de Forton et Jehan de Fortevisse ses
embaxadeurs et procureurs pur lui porter et bailler par maniere de se-
cours et a prest pour[2] commencer la guerre a cellui qui se disoit
Daulphin et ses adherens pour recouvrer et remectre en lobeissance
diceulx le pays de Languedoc qui le dit soy disant Daulphin occupoit
et encore occupe et dont iceulx embaxadeurs et procureurs furent
daccord.

Item diront les ditz embaxadeurs que pour la dit cause et pour recevoir
de lui en sa personne le serement de la dit paix come promis et accorde
avoit este par les dits embaxadeurs et procureurs et bailler ses lettres
aprobatoires de celles de ses ditz embaxadeurs et procureurs et fere
autres choses dont en avoit traictie et accorde avecques iceulx procureurs les ditz roys envoierent diligemment par devers lui ses embaxadeurs, cest assavoir les dits conte de Longueville frere du dit
conte, Jehan Radclif lors connestable de Bordeaulx,[3] et maistre Guillem
Barrau et Perre Guirault secretaires des ditz roys et autres.

Item que les ditz embaxadeurs des ditz feux roys se partirent et sen
alerent a Bordeaulx avec les dits embaxadeurs et procureurs du dit
conte de Foix ou ilz arriverent le samedi xxiijᵉ jour de may lan mil
iiijᶜ xxij et fut conclud entre eulx que les ditz embaxadeurs et procureurs du dit conte yroient devant devers[4] le dit conte pour lui
exposer ce quil avoient traictie et accorde avecques les ditz feux roys.
Et que les ditz embaxadeurs des ditz roys partiroient iiij ou v jours
apres le dit partement pour eulx traire devers le dit conte.

Item que cependant le dit conte envoya devers eulx messire Jehan
de Bearn' son chivaler et conseiller pour leur dire prier et requerir
de par icelui conte que pour le bien des ditz roys et de la besoigne pour
laquelle ilz venoient, ilz nalassent point devers lui jusques en la fin
du mois de juing lors prochain ensuivant ou jusques ad ce quilz les
mendast, car il estoit lors en certain traictie avecques aucuns de
Tholose[5] pour avoir icelle ville et autres villes du dit pais de Languedoc
pour la quelle cause les ditz embaxadeurs des ditz roys demourerent

---

[1] This word is followed by *livres* struck through.
[2] This word is followed by a false start for *commencer*.
[3] Bordeaux, France, *dép.* Gironde.   [4] MS., *deves*.
[5] Toulouse, France, *dép.* Haute-Garonne.

au dit lieu de Bordeaux jusques au ixe jour de juillet ensuivant que le dit conte les manda querir par le dit mess^r Jehan de Bearn'.

[*f. 230^r*] Item ariverent les ditz embaxadeurs des ditz roys par devers le dit conte en sa ville Dortes[1] en Bearne[2] le lundi xiij^e jour du dit mois de juillet. Et apres plusieurs traictemens parlemens et communicacions eues ensemble le dit conte bailla ses responces contenues en certaines lettres patentes[3] scellees de son scel contenant entre autres choses certeines modifficacions a lui estre passees et accordees par les ditz roys avant quil feist la serement de la dite paix ne baillast ses dites lettres approbatoires pour la quelle cause les ditz Barrau et Guirault se mirent en chemin de retourner avecques les dits roys messe^r Guillem Remond ? viscounte de Lescat[4] et Remond Arnault de Lebreto escuier conseiller et embaxadors dudit conte mais quant il furent en Artemue[5] en Angleterre ilz sceuent la mort des ditz roys dont ilz furent moult dolens et alerent devers le conseil du roy nostre dit s^r qui apud est[6] in sa ville et cite de Londres.

Item et devers icellui s^r par ladvis et deliberacion tant du conseil de France comme Dengleterre obtindrent lettres patentes[3] par les quelz le roy nostre s^r a conferme et octroye au dit conte tout ce [que] par du dit conte feux roys lui avoit este accorde et octroie. Et aussi les dites modificacions et reparacions demandees et requises par lettres patentes[3] de dit les quelles lettres furent envoiees et baillees pour porter au dit conte signee du sing manuel de certain tabellion ou noteires collacionees[7] a loriginal et a luy envoyees par le poursuivant du conte de Longueville. Et tout ce aussi a peu savoir par le raport de ses dits embaxadeurs.

Item et pour les causes dessus dites le conseil du roy estant a Bordeaux les ditz conte de Longueville, senechal de Guienne et Perre Guirault lui escripvirent par plussieurs fois en declarent tout au long la dite matiere et requerans que veu icelle et que les ditz roys avoient fait tout ce quil avoit requis il voulist aussi faire tout ce quil devoit faire et acomplir de son coste dont il na baille sur ce certaine ne clere responce.

Item et ce pour ce que le roy nostre s^r a la dite matiere a cueur et que cause du dit retardement il a eu plusieurs grans frais et dommaiges, et aussi quil a entencion[8] de renvoyer[9] le dit pais[10] par le moyen du dit conte ou par autre derechief il envoye ses ditz embaxadeurs par devers le dit conte pour refreschir et remonstrer les choses dessus

---

[1] Orthez, France, *dép.* Basses-Pyrénées.   [2] Béarn.
[3] MS., *paten.*   [4] ? read *Lescar, dép.* Basse-Pyrénées, *arr.* Pau.
[5] Dartmouth, England, *co.* Devon.   [6] *Sic* in MS.
[7] MS., *collacionnaire.*   [8] MS., *entencon.*   [9] MS., *renvoyez.*
[10] MS., this word is followed by a false start.

ditz et lui requerir quil [*f. 230ᵛ*] veulle fere et acomplir et mectre a execucion deue tout ce que par icellui a este accorde en ceste partie.

Cest assavoir quil jure en sa personne la paix final faicte et conclue et fermee entre les ditz feux roys de France et Dangleterre, leurs royaumes et subgetz et les articles en icelle contenuz.

Item et aussi les autres articles passez et acordez entre les ditz feux roys dune part et ses ditz embaxadeurs et procureurs pour et ou nom de lui dautre part. Et quil voille ses lettres ratifficatoires et approbatoires jonctes les dites modificacions de celles lettres que ses ditz embaxadeurs et procureurs ont sur ce baillees a iceulx feux roys.

Item et que sur ce il leur face responce certaine et clere.

Item ou cas que le dit conte sera refusant ou tropt delayans ou en demeure de fere ou acomplir ce que dit est, les dits embaxadeurs lui requerront quil leur rende, baille et delivre pour et ou nom du roy nostre dit sʳ ladit somme de xijᵐ vᶜ ¹ escuz dor ou la valeur diceulx en baillant au dit conte et autres la quietance quil appartiendra.

Item et que les dits embaxadeurs signiffieront par deca le plus deligemment quil pourront ce que fait aura este sur ce.

Item et que sur toutes les choses devant dictes et dependances dicelles les ditz embaxadeurs procederont selon lexigence des cas et qui soffiront aux mieulx que pouront selon leur discrecion.

8. *Instructions for the ambassadors of the Duke of Bedford to the King of Castile. Circa January 1423.* [*B.N., MS. Dupuy 223, ff. 231ʳ–232ʳ. Contemporary copy.*]

[*f. 231ʳ*] Instrucciones² Castelle

Instrucciones ex parte illustrissimi principis Henrici Francie et Anglie regis et incliti principis Johannis regentis regnum Francie ducis Bedfordie super³ hiis, que dominus Bernardus⁴ de Monferrant miles,⁵ magistri Guillelmus Britonis in jure canonico licenciatus [archidiaconus] Pravinin'⁶ in ecclesia Senon',⁷ et Guillelmus Eim[e]rie in theologica doctor decanus Remensis,⁸ consiliarii domini nostri regis, qui presencialiter destinantur⁹ ad serenissimum principem regem Castelle et Ligionis¹⁰, habebunt eidem exponere.

Primo post reverenciarum condignarum exhibicionem litteras clausas status et credencie quas deferunt presentabunt.

---

¹ This word is followed by *livres* struck through.   ² MS., *instruciones*.
³ MS., *surper*.   ⁴ MS., *Benardus*.   ⁵ MS., *milles*.
⁶ MS., *Preveniensis*. Provins, France, *dép*. Seine-et-Marne.
⁷ Sens, France, *dép*. Yonne.   ⁸ Reims, France, *dép*. Marne.
⁹ MS., *destnantur*.   ¹⁰ *Sic* in MS.

Item in exposicione sue credencie dicent in primis quod habent pro repetito id quod dudum fuit sibi expositum[1] et relatum per[2] ambassatores celebris recordacionis principis regis Francie super abhominanda et dampnabili prodicione per Karolum pro Delphino[3] se gerentem[4] conspirata in mortem inclite memorie Johannis[5] ducis Burgundie, cui Deus propicietur, et eciam[6] super sacerrima pace inter deffunctum[7] regem Francie et bone memorie Henricum regem Anglie et regentem Francie dum viveret ac eorum regna facta et jurata. Quod insuper fuit sibi expositum ex parte dicti deffuncti[8] regis Anglie super requisicione treugarum inter regna Anglie et Castelle et subditos eorum sub affeccione confederacionum inter eos subscandarum.[9]

Item dicent quod post decessum prefatorum[10] Francie et Anglie regum,[11] dictus dominus noster rex filius dictorum regum eis successit in regnis supradictis, effectusque est ipsorum rex et dominus habens Dei gracia equalem ymo majorem obedienciam precipue[12] in[13] dicto regno Francie quam dicti sui predecessores haberent post tractatum pacis. Et jure proximitatis dictus dominus dux Bedfordie paternus ipsius domini nostri regis est regens Francie.

Item et cum ipse sit dictorum duorum potentissimorum regnorum Francie et Anglie rex et dominus et dicti predecessores sui intimo quesierunt desiderio mutuas amicicias, alligancias et confederaciones ab olim inter eos et reges Castelle initas et hereditas[9] perdurare que res quamvis apud ipsum regem Castelle ut separatur in bono mentis affectu[14] resederit non fuerit ad finem cupitum [f. 131[v]] perducta[15] sed remanserit[16] in suspenso. Prefatus dominus[17] noster rex ac dictus dominus regens considerantes proximitatem sanguinis qua inter se et regem Castelle connexi sunt rememorantes insuper[18] confederaciones, ligas et amicicias inter progenitores suos quondam contractatas et diu observatas, attendentes preterea bonum et securitatem[19] toti Christianitati redundantem.[20] Si Christianissima regna Francie et Anglie et Castelle pace bona et sancta concordia convenirent, illud bonum federis conceperunt et suis morigerendo predecessoribus eadem benevola vota ad Dei laudem et[21] honorem amplexi[22] sunt.

---

[1] MS. repeats *fuit*.   [2] MS. repeats *per*.
[3] MS. corrected from *delphinum*.   [4] MS., *geremtem*.
[5] MS., *Johannem*.   [6] MS., *ecciam*.   [7] MS., *deffuctum*.
[8] MS., *deffincti*.   [9] *Sic* in MS.   [10] MS., *prefactorum*.
[11] MS., *regem*.   [12] MS., *principue*.
[13] This word is followed by *dominio* struck through.
[14] MS., *affecta*.   [15] MS., *produta*.   [16] MS., *remenserit*.
[17] MS., *dus*.   [18] This word is followed by *confederantes* struck through.
[19] This word is followed by *toit st* struck through.
[20] This word is followed by *in* struck through.
[21] MS. repeats *et*.   [22] MS., *emplex'*.

Item licet post decessum prefatorum regum illa pars regni Francie que eis obediebat in sincera[1] permanserit obediencia dicti domini nostri regis absque divisione seu alienacione[2] aliquali nichilominus predictorum domini nostri regis et regentis bona voluntas non[3] valuit adeo curiose[4] intimari sicut[5] in eorum residebat[6] pectoribus obstantibus multis[7] occupacionibus per dictum decessum provenientibus quibus existebat necessitas vigilare, sed tandem multa Dei[8] dona splendida in triumphis et subjugacione hostium dominus noster rex et regens prefati adepti sunt qui[9] occupaciones predictas pro majori parte subtraxerunt et vias embassatorum apparuerunt.

Item idcirco illis occupacionibus et impedimentis relaxatis et in potentissima parte amputatis mittuntur dicti ambassatores ad exponendum predicta et requirendum dicto regi Castelle quod federa, ligas et amicicias facere velit cum prefatis domino nostro rege et regente Francie sicut hactenus [a] predecessoribus partis utriusque fuerunt[10] contracte et observate.

Item et ut regni Francie rebelles ad dicti domini regis obedienciam[11] facilius reducantur quod velit armatos per mare et per terram si opus sit et quando requisitus fuerit quam majori numero fieri poterit in subsidium regis transmittere.

Item domino Karolo nullum prestet auxilium contra regem quinymo si ? aliquos[12] auxiliatores[13] eidem[14] destinaverit seu aliqui de suis regnis eidem[15] repetere[16] ac contramandare velit.

Item quod in casu quo dictus rex differre vellet contrahere dicta federa, ligas et amicicias ipsi ambassatores tractabunt quod velit mittere suos ambassiatores ad dominum nostrum regem et dominum regentem[17] in Franciam quam cicius fieri poterit ad eis notificandum suam bonam voluntatem.

Item quod interim nullum per se aut suos adversarios domini nostri regis ac[18] domini regentis prestet auxilium[19] aut succursum et[20] precipue illi qui se pro Delphino gerebat ymo si quos jam in auxilium ejus miserit revocet.

[f. 232[r]] Item quod super omnibus premissis et eorum dependentibus dicti ambassiatores procedent secundum casuum[21] emergencium

---

[1] MS., *sincere.*   [2] MS., *alternacione.*   [3] MS., *no.*
[4] *Sic* in MS.   [5] MS. repeats *sicut.*   [6] Expunged by mistake in MS.
[7] MS., *multus.*   [8] This word is followed by *bona* struck through.
[9] MS., *que.*   [10] MS., *fuerit.*   [11] MS., *obedianciam.*
[12] MS., *? aiquos.*   [13] MS., *auxiliares.*   [14] MS., *eadem.*
[15] MS., *eodem.*   [16] This word is followed by *et* struck through.
[17] MS., *regem.*   [18] MS. corrected from *ad.*   [19] MS., *axiliam.*
[20] MS. repeats *et.*   [21] MS., *casus.*

exigenciam prout melius poterunt quantum Deus eorum discreccionibus[1] dignabitur inmittere.

9. *Letters of proxy for the ambassadors of Alfonso V to treat for a league with the English. 15 November 1430.* [*A.C.A.,* *Registro 2692, f. 117ʳ⁻ᵛ. Contemporary copy.*]

[*f. 117ʳ*] Pateat universis quod nos Alfonsus, Dei gracia rex Aragonum etc', quia ut rerum diuturna experiencia in apertum deducit dum aliqui ex terrenis principibus confederacionis affectu et amicicie vinculo alligantur tunc illorum naturales et subditi se ad invicem confovendum et bene tractandum in personis et bonis et ad vicissim comerciandum ferventius inducuntur et ad quoscumque communes hostes et emulos expellendos pro eorum conservandis mutuis honoribus et valitoribus forcius animantur. De vestri, dilectorum et fidelium Jacobi Pelegrini legum doctoris vicecancellarii et Mathei Pujades militis camerarii consiliariorum et ambassiatorum nostrorum, fidelitate industria et probitate ab experto plenarie confidentes tenore presentis publici instrumenti de certa nostri sciencia deliberate et consulte facimus, constituimus, creamus et ordinamus nostros veros certos et indubitatos procuratores, vos eosdem Jacobum Pelegrini et Matheum Pujades vobisque simul nostrum posse conferimus et plenissimam facultatem videlicet quod vice et nomine nostris ac pro nobis et successoribus nostris quibuscumque Aragonum et Sicilie regibus imperpetuum atque subditis et vassallis nostris et eorum possitis et libere valeatis cum illustrissimo et potentissimo principe Enrico eadem gracia rege Anglie et Francie, fratre et consanguineo nobis carissimo, seu ejus ad hec procuratoribus et ambaxiatoribus ac quibusvis magnatibus et aliis de ejus consilio ac dominio cujusvis preheminencie status dignitatis vel condicionis existant, simul vel divisim ac pro se et suis successoribus Anglie et Francie regibus ac subditis et vassalis utriusque dictorum regnorum Anglie et Francie tractare, acceptare, firmare et concedere quascumque ligas amicicias confederaciones promisiones conveniencias et concordias imperpetuum, et propterea quascumque convenciones promissiones pacta capitula condiciones juramenta homagia et obligaciones facere inhire, concedere et firmare, cum et sub adjeccionibus clausulis formis et modis vobis visis et cum dicto rege seu ejus ambassiatoribus et procuratoribus et aliis supradictis simul vel divisim melius concordare poteritis et noveritis posse aut debere firmari et concedi cum cartis instrumentis cartellis et aliis publicis et auctenticis scripturis ac verborum serie tenoribus et expressionibus quibus vobis videbitur. Necnon possitis eciam et valeatis prestare pro nobis dicta

___
[1] MS., *discrescionnibus.*

homagia et juramenta [*f. 117ᵛ*] super crucem Domini et ejus sancta quatuor ewangelia et cum alia quacumque validiori seu firmiori solemnitate forma et modo quibuscumque, et dictis nostris successoribus regibus Aragonum et nomine nostro concordare poteritis. Et ab ipso rege et ejus ut prefertur procuratoribus et ambassiatoribus ac aliis predictis utique consimilia juramenta et homagia, obligaciones et securitates nostri nomine exhigere et recipere et quecumque instrumenta cartas cartella aut scripturas per eum vel eosdem seu ipsorum partem faciendas et firmandas ac concedendas pro nobis et nostro[1] nomine recuperare et habere et per vos firmandas et faciendas in vim hujusmodi eisdem tradere et liberare aut tradi et liberari facere et permittere. Et demum possitis et valeatis insimul in et circa premissa et eorum quodlibet nostri nomine et pro nobis dictisque nostris successoribus ac subditis facere firmare concedere jurare et promittere quecumque nos possemus. Inde personaliter constituti eciam si talia forent que de jure vel de facto aut alias mandatum exhigerent magis speciale ac sine quibus predicta aut eorum aliqua ad debitum effectum deduci nequirent. Quoniam nos in et super eisdem omnibus et singulis et circa ea et eorum quodlibet vobis, dicto Jacobo Pelegrini et Matheo Pujades, procuratoribus nostris simul concedimus damus et committimus totum nostri posse ac omnimodam facultatem cum libera et generali administracione et plenissima facultate. Promittentes vobis in nostra regia bona fide in manu et posse notarii et secretarii nostri subscripti tanquam publice persone pro vobis et aliis personis eciam quibuscumque quarum intersit stipulantibus et acceptantibus, ac eciam juramus per crucem Domini et ejus sancta quatuor evangelia manibus nostris corporaliter tacta quod semper habebimus ratum gratum validum atque firmum quicquid per vos dictos procuratores nostros simul tractatum conventum inhitum paccatum, concordatum, concessum, firmatum et juratum fuerit, nulloque tempore revocabimus aut eisdem contrafaciemus vel veniemus aut contrafieri permittemus vel consenciemus quavis racione seu causa sub bonorum nostrorum quantumcumque privilegiatorum omnium obligacione. In cujus rei testimonium presentem fieri jussimus nostro sigillo pendenti munitam. Dat' Ilerde[2] xv die novembris anno a nativitate Domini millesimo quadringentesimo xxx⁰ regnique nostri xv⁰.

Signum[3] Alfonsi Dei gracia regis Aragonum etc' qui predicta laudamus concedimus juramus. Rex Alf[onsus].

Testes sunt qui[4] predictis interfuerunt: Franciscus Sarcola thesaurarius

---

[1] This word is interlined.
[2] Lérida, Spain, *prov.* Lérida.
[3] This word is followed by a blank in the MS.
[4] This word is followed by *in* struck through.

et Martinus Didici,[1] Davig locumtenens bajuli generalis regni Aragonum milites consiliarii domini regis predicti.

10. *Letters of credence for envoys from Alfonso V to the Queen of Navarre. 6 April 1431. [A.C.A., Registro 2689, f. 31ᵛ. Contemporary copy.]*

[*f. 31ᵛ*] A la muy alta princessa dona Blancha[2] por la gracia de Dios reyna de Navarra nostra muy cara e muy amada hermana, nos el rey Daragon e de Sicilia vos embiamos muyto a saludar como aquella que muyto amamos e por a quien querriamos diesse Dios tanta honrra e buena ventura quanta para nos mesmo deseamos. Reyna muy cara e muy amada hermana, nos tornamos embiar de present a la ciudat de Banyona los amados e fieles conselleros e vicicanciellero micer Jaume Pelegri doctor en leys, mossen Lois de Falces mayordomo e mossen Matheu Pujades cambrero embaxadores nostros por los afferes que vos sabeds e[3] ellos vos explicaran de nostra part a las peraulas de los quales vos rogamos querades dar ferma fe e creença como si nos personalment[4] las vos deziamos, mandando los dar quanto en vos sera toda endreça necessaria por que aquellos puedan salvament[5] e sin recelo o danyo fazer su camino. E si cosas algunas, reyna muy cara e muy amada ermana, vos son plazientes de las partes de la qua embiat las nos dezir, car nos las compliremos de muy buena voluntat. E sea vostra guarda la santa trinidat. Dada en Barchna'[6] dins nostro siello secreto a seys dias de abril del anyo mil cccc xxxj. Rex Alfonsus.

A la muy alta princessa dona Blancha
per la gracia de Dios reyna de Navarra
nostra muy cara e muy amada ermana.

> Dominus rex mandavit
> mihi Johanni Olzina.

11. *Letter from Alfonso V of Aragon to the English ambassadors at Bayonne. 6 April 1431. [A.C.A., Registro 2689, ff. 31ᵛ–32ʳ. Contemporary copy.]*

[*f. 31ᵛ*] Lo rey Darago e de Sicilia.

Embaxadors, vostra letra havem reebuda e vista aquella per que alguns dels embaxadors que trameten aqui no eren en nostre cort, havien haut licencia de nos de anar a lurs[7] cases per propris affers

---

[1] *Sic* in MS. corrected from *Diadici.*
[2] MS., corrected from *Blncha.*
[3] This word is interlined.
[4] MS., corrected from *personalmente.*
[5] MS., corrected from *salvamente.*
[6] Barcelona, Spain.
[7] This word is followed by *coses* struck through.

la qual los haviem donada per no haver haut ardit o sentiment algu
de vostra venguda aqui en deniers ja esser per tot lo mes de noembre
prop passat. Creents que puys per tot lo mes de febrer o la major
part de aquell no haviem sentiment de vostra venguda no enteniets
venir, los dits nostres embaxadors no se sen postuts axi comprestament
desempachat car haver haut a creure per alguns dells a com nous
posguessen attenyer en Leyda¹ son se hauts a largar se aci de present
empero trametre aqui les dits nostres embaxadors, ço es los amats
consellers micer Jacme Pelegri vicecanceller, mossen [f. 32ʳ] Luis
de Falces majordom e mossen Matheu Pujades cambres nostres
informats plenerament de nostra intencio. A les peraules dels quals vos
pregam donets plenera fe e creença com a nostra propria persona.
Dada en Barchna'² sots nostre sigel secret a vj dies de abril del any³
de la nativitat de nostre senyor mil cccc xxxj. Rex Alfonsus.

Als venerable pare en Christ nobles e amats nostres
los embaxadors del molt illustre rey Danglaterra
residents en la ciutat de Banyona.⁴

> Dominus rex mandavit mihi
> Johanni Olzina

12. *Letter from Alfonso V of Aragon to his ambassadors at
Bayonne. 10 May 1431.* [*A.C.A., Registro 2692, ff.
137ᵛ–138ʳ. Contemporary copy.*]

[f. 137ᵛ] Lo rey

Embaxadors, oit lamat nostre mestre Garcia de Falces sobre lo contengut en vostres instruccions, vos certificam primerament quant al
caps de les dites instruccions fahent mencio de les valences o soccors
fahedors axi per nos al rey de Anglaterra com per aquell a nos en
virtud de la liga e confederacio entrecambiadament fahedora, ço es
que en compensacio o esmena dels mil rocins dels quals nos haurem en
son cas a soccorrer al dit rey de Anglaterra dada a nos eleccio sobre
aco etc'. Es nostre parer e intencio lo dit rey Danglaterra deja soccorrer
a nos en son cas de nos mil archers comptant dos arches per cascun
roci o si mes volrem nos, axi mateix li puixam soccorrer de dos milia
ballesters en axi que vinga a raho de un archer per cascun ballester e
de dos arches per cascun roci. On empero sobre aço no poguessets
finar per aquesta forma, som [f. 138ʳ] contents finets en la manera
en les dits vostres instruccions sobre aquest cap contengueda. Quant a
cap de la valenca o soccors fahedors en son cas per lo rey de Navarra

¹ Lérida, Spain.   ² Barcelona, Spain.
³ This word is followed by *mil cccc xxxj* struck through.
⁴ Bayonne, France, *dép.* Basses-Pyrénées.

al dit rey Danglaterra par a nos sia assats competent que sia la terca part de la valenca o soccors que nos farem al dit rey Danglaterra entes, empero que la dita valenca fahedora per lo dit rey de Navarra no sia punt compressa en la que nos haurem a fer segons dit es. Quant al matrimoni fahedor o tractador entrel dit rey de Anglaterra et la una de les infantes filles del dit rey de Navarra, som de intencio e parer dejats instar e procurar per tot poder que lo dit matrimoni[1] se faca ab la infanta e filla menor; on empero en altre manera passar no pogues, e del tot volguessem la filla major ladonchs entrarets en pratica ab los embaxadors del dit rey de Anglaterra del dit matrimoni ab la filla major del dit rey de Navarra, pregants e encarregants vos que sobre aço e altres coses en los dits vostres instruccions contengudes vos hajats ab la diligencia e sollicitud que de vosaltres confiam, e a utilitat e honor de nostre part conexents esser expedient, rescrivint sovent dels dits affers. Dada in Valldaura[2] a x dies de maig del any mil cccc xxxj Rex Alf[onsus]

Dominus rex mandavit mihi
Johanni Olzina pro[thonotario]

Als amats e feels consellers[3]
los embaxadors nostres residents en Bayona

13. *Letter from John II of Aragon to Vicent Clement. 13 July 1459. [A.C.A., Registro 3408, f. 25ᵛ. Contemporary copy.]*

[*f. 25ᵛ*] Lo rey Darago de Navarra e de Sicilia etc', venerable amat e devot nostre. Per la via de Barchinona[4] vos havem respost ara dos o tres jorns ha remeses les letres an Francescho But' de Junyent per medi dels quals nos tenim per dits vos seran trameses ab bon recapte, e segons que en les dites nostres letres es feta mencio per lo serenissimo rey de Anglaterra nostre molt car et molt amat cosi nos es stat trames un gentilhome de casa sua appellat Luis de Brutals ab una molt graciosa letra sua. A la qual havem respost e per avis vostre vos trametem copies axi de la letra sua com de la resposta nostra. Veritat es que en virtut de la crença al dit gentilhom aco manada per ell nos fou dit de peraula per part del dit illustrissimo rey de Anglaterra quell serra molt content pendre ab nos bona inteligencia e confederacio, e de molt bon grat oyria nostres ambaxadors en cas quels hi volguessem trametre. O si a nos venie en plaer ell nos trametria ambaxada sua. E tant com es a aquest article havem comes al dit Luis

---

[1] This word is followed by *per* struck through.
[2] A hunting lodge now in Sardaynola near Sabadell, *prov.* Barcelona.
[3] This word is followed by *nostres* struck through.
[4] Barcelona, Spain.

que diga la intencio nostra de peraula al dit rey la qual es aquesta: que per ço com ara en lo mes de juny prop passat stant en la nostra ciutat de Valenc'[1] son venguts a nos ambaxadors del rey de França nous es stat vist fos cosa decent ne pertinent nos deure trametre de present la dita ambaxada. Si empero al dit serenissimo rey[2] Dinglaterra plaura trametre a nos ambaxada sua ab molt gran plaer e bona voluntat la reebrem[3] e oyrem. E per que sabem que vos sou persona grata e accepta al dit rey per vostres merits e virtuts e per semblant tenim de vos molta confianca per aquell mateix respecte e encara per esser subdit e natural nostre; nostre havem delliberat donar vos avis de totes les dites coses segons que son passades per que de aquelles puxats conferir en lo modo e forma que vist vos sera ab lo dit rey. E per medi vostre[3] siam avisats de ço que per ell sera acordat e delliberat havents per molt cert que aquests affers e altres que redundar poguessen en honor nostra e sua per vos seran menejats ab tota fidelitat e intencio recta. Dat' en la nostra vila de Murvedre[4] a xiij dies de juliol del any mil cccc lviiij. Rex Joannes.

Al venerable amat e devot nostre
mestre Vicent Clement collector de la
cambra apostolical en lo regne de
Anglaterra

A[nthonius] Nogueras protho-
notarius

---

[1] Valencia, Spain.
[3] MS., corrected from *vostres*.

[2] This word is interlined.
[4] Sagunto, Spain.

BIBLIOGRAPHY

Note: The works mentioned in the list of abbreviations are not repeated here.

I. MANUSCRIPT SOURCES

Barcelona, *Archivo de la Corona de Aragón*
    REGISTROS DEL REY: 2655, 2658, 2678, 2680, 2687, 2689, 2692, 2939, 3408.

Barcelona, *Archivo Histórico de la Ciudad de Barcelona*
    LLETRES CLOSES: 1436–8, 1442–4.

Brussels, *Archives Générales du Royaume*
    CONSEIL DE FLANDRES: 21799, 21801 (accounts of the receiver of fines imposed by the Council of Flanders).

Cambridge, *Cambridge University Library*
    Manuscript Mm. I. 45 (a collection of documents by Dr. Brady).

Cambridge, *Corpus Christi College*
    Manuscript 170 (N. Colly's letter-book).

Copenhagen, *Rigsarkivet*
    ANGLO-DANISH TREATIES OF THE FIFTEENTH CENTURY (originals).

Düsseldorf, *Staatsarchiv*
    URKUNDE KURKÖLN: 1928, 1944, 1947, 1979, 2209, 2216, 2243, 2247, 2302, 2348, 2364; URKUNDE KLEVE-MARK: 1581, 1603 (original letters and treaties).

Florence, *Archivio di Stato*
    MEDICEO AVANTI IL PRINCIPATO: filza xi, carta 202 (an original signet letter).

London, *British Museum*
    ADDITIONAL CHARTERS: 87, 1397, 3396, 3579, 3580, 8121, 11484, 11486, 11802 (originals and contemporary drafts).
    ADDITIONAL MANUSCRIPTS: 13961 (claims of the English to the crown of France), 15380, 15381, 15384 (transcripts of papal registers), 24062 (Hoccleve's formulary), 25247 (a seventeenth-century collection of documents), 34324 (a collection of political papers made by Sir Julius Caesar), 35204 (Issue roll for Easter 6 Henry VI), 36541, (chronicle of Richard II, etc.), 38690 (transcripts of documents), 48001 (transcripts of treaties), 48005 (Henry VI's claims to the crown of France), 48008 (transcripts of negotiations with foreign powers), 48009 (transcripts relating to the Hansa), 48031 (copies of miscellaneous state papers).
    COTTON CHARTERS: IV, 61; X, 5, 19, 20; XI, 26, 29, 62; XIII, 30 (1); XXIV, 6 (originals and contemporary drafts).
    COTTON MANUSCRIPTS: Caligula D. V (fragment of a volume on Anglo-French relations temp. Henry V and VI), Nero B. I (original letters and

drafts), Nero B. II (original letters and drafts), Nero E. V (Gloucester's collection of canons), Vespasian C. XII (originals and copies of documents concerning Spain), Cleopatra C. IV (William Swan's letter-book), Cleopatra E. III (originals and copies of documents concerning the Church).

HARLEY MANUSCRIPTS: 431 (contemporary copies of diplomatic documents), 861 (Beckington's collection of diplomatic documents).

LANSDOWNE MANUSCRIPT: 223 (a translation into English of Bodley MS. 885).

London, *Public Record Office*

CHANCERY: Miscellanea of the Chancery (C 47), Parliamentary and Council Proceedings (C 49), Close Rolls (C 54), Gascon Rolls (C 61), Treaty Rolls (C 76), Warrants for the Great Seal, Series I (C 81), Petty Bag Series (C 202).

EXCHEQUER:

A. Treasury of the Receipt: Council and Privy Seal Files (E 28), Diplomatic Documents (E 30), Scottish Documents (E 39).

B. King's Remembrancer: Accounts Various (E 101), Memoranda Rolls (E 159).

C. Lord Treasurer's Remembrancer and Pipe Office: Rolls of Foreign Accounts (E 364), Memoranda Rolls (E 368).

D. Exchequer of Receipt: Enrolments and Registers of Issue (E 403), Writs and Warrants for Issues (E 404), Tellers' Books or Rolls (E 405/2).

PRIVY SEAL OFFICE: Signet Warrants for the Privy Seal (P.S.O. I).

PUBLIC RECORD OFFICE TRANSCRIPTS: Milan Archives Transcripts (P.R.O. 31/3), Record Commission Transcripts Series I (P.R.O. 31/7), Record Commission Transcripts Series II (P.R.O. 31/8, 9).

SPECIAL COLLECTIONS: Ancient Correspondence (SC I), Ancient Petitions (SC 8).

STATE PAPER OFFICE: State Papers Domestic, Charles II (SP 29).

London, *Somerset House*

REGISTER OF WILLS PROVED IN THE PREROGATIVE COURT OF CANTERBURY: 16 Godyn, 19 Milles.

Norwich, *Norwich Diocesan Registry*

BISHOPS' REGISTERS: REG 5, Book 10 (Thomas Brouns).

Oxford, *Bodleian Library*

ASHMOLE MANUSCRIPTS: 758, 789 (fifteenth-century copies of various letters and treaties), 859 (Ashmole's transcriptions).

BODLEY MANUSCRIPTS: 710 (an English translation of MS. 885), 885 (claims of the English to the crown of France).

Pamplona, *Archivo General de Navarra*

CAJÓN: 107, 119, 125, 129, 139.

COMPTOS DEL TESORERO: vols. 365, 398, 402, 403, 427.

Paris, *Archives Nationales*

J. 520 no. 34, J. 643, JJ. 616 nos. 25, 26 (originals).

Paris, *Bibliothèque Nationale*

COLLECTION DOAT: vol. 214 (transcripts of letters).

MANUSCRIT DUPUY: 223 (contemporary copies of letters).

Paris, *Bibliothèque Nationale* (cont.):
MANUSCRITS FRANÇAIS: 4054 (original letters and drafts), 4485, 4491 (accounts of the receiver general), 26048.
MANUSCRIT LATIN: 5956a.
Vienna, *Nationalbibliothek*
Manuscript 4933 (John Stokes's disputation with Hus).

2. PRINTED SOURCES

Anglo-Saxon Wills, ed. D. Whitelock, Cambridge, 1930.

Basin, T., *Histoire de Charles VII*, ed. C. Samaran (Les Classiques de l'histoire de France au moyen âge), 2 vols., Paris, 1933–44.

Beccadelli, A., *De Dictis et factis Alfonsi regis Aragonum libri iv*, Basel, 1538.

Bisticci, V. de', *Renaissance Princes, Popes and Prelates*, ed. M. Gilmore, trans. W. George and E. Waters, New York, 1963.

Bonet, H., *The Tree of Battles*, ed. and trans. G. W. Coopland, Liverpool, 1949.

Bronnen tot de geschiedenis van den handel met Engeland, Schotland en Ierland, 1150–1485, ed. H. J. Smit, The Hague, 1928.

The Brut, or the Chronicles of England, ed. F. W. D. Brie (Early English Text Society, original ser., no. 131, pt. 2), London, 1906.

Brutails, J. A., *Cartulaire de l'église collégiale Saint-Seurin de Bordeaux*, Bordeaux, 1897.

But, A. de, 'Chronicon Flandriae', ed. J.-J. de Smet, Corpus chronicorum Flandriae, vol. i, Brussels, 1837, pp. 259–367.

—— *Chronique d'Adrien de But*, ed. J. M. B. C. Kervyn de Lettenhove (Chroniques relatives à l'histoire de la Belgique sous la domination des ducs de Bourgogne, vol. i), Brussels, 1870.

Cacheux, P. le, ed., *Actes de la chancellerie d'Henri VI concernant la Normandie sous la domination anglaise* (Société de l'histoire de Normandie), 2 vols., Rouen and Paris, 1907–8.

Calendar of Letter-Books Preserved among the Archives of the Corporation of the City of London: Letter-Book K, ed. R. L. Sharpe, London, 1911.

Calendar of State Papers and Manuscripts Existing in the Archives and Collections of Milan, ed. A. B. Hinds, London, 1912.

Campbell, N., *Materials for a History of the Reign of Henry VII* (Rolls Series), 2 vols., London, 1873–7.

Champion, P., *Procès de condamnation de Jeanne d'Arc*, 2 vols., Paris, 1920–1.

Chaplais, P., 'Some Documents Regarding the Fulfilment and Interpretation of the Treaty of Brétigny (1361–1369)', *Camden Miscellany* vol. xix, third ser. lxxx (1952), 51–84.

Chartularium universitatis Parisiensis, ed. H. Denifle and H. Chatellain, vol. iv, Paris, 1897, repr. Brussels, 1964.

Chastellain, G., *Œuvres*, ed. J. M. B. C. Kervyn de Lettenhove, 8 vols., Brussels, 1863–6.

A Chronicle of London from 2089 to 1483 ed. E. Tyrrell and N. H. Nicolas, London, 1827.

Chronicles of London, ed. C. L. Kingsford, Oxford, 1905.

Chronicles of the White Rose of York, ed. J. Giles, London, 1845.

Chronique du Mathieu d'Escouchy, ed. G. du Fresne de Beaucourt (Société de l'histoire de France), 3 vols., Paris, 1863–4.

Chronique des Pays-Bas, de France, d'Angleterre et de Tournai, ed. J.-J. de Smet (Corpus chronicorum Flandriae, vol. iii), Brussels, 1856.

Chronique du Mont-Saint-Michel, ed. S. Luce (Société des anciens textes français), 2 vols., Paris, 1879–83.

Clay, J. W., *North Country Wills* (Surtees Society, cxvi, cxxi), 2 vols., London, 1908–12.

Cochon, P., *Fragment de la chronique normande*, ed. M. Vallet de Viriville, Paris, 1845.

Coke, E., *The Fourth Part of the Institutes of the Laws of England . . .*, 6th edn., London, 1681.

—— *The Third Part of the Institutes of the Laws of England . . .*, 6th edn., London, 1680.

Cooper, C. P., *Appendix A to the Report on the Foedera*, London, 1869.

—— *Appendix C to the Report on the Foedera*, London, 1869.

Le Cotton MS. Galba B. I, ed. E. Scott and L. Gilliodts-van Severen, Brussels, 1896.

Cotton, R., *An Exact Abridgement of the Records in the Tower of London*, ed. W. Prynne, London, 1657.

Cousinot, G., *Chronique de la Pucelle*, ed. M. Vallet de Viriville, Paris, 1892.

Dacher, E., *Historia magnatum in Constantiensi Concilio*, ed. H. von der Hardt (Rerum Universalis Concilio Constantiensi, vol. v), Frankfurt and Leipzig, 1699.

Devon, F., ed., *Issues of the Exchequer, Henry III to Henry VI*, London, 1837.

Diplomatarium Islandicum, ed. J. Sigurðsson *et al.*, 5 vols., Copenhagen, 1857–1922.

Diplomatarium Norvegicum, eds. C. A. Lange, C. R. Unger, *et al.*, 20 vols., Christiania, 1849–1919.

Doncœur, P., and Lanhers, Y., eds., *La Réhabilitation de Jeanne la Pucelle, l'enquête du cardinal d'Estouteville en 1452* (Documents et recherches relatifs à Jeanne la Pucelle, vol. iv), Paris, 1958.

Douët d'Arcq, L., *Choix de pièces inédites relatives au règne de Charles VI* (Mémoires pour servir à l'histoire de France), Paris, 1863.

Dumont, J., *Corps universel diplomatique de droit des gens . . .*, 8 vols., Amsterdam and The Hague, 1726–31.

Dupré Theseider, E., *L'idea imperiale di Roma nella tradizione del Medioevo*, Milan, 1942.

Dynter, E. de, *Chronique des ducs de Brabnt*, ed. P. de Ram, 3 vols., Brussels, 1854–60.

Elmham, T. de, *Vita et gesta Henrici Quinti*, ed. T. Hearne, Oxford, 1727

England und Köln: Beziehungen durch die Jahrhunderte in archivalischen Zeugnissen, ed. H. Stehkamper, Cologne, 1965.

English Historical Documents, vol. ii, ed. D. C. Douglas and G. W. Greenaway, London, 1953.

Epistolae pontificiae ad concilium Florentinum spectantes, ed. G. Hofmann, Rome, 1940.

Fauquembergue, C. de, *Journal de Clément de Fauquembergue, 1417–35*, ed. A. Tuetey (Société de l'histoire de France), 3 vols., Paris, 1903–15.

Fazio, B., *De Rebus gestis ab Alphonso primo Neapolitanorum rege commentariorum libri decem*, Lyons, 1560.

Finke, H., ed., *Acta Concilii Constanciensis*, 4 vols., Münster, 1896–1928.

Fleta, ed. H. G. Richardson and G. O. Sayles (Selden Society, vol. lxxii for 1953), vol. ii, London, 1955.

45th Report of the Deputy Keeper of the Public Records, London, 1884.

Frankfurts Reichs-Correspondenz nebst andern verwandten Aktenstücken von 1376–1519, ed. J. Janssen, 2 vols., Freiburg im Breisgau, 1863–72.

Gert's van der Schüren Chronik von Cleve und Mark, ed. L. Tross, Hamm, 1824.

Gruel, G., *Chronique d'Arthur de Richemont*, ed. A. le Vavasseur (Société de l'histoire de France), Paris, 1890.

Grunzweig, A., ed., *Correspondance de la filiale de Bruges des Medici* (Commission royale d'histoire), Brussels, 1931.

—— *Le Fonds du consulat de la mer aux archives de l'État à Florence* (Bulletin de l'Institut historique belge de Rome, fasc. 10), Rome, 1930.

Guden, V. F. von, *Sylloge variorum diplomatariorum res Germanicas in primis moguntinas illustrantium*, Frankfurt am Main, 1728.

Hall, E., *Chronicle of Lancaster and York (1399–1547)*, ed. H. Ellis, London, 1809.

Haller, J., ed., *Piero del Monte*, Rome, 1941.

—— et al., *Concilium Basiliense: Studien und Quellen zur Geschichte des Concils von Basel*, 8 vols., Basel, 1896–1936.

Hanserecesse, 1431–1476, ed. G. von der Ropp (Verein für hansische Geschichte), zweite Abteilung, 7 vols., Leipzig, 1876–92.

Hansisches Urkundenbuch, ed. K. Höhlbaum, K. Kunze, and W. Stein (Verein für hansische Geschichte), 10 vols., Halle and Leipzig, 1876–1907.

Hemmant, M., ed., *Select Cases in the Exchequer Chamber before all the Justices of England, 1377–1461* (Selden Society, vol. ii), London, 1933.

Höfler, K., *Geschichtsschreiber der husitischen Bewegung in Böhmen*, 3 vols., Vienna, 1856–66.

Hofmann, G., 'Briefe eines päpstlichen Nuntius in London über das Konzil von Florenz', *Orientalia Christiana Periodica*, vol. v (1939), pp. 407–33.

Hostiensis (Henry of Segusio), *Aurea Summa*, Cologne, 1612.

Hrabar, V. E., *De Legatis et Legationibus tractatus varii*, Dorpat, 1905.

Hus, J., and H. Pragensis, *Historia et monumenta* . . ., Nuremberg, 1558.

Imperatoris Iustiniani Institutiones, ed. J. B. Moyle, 5th edn., Oxford, 1912.

John of Legnano, *Tractatus de bello*, ed. J. E. Holland, Oxford, 1917.

Jorga, N., *Notes et Extraits pour servir à l'histoire des croisades au xve siècle*, Paris, 1899.

Journal d'un bourgeois de Paris, 1405–1445, ed. A. Tuetey (Société de l'histoire de Paris), Paris, 1881.

Le Fèvre, J., *Chronique de Jean le Fèvre, seigneur de Saint-Rémy*, ed. F. Morand (Société de l'histoire de France), 2 vols., Paris, 1876–81.

Leibnitz, G. W., *Codex juris gentium diplomaticus; Mantissa codicis juris gentium diplomatici*, 2 vols., Hanover, 1693–1700.

Lettres de Louis XI, roi de France, ed. E. Charavay *et al.* (Société de l'histoire de France), 11 vols., Paris, 1883–1909.

Liber regie capelle, ed. W. Ullmann (Henry Bradshaw Society, vol. xcii), London, 1961.

Livius, T. (Frulovisi), *Vita Henrici Quinti, regis Angliae (1413–22)*, ed. T. Hearne, Oxford, 1716.

Longnon, A., *Paris pendant la domination anglaise, 1420–1436* (Société de l'histoire de Paris), Paris, 1878.

Ludewig, J. P. von, *Reliquiae manuscriptorum omnis aevi diplomatum ac monumentorum ineditorum adhuc*, 12 vols., Frankfurt and Leipzig, 1729–41.

Lünig, J. C., *Das Teutsche Reichs-Archiv*, 24 vols., Leipzig, 1713–22.

Madurell Marimón, J. M., *Mensageros barcelonenses en la corte de Nápoles de Alfonso V de Aragón, 1435–1458*, Barcelona, 1958.

Martel, G., *Forma de celebrar cortes en Arragón*, Zaragoza, 1641.

Martène, E., and Durand, U., *Veterum scriptorum et monumentorum historicorum, dogmaticorum, moralium amplissima collectio*, 9 vols., Paris, 1724–33.

Monstrelet, E. de, *Chronique*, ed. L. Douët d'Arcq (Société d'histoire de France), 6 vols., Paris, 1857–62.

Morice de Beaubois, P. H., *Mémoires pour servir de preuves à l'histoire ecclésiastique et civile de Bretagne*, 3 vols., Paris, 1742–6.

Morosini, A., *Chronique d'Antonio Morosini*, ed. G. Lefèvre-Pontalis and L. Dorez (Société de l'histoire de France), 4 vols., Paris, 1898–1902.

Muratori, L. A., *Rerum Italicarum scriptores*, 25 vols., Milan, 1723–51.

Narratives of the Expulsion of the English from Normandy, ed. J. Stevenson (Rolls Series), London, 1863.

Nicholls, W., *Leges marcharum*, London, 1747.

Ordonnances des rois de France de la troisième race, ed. D. F. Secousse *et al.*, 21 vols., Paris, 1733–1849.

Original Letters Illustrative of English History, ed. H. Ellis, 2nd ser., 4 vols., London, 1827; 3rd. ser., vol. i, 1846.

Palacký, F., *Documenta Magistri Johannis Hus* . . ., Prague, 1869.

Paston Letters, 1422–1509, ed. J. Gairdner, 3 vols., London, 1900.

Pérez de Guzmán, F., *Crónica del Rey Don Juan II* (Biblioteca de autores españoles, xviii), Madrid, 1877.

—— *Generaciones, semblanzas, e obras* . . ., Madrid, 1775.

Pisan, Christine de, *The Book of Fayttes of Arms and of Chyvalrye*, ed. A. T. P. Bayles (Early English Text Society, original ser., no. 189), London, 1932.

Pius II, *Der Briefwechsel des Eneas Silvius Piccolomini*, ed. R. Wolkan (Fontes rerum austriacarum, vols. lxi–lxii), Vienna, 1909.

—— *Commentaries*, ed. F. A. Gragg and L. C. Gabel (Smith College Studies in History, xvii, nos. 1–2, xxv, nos. 1–4, xxxv), Northampton, Mass., 1937–40.

Poquet du Haut-Jussé, B.-A., *La France gouvernée par Jean sans Peur*, Paris, 1959.

Quellen zur Geschichte des Kölner Handels und Verkehrs im Mittelalter, ed. B. Kuske, 4 vols., Cologne, 1917–38.

Raynaldus, O., *et al.* [C. Baronius], *Annales ecclesiastici a Christo nato*, 41 vols., Lucca and Rome, 1738–1856.

Recueil des chroniques de Flandre, ed. J.-J. de Smet (Corpus chronicorum Flandriae), 4 vols. (Commission royale d'histoire), Brussels, 1837–65.

Regesta Imperii, XI: *die Urkunden Kaiser Sigmunds (1410–1437)*, ed. W. Altmann, 2 vols., Innsbruck, 1896–1900.

Regesten der Markgrafen von Baden und Hachberg, 1050–1515, ed. R. Fester, 4 vols., Innsbruck, 1900–15.

The Register of Nicholas Bubwith, Bishop of Bath and Wells, ed. T. S. Holmes (Somerset Record Society, vols. xxix–xxx), 2 vols., London, 1914.

Registrum Thome Spofford, ed. A. T. Bannister (Canterbury and York Society, vol. xxiii), London, 1919.

Richental, U. von, *Chronik des Constanzer Conzils*, Hildesheim, 1962.

Salter, H. E., ed., *Registrum cancellarii Oxoniensis (1434–1469)* (Oxford Historical Society, vols. xciii–xciv) 2 vols., Oxford, 1932.

Stavelot, J. de, *Chronique de Jean de Stavelot*, ed. A. Borgnet (Commission royale d'histoire), Brussels, 1861.

Stevenson, J., ed., *Letters and Papers Illustrative of the Wars of the English in France during the Reign of Henry VI* (Rolls Series), 2 vols. in 3 parts, London, 1861–4.

Suárez Fernández, L., *Castilla, el cisma y la crisis conciliar (1378–1440)* (Escuela de estudios medievales, vol. xxxiii), Madrid, 1960.

—— *Relaciones entre Portugal y Castilla en la época del infante Don Enrique, 1393–1460* (Escuela de estudios medievales, vol. xxxiv), Madrid, 1960.

Tomic Caualler, P., *Historias e conquestas dels excellentissims e catholics reys de Aragó e de lurs antecessors los comtes de Barcelona*, Barcelona, 1886.

Upton, N., *De Studio militari*, ed. E. Bysshe, London, 1654.

Urkundenbuch für die Geschichte des Niederrheins, ed. T. J. Lacomblet, 4 vols., Düsseldorf, 1840–58.

Urkundliche Geschichte des Hansischen Stahlhofes zu London, ed. J. M. Lappenberg, Hamburg, 1851.

Vielliard, J., and Avezou, R., 'Lettres originales de Charles VII conservées aux archives de la couronne d'Aragon', *Bibliothèque de l'École des Chartes*, vol. xcvii (1936), pp. 317–73.

Les Vies et quelques gestes des roys de Navarre, Paris, 1595.

Waurin, J. de, *Recueil des croniques et anchiennes istories de la Grant Bretaigne*, eds. W. Hardy and E. L. C. P. Hardy (Rolls Series), 5 vols., London, 1864–91.

Wilkins, D., *Concilia Magnae Britanniae et Hiberniae*, 4 vols., London, 1737.

Wykeham's Register, ed. T. F. Kirby (Hampshire Record Society), 2 vols., London, 1896–9.

Zurita, G., *Anales de la corona de Aragon*, Zaragoza, 1610.

3. SECONDARY WORKS

Allain, R., 'La politique domaniale du roi René en Provence (1431–1480)', *Positions des thèses* ... (École Nationale des Chartes), (1947), pp. 9–16.

Allmand, C. T., 'The Anglo-French Negotiations, 1439', *Bulletin of the Institute of Historical Research*, xl (1967), 1–33.

—— 'Normandy and the Council of Basel', *Speculum*, xl (1965), 1–14.

Andersson, I., *A History of Sweden*, trans. C. Hannay, London, 1956.

Armstrong, C. A. J., 'La double monarchie France–Angleterre et la maison de Bourgogne (1420–35)', *Annales de Bourgogne*, xxxvii (1965), 81–112.

Aubenas, R., and R. Ricard, *L'Église et la Renaissance, (1449–1517)* (*Histoire de l'Église*, ed. A. Fliche and V. Martin, vol. xv), Paris, 1951.

Balasque, J., *Études historiques sur la ville de Bayonne*, vol. iii, Bayonne, 1862.

Baldwin, J. F., *The King's Council in England during the Middle Ages*, Oxford, 1913.

Balfour-Melville, E. W. M., *James I, King of Scots, 1406–1437*, London, 1936.

Baron, H., *The Crisis of the Early Italian Renaissance*, 2 vols., Princeton, 1955.

Barraclough, G., *Papal Provisions*, Oxford, 1935.

Bartoš, F., 'An English Cardinal and the Hussite Revolution', *Communio Viatorum*, i (1963), 49.

Beaurepaire, C. de, *Les États de Normandie sous la domination anglaise*, Évreux, 1859.

Beer, S., 'An Operational Research Approach to the Nature of Conflict', *Political Studies*, xiv (1966), 119–32.

Behrens, B., 'The Office of English Resident Ambassador', *Transactions of the Royal Historical Society*, 4th ser. xiv (1933), 161–92.

—— 'Treatises on the Ambassador Written in the Fifteenth and Early Sixteenth Centuries', *English Historical Review*, li (1936), 616–27.

Beltrán de Heredia, V., 'La embajada de Castilla en el concilio de Basilea y su discusión con los ingleses acerca de precedencia', *Hispania sacra*, x (1957), 5–31.

Beltz, G., *Memorials of the Most Noble Order of the Garter from the Foundation until the Present Time*, London, 1841.

Betcherman, L.-R., 'The Making of Bishops in the Lancastrian Period', *Speculum*, xli (1966), 397–419.

Biscaro, G., 'Il Banco Filippo Borromei e Compagni di Londra (1436–39)', *Archivio storico lombardo*, 4th ser. xix (1913), 37–126, 283–386.

Biskup, M., 'Die Polnisch-preussischen Handelsbeziehungen in der ersten Hälfte des 15. Jahrhunderts', *Hansische Studien: Heinrich Sproemberg zum 70. Geburtstag*, Berlin, 1961, pp. 1–6.

—— *Zjednoczenie Pomorza Wschodniego z Polską w połowie XV w.*, Warsaw, 1959.

Bjork, D., 'The Peace of Stralsund, 1370', *Speculum*, vii (1932), 447–76.

Boase, C. W., ed., *Register of the University of Oxford*, vol. i, Oxford, 1885.

Bonenfant, P., *Du meurtre de Montereau au traité de Troyes* (Académie royale de Belgique, Mémoires, vol. lii), Brussels, 1958.

—— *Philippe le Bon*, Brussels, 3rd edn., 1955.

Bossuat, A., 'La littérature de propagande au xvᵉ siècle: le mémoire de Jean de Rinel, secrétare du roi d'Angleterre, contre le duc de Bourgogne (1435)', *Cahiers d'histoire*, i (1956), 131–46.

—— 'Le Parlement de Paris pendant l'occupation anglaise', *Revue historique*, ccxxix (1963), 19–40.

—— *Perrinet Gressart et François de Surienne, agents de l'Angleterre*, Paris, 1936.

—— 'Les prisonniers de guerre au xvᵉ siècle, la rançon de Guillaume, seigneur de Châteauvillain', *Annales de Bourgogne*, xxiii (1951), 7–35.

—— 'Le rétablissement de la paix sociale sous le règne de Charles VII', *Le Moyen Âge*, lx (1954), 137–62.

Brandt, A. von, 'Recent Trends in Research on Hanseatic History', *History*, xli (1956), 25–37.

Bridbury, A. R., *Economic Growth*, London, 1962.

—— *England and the Salt Trade in the Later Middle Ages*, Oxford, 1955.

BIBLIOGRAPHY 261

Buckland, W. W., *The Main Institutions of Roman Private Law*, Cambridge, 1931.

Bugge, A., 'Handelen mellem England og Norge indtil beyguldelaen af det 15de aarhundrede', *Historisk tidsskrift*, iv (1898), 1–148.

Bukofzer, M. F., 'English Church Music of the Fifteenth Century', *The New Oxford History of Music*, ed. A. Hughes and G. Abraham, iii, London, 1960, pp. 165–213.

Calmette, J., *Histoire de l'Espagne*, Paris, 1947.

—— *Louis XI, Jean II et la révolution catalane, 1461–1473*, Toulouse, 1903.

The Cambridge Economic History of Europe, vol. i, 2nd edn., ed. M. M. Postan, Cambridge, 1966; vol. ii, ed. M. M. Postan and E. Rich, 1952; vol. iii, ed. M. Postan, E. Rich, and E. Miller, 1965.

The Cambridge Medieval History, vol. vii, ed. J. R. Tanner, C. W. Previté-Orton and Z. N. Brooke, Cambridge, 1932; vol. viii, ed. C. W. Previté-Orton and Z. N. Brooke, 1936.

Carleton Williams, E., *My Lord of Bedford, 1389–1435*, London, 1963.

Caro, J., *Das Bündniss von Canterbury: eine Episode aus der Geschichte de Constanzer Conzils*, Gotha, 1880.

Carsten, F. L., *The Origins of Prussia*, Oxford, 1954.

Carus Wilson, E. M., 'The Icelandic Trade', *Studies in English Trade in the Fifteenth Century*, ed. E. Power and M. Postan, London, 1933, pp. 155–82.

—— 'The Overseas Trade of Bristol', *Studies in English Trade in the Fifteenth Century*, ed. E. Power and M. Postan, London, 1933, pp. 224–30.

—— and O. Coleman, *England's Export Trade, 1275–1547*, Oxford, 1963.

Champion, P., *Vie de Charles d'Orléans, 1394-1465*, Paris, 1911.

—— 'La librairie de Charles d'Orléans', *Bibliothèque du XVe siècle*, vol. xi, Paris, 1910.

Chaplais, P., 'The Anglo-Saxon Chancery: from Diploma to Writ', *Journal of the Society of Archivists*, iii (1966), 160–76.

—— 'English Diplomatic Documents to the End of Edward III's Reign', *The Study of Medieval Records: Essays in honour of Kathleen Major*, ed. E. Bullough and R. L. Storey, Oxford, 1971.

—— 'Règlement des conflits internationaux franco-anglais au xive siècle (1293–1337)', *Le Moyen Âge*, lvii (1951), 269–302.

—— 'Le sceau de la cour de Gascogne ou sceau de l'office de sénéchal de Guyenne', *Annales du Midi*, lxvii (1955), 19–29.

Cohn, H. J., *The Government of the Rhine Palatinate in the Fifteenth Century*, Oxford, 1965.

Coleman, O., 'Trade and Prosperity in the Fifteenth Century: Some Aspects of the Trade of Southampton', *Economic History Review*, xvi (1963–4), 9–22.

Coll Julià, N., 'Aspectos del corso catalán y del comercio internacional en el siglo XV', *Estudios de historia moderna*, iii (1953), 159–93.

Cosneau, E., *Le Connétable de Richemont, Artur de Bretagne, 1393–1458*, Paris, 1886.

Crowder, C. M. D., 'Henry V, Sigismund and the Council of Constance, a Re-examination', *Historical Studies*, iv (1963), 93–110.

Cuttino, G. P., *English Diplomatic Administration, 1259–1339*, 2nd edn., Oxford, 1971.

Daae, L., 'Erik af Pommerns, Danmarks, Sveriges og Norges konges gifter-maal med Philippa, Prindsesse af England', *Historiske Tidskrift*, ii (1880), 332–74.

Daumet, G., *Étude sur l'alliance de la France et de la Castille au XIVe et au XVe siècles* (Bibliothèque de l'École des Hautes Études, fasc. 118), Paris, 1898.

Delaruelle, E., Labande, E. R., and Ourliac, P. *L'Église au temps du Grand Schisme et la crise conciliaire (Histoire de l'Église, ed. A. Fliche and V. Martin, vol. xiv)*, Paris, 1962.

Denholm-Young, N., *History and Heraldry, 1254–1310*, Oxford, 1965.

Déprez, E., 'La conférence d'Avignon (1344), l'arbitrage pontifical entre la France et l'Angleterre', *Essays Presented to T. F. Tout*, ed. A. G. Little and F. M. Powicke, Manchester, 1925, pp. 301–20.

—— *Études de diplomatique anglaise de l'avènement d'Édouard Ier à celui de Henri VII (1272–1485): Le Sceau privé, le sceau secret, le signet*, Paris, 1908.

Desplanque, A., *Projet d'assassinat de Philippe le Bon par les Anglais (1424–1426)* (Mémoires de l'Académie royale de Belgique: Savants étrangers, vol. xxxiii), Brussels, 1867.

Deville, A., *Tombeaux de la cathédrale de Rouen*, Rouen, 1833.

Dicks, S. E., 'Henry VI and the Daughters of Armagnac', *The Emporia State Research Studies*, xv (1967), 5–12.

Dictionnaire topographique du département de Seine-et-Marne, ed. H. Stein and J. Hubert, Paris, 1954.

Dollinger, P., *La Hanse (XIIe–XVIIe siècles)*, Paris, 1964.

Doucet, R., 'Les finances anglaises à la fin de la guerre de cent ans (1431–1433)', *Le Moyen Âge*, xxxvi (1926–7), 265–332.

Droege, G., *Verfassung und Wirtschaft in Kurköln unter Dietrich von Moers (1414–1463)* (*Rheinisches Archiv*, i), 1957.

Du Boulay, F. R. H., 'The Fifteenth Century', *The English Church and the Papacy in the Middle Ages*, ed. C. H. Lawrence, London, 1965, pp. 195–242.

Dunlop, A. I., *The Life and Times of James Kennedy, Bishop of St. Andrews* (St. Andrews University Publications, no. xlvi), Edinburgh, 1950.

Dupont-Ferrier, G., 'Les avocats à la cour du trésor de 1401 à 1515', *Bibliothèque de l'École des Chartes*, xcvii (1936), 50.

Dupré Theseider, E., *La politica italiana di Alfonso d'Aragona*, Bologna, 1956.

Einstein, L., *The Italian Renaissance in England: Studies*, New York, 1902.

Elton, G. R., *Reformation Europe, 1517–1559*, London, 1963.

Engel, K., 'Die Organisation der deutsch-hansischen Kaufleute in England im 14. und 15. Jahrhundert bis zum Utrechter Frieden von 1474', *Hansische Geschichtsblätter*, xix (1913), 445–517; xx (1914), 173–225.

Entrèves, A. P. d', *Natural Law*, London, 1951.

Felici, G., 'Protonotari apostolici', *Enciclopedia cattolica*, vol. x (1953), coll. 200–2.

Fellmann, W., 'Die Salzproduktion im Hanseraum', *Hansische Studien: Heinrich Sproemberg zum 70. Geburtstag*, Berlin, 1961, pp. 56–71.

Fellowes, E. H., *The Knights of the Garter, 1348–1939*, London, 1939.

Fernández Torregrosa, A., 'Aspectos de la política exterior de Juan II de Aragón', *Estudios de historia moderna*, ii (1952), 99–132.

—— and Tate, R. B., 'Vicent Clement, un valenciano en Inglaterra', *Estudios de historia moderna*, vi (1956–9), 115–68.

Figgis, J. N., *Political Thought from Gerson to Grotius, 1414–1625*, 2nd edn., Cambridge, 1916, repr. New York, 1960.

Fink, K. A., 'König Sigismund und Aragon; die Bundesverhandlungen vor der Romfahrt', *Deutsches Archiv für Geschichte des Mittelalters*, ii (1938), 149–71.

—— 'Martin V und Aragon', *Historische Studien*, Heft 340, Berlin, 1938.

Finke, H., *Forschungen und Quellen zur Geschichte des Konstanzer Konzils*, Paderborn, 1889.

Flenley, R., 'London and Foreign Merchants in the Reign of Henry VI', *English Historical Review*, xxv (1910), 644–55.

Flourac, L., *Jean Ier, comte de Foix, vicomte souverain de Béarn*, Paris, 1884.

Folz, R., *L'Idée d'empire en Occident du ve au xive siècle*, Paris, 1953.

Foreville, R., *Le Jubilé de saint Thomas Becket*, Paris, 1958.

Gade, J. A., *The Hanseatic Control of Norwegian Commerce during the Late Middle Ages*, Leiden, 1951.

Gallia Christiana, ed. D. de Sainte-Marthe, *et al.*, 16 vols., Paris, 1716–1865.

Ganshof, F.-L., *Le Moyen Âge* (Histoire des relations internationales, vol. i), Paris, 1953.

Geanakoplos, D. J., *Byzantine East and Latin West: Two Worlds of Christendom in Middle Ages and Renaissance*, Oxford, 1966.

Giesey, R. E., 'The Juristic Basis of Dynastic Right to the French Throne', *Transactions of the American Philosophical Society*, n.s. li (1961), pp. 3–47.

Giesey, R. E. (*cont.*):

—— *The Royal Funeral Ceremony in Renaissance France* (Travaux d'humanisme et Renaissance), Geneva, 1960.

Gill, J., *The Council of Florence*, Cambridge, 1961.

—— *Personalities of the Council of Florence*, Oxford, 1964.

Gjerset, K., *History of the Norwegian People*, New York, 1932.

Graham, A. J., *Colony and Mother City in Ancient Greece*, Manchester, 1964.

Graves, E. B., 'The Legal Significance of the Statute of Praemunire of 1353', *Haskins Anniversary Essays*, Cambridge, Mass., 1929, pp. 57–80.

Hale, M., *Historia placitorum coronae: The History of the Pleas of the Crown*, vol. i, London, 1736.

Halecki, O., 'Problems of the New Monarchy: Jagello and Vitold, 1400–34', *The Cambridge History of Poland to 1696*, ed. W. Reddaway, J. H. Penson, *et al.*, Cambridge, 1950, pp. 210–31.

Haller, J., *England und Rom unter Martin V.*, Rome, 1905.

Hay, D., 'Italy and Barbarian Europe', *Italian Renaissance Studies: A Tribute to the Late Cecilia M. Ady*, ed. E. F. Jacob, London, 1960, pp. 28–68.

Heers, J., *Gênes au XVe siècle* (École pratique des hautes études — VIe section: Centre de recherches historiques), Paris, 1961.

—— 'Les Génois en Angleterre: la crise de 1458–66', *Studi in onore di Armando Sapori*, Milan, 1957, vol. ii, 809–32.

—— *L'Occident aux XIVe et XVe siècles: Aspects économiques et sociaux* (Nouvelle Clio, no. 23), Paris, 1963.

Heers, M.-L., 'Les Génois et les commerces de l'alun à la fin du Moyen Âge' *Revue d'histoire économique et sociale*, xxxii (1954), 31–53.

Hefele, C. J. von, *Histoire des conciles d'après les documents originaux*, ed. and trans. H. Leclercq, 10 vols., Paris, 1907–38.

Hillard-Villard, D., 'Les relations diplomatiques entre Charles VII et Philippe le Bon de 1435 à 1445', *Positions des thèses* . . . (École Nationale des Chartes), Paris, 1963, pp. 81–5.

Historia social y económica de España y América, ed. J. Vicens Vives, vol. ii, Barcelona, 1957.

Holdsworth, W., *A History of English Law*, 16 vols., London, 1903–66.

Holmes, G. A., 'Florentine Merchants in England, 1350–1450', *Economic History Review*, 2nd ser. xiii (1960), 193–208.

Holtzmann, W., 'Die englische Heirat Pfalzgraf Ludwigs III.', *Zeitschrift für die Geschichte des Oberrheins*, n.s. xlii (1929), 1–38.

Italia sacra, ed. F. Ughelli, 10 vols., Venice, 1717–22.

Jacob, E. F., 'Archbishop John Stafford', *Transactions of the Royal Historical Society*, 5th ser. xii (1962), 18–22.

Jacob, E. F. (*cont.*):

—— *Essays in the Conciliar Epoch*, 2nd edn., Manchester, 1953.

—— *The Fifteenth Century, 1399–1485* (The Oxford History of England, vol. vi), Oxford, 1961.

—— *Henry Chichele and the Ecclesiastical Politics of His Age*, London, 1952.

—— *Henry V and the Invasion of France*, London, 1947.

—— 'Thomas Brouns, Bishop of Norwich, 1436–45', *Essays in British History Presented to Sir Keith Feiling*, ed. H. R. Trevor-Roper, London, 1964, pp. 61–83.

—— 'To and from the Court of Rome in the Early Fifteenth Century', *Studies in French Language and Medieval Literature presented to Professor Mildred K. Pope*, Manchester, 1939, pp. 161–83.

—— 'Two Lives of Archbishop Chichele', *Bulletin of the John Rylands Library*, xvi (1932), 428–81.

Jenkinson, H., *Catalogue of an Exhibition of Treaties at the Public Record Office*, London, 1948.

Jones, J. Mervyn, *Full Powers and Ratifications*, Cambridge, 1946.

Joubert, A., 'Le mariage de Henri VI et de Marguerite d'Anjou', *Revue historique et archéologique du Maine*, xiii (1883), 313–32.

Keen, M. H., 'Brotherhood in Arms', *History*, xlvii (1962), 1–17.

—— *The Laws of War in the Late Middle Ages*, London, 1965.

—— 'Treason Trials under the Law of Arms', *Transactions of the Royal Historical Society*, 5th ser. xiii (1963), 85–103.

Kendall, P. M., *Warwick the Kingmaker*, London, 1957.

Kerling, N. J. M., *Commercial Relations of Holland and Zeeland with England from the late 13th Century to the Close of the Middle Ages*, Leiden, 1954.

Keutgen, F., *Die Beziehungen der Hanse zu England im letzten Drittel des vierzehnten Jahrhunderts*, Giessen, 1890.

Kingsford, C. L., *English Historical Literature in the Fifteenth Century*, Oxford, 1913.

—— *The First English Life of King Henry the Fifth*, Oxford, 1911.

—— *Prejudice and Promise in Fifteenth-Century England*, Oxford, 1925, repr. 1962.

Kirby, J. L., 'The Issues of the Lancastrian Exchequer and Lord Cromwell's Estimates of 1433', *Bulletin of the Institute of Historical Research*, xxiv (1951), 121–51.

—— 'Sir William Sturmy's Embassy to Germany in 1405–6', *History Today* (January 1965), 39–47.

Kirsch, J. P., 'Prothonotary Apostolic', *The Catholic Encyclopedia*, vol. xii (1913), p. 503.

Knowlson, G. A., *Jean V, duc de Bretagne, et l'Angleterre*, Rennes, 1964.

Koczy, L., *The Baltic Policy of the Teutonic Order*, Toruń, 1936.

Kunz, K., 'Das erste Jahrhundert der deutschen Hanse in England', *Hansische Geschichtsblätter*, iv (1891), 129–52.

Lander, J. R., 'Henry VI and the Duke of York's Second Protectorate, 1455 to 1456', *Bulletin of the John Rylands Library*, xliii (1960–1), 49–69.

—— *The Wars of the Roses*, London, 1965.

Lannoy, B. de, *Hugues de Lannoy, le bon seigneur de Santes*, Brussels, 1957.

Le Blant, E., *Les Quatre Mariages de Jacqueline, duchesse en Bavière*, Paris, 1904.

Legai, A., *Histoire du Bourbonnais*, Paris, 1960.

Le Neve, J., *Fasti Ecclesiae Anglicanae, 1300–1541*, vol. vi, London, 1963.

Le Patourel, J., 'The Plantagenet Dominions', *History*, l (1965), 289–308.

Lewis, P. S., 'Two Pieces of Fifteenth-Century Political Iconography', *Journal of the Warburg and Courtauld Institutes*, xxvi (1964), 317–20.

—— 'War Propaganda and Historiography in Fifteenth-Century France and England', *Transactions of the Royal Historical Society*, 5th ser. xv (1965), 1–21.

Lipson, E., *The Economic History of England*, i, 10th edn., London, 1949.

Livermore, H., *A New History of Portugal*, Cambridge, 1966.

Löher, F., von, *Jakobäa von Bayern und ihre Zeit*, 2 vols., Nordlingen, 1862–9.

Loomis, L., 'Nationality at the Council of Constance', *American Historical Review*, xliv (1939), 508–27.

Lopez, R., Miskimin, H. A., and Cipolla, C. M., 'Economic Depression of the Renaissance?', *Economic History Review*, xvi (1963–4), 519–29.

Loyn, H., *The Norman Conquest*, London, 1965.

Lucas, H. S., 'The Machinery of Diplomatic Intercourse', *The English Government at Work*, eds. J. F. Willard and W. A. Morris, Cambridge, Mass., 1940, i, pp. 300–31.

Luce, S., *Jeanne d'Arc à Domrémy*, Paris, 1886.

Lunt, W. E., *Financial Relations of the Papacy with England, 1327–1534* (Studies in Anglo-Papal Relations during the Middle Ages), Cambridge, Mass., 1962, vol. ii.

Macdonald, I., *Don Fernando de Antequera*, Oxford, 1948.

Mallett, M. E., 'Anglo-Florentine Commercial Relations, 1465–91', *Economic History Review*, 2nd ser. xv (1962), 250–65.

—— *The Florentine Galleys in the Fifteenth Century*, Oxford, 1967.

Marchesi Buonaccorsi, G., *Antichità ed eccellenza del protonotariato appostolico partecipante*, Faenza, 1751.

Marinis, T. de, *La biblioteca napoletana dei re d'Aragona*, 4 vols., Milan, 1947–52.

Marle, R. van, *Le Comté de Hollande sous Philippe le Bon (1428–67)*, The Hague, 1908.

Mattingly, G., *Renaissance Diplomacy*, London, 1955.

Maulde, R. de, 'Les instructions diplomatiques au Moyen-Âge', *Revue d'histoire diplomatique*, vi (1892), 602–32.

Maxwell-Lyte, H. C., *Historical Notes on the Use of the Great Seal of England*, London, 1926.

McFarlane, K. B., 'England and the Hundred Years War,' *Past and Present*, 22 (July 1962), 3–13.

—— 'Henry V, Bishop Beaufort and the Red Hat, 1417–21', *English Historical Review*, lx (1945), 316–48.

—— 'Loans to the Lancastrian Kings: the Problem of Inducement', *Cambridge Historical Journal*, ix (1947–9), 51–68.

—— 'The Wars of the Roses', *Proceedings of the British Academy*, l (1965), 87–119.

McKenna, J. W., 'Henry VI of England and the Dual Monarchy: Aspects of Royal Propaganda, 1422–1432', *Journal of the Warburg and Courtauld Institutes*, xxviii (1965), 145–62.

Mirot, L., 'Un conflit diplomatique au xvᵉ siècle: l'arrestation des ambassadeurs florentins en France (1406–1408)', *Bibliothèque de l'École des Chartes*, xcv (1934), 74–115.

Miskimin, H. A., 'Monetary Movements and Market Structure—Forces for Contraction in Fourteenth and Fifteenth Century England', *Journal of Economic History*, xxiv (1964), 470–90.

Mitchell, R. J., *John Tiptoft, 1427–1470*, London, 1938.

—— *The Laurels and the Tiara, Pope Pius II, 1458–1464*, London, 1963.

Murdock, V., 'John Wyclyf and Richard Flemyng, Bishop of Lincoln: Gleanings from German Sources', *Bulletin of the Institute of Historical Research*, xxxvii (1964), 239–45.

Myres, A. L., 'The Household of Queen Margaret of Anjou, 1452–53', *Bulletin of the John Rylands Library*, xl (1957–8), 79–113, 391–431.

Newhall, R. A., *The English Conquest of Normandy, 1416–1424* (Yale Historical Publications), New Haven, 1924.

—— 'The War Finances of Henry V and the Duke of Bedford', *English Historical Review*, xxxvi (1921), 172–97.

Oman, C., *The Art of War in the Middle Ages, A.D. 1378–1515*, rev. and ed. J. H. Beeler, Ithaca, N.Y., 1953.

Ortolan, T., 'Cour romaine', *Dictionnaire de théologie catholique*, vol. iii (1908), coll. 1965–8.

Otway-Ruthven, J., *The King's Secretary and the Signet Office in the Fifteenth Century*, Cambridge, 1939.

Pagel, K., *Die Hanse*, Brunswick, 1963.

Palle, L., *A History of the Kingdom of Denmark*, Copenhagen, 1960.

Passerini, L., *Gli Alberti di Firenze*, 2 vols., Florence, 1869–70.

Pérouse, G., *Le Cardinal Louis Aleman president du concile de Bâle, et la fin du grand schisme*, Paris, 1904.

Plancher, U., *Histoire générale et particulière de Bourgogne . . .*, 4 vols., Dijon, 1739–81.

Post, G., *Studies in Medieval Legal Thought*, Princeton, 1964.

Postan, M., 'The Economic and Political Relations of England and the Hanse from 1400 to 1475', *Studies in English Trade in the Fifteenth Century*, ed. E. Power and M. Postan, London, 1933, pp. 91–153.

Power, E., *The Wool Trade in English Medieval History*, London, 1941.

Previté-Orton, C. W., 'The Early Career of Titus Livius de Frulovisis', *English Historical Review*, xxx (1915), 74–8.

Queller, D. E., *The Office of Ambassador in the Middle Ages*, Princeton, 1967.

—— 'The Thirteenth-Century Diplomatic Envoys: *Nuncii* and *Procuratores*', *Speculum*, xxv (1960), 196–213.

Radford, L. B., *Henry Beaufort: Bishop, Chancellor, Cardinal*, London, 1908.

Richardson, H. G., 'The Commons and Medieval Politics', *Transactions of the Royal Historical Society*, 4th ser. xxviii (1946), 21–45.

Richmond, C. F., 'The Keeping of the Seas during the Hundred Years War: 1422–1440', *History*, xlix (1964), 283–98.

Rickert, M., *Painting in Britain: The Middle Ages*, London, 1954.

Roncière, C. de la, *Histoire de la marine française*, 6 vols., Paris, 1899–1932.

Roover, R. de, *The Rise and Decline of the Medici Bank, 1347–1494*, New York, 1966.

Roskell, J. S., *The Commons and their Speakers in English Parliaments, 1376–1523*, Manchester, 1965.

—— *The Commons in the Parliament of 1422: English Society and Parliamentary Representation under the Lancastrians*, Manchester, 1954.

Rowe, B. J. H., 'The Estates of Normandy under the Duke of Bedford, 1422–1435', *English Historical Review*, xliv (1931), 551–78.

—— 'The *Grand Conseil* under the Duke of Bedford', *Oxford Essays in Medieval History Presented to Herbert Edward Salter*, Oxford, 1934.

Ruddock, A. A., *Italian Merchants and Shipping in Southampton, 1270–1600*, Southampton, 1951.

Runciman, S., *The Fall of Constantinople, 1453*, Cambridge, 1965.

Russell, P. E., *The English Intervention in Spain and Portugal in the Time of Edward III and Richard II*, Oxford, 1955.

Ryder, A. J., 'The Evolution of Imperial Government in Naples under Alfonso V of Aragon', *Europe in the Late Middle Ages*, eds. J. R. Hale, J. R. L. Highfield, B. Smalley, London, 1965, pp. 332–57.

Ryder, T. T. B., *Koine Eirene; General Peace and Local Independence in Ancient Greece*, Oxford, 1965.

Samaran, C., *La Maison d'Armagnac au xve siècle et les dernières luttes de la féodalité dans le Midi de la France*, Paris, 1907.

Sanders, G. W., *Orders of the High Court in Chancery . . .*, vol. i, London, 1845.

Schanz, G., *Englische Handelspolitik gegen Ende des Mittelalters, mit besonderer Berücksichtigung des Zeitalters der beiden ersten Tudors, Heinrich VII. und Heinrich VIII.*, vol. i, Leipzig, 1881.

Schevill, F., *Medieval and Renaissance Florence*, 2 vols., New York, 1963.

Schneider, F., *Rom und Romgedanke im Mittelalter*, Munich, 1926.

Schofield, A. N. E. D., 'England, the Pope, and the Council of Basel, 1435–1449', *Church History*, xxxiii (1964), 248–78.

—— 'The First English Delegation to the Council of Basel', *Journal of Ecclesiastical History*, xii (1961), 167–96.

Schulz, F., 'Die Hanse und England: von Eduards III. bis auf Heinrichs VIII. Zeit', *Abhandlungen zur Verkehrs- und Seegeschichte im Auftrag des hansischen Geschichtsvereins*, ed. D. Schäfer, vol. v, Berlin, 1911.

Scofield, C. L., *The Life and Reign of Edward the Fourth*, 2 vols., London, 1923.

Sheenan, M. M., *The Will in Medieval England*, Toronto, 1963.

Soldevila, F., *Història de Catalunya*, ii, Barcelona, 1935.

Steel, A., *Receipt of the Exchequer, 1377–1485*, Cambridge, 1954.

Stein, W., *Beiträge zur Geschichte der deutschen Hanse bis um die Mitte des fünfzehnten Jahrhunderts*, Giessen, 1900.

—— 'Die Hanse und England beim Ausgang des hundertjährigen Krieges', *Hansische Geschichtsblätter*, xxvi (1920–1), 27–127.

Storey, R. L., *The End of the House of Lancaster*, London, 1966.

Suárez Fernández, L., 'Política internacional de Enrique II', *Hispania*, xvi (1956), 16–129.

Tawney, R. H., *Business and Politics under James I*, Cambridge, 1958.

Thielemacks, M.-R., *Bourgogne et Angleterre* (Travaux de la Faculté de Philosophie et Lettres, vol. xxx), Brussels, 1966.

Thompson, A. H., *The English Clergy and their Organization in the Later Middle Ages*, Oxford, 1947.

Tooke, J., *The Just War in Aquinas and Grotius*, London, 1965.

Toussaint, J., *Les Relations diplomatiques de Philippe le Bon avec le concile de Bâle*, Louvain, 1942.

Trame, R., *Rodrigo Sánchez de Arévalo, 1404–1470* (Catholic University of America, Studies in Medieval History), Washington, D.C., 1958.

Trautz, F., *Die Könige von England und das Reich, 1212–1377*, Heidelberg, 1961.

Tucoo-Chala, P., *Gaston Fébus et la vicomté de Béarn*, Bordeaux, 1959.

—— *La Vicomté de Béarn et le problème de sa souveraineté*, Bordeaux, 1961.

Überweg, F., *Grundriss der Geschichte der Philosophie*, 11th edn., vol. ii, Berlin, 1928.

Ullmann, W., 'The Bible and Principles of Government in the Middle Ages', *La Bibbia nell'alto Medioevo*, Spoleto, 1963, pp. 181–227.

—— 'The Development of the Medieval Idea of Sovereignty', *English Historical Review*, lxiv (1949), 1–33.

—— 'Eugenius IV, Kemp and Chichele', *Medieval Studies Presented to Aubrey Gwynn, S.J.*, ed. J. A. Watt, *et al.*, Dublin, 1964, pp. 359–83.

—— *The Growth of Papal Government in the Middle Ages*, London, 1955.

—— 'The Papacy as an Institution of Government in the Middle Ages', *Studies in Church History*, ii, ed. C. J. Cuming, London, 1965, pp. 78–101.

—— *Principles of Government and Politics in the Middle Ages*, London, 1961.

Unwin, G., 'The Economic Policy of Edward III', *Studies in Economic History: The Collected Papers of George Unwin*, ed. R. H. Tawney, London, 1927, pp. 117–32.

Valois, N., *Histoire de la pragmatique sanction de Bourges sous Charles VII*, Paris, 1906.

—— *Le Pape et le concile (1418–50)*, 2 vols., Paris, 1919.

Van Houtte, J., 'La Genèse du grand marché international d'Anvers à la fin du Moyen Âge', *Revue belge de philologie et d'histoire*, xix (1940), 87–126.

Varenbergh, E., *Histoire des relations diplomatiques entre le comté de Flandre et l'Angleterre au Moyen Âge*, Brussels, 1874.

Vaughan, R., *John the Fearless*, London, 1966.

Veale, E. M., *The English Fur Trade in the Later Middle Ages*, Oxford, 1966.

Vecchio, A. del, and Casanova, E., *Le rappresaglie nei comuni medievali e specialmente a Firenze*, Bologna, 1894.

Vic, C. de and Vaissete, J., eds., *Histoire générale de Languedoc*, vol. iv, Paris, 1742.

Vicens Vives, J., *Aproximación a la historia de España*, 2nd edn., Barcelona, 1960.

—— *Juan II de Aragón 1398–1479: monarquía y revolución en la España del siglo XV*, Barcelona, 1953.

—— *Manual de historia económica de España*, 3rd edn., Barcelona, 1964.

—— *Els Trastàmares*, Barcelona, 1961.

Vickers, K. H., *Humphrey, Duke of Gloucester*, London, 1907.

Villey, M., *Le Droit romain*, Paris, 1964.

Vitale, V., *Breviario della storia di Genova*, i, Genoa, 1955.

Vollbehr, F., *Die Holländer und die deutsche Hanse* (Pfingst-Blätter des Hansischen Geschichtsvereins), Lübeck, 1938.

Wagner, A. R., *Heralds and Heraldry in the Middle Ages*, 2nd. edn., London, 1960.

Wasner, F., 'Fifteenth-Century Texts on the Ceremonial of the Papal "Legatus a latere" ', *Traditio*, xiv (1958), 295–358.

Watson, A., *Contract of Mandate in Roman Law*, Oxford, 1961.

Watson, W. B., 'The Structure of the Florentine Galley Trade with Flanders and England in the Fifteenth Century', *Revue belge de philologie et d'histoire*, xxxix (1961), 1073–91; xl (1962), 317–47.

Waugh, W. T., 'The Great Statute of Praemunire', *English Historical Review*, xxxviii (1922), 173–205.

Weiss, R., 'Humphrey, Duke of Gloucester, and Tito Livio Frulovisi', *Fritz Saxl, 1890–1948: a Volume of Memorial Essays from His Friends in England*, London, 1957, pp. 218–27.

Wernham, R., *Before the Armada*, London, 1966.

Wieacker, F., *Recht und Gesellschaft in der Spätantike*, Stuttgart, 1964.

Wilkinson, B., *Constitutional History of England in the Fifteenth Century, 1399–1485*, London, 1964.

Wilks, M. J., *The Problems of Sovereignty in the Later Middle Ages*, Cambridge, 1963.

Wylie, J. H., 'Decembri's Version of the Vita Henrici Quinti by Tito Livio', *English Historical Review*, xxiv (1909), 84–9.

—— *History of England under Henry the Fourth*, 4 vols., London, 1884–98.

—— and Waugh, W. T., *The Reign of Henry the Fifth*, 3 vols., Cambridge, 1914–29.

Yanguas y Miranda, J., *Diccionario de antigüedades del reino de Navarra*, Pamplona, 1840.

Zanelli, A., 'Pietro del Monte', *Archivio storico lombardo*, serie 4a, vii (1907), 317–78; viii (1907), 46–115.

Zellfelder, A., *England und das Basler Konzil*, Berlin, 1913.

INDEX

Gloucester, abbot of St. Peter's, *see* Boulers, R.
— duchess of, *see* Hainault, J.
— herald, 53, 167, 202.
— Humphrey, duke of (1414–47), xix, xx, xxii, xxiv, 1, 4, 8–12 n. 1, 14, 16, 19–26, 32, 38, 44, 46, 51, 56, 122, 125–6, 129 n. 5, 131–2 n. 1, 135, 154, 161–2, 166, 176.
Godart, Jacques, secretary of the duke of Brittany, 197.
Godry, Colard, 195.
Gogh, Matthew, esquire, 180.
Golden Fleece, order of the, 13.
Goldener, Johannes, bishop of Acre, 216.
Goldyn, Reginald, master, 197.
Gosne, Charles de, 186.
Gosselyn, John, 207.
Grau, Pere, 201.
Gravelines, *dép.* Nord, 22–4.
Gray, William, bishop of London, bishop of Lincoln (1431–6), 113, 128, 141, 200, 210, 216.
Greenfield, Thomas, 180.
Gregory VII (1073–85), 149.
Grenevill, John, 210.
Grevenstein, Heinrich, 106, 208.
Grez-sur-Loing, *dép.* Seine-et-Marne, *arr.* Melun, *c.* Nemours, 42.
Grimeston, Edward, 180, 189.
Grivyne, pursuivant, 197.
Grymesby, John, 92.
Guelders, duke of, 34, 60, 66 n. 2.
Guéménée, siegneur de, 197.
Guidecheon, Marc, 195.
Guido, Antonius, 212.
Guiraud, Pierre, master, 6 n. 5, 202.
Guyenne, herald, 189.

Hainault, 9, 12.
— Jaqueline, countess of, duchess of Bavaria, Holland, Gloucester, xix, 8–9 n. 2, 11–12, 19 n. 3, 122, 125.
Hall, E., 163.
— Robert, master, 189.
Hälsingborg, Sweden, Oresund, 90.
Hamburg, *L.* Holstein, 95, 97, 112 n. 7.
Hanseatic League, 72–3, 83–4, 86–8, 91–4, 96–7, 99–107, 112, 176.
— — merchants of, xxi.
Harcourt, xviii.
Hardenurst, Eberhard, 208.

Harfleur, *dép.* Seine-Maritime, *arr.* Le Havre, *c.* Montivilliers, 45, 161.
Harrington, Richard, bailiff of Caen, 180.
Harley, Nicholas, clerk, 190.
Harton, William, esquire, 190.
Hastings, battle of (1066), xiii.
Havart, Jean, 28, 186.
Hawsenore, George de Bavoir', 209.
Hazeltine, H. D., 160.
Heligoland, 98.
Henry IV, king of England (1399–1413), 36, 59, 86.
Henry V, king of England (1413–22), xi, xii, xiii, xvii, xviii, xxi, 1 n. 1, 4–10, 12 n. 3, 19 n. 3, 24, 28 n. 1, 36–43, 45, 59–60 n. 1, 62, 69–72, 88–9, 108–11, 120–2, 150, 152, 169 n. 5, 171–3, 175.
Henry VI, king of England (1422–61), xiii, *et passim.*
Henry VII, king of England (1485–1509), 31, 58.
Herald, 186, 195, 201, 203.
Heralds, *see* Algarve, Artois, Asturias, Barchelone, Bretaigne, Byllestrayne, Chester, Clarenceaux, Denmark, Ermine, Garter, Guyenne, Hereford, Ireland, Lisbon, Pamplona, Portugal, Sicily, Stiparlo, Styrand, Suffolk, Toisson d'Or, Valis, Valois.
Herbert, William, esquire, 190.
Herburg, Henry, 48 n. 1, 200.
Hereford, bishop of, *see* Polton, T., Spofford, T.
— herald, 166.
Herkyn, Reynaldo, 206.
Herring, battle of the (1429), xiii.
Hertze, Johannes, 208.
Heyworth, William, bishop of Coventry and Lichfield (1420–47), 207.
Hogge, Hermann van der, 212.
Hoiger, Heinrich, 208.
Holes, Andrew, master, 48 n. 1, 134, 200, 216.
Holland, 9, 85, 97,
— duchess of, *see* Hainault, J.
— John, earl of Huntingdon (1417–47), 180, 211, 216.
Holstein, count of, 90.
Holy Roman Emperor, *see* Rupert, Sigismund, Alberecht, Frederick III.
Holy Roman Empire, 59, 76.